BECOMING CITIZENS

WOMEN IN AMERICAN HISTORY

Series Editors

Mari Jo Buhle

Nancy A. Hewitt

Anne Firor Scott

Stephanie Shaw

*A list of books in the series appears
at the end of this book.*

BECOMING CITIZENS

THE EMERGENCE AND DEVELOPMENT OF THE CALIFORNIA WOMEN'S MOVEMENT, 1880–1911

❖

GAYLE GULLETT

UNIVERSITY OF ILLINOIS PRESS
URBANA AND CHICAGO

Library of Congress Cataloging-in-Publication Data
Gullett, Gayle Ann.
Becoming citizens : the emergence and development of the
California women's movement, 1880–1911 / Gayle Gullett.
p. cm.—(Women in American history)
Includes bibliographical references and index.
ISBN 0-252-02503-2 (cloth)
ISBN 0-252-06818-1 (pbk.)
1. Feminism—California—History. 2. Women in politics—
California—History. 3. Women—Suffrage—California—History.
I. Title. II. Series.
HQ1438.C2 G85   2000
305.42′09794—dc21   99-6028
CIP

1   2   3   4   5   C   P   5   4   3   2   1

University of Illinois Press
1325 South Oak Street
Champaign, IL 61820-6903
www.press.uillinois.edu

For my parents,
Pat and Bill Gullett

Contents

Acknowledgments

This book has taken me a very long time to write. But I could not have written it at all without the support of many individuals, families, communities, and institutions. I am solely responsible for the mistakes, errors in judgment, and other failings, but everyone mentioned (and many more) helped make this book possible.

I could not have written a history of the California women's movement without reading the materials that organized women left behind, a task enriched by the fact that in several cases I read materials still held by the original organizations. Esther Depew, president of the southern California Woman's Christian Temperance Union, went out of her way to make sure that I had access to everything that I needed in the organization's Los Angeles archives. The women of the northern California WCTU operated from a small office in Oakland, but Cynthia Nelson, their president, kindly made space for me in her cramped quarters. All the temperance women told me stories of their former leaders and past political successes, stories that still live for them.

Club women were also generous. The late Margaret Grey of the Friday Morning Club in Los Angeles gave me access to the club's archives (now housed at the Huntington Library). She shared with me her extensive oral history of the club and made me welcome in the clubhouse, which dates from the 1920s. I am sure that I first began to understand the relationship between club buildings and club life when she graciously gave me an extensive tour of the beautiful building. Mrs. Albert Crichton, president of the California

Federation of Women's Clubs, allowed me to read files at the federation office in Fresno; these are now held at the University of California at Santa Cruz.

I also want to thank librarians and staff members at numerous research libraries, including the Bancroft Library at the University of California at Berkeley; the California Historical Society, San Francisco; the Hoover Institution Archives, Stanford University; the special collections sections at the University Research Library at the Green Library of Stanford University and at the Universities of California at Santa Cruz and Los Angeles; the California State Library, Sacramento; the Gilroy Museum, Gilroy; and the Huntington Library, San Marino. For their help in collecting pictures, I want to thank Ellen Harding at the California State Library, Emily Wolf at the California Historical Society, and Erin Wardlow at the Huntington Library; I especially want to thank Janet Soper, a graphic designer at Arizona State University, for her technical skills, which greatly assisted me in preparing the cartoons for publication. For her insistence that I *must* have pictures, I thank Vicki Ruiz.

I want to thank several institutions for their financial support, which helped pay for research trips and gave me time to write: the women's studies and faculty grant-in-aid programs at Arizona State University; the Summer Faculty Fellowship and faculty grant-in-aid program at Indiana University Northwest; and the summer stipend program of the National Endowment for the Humanities.

Everyone at the University of Illinois Press has been immensely helpful. I do not know how to begin to thank Anne Firor Scott. Her long-term interest and her wise critiques have done much to strengthen this book and make it possible. Karen Hewitt is an ideal editor; she guided me through each step and kept me informed. Melanie Gustafson provided exceptionally insightful comments. I also wish to thank Theresa Sears and Polly Kummel for their patience and support.

My ideas for this book first developed during graduate school at the University of California at Riverside. Hal Bridges, Carlos Cortés, Barbara Deckard, Bob Hine, and Sarah Stage taught me how to think critically about politics. Alice Clement, in her tutorials on American women's history and in her leadership role in the West Coast Association of Women Historians, taught me about the meaning and craft of politics. Bob Chandler, a friend and fellow student at Riverside, continues to share with me his research in California history. The late Bonnie Gordon and I always shared notes about work and life; her humor and shrewd analysis made a great difference in my life.

At a crucial time in my graduate career Estelle Freedman and her graduate students at Stanford University welcomed me into their Women's History Dissertation Support Group. Their support, discerning questions, and enthusiasm for intellectual inquiry made an immense difference to me; without them I might not have finished the dissertation on which the first half of this book is based. Members of the group included Antonia Casteñeda, Camille Guerin-Gonzalez, Gary Sue Goodman, Lois Helmbold, Gail Hershatter, Emily Honig, Sue Lynn, Valerie Matsumoto, Joanne Meyerowitz, Katherine Poss, Vicki Ruiz, Linda Schott, and Frances Taylor.

So many wonderful people made Indiana University Northwest such a collegial place to work that I wish I could thank them all. Ruth Needleman read early portions of the manuscript, helped organize a women's reading group, and greatly enlarged my thinking about the labor movement and the complexities of gender, class, and race. She and Ron Cohen always encouraged me to go forward, do more—and did this, most of all, through their confidence in me. Jack Bloom, Fred Chary, Tanice Foltz, Charles Gallmeier, Paul Kern, Angeline Komenich, Jim Lane, Inma Minoves-Myers, Rhiman Rotz, Stephanie Shanks Meile, Mary Veeder, and Dorothy Williamson Ige provided important critiques and support. The IUN library is not a research library, but librarians Bob Moran and Cindy Bauer did much to make it a place that furthered my research. Chancellor Peggy Elliott made IUN a hospitable place for women in general and me in particular to study. Among many other things, she supported the creation of a women's studies program.

I brought boxes of research to Arizona State University and here in the desert they flowered into a book. Retha Warnicke, chair of the history department, provided wise guidance and excellent advice. Susan Gray and Wanda Hendricks took time during my first year to make sure that I adjusted easily and well. The Women's History Reading Group, now in its fourth year, gave me insightful readings of chapter drafts; members included Michelle Curran, Rachel Fuchs, Susan Gray, Timothy Hodgdon, Terri Hurt, Asuncion Lavrin, Mary Melcher, Sybil Thornton, and Vicki Ruiz. I especially want to thank Rachel for her careful and incisive reading of the entire manuscript. Special thanks also go to Vicki, who gave me extended comments at crucial points, always recommended exactly the right book—no matter at what inconvenient time I asked, and who continually serves as a model of committed, caring scholarship. Art Rosales generously shared his research, and Al Hurtado provided encouraging words. Peter Iverson contributed a much appreciated mentoring in the process of writing and publishing, as did Beth Luey. I strongly urge everyone who does not have the privilege of working down the hall from Beth to read her book, *Handbook for Academic Authors.* Mary Roth-schild, who wears the two hats of historian and women's studies director, helped nurture this project. Several research assistants participated in the final gathering of data; Terri Hurt and Elizabeth Carney Sowards did outstanding work. Emily Neilan provided several different kinds of research skills that helped complete this manuscript. The women's studies librarian, Kimble Blouin, and everyone in the interlibrary loan office have been very helpful.

Scholars at other institutions have contributed in important ways to the research and writing of this book. I have met several historians at research libraries who offered most useful suggestions in how to navigate those institutions and often sage advice about this project as well. They include Karen Blair, Sherry Katz, Rebecca Mead, and Margaret Rossiter. I have presented various drafts of this work at conferences; people who have commented include Karen Blair, Ellen DuBois, Al Hurtado, Gloria Ricci Lothrop, Michael McGerr, Anne Firor Scott, Carole Srole, Sarah Stage, Vicki Ruiz, and Marjorie Spruill Wheeler.

My research trips would have been short and unproductive had friends and family not opened their homes to me. Linda and Dan Guerra let me stay for weeks, a tremendous imposition, but they always made me feel like family. Their kindness allowed me to finish my research in San Francisco and Berkeley. Mark and Guadalupe Levine's hospitality helped me complete my research in Palo Alto, and Diana and Brent Bills did the same for my work in Fresno. In southern California Alice and David Clement and my aunt and uncle, Mary and Harold Richards, made room for me in their homes and busy lives.

I am fortunate to belong to many families that have encouraged me and supported my work. My parents, Pat and Bill Gullett, taught me how to live and work through their faith in me and love for me. My parents, my sister, Patrea, and my brother, Bill, and their families; my aunts Gerry and Mary; my cousins, especially Tom, Jim, and Sandi; and my father's cousin, Tom Patterson, a historian long before me, have all sustained me, made me laugh at myself, and kept me going. The extended Escobar family, mine by marriage and love, has taught me much about family and work and has done much to make both possible—thank you, Carmen, and the late Steve Escobar, Al and Becky, and their families. The Gullett Escobar family has made me the most fortunate of people. My children, Marcos and Cristina, do not remember when their mother was not distracted by "the book," but they have always reminded me what is most important in life and filled my life with tremendous pride and happiness. My husband, Ed, although busy writing his own book, never failed to help me with mine, reading innumerable drafts, serving as my most thorough and truest critic. Much more, his confidence in me and love for me have made my life and work a joy. Because of him, I have been able to find a balance that makes life worth living.

.

INTRODUCTION

When California became the sixth state to grant women the right to vote in 1911, suffragists believed it marked a turning point for the national women's movement. For the first time women had become voters in a state with a city, San Francisco, that mirrored eastern cities in size and immigrant working-class population. To gain the vote California women had developed innovative political techniques and cross-class alliances that attracted wide attention. National suffrage leaders, especially, hoped that the link between California suffragists and progressivism—clearly a reform movement of growing national importance—was a harbinger of future success.[1]

California was also a significant victory in its own right; as Alice Stone Blackwell, editor of the *Woman's Journal,* the national organ of the suffrage movement, wrote in 1911, California was "the greatest single advance that the suffrage movement in America has yet made." Women had won the vote in five other western states, but these lightly populated states commanded few electoral votes in presidential elections. Thus women voters in Wyoming, Utah, Colorado, Idaho, and Washington had little influence in national elections, an equation that suffragists believed California would begin to change significantly. Yet, despite the importance of the California campaign, we know little about the state women's movement that achieved such a vital victory and so profoundly changed regional and national definitions of gender, politics, and citizenship.[2]

California women achieved the vote by creating a social movement; this is the story of that movement from the 1880s to 1911. Movement activists—predominantly white and affluent—created a new kind of women's politics. These women developed new values, established new organizations, and linked them together in a new collectivity—a new mass movement. The women called their movement "organized womanhood" to emphasize what they saw as the source of their power, politicized solidarity. This movement not only gained women citizenship but transformed the politics of the white middle class and contributed to the political movement that we now call progressivism. This book documents, then, how women's collectivity transformed women—and their world.[3]

Organized women transformed themselves, their gender, and their politics, but they did so in a process that borrowed from and in some ways maintained older understandings of gender, politics, and citizenship. They gained citizenship and developed a place for women in politics, but it was not the same kind of citizenship or place in politics that men held. They became female citizens who did not possess the same power or rights as male citizens. Most noticeably, although California women won the right to vote in 1911, male lawyers and judges successfully contended that this did not grant women the right to serve on juries. To become jurors the women had to engage in yet another campaign, which they did not win until 1917. Women entered politics, but they did so as women committed to what they understood as womanly politics—those that were moral, altruistic, and civic minded. The women felt ambiguous about partisan politics—an arena they saw as male, amoral, and self-seeking. Organized women attempted to link terms they saw as opposites—such as the good woman and politics—but they found that they could do so only by qualifying their terms. The woman citizen who engaged in politics in 1911 represented a transformation that both challenged and maintained traditional notions of gender.[4]

Because this is a study of how women in a social movement transformed political definitions, it looks closely at the various kinds of politics that helped create, shape, and maintain organized womanhood. It examines how women created organizations to enlarge women's public opportunities, how those organizations coalesced into a movement, and how women in that movement developed a dynamic sense of themselves as something greater than their many parts—a sense of themselves as an organized womanhood.[5]

The name women gave themselves, organized womanhood, explains what they saw as the source of their power—their numerous groups were so systematically united that they could speak as one and thus for all women. They reached this conclusion because they struggled to build a movement composed of many different women and because they assumed that women like themselves—white, native-born affluent Protestants—represented the true essential woman of "womanhood." Organized women understood womanhood as meaning that all women shared a commitment to moral domesticity and that the term referred only to women who were white and elite. As organized women, their greatest political strength and fragility came from their struggles to build a movement based on the assumed ties of womanhood.[6]

The statements and actions of Caroline Severance, a Los Angeles club woman who did much to build the state women's movement, illustrate the complex way activists viewed organized womanhood. Severance understood this concept as a source of empowerment. Women's ability to organize themselves meant they had the ability to change the world around them, to be political. She captured this sense of empowerment when she said—as she frequently did—that "there is nothing that is impossible for an organized womanhood, united in aim and effort." On the other hand, Severance, a former abolitionist and someone who always proclaimed her belief in the unity of all women, supported the exclusion of African American women from the national association of club women, the General Federation of Women's Clubs, at its 1902 convention in Los Angeles. She did this to empower organized womanhood. She contended that if white women built a national organization that unified northern and southern white women, they would have greater strength to achieve their goals for all women.

Organized women were always engaged in politics—a struggle over power relations—but this book examines only some of those struggles, the public campaigns that organized women saw as most relevant to their movement. Women formed the movement to "advance women's work." They meant that they intended to make women more powerful in their private and public affairs by gaining greater recognition for the work women already performed and by expanding women's opportunities for work. To this end activists defined women's work holistically, in a way that embraced the work of the home, work for wages, social service, and political activism. All tasks, paid and unpaid, were legitimately women's work—so long as women could be seen as fulfilling, in some way, the moral responsibilities women held as women. Organized women's efforts to advance their work both expanded the accepted definitions of women's work and maintained their position in society as those who preserved the nurturing morality of the home.[7]

Almost immediately after California women created a state movement in the early 1890s, dedicated to advancing women's work, they declared for suffrage and thus launched their second campaign, their fight for citizenship.

Caroline Severance, 91, mailed numerous copies of this personally inscribed photograph to her friends in celebration of the 1911 suffrage campaign. (The Huntington Library, San Marino, California)

The two campaigns were closely related to each other. In the United States people commonly understood citizenship to mean those who can support themselves and thus think and vote independently. As organized women struggled to expand women's work, they came to see themselves as capable of sustaining an autonomous life of the mind and spirit, if not necessarily economically, especially the wives. Moreover, because they believed that their work proved their abilities in political, economic, and civil life, they believed that their citizenship gave them the right to demand their political, economic, and civil rights.[8]

California women entered and lost a state campaign for suffrage in 1896. In the years that followed, club women, who became the dominant group within the state's organized womanhood in the early twentieth century, played a crucial role in rebuilding a movement dedicated to expanding women's work. Despite the club women's successes in such highly political efforts as building community playgrounds and a state juvenile court system, they insisted that they were performing nonpolitical work, an effort they labeled "civic altruism." Such work, they insisted, was not political because, although they became more powerful, they did not seek power for themselves. They sought the public good and did so only through activities that could easily be seen as an expansion of women's domestic role; some activists referred to urban civic altruism as acting as "city mothers." Finally, club women contended that civic altruism was not political because it was not partisan or, to use a term they saw as synonymous, corrupt.[9]

Organized women's civic activism helped develop a political role for women, create progressivism, and win women's citizenship; however, women remained uncertain about their role in politics, their political relation to male progressives, and the kind of political power that women citizens should and could make their own. Club women's civic altruism facilitated an alliance with male reformers who agreed that partisan politics had done much to corrupt California. These men and women were soon working together in campaigns for "good government" that both insisted were political but nonpartisan. Their joint efforts developed progressivism. After male progressives gained control of California state government in 1910, they felt compelled to repay such support by supporting women's suffrage. Women became citizens. They could selflessly contribute to the public good; they could support nonpartisan reform politics. They had gained a moral citizenship that placed them far above the power struggles of men; and thus out of reach from an equal distribution of power.

Organized women understood that their "politics"—their analysis of wom-

THE SENATE WILL NOW "TAKE TO THE BRUSH"

The female suffragists have secured the scalp of the House and are after the Senate.

(*Los Angeles Times,* February 17, 1895)

en's position in society and struggles to change it—fundamentally challenged a social order based on traditional notions of gender. But even if they had been oblivious to the larger implications of their politics, their opponents lost no time in pointing it out—in a highly political manner. Antisuffragists denounced and, in what probably was their most effective tactic, ridiculed women for attempting to transform the social order. According to the antisuffragists, men held the franchise because they possessed the ability to support themselves; they could make their way in the world as individuals and could therefore vote as individuals. Men dominated the marketplace and the political system of parties and elections, up to and including the full rights of citizenship, because only men were qualified to enter these public struggles. When suffragists made counterclaims, they were attempting to overthrow the social order.

Today one might have trouble linking social revolution to women's suffrage; certainly in the recent celebration of the seventy-fifth anniversary of women's winning the vote, no one took to the streets to denounce women's voting as a crime against society. Two political cartoons from the period illustrate how some Americans once viewed women's demand for citizenship. In 1895 California suffragists persuaded the state House of Representatives to pass a bill that would give women the vote and sought to convince the state Senate to do the same. An 1895 *Los Angeles Times* cartoon represented the lobbying suffragist as an avenging woman "on the warpath." She is running with the scalp of the state House in one hand and a large knife in the other as she seeks to scalp the state Senate. Her pursuit of a power that only men can have, a quest that takes her outside the bounds of civilized society, has transformed her into a "savage." If she should succeed in scalping men, she would not win political equality. But she would have stopped progress and created anarchy.

After California women won their enfranchisement in 1911, the *New York Evening Globe* suggested the meaning of their victory in a cartoon that was reprinted by the *California Outlook,* the journal of the state's progressive movement. California, depicted as a conventionally feminine and attractive young woman dressed in fringed buckskin and wearing a sombrero, has just stepped from the voting booth, a log cabin. She is armed, dangerous, and shooting at a man. Of course, perhaps comforting, she is only shooting at his feet and he represents "Corrupt Politics." Woman has gained power that men once monopolized and quite skillfully wields her two six-shooters to further progress and maintain a just social order. Yet I suspect that readers, then and now, cannot help but wonder: where will she point her guns next? The chief political issue of these two cartoons, the distribution of power between men and women, remains a vital, unsettling, and unsettled issue.

❖

The story of California's organized womanhood illuminates the histories of the state and national women's movement. The state movement shares much

"Now Dance!"   Evening Globe. New York City

(*California Outlook,* November 4, 1911)

in common with the national movement; the local story tells a nationally representative history. However, because this work analyzes movement politics as local politics, it changes our understanding of movement history. We see the national movement as it looked from the grassroots; we also see the way national leaders viewed, participated in, and sometimes were changed by local situations.

This California history increases our understanding of state, regional, and national politics. Some of the history of the California movement is a distinctly western story. The California 1896 suffrage campaign shares with other western suffrage campaigns of the 1890s an involvement with populism; similarly, the California victory of 1911 formed part of a wave of western state victories during the progressive era. As western history, this book corrects the assumption in much of U.S. women's history that still assumes national history stops at the Mississippi. California history also stands alone as its own story; as historian Michael Goldberg argues, politics in each state is distinctive. The thread that ties together the political histories of state, region, and nation, and that reconfigures our past understandings of politics, is that this history analyzes women's struggles for power.[10]

❖

The book examines the two stages of the California women's movement in four chapters whose organization is meant to encourage comparison. Chapter 1 examines how women created a mass movement in the late 1880s and early 1890s that sought to empower them through participation in public life, in particular through advancing women's work. Chapter 2 studies how this movement helped create, directed, and was changed by the suffrage campaign of 1896. Chapter 3 looks at how club women recreated the movement at the beginning of the century, making its emphasis one particular kind of women's work, civic altruism. Chapter 4 documents how this revived movement helped create, directed, and was changed by the suffrage campaign of 1911.

I have tried to make this book the story of organized women in California, to explain how they saw the world and understood themselves. To that end, I tried to use the names that the women preferred; therefore, some are Jane Smith and some are Mrs. John Smith. But I acknowledge that I also break this rule or at least bend it to make it fit the spirit of the rule. If a woman was known in the latter part of her life by a certain name, that is the one I used, even if she did not choose that name until after the period discussed here. Charlotte Perkins Gilman, for example, was Charlotte Perkins Stetson in the period encompassed by this book, but I used Charlotte Perkins Gilman— because that was the final name she chose for herself and how she is better known.

THE POLITICS OF WOMEN'S WORK:
BUILDING THE CALIFORNIA WOMEN'S
MOVEMENT, 1880–93

IN THE 1870s a few extraordinary pioneers for women's rights entered California's political arena, demanding women's enfranchisement. They based their demand on a fundamental principle: fathers and husbands should not vote for women; women must speak for themselves. The suffragists envisioned that women, with the gain of citizenship, would become a powerful force that could greatly improve women's position in society. Yet despite the hours these women spent organizing the suffrage movement, it remained small. Most women saw themselves as living private lives and did not see a relationship between angers many felt about their lives and the demand for the vote.

Although women lacked enthusiasm for the vote, they did develop a public role. During the 1870s women in San Francisco and Los Angeles built public institutions, such as philanthropic organizations that managed urban social welfare services. But the women who created these associations understood them as extensions of women's private domestic responsibilities and not as a challenge to their lives or duties. Just as the woman in the home, supported financially by her husband, created a place of moral influence, so women in charities created places of morality that depended upon male support. These women differentiated between women's role in public service and the role of women in electoral politics. The first was an extension of their domestic lives. The second was the realm of men.

In the 1880s women's organizations developed new ways of thinking about the relationship between women's work and politics. Organized women worried that they were losing their traditional ability to influence national morality through their work in the home, church, and community because of forces they called the "factory," the "city," and the "immigrant." Women turned to politics as a means to bolster their moral guardianship and thus advance themselves as a group; with this understanding they campaigned for, among other things, prohibition, women members on school boards, and a "pure," or nonsensational, press.

Women did not initially call their efforts political, which they understood as male partisan endeavors that were sectarian and opportunistic and, more often than not, corrupt. Organized women felt more comfortable labeling their political campaigns as women's work, a term that evoked for them the traditions of womanly service and obligation. When organized women spoke, as they commonly did, of "advancing women's work," they referred to their work in the home, volunteer work for churches and charities, paid work, and the work of civic activism. Women created an elastic and holistic definition that expanded their work and enhanced their power. When women did this, they were acting politically.

The Woman's Christian Temperance Union (WCTU) pioneered in arguing that politics could facilitate women's traditional task of providing moral influence. For WCTU women this meant lobbying for temperance legislation in order to protect the home from the ravages of male alcoholism. Club women, college-educated women, and professional women followed the WCTU's example of using politics for "home protection." Generally, they became involved in school elections, actions that they justified in terms of women's traditional work, their familial responsibilities.

Women's clubs and women's professional groups focused much of their attention on women's paid labor. They were influenced by the rising number of women attending college and the growing number of women who were entering the paid labor force. During the mid- to late 1880s club women in San Francisco and Los Angeles created institutions that sought to aid working-class wage-earning women as workers and protect them as women from public dangers. The club women who led these institutions—and thus worked both as moral guardians and as public servants—spoke of women's right to work and how women themselves, if united, could expand women's opportunities. During this period college-educated and/or professionally skilled middle-class women organized specifically to advance their employment opportunities, which were also linked to the dual concerns of moral service and professional development.

As women expanded their work, they built a new identity for themselves as women citizens. Their claim to public moral authority marked—and limited—them as a different kind of citizen than men; women were still confined to a moral sphere, albeit a more public one. But women's activism as moral guardians also aided their entrance into politics. Women argued that they could provide what men did not and what the women contended an industrial society needed in order to achieve true progress—an ethical nonpartisan public voice that spoke for women and children. By assuming such civic duties, through women's organizations that they controlled, directed, and staffed, women declared themselves citizens; they were performing independent work that sustained the Republic.

A social movement emerges when individuals and organizations form a collectivity, but this is not a process that necessarily runs in a smooth uninterrupted line. Women entered campaigns that were lost, formed groups that disintegrated; much of their story is therefore episodic. But women who engaged in this process developed a new consciousness about themselves; they began seeing themselves part of a movement they called *organized womanhood.* This label reflected their traditional belief that all women shared the womanly concerns of home and morality as well as their newly gained insight—that they could organize and gain strength from each other. Slowly, many began to feel that such power made them citizens.

❖

In January 1870 a group of women met in San Francisco to unite the scattered suffrage societies in the northern part of the state into the first state suffrage society. As Laura de Force Gordon told a reporter, "When questions were put to the meeting not more than a dozen timid voices could be heard saying 'aye,' or 'no.'" She urged the women to "open their mouths and vote audibly." To do otherwise, she declared, would discredit the women's movement. The audience cheered and thereafter "unequivocal demonstration of voices were made" at each vote. Gordon's confidence reflected her years on the lecture circuit. Born in 1838, she toured the eastern states during the early 1860s, speaking for spiritualism, a popular movement on the left of religious liberalism. After moving west with her physician husband in 1867, she continued to speak publicly but dedicated more of her lectures to women's rights.[1]

Gordon belonged to a small but vigorous national band of women that included Elizabeth Cady Stanton and Susan B. Anthony and was creating a women's movement. Gordon made several crucial contributions to the early western suffrage movement. She delivered the first suffrage speech in Califor-

Laura de Force Gordon (California History Room, California State Library, Sacramento)

nia, at San Francisco in 1868. She spent countless hours and miles touring California and other western states for suffrage in the early 1870s. Most of all, she brought to the movement a militant individualism, a deep belief in everyone's natural rights. Soon after that first San Francisco speech, she presented her perspective on the national debate about citizenship as the nation considered what should be the legal status of ex-slaves during the post–Civil War years. "Let the Constitutions of the several States be amended," she demanded, "so that white and black, red and yellow, of both sexes, can exercise their civil rights."[2]

California suffragists split into two factions, which they labeled "radical" (those linked to the Stanton-Anthony National Woman Suffrage Association) and "conservative" (Henry Blackwell's and Lucy Stone's American Woman Suffrage Association); nonetheless, the California women hoped that their divisions would become a source of strength. As separate groups, each could recruit from their constituencies. Although this could have occurred, it did not. Instead, the 1870s movement failed to grow. This occurred both in California and nationally, more because politics grew conservative as the nation retreated from its Reconstruction promises of equal rights than because suffragists were split internally.[3]

Those divisions, however, fueled by a disheartening decline in popular support, quickly became very bitter and very public. The local press accused California radicals, such as Gordon, of promoting socially dangerous free thinking; according to the *San Francisco Chronicle* in 1872, they supported socialism, spiritualism, and free love. Within a year conservative suffragists used the same paper to publicly charge a suffragist, Emily Pitts Stevens, with "free love"—which she and other radicals denied. Nonetheless, the conservatives purged her from the movement and soon thereafter the suffrage organ that Pitts Stevens edited, the *Pioneer,* died.[4]

Suffragists achieved a significant legislative victory in the early 1870s through the work of San Jose suffragists. In 1874 Sarah Louise Knox Goodrich and other San Jose women persuaded the state legislature to pass a law that allowed women to hold educational offices, such as seats on school boards. Knox Goodrich, a wealthy and politically well-connected woman, whom scholar Barbara Babcock characterizes as "maternal, sweet and very tough," served as leader of the San Jose society, which had an impressive two hundred members. Her first husband, William J. Knox, a physician, town booster, and state senator, secured a bill aiding married women's property rights shortly before his death in 1867; a few years later she married Levi Goodrich, a prominent architect, and thereafter used both names.[5]

All the California suffragists supported the educational office bill because all shared with Knox Goodrich the belief that their struggle for women's citizenship was also a fight to increase women's opportunity to engage in public work, from civic activism to paid labor. Knox Goodrich explained that women sought the ballot in order to be "acknowledged as citizens, respected as citizens, accorded the same rights and privileges as other citizens, and given the same chance to earn an honest living."[6]

Suffragists gained victories in other areas as well. In 1878 Gordon and Clara Shortridge Foltz, another suffragist committed to radical individualism, successfully lobbied the state legislature for the Woman Lawyer's Bill. It changed the state requirement to practice law from "white male" to "person." The state suffrage movement aided and supported their efforts, but the work and the victory were mostly theirs. Approximately a year later the state constitutional convention, meeting in Sacramento, approved two clauses key to women's rights; one protected women's right to work and the other their right to higher education. The two women wrote the first clause and lobbied for it.[7]

Despite these efforts and largely because of the growing conservatism of the Gilded Age, the state suffrage movement disintegrated in the 1880s. Although individuals and local societies continued to call for the vote, they did so in increasing isolation as the organizational and communication links that once held the movement together fell apart. As early as 1878 California suffragist Mary Snow reported that there was not "the same amount of activity in the movement as formerly." She observed that only "counties and individuals" gathered petitions; the state society did not. In 1886 a suffragist reported to the American Woman Suffrage Association that no state suffrage association existed; however, Foltz and Gordon continued a society affiliated with the National Woman Suffrage Association.[8]

Los Angeles suffragist Elizabeth Anne Kingsbury toured California in 1887 to determine the condition of the state suffrage movement. A spiritualist and abolitionist, she had worked for suffrage in the East since 1856. She moved west in 1883, and in the spring of 1884 she formed the Los Angeles Woman's Suffrage Association. After her trip up and down California, Kingsbury announced that she had failed to find a single "earnest suffragist" in San Francisco and that Knox Goodrich was "discouraged regarding organized effort." Kingsbury used the columns of the *Woman's Journal,* a national organ of the suffrage movement, to plaintively inquire, "Is our little suffrage club of Los Angeles with seventeen members the only one in the state?"[9]

As suffrage receded, women's temperance activism increased. Suffragists appraised this shift differently. Knox Goodrich complained in 1882 that "there is not as much interest taken in suffrage work directly as I would like to see, a great many of our old workers having gone off into other channels, such as temperance work." She conceded that "it may be that these will all lead to suffrage in the end," but she was "too impatient to secure the ballot to be even interested in any side issues." For her, temperance represented a retreat from women's struggle for citizenship.[10]

Other suffragists, however, saw the WCTU as a vehicle to promote women's issues. The radical suffragist Pitts Stevens became a leader within the WCTU. As historian Nancy Yamane notes, the WCTU provided Pitts Stevens with a "safe refuge" from personal assaults. Temperance women entered politics as Christians on a crusade to protect the home; such women were not necessarily popular in fashionable society, but their moral reputations were beyond attack. Pitts Stevens developed a regional reputation as a noted temperance orator and writer. Because she watched the temperance movement as it eventually embraced suffrage, she no doubt perceived the WCTU as a powerful resource for the women's movement.[11]

The WCTU served as a retreat, refuge, and resource for suffragists. Its greatest strength and weakness came from its contradictory combination of contained militancy—temperance women entered politics to protect women's place in the family. This focus represented a retreat from the suffragists' struggle to expand rights for women in and out of the family. Temperance women defended the homes of white, native-born, Protestant Americans, which won them much support and shelter from public attack. On the other hand, the WCTU argued that women could best guard the family by developing a politically powerful women's organization, so powerful that it could change laws. Not surprisingly, women who did this successfully rather quickly developed new definitions of *womanhood, women's work,* and *politics* that contrasted sharply with their defense of the status quo.

The WCTU developed into a resource for another reason—Frances Willard, the charismatic leader of the national WCTU. She became president in 1879 and soon transformed the small timid organization chiefly concerned with persuading individuals to support prohibition into the largest women's civic (or political) organization in the United States during the 1880s. By 1890, 150,000 women belonged to the WCTU, whereas only 13,000 were members of the national suffrage organization, which at that point was the National American Woman Suffrage Association (the separate groups had merged). Nationally, the suffrage movement remained, as in California, a small group of women clustered around extraordinary individuals. But Willard built an exceptionally well-organized movement with ten times as many members.[12]

Willard rallied women when she asked them to enter politics for home protection—to shield themselves and their children from alcoholic husbands and fathers. Her request evoked two deeply emotional images for the white, native-born, Protestant women, neither rich nor poor, who formed the bulk of the WCTU's membership: the wife, brutalized by a raging alcoholic husband, and the home, a place where women's moral influence transformed husbands into saintly men. Willard's call for home protection criticized male failure in the home and informed women that if they wished to continue as the moral guardians of the home, they must organize, enter politics, and lobby for temperance legislation. As a group they could develop the power they needed to transform America. To quote Willard—whose power rested at least in part on her ability to create such effective political slogans—home protection was "For God and Home and Native Land."[13]

California women, encouraged by Willard, formed a state WCTU in 1879; they started with fewer than two hundred members. (Initially, one organization covered the entire state, but in 1884 southern California women formed a separate group.) At the first state convention in 1880, they made the national slogan of "Home Protection" their own. They declared in their constitution that because the "woman is and always has been the greatest sufferer from this vice [alcoholism], which invades her home, and destroys her loved one," they would therefore "covenant with one another in a sacred and enduring compact against the wicked sale of alcoholic stimulants." In particular, they pledged to "work for such a change in those laws as will give us power to reclaim the fallen" and to create "a high moral and religious sentiment in favor of total abstinence."[14]

When the California WCTU pledged to change laws and develop public opinion to defend the home, it did so for the values that supported Protestant homes. At the heart of WCTU members' political strategy stood their commitment to coercive Christianity. If they could not persuade people to be temperate and religiously observant, they would legislate this behavior. At their first convention they promised to work for state-imposed prohibition and to pass laws to "protect the [Christian] Sabbath as a day of rest and worship"; through the years, the women would continue these efforts.[15]

The women understood such goals as religiously and culturally—perhaps even racially—imperative for the nation. To emphasize this point, and to gain public support in a country with growing anti-immigrant sentiment, temperance women contrasted themselves and their values to immigrant men and their supposedly un-American ways of living. Mary Frank Browne, first state president, referred to immigrants as "enemies of our free institutions." Frank Browne, whose paternal grandfather came from Germany, acknowledged that "some of our best citizens are foreigners, and that our own ancestors, at some period of their history, must have been such." Nonetheless, she blamed immigrant males for the high social costs of intemperance; furthermore, she

argued that immigrant men were deeply involved in the liquor business because they could not work as well as the "sons of New Englanders."[16]

Although temperance women marched under a banner of service for "God
and Home and Native Land," they declared that they had organized "with a
profound sense of our own weakness." Frank Browne illustrated their trep-
idation. After she was elected president, she refused to promise to preside over
future public meetings. She would not sit on the platform of the organizing
convention, even though it was held in a church.[17]

A closer look at Frank Browne's life helps explain the causes of WCTU
fearfulness. Ironically, she, like many other temperance women, came to the
WCTU with a record of church activism. Her achievements were particularly
noteworthy. Born in New York State in 1835, she moved to Montreal with her
banker husband and helped organize and manage, among other things, the
Young Women's Christian Association and the Ladies' Canadian Foreign Mis-
sionary Society. After her husband suffered business reverses, she and their
three children moved with him to San Francisco in 1876; she quickly established a YWCA in that city and in Oakland and became president in 1877 of
the Woman's Occidental Board of Foreign Missions. But Frank Browne and
others saw religious activism as private and, probably more to the point,
traditional; as temperance women, they were pledging to storm the citadel of
male power, the statehouse.[18]

Frank Browne, over time, like so many other temperance women, became
an accomplished public leader and speaker. This transformation is clearest in
the WCTU's successful campaign to achieve compulsory temperance education in the state's public schools. Although WCTU policy granted much au-
tonomy to its local chapters, the entire state organization, with enthusiastic
local support, dedicated itself to achieving mandated temperance education.
Nor did California women stand alone. They made this decision because of
the influence of the national WCTU; it had promoted temperance education
since the 1870s and with great success. By 1901 all states had legislation requiring temperance education.[19]

One reason that temperance women were so successful was internal. Their
campaign, with its focus upon educating children, appealed strongly to wom-
en who were still uncertain about participating in politics. California WCTU
women justified their activism by calling upon the principles of home protection, resolving that "by virtue of our motherhood, we feel the work of moral
[temperance] education to be our special province." Furthermore, the nature
of the temperance education campaign permitted mothers who were politically timid to become involved in politics slowly and cautiously. But the ineffi-

ciency of these efforts soon encouraged women to take steps that were more public, political, controversial, and successful.[20]

The temperance education campaign succeeded for external reasons as well. WCTU women accurately calculated that the general public would accept laws that asked for a "scientific" temperance education much more readily than those that sought to restrict public access to alcohol. As Willard commented, the immigrant "scoffed at the 'crusading women,' but the dignity of science will do much to silence him, and it will convince his children."[21]

Reassured by the national organization that they belonged in politics, California temperance women went after temperance education by first lobbying local boards of education to permit them to hold temperance essay competitions in public schools. In the first year, 1881, in San Francisco schools alone, twenty thousand children competed for the temperance prizes. After these competitions developed public support, WCTU members asked school boards to place a temperance textbook (one approved by the WCTU) in the school library.[22]

Despite these early successes, temperance women could see that they were still far from ensuring that all children received temperance indoctrination in the public schools. In 1883, therefore, they enlarged their plan of action and, in the process, expanded their political role. That year Mary Congdon, a music teacher and organizer and officer of the WCTU, urged temperance women to seek to have women elected to school offices. We must, she declared, be "progressive and aggressive." She then followed her own advice. Although three years earlier she had successfully pushed for a resolution that prohibited WCTU women from officially discussing women's suffrage, she now broke the resolution. She urged members to support women's "right of expressing their opinion in the form of ballots." She may have been influenced in part by Francis Willard, who visited California that year; she had persuaded the national WCTU to support votes for women two years earlier. But after hearing its first official request for women's suffrage, the California WCTU rejected it.[23]

The state WCTU women, however, continued their work for temperance education and did so with increased energy and daring. In 1884 they acquired the endorsement of six counties for temperance education. Temperance women ran for seats on the San Francisco school board that year, nominated by the Prohibition Party. All the women lost. But the very fact that they had campaigned for public office in what was the ninth-largest city in the nation, the gold rush city known for its hostility to prohibition, says much about their changing notions of women's place in politics.[24]

Undaunted by their setback, temperance women pushed forward. By 1886 the WCTU achieved temperance education in twenty counties, as well as in San Francisco and other cities. They gained so many local victories that at the 1886 temperance convention they announced that nearly 90 percent of public schoolchildren were using a temperance textbook. This achievement electrified the convention. Emboldened by their victories at the local level, the women resolved to lobby for a state law requiring temperance education, their most ambitious political activity to date. The WCTU women concentrated all their energies on this one very well-organized campaign. For the first time the northern California WCTU cooperated with the WCTU of southern California.[25]

The 1886 temperance convention represented a turning point for another reason. Temperance women decided—54-45—to support women's suffrage. Their suffrage resolution justified women's enfranchisement in limited terms as the instrument to "not only gain but maintain prohibitory laws." But they took steps that soon helped them expand their objectives; they established a franchise department and named Sarah M. Severance as its superintendent. She remained for twenty years.[26]

Severance contributed passion, organizing skills, and vision to the cause; a San Jose newspaper described her as "argumentative, witty, pertinent and strong." Years later California suffragist Mary McHenry Keith named Severance the "war horse" of the state suffrage movement, a fitting name for someone who always charged ahead and worked exceptionally hard. Born and educated in New York State, she taught school there before moving to California in 1862. After teaching for five years at the San Jose Institute, she established a boarding school in Gilroy, a small farming community south of San Jose. After she accepted the position as franchise superintendent from the state WCTU, she began systematic, energetic organizing.[27]

About the same time that the state WCTU committed itself to working for women's enfranchisement, it began developing new ways of thinking about race and ethnicity. During a prayer session at its 1885 state convention, both an African American woman and a woman who spoke with a German accent offered prayers. A local WCTU group resolved in 1886 that "when sex and race prejudices are educated out of people, and a taboo put upon alcohol, we shall have a millennium on this earth." That same year an African American woman served as a vice president of the San Jose chapter. By 1889 San Francisco's temperance women boasted African American, Swedish American, and German American members and attempted to organize Russian Finns and Japanese women. Although earlier WCTU remarks about immigrants were attacks upon immigrant men, these newer efforts underscored its in-creased commitment to gender as a positive identity and the growth of tolera-tion, at least for women, within its ranks.[28]

The WCTU temperance education campaign increased women's political activism. When they lobbied the 1887 state legislature for temperance educa-tion, an unprecedented number of women participated. Dorcas Spencer was largely responsible. She felt her life had changed forever in the early 1870s when she led church women in a crusade against liquor in a California mining town, Grass Valley, and she developed the campaign with the intent of en-couraging wide participation. She called upon every woman to take political action—to collect petitions and write letters.[29]

The compulsory temperance education bill quickly passed the state Senate but languished in the Assembly. Spencer had anticipated this, and WCTU petitions, signed by fifteen thousand and representing nearly every county in the state, were presented in the Assembly. Spencer next gave the signal to begin a letter-writing campaign. Still, the bill did not move until late on the last day of the session when it passed with only a three-vote margin. After the session a senator remarked to Spencer that "there had never been so many personal letters written to members in behalf of any bill as this one." She held out a directory of local chapters and proudly stated, "Every name there repre-sents a woman with a pen in her hand."[30]

In the year after this legislative victory the northern California WCTU more than doubled its membership, from 1,300 members in 1887 to 3,300 in 1888. In addition, successful political activism dramatically changed temper-ance women's opinions regarding women's rights. In 1886 the women had asked for suffrage only as a means to gain prohibition; by 1888 they resolved to work for the ballot because the "franchise is the symbol of freedom, and half the members of the republic are deprived of that right." Temperance women declared themselves citizens because they had acted as citizens.[31]

WCTU activists were conscious of how their temperance efforts empow-ered them as women. When Spencer surveyed all that temperance women had accomplished, she concluded that it "showed how the women are being developed by their work; and it showed how we have outgrown the conditions under which we began." She gave a "special call to the rank and file of our women . . . to cultivate their own capacity for usefulness."[32]

She now asked WCTU members to work for home protection and suffrage; she and many others saw the two as complementary objectives. WCTU wom-en's growing sense of entitlement developed from their ability to successfully lobby for legislation based on the moral values of their homes; therefore, they continued to see their political gains as growing from and made legitimate by their defense of the home. In 1889 temperance women sought the ballot "because it is the 'inherent right' of the governed, and because it is needed and right to make our zeal effective." The women supported suffrage both because of their "sameness" with men—their shared natural rights—and because of women's "difference"—their unique moral nature and responsibilities, a position that they shared with most suffragists of the era.[33]

The WCTU lobbied for its first suffrage bill at the state legislature in 1889 and did so as part of a coalition with suffragists. Both groups collected petitions and both lobbied state legislators. The temperance women reported themselves pleased to be able to work with Laura de Force Gordon, a "clear-headed lawyer, [who] was able to do splendid work in our common cause." She delivered key speeches; the WCTU women collected most of the petitions. Their joint efforts were rebuilding the women's movement and, in a pattern that was common in the West, the temperance women dominated the movement with their numbers and grassroots organizational skills. In a few years their coalition would dramatically expand.[34]

❖

Some California women's clubs joined the temperance-suffrage coalition in the 1890s; the clubs, which encouraged their members to educate themselves and engage in reform, also fostered members' commitment to suffrage. The New England Woman's Club, founded in 1868 by Caroline Severance in Boston, served as a model for such pioneering clubs. Severance, active as an abolitionist and suffragist before the Civil War, created the club as a place where women could study together, presenting papers and commenting upon them. She felt certain that women educated in such a manner would take up the work of reform and civic activism. Her confidence was affirmed. Members of the New England Woman's Club quickly investigated "needle women," or women who sewed in sweatshops; established a horticultural school for women; and placed four women on the Boston school board. Severance believed, as did Francis Willard, that women could build a new and better world but only if they worked in that world—a process that not coincidentally would also make them public citizens.[35]

In the mid-1870s Severance and her husband, a retired banker, seeking to recover from illness and fatigue, left Boston and eventually settled in Los Angeles, a small, dusty cattle-ranching town. In 1878 Severance, then fifty-eight, began a new phase of her life by organizing the Los Angeles Woman's Club, following the model of her earlier club. Such ideas—women's organizing to educate themselves and seeking reform legislation as women to aid women, without the shelter of religious or social welfare institutions—were daring in Boston in 1868. Ten years later Los Angeles still found such notions radical. Just as the Boston press criticized the New England Woman's Club, so the Los Angeles press censured the Los Angeles Woman's Club. The *Los Angeles Herald* editorialized that virtue and intellect were not compatible in women. Local clergymen prayed that women club members would see the error of their ways.[36]

Twenty women caused this uproar in Los Angeles. Many also belonged to the Unitarian church, an institution of religious liberalism founded by Severance as soon as she arrived in town. The church provided space for the club to meet. "I doubt," stated Mary Spalding, a club member, Unitarian, wife of a *Los Angeles Times* editor, and mother of seven, "if we would have been permitted to assemble anywhere else." The most severe limitation faced by the club was its size; the Boston club began with six times as many members. Although many of the Los Angeles women were well educated (Spalding was a Vassar graduate), the intellectual life of the small club centered around Severance. When she returned to Boston for a visit that stretched into years, the Los Angeles Woman's Club disintegrated.[37]

In 1885 Severance, again living in Los Angeles, resuscitated the Los Angeles Woman's Club; the second club was more successful. The city was booming in the 1880s and the new club benefited; it began with thirty members and expanded to fifty by the end of the year. Half the officers of the 1885 club, including Severance as president, had been members of the first club. The new club, founded on the same principles as the earlier one, took up the study of the arts and community projects; it established a free kindergarten system for working-class children. Some members found such a public role uncomfortable; in response, the club organized itself into committees so that members could choose whether to engage in public affairs or limit themselves to intellectual pursuits.[38]

Those club members who were interested in reform joined the Work Committee. In March 1885 the Work Committee, whose elite members included Mary Gibson, wife of a banker; Mary Barnes Widney, wife of a judge; and Mrs. H. H. Boyce, wife of the business manager of the Times-Mirror Company, began investigating "the conditions and wages of working women in Los Angeles." The committee determined that many "thoroughly respectable" women came to the city expecting to immediately "find plenty of work at a fair compensation." Instead, the female job seekers found that securing a position often took some time and that their wages were frequently inadequate to pay for decent housing. The committee decided to solve these problems by building a women's boarding home with progressive, subsidized rates.[39]

The club women's worries about the difficulties of women wage earners stemmed from the city's period of rapid growth and development. In 1880, in a town of 11,000, fewer than 15 percent of women residents worked for wages; by 1900, in a city of 100,000, more than 20 percent worked for wages, a 46 percent increase. Club women's worries may have been heightened because women workers were mostly young and single and because they were performing work that seemed dramatically more public than that performed by earlier residents. In 1880 many women in the ranching town of Los Angeles still engaged in household production, such as food preservation, and one third of those who worked for wages did so as domestic servants. Twenty years later only 19 percent of working women were employed in household production or as servants; young women took up newly created jobs in clerical, sales, and professional areas of employment.[40]

The Los Angeles women's decision to build a boarding home also reflected and grew from the thinking of the national women's movement. Other urban organized women witnessed a great increase in the numbers of young unmarried women who were entering the paid labor force, especially during the 1870s and 1880s. Nationally, 16 percent of women worked for wages in 1880, and this increased to about 20 percent in 1900, rates close to those of Los Angeles. In response to this change, women's groups, especially the Young Women's Christian Association, built homes for wage-earning women. By 1888 about forty of these homes served women workers in the country's cities. The women who built these homes, middle-aged and middle-class matrons, saw themselves as protecting "working girls," young unmarried women workers, from an exploitative labor market and from sexual transgressions.[41]

To build the same kind of home in Los Angeles, the Work Committee formed an umbrella organization, the Women's Cooperative Union, that welcomed interested women. Judging by the union's advisory board, most women who joined probably came from women's groups already working in the public sphere. Ira More from the WCTU sat on the board, as did Mary Gibson of the Orphans' Home Society and Mrs. Ducommun of the Ladies Benevolent Society. Through the latter two institutions elite women managed the city's public welfare system. The Ladies Benevolent Society, working closely with the police and city supervisors, distributed public funds and services. Gibson and other women made the city orphanage possible; they conducted private fund-raising and secured state aid. The women soon ran the orphanage as well. Women who engaged in benevolent charities no doubt

Women promoting the Los Angeles Flower Festival, probably in 1888. (The Huntington Library, San Marino, California)

saw the construction of a boarding home as yet another "ladies' benevolent endeavor"; instead of rescuing poor widows or orphans, these affluent matrons would provide maternal protection for the "working girls."[42]

The Women's Cooperative Union decided to hold a flower festival to raise the large sum needed to build a boarding home. The women were so successful in their venture that they changed the name of their organization to the Flower Festival Society and made the festival an annual spring event in Los Angeles. With the impressive amounts of money they raised through the festivals, they were able first to rent and then to build a home for women. It opened with a triumphant reception in the spring of 1887, only two years after the first festival.[43]

The Flower Festival Society wanted the home to become a "center for women's work in this city," and the three-story house sheltered a variety of services. It provided "thirty-six sleeping apartments" with prices "graduated to the income of the applicant, and often remitted entirely" until the woman found employment. The apartments quickly filled and developed a long waiting list.

The home also housed the Woman's Exchange and the Bureau of Information. The exchange provided a place to sell "everything that a woman can make well, for which there is a market," while the bureau sought to help women find jobs. Within a year the Bureau of Information had aided three hundred women in their search for employment, while two hundred women were said to support themselves, for the most part, by what they sold at the exchange.[44]

The Flower Festival Society built the home to help women in the paid labor force. Mary Barnes Widney, president of the society, readily acknowledged that providing subsidized housing was only a stopgap measure for the problems of working women. Their advancement required, Widney asserted, that women become skilled workers who received just compensation. Women should be prepared for the labor force by an industrial education provided for both sexes and all classes. Widney perceived the limitations of the home, but she defended it as well. It was something that could be done by the club women immediately; it symbolized that women could legitimately participate in the marketplace, that it was to women's credit "that they are willing to work for an honest living."[45]

The Flower Festival Society built the home for another reason: its mature affluent members worried that young women, without adequate housing or wages, would engage in sex outside of marriage, an act that would prove disastrous to them personally and to society. According to leaders of the society, poor living and working conditions exposed women "to ruin a hundred times worse than death" and fostered "demoralization that may invade the most happy and respectable families." Members of the society did not blame the working women for this situation. "What right have we," asked Mary Widney, "with money always at our command, to look with contempt upon the frail, helpless, unprotected, unloved and half-paid girl who, in a moment of desperation, for want of money, yields to the tempter's voice?" Yet, as Widney made clear, although the society did not condemn "frail, helpless" young women, neither did it trust them on their own.[46]

Members of the Flower Festival Society made themselves protectors of the young women and chose the home as the best means to do so. It protected the boarders as if "they were hedged in by parental care," the *Los Angeles Herald* reported: a matron watchfully oversaw the home, boarders were "affectionately invited to be present" at daily worship services (as the home's rules put it), and gentlemen callers were received only in the library or parlor. The society decided when young women must return home at night as well as at which hour the lights must be turned out. The *Los Angeles Herald* praised the society for managing the home so as "to make every woman in the home *feel* thoroughly independent" (emphasis added). Yet the strict rules of the Flower Festival Society undercut those lessons of independence that it wished to instill. By building the home, the society both supported women's entrance into the paid labor force and sought to limit the social independence women might gain from their small wages.[47]

The Flower Festival Society was more successful at providing a means for its members to participate in the public sphere, developing work for themselves. Not the least of these accomplishments was the financial success of the Flower Festivals. They began in years of prosperity for Los Angeles and climaxed with the height of the real estate boom of 1886. Opening in 1885, the festival netted $2,000, doubled that sum in 1886, and earned almost as much again in 1887. In 1888 the women gave $4,500 from their profits to the Orphans' Home. They were soon wishing they had kept the money. The economic boom of the 1880s collapsed. The subsequent sluggish business economy stopped the festivals, even though more young women than ever needed the services of the home.[48]

During the boom years, however, tourists and natives alike flocked to see this early southern California forerunner of the Rose Parade and Disneyland. The women rented a large hall and filled it with floral displays, such as the nine-foot-long replica of Mission San Gabriel, with walls of white margue-rites and a roof of double red geraniums. In 1887 the *Los Angeles Herald* de-clared that "the efforts of the ladies are worth many hundreds of thousands of dollars to us in the way of advertising." Because Los Angeles depended on real estate speculation and tourism, the Flower Festivals undoubtedly brought important amounts of money into the city. The festivals became so popular that eastern travel agents arranged special excursions to Los Angeles during the festivals.[49]

Both the Flower Festivals and the home built by festival money represented women's struggle and ability to participate in the commercial life of the city. Yet the festivals, like the home, represented a dual symbol of women's depen-dence and independence. The society members earned large sums for the city and their charity, yet their own work was unpaid, testimony to their depen-dence on male wages.

But society members made two important gains. They recognized that all women, young working women and middle-aged matrons, suffered from their exclusion from public life. Widney noted that society regretted the burn-ing of famous old books or the untimely death of talented men but, she asked, "what are all these compared to that which has been going on in all lands and ages in the lives of women . . . [the] waste of their faculties?" She may have been reflecting on her own life. Before her marriage to Robert M. Widney, attorney, founder of the city's Board of Trade in 1873, and leading real estate agent—the father of gringo boosters, according to one source—she was known as a student with "brilliant intellectual attainments." She met her husband at the University of the Pacific where he was a professor and she was a student. Widney and other Flower Festival Society members also gained through their experience the recognition that women could change their public lives if they developed, in her words, "clear sympathy with all womankind."[50]

In April 1891 Caroline Severance and twenty other women organized the Friday Morning Club, the most important and long-lived women's club in southern California history; with this club Severance at last saw her club ideals take permanent root in Los Angeles. Its predecessor, the second Los Angeles Woman's Club, had died, because of Severance's prolonged absences from the city and the energy that members were expending for the Flower Festival. The Friday Morning Club, however, prospered. Several reasons account for its success. Severance remained in Los Angeles, but more important was that this club quickly outgrew its dependence on one person. An important factor was its size. Within a year the club boasted two hundred members. This growth reflected the growth of Los Angeles; by 1890 the city was five times larger than it was when Severance organized a woman's club in the 1870s.[51]

Part of the Friday Morning Club's success resulted from the varied nature of its membership. The initial membership consisted, Severance recounted in 1899, "of some of the advance guard and old standbys of the woman's movement." Women who were socially prominent in the community joined the club; these included Margaret Sartori, wife of a banker; Eliza Otis, wife of the owner of the *Los Angeles Times*; and Olive Cole, wife of a former U.S. senator. Unlike the earlier clubs, where Unitarians dominated the membership, so many new women joined the Friday Morning Club that most members belonged to mainstream Protestant churches. On the other hand, women known for their advanced views regarding suffrage and other matters also joined the club. By 1891 several different kinds of Los Angeles women felt comfortable joining a women's club.[52]

Only months after the Friday Morning Club opened its doors it became involved in a heated public battle about women's work. The contest began in July 1891, when the Teachers' Committee of the Los Angeles School Board dismissed twenty-one teachers—all women. All, regardless of their qualifications, were discharged in a singularly unjust fashion: without a hearing, without an explanation, without any warning. The club members assumed—and they were supported in this by the *Los Angeles Times*—that the women were dismissed so they could be replaced by "political" appointees.[53]

The Friday Morning Club appointed a committee chaired by Severance to publicly ask the school board members why they had "removed so many able and competent teachers from the city's schools" in such a manner. In reply, the board, surprised by the women's visit, could say only that the teachers were "inefficient" and the board members "could do better" by hiring others. The board did not know that a woman reporter was present at the confrontation. According to the reporter, who favored the club women, the board was "dumbfounded" by the women's visit and responded to their pointed questions in a "weak voice" with even weaker answers. Women's powerful voice proved potent. Within three months the club, with the aid of "public opinion," was able to restore half the teachers to their positions.[54]

The controversy with the school board spurred the club women into further political activity. The Friday Morning Club decided that the best means to prevent such an incident from recurring was to put a woman on the school board. Fortunately for the club, a board member resigned and the board had to appoint someone to serve until the next election. The club ensured that a club member, Margaret Hughes, was nominated for the position. But the city attorney refused to let her sit on the board because the city charter did not permit women to hold public office. Hughes correctly noted that the city charter was superseded by a state law that permitted women to hold all educational offices—the law suffragists had lobbied for and won in 1874. The matter was taken to court, but the court did not decide in Hughes's favor until three months before the end of her term.[55]

Placing Hughes on the school board represented the Friday Morning Club's entry into politics. After Hughes's appointment the club became increasingly involved in local politics and came to see itself as a legitimate participant in political debates regarding public services. In the fall of 1892 the club successfully supported Hughes in a school board election campaign. By the end of 1893 the club suggested that its members visit schools, appear at school board meetings, and attend local election primaries in order to "fit themselves for future efforts toward improvement"—advice that the club members followed. They launched a campaign in the spring of 1894 to make Kate Tupper Galpin, an honorary club member, normal school professor, and nationally known educator, the county superintendent of schools. The women lost that campaign but not their commitment to civic activism.[56]

Through such reform efforts the Friday Morning Club believed it had found a resolution to a question it had endlessly debated in the 1890s, finding the appropriate public work for elite women. Club women believed women had a right to education and freedom of choice in selecting an occupation. They especially emphasized that they wanted this for their daughters, probably because in Los Angeles, as elsewhere, middle-class young women often worked for wages before their marriage. Yet club members were also concerned that women continue their domestic responsibilities, and in fact wives of all classes seldom engaged in paid labor. Club members argued, however, that contemporary wives had less to do at home than their mothers because machines had taken over much of women's household production. Club work, from self-education to civic activism, presented a solution: work that was personally rewarding, socially useful, and easily adjusted to the demands of domestic duties.[57]

Friday Morning Club members decided that they would especially pursue the work of civic activism because it promised the greatest rewards for them and for society; they were explicitly advised to do so only a few months before they organized their club. In January 1891 Charlotte Perkins Gilman, who was just beginning to develop a national reputation as an iconoclastic feminist writer, spoke to the last remnants of the Los Angeles Woman's Club. She was living with friends in Pasadena while recovering from a mental collapse caused by the tension of living a life restricted to "domestic service" while she longed to serve the world. She first urged the women to perform public work, declaring that "you cannot belong to the human race till you do *human work*" (her emphasis). But she especially urged the club women to take up political work, declaring that Los Angeles "is composed half of men and half of women. It is your city as much as theirs." Gilman concluded, "By the side of man where God placed us—doing the work of the world of which we are half . . . in the forefront of a race which has no sovereign save God—this is Our Place Today!"[58]

When Gilman spoke of club women standing "in the forefront of a race," she meant the human race but with the white race serving as the vanguard of all races. She made this quite clear in her speech to the Los Angeles Woman's Club when she referred to the "civilized world" as Europe, America, and Australia and to the rest of the planet, those places filled with people she saw as nonwhite, as the "savage world." Gilman, a fervent evolutionist, called upon club women to perform "the work of the world" so that they would push forward what she saw as inextricably linked, the evolution of the white race and half its members, white women. Other women shared her views. When Spalding gave her speech, "The New Woman," in 1895 before the Friday Morning Club, she celebrated the college-educated women's achievements in private and public life; she did not ask why the few women who attended college were mostly white and wealthy. Instead, Spalding concluded that women faced no limit except "the law of the survival of the fittest." The club responded with "earnest applause."[59]

To further women's public work, a group of Los Angeles women established the Women's Parliament of Southern California in the fall of 1892. An umbrella organization for women's associations in the region, the parliament's role was "to bring the progressive women of Southern California into closer relation" so that they might participate in a "full and free discussion of reform necessary to the progress of woman's work in the church, home, and society." In the minds of the activists, "progressive" and the "progress of woman's work" were linked.[60]

Although Unitarian women, with a shared background in women's clubs, created the Women's Parliament, they believed that in order for the parliament to succeed, it must build a more diverse movement. Elmira Stephens, president of the parliament, felt certain that when women came together to discuss women's work, they could learn to "council with each other" and realize "that in organization there is strength." To ensure that this occurred, invitations were sent through the press to women in churches, societies, and clubs. At the second session of the parliament, in February 1893, the treasurer, Sarah Judson, resigned and was replaced by Lucy Blanchard, a Methodist and WCTU leader. The officers stated publicly that Judson "voluntarily resigned in order that another denomination besides the Unitarian might be officially recognized."[61]

The parliament achieved great popularity. Five hundred women attended the first session, and this grew to one thousand by the second session. An examination of those who came as delegates, a smaller number than the audience at large, reveals that although parliament organizers sought diversity, most members were Protestant and all were white. The WCTU sent about 25 percent of the delegates, about the same as women's clubs. Women from denominational groups composed another fourth of the delegates, with mainstream Protestants more than half the group. No Catholic or Jewish women were listed as delegates from their respective religious groups. The last quarter of the delegates was composed of a small group of suffragists; women from interdenominational charity groups, such as the King's Daughters; and representatives from charities and philanthropies.[62]

At the three sessions of the parliament from the autumn of 1892 to the autumn of 1893, papers were presented on a wide range of women's activities, with the emphasis upon furthering elite women's work. Professional women spoke to encouraging audiences. Various organizations presented women-supported institutions, such as the Santa Barbara Cottage Hospital.[63]

Speakers discussed, especially at the first parliament, how to increase the efficiency of women's philanthropic organizations and thus establish women managers as powerful experts who policed class lines. Gibson in particular wanted the parliament to become a "benevolent clearing house" that would ensure charity was dispensed to the "worthy poor" on a "business basis." She used this language of corporate America because she shared with men of her class a belief in the importance of maintaining and protecting class interests.[64]

Gibson, a public schoolteacher, came to Los Angeles in the late 1870s and married Frank Gibson, a banker, in 1881 when she was twenty-six. She had four children but only one survived. As noted earlier, she became deeply involved in women's voluntary groups, such as the Orphans' Home Society. At the parliament, which she helped build and where she served as an officer—the better to make an organized womanhood—she emphasized that women must make their work systematic, scientific, and consolidated. She saw such efforts as increasing the influence of elite woman experts and felt all women's groups could gain from such bureaucratic rationalization, noting that the WCTU under Frances Willard had developed a "perfect system [where] every question of reform and progress is reported on by bands of women all over the United States."[65]

Gibson further observed that although the WCTU began "with every shade of opinion on the Woman Suffrage question, . . . they now acknowledge [it] as the keynote of all reforms." Two other speakers at the first session of the Women's Parliament mentioned suffrage in their papers—although the parliament, when it was organized in the fall of 1892, had announced that it was "not a woman's rights society." Yet each time the parliament met, it increased its support for women gaining the vote. At the first session no one gave an entire lecture about women's enfranchisement. At the February 1893 session Spalding delivered a suffrage speech. According to the *Los Angeles Times,* her talk "caused more enthusiasm than any preceding it" and was "frequently interrupted by applause long and loud." At the end of this session the parliament sent a telegram to the California legislature requesting passage of the pending suffrage bill. Not a single woman spoke or voted against this action.[66]

Alice Moore McComas, president of the Los Angeles Woman's Suffrage Association, claimed she was not surprised by this rapid transformation of the Women's Parliament into a suffrage organization. McComas, a journalist who was the daughter of an Illinois congressman and wife of a Los Angeles judge, stated she realized ahead of time that a woman's organization that discussed all aspects of women's work would soon notice women's political limitations. Her insight was correct. The efforts to advance women's public work, paid or unpaid, were attempts to increase and legitimize women's public power in society; the ballot aided women's work in a narrow pragmatic sense and in a much larger ideological manner. As Mary Lynde Craig, lawyer and Redlands club woman, stated at the 1893 fall session of the Women's Parliament, justice will be done "when women, rich and poor, high and low, black and white" realize they are citizens "not only in name . . . but in power, and in dignity that always accompanies power."[67]

❖

San Francisco women also formed organizations aimed at advancing women into public life. Northern California women's experience differed from that of their Los Angeles counterparts in that the two key organizations (other than the WCTU) that led elite women into politics were not groups open to a broad range of middle-class women, such as the Friday Morning Club and the Women's Parliament. Instead, the two path-breaking associations, the Pacific Association of Collegiate Alumnae and the Pacific Coast Woman's Press Association, opened their doors to highly specialized groups, college educated and/or professional women. Both came to believe in the importance of political actions for themselves as professional women and for the status of women as a group.

In 1885 Marion Talbot, founder of the National Association of Collegiate Alumnae, wrote a friend in San Francisco, Sarah Dix Hamlin. Talbot urged her to form a Pacific branch of the association. The three-year-old organization of college-educated women sought to solve two pressing problems of female baccalaureates in the 1880s: their limited options for employment and the isolation produced by their unemployment. Hamlin responded positively to Talbot's suggestion. The Pacific Association of Collegiate Alumnae, a San Francisco–based organization, began in 1885 with twenty-five members who pledged to "stand ready to help . . . in investigations . . . and in efforts to extend and improve the collegiate education of women."[68]

The twenty-five women were young, affluent, and accomplished. None had been out of school for longer than eleven years and one third were listed in San Francisco's *Elite Directory*, or Blue Book. Most Collegiate Alumnae members were listed in terms of the accomplishments of their fathers or husbands, a reflection of both the elite status of a college education and the small number of employment opportunities for college women. Nonetheless, a few alumnae were mentioned for their own achievements; Hamlin founded and taught at an exclusive school for girls. She was not a wealthy woman, but wealth was not the only criterion for admission into the city's elite. Other alumnae benefited from family connections as well as talent; Dr. Emma Sutro Merritt, the daughter of Adolph Sutro, a Jewish immigrant mining engineer who became a millionaire reformer, was listed in the elite directory.[69]

Despite their pledge to concentrate on efforts to improve collegiate education, the Collegiate Alumnae focused on increasing employment opportunities for women college graduates. They put some energy toward lessening the discriminatory practices of public schools, which "almost invariably" hired normal school graduates for teaching positions rather than women with college degrees. But mostly they worked to increase women's employment within community service. The association carefully chose its areas of endeavor within social services, selecting those with the maximum potential for using the skills of college women, in particular, the skills of social science research. The association's community service increased voluntary yet meaningful employment opportunities for college women as it developed progressive reforms, an effort characterized by a potent blend of self-interest, altruism, elitism, and social science methodology.[70]

The Pacific Association of Collegiate Alumnae took its first step into social service in 1887. It helped create the Associated Charities of San Francisco, part of a national movement to rationalize urban philanthropy through organizational consolidation and unified standards of welfare distribution—standards achieved through social science. Caroline Jackson, an accepted member of San Francisco's elite as well as an active member of the Collegiate Alumnae, helped form the Associated Charities. Jackson sat on the board of directors of the Associated Charities for five years as the Collegiate Alumnae representative.[71]

In 1889 Milicent Shinn, Collegiate Alumnae officer and editor of the *Overland Monthly,* an important local magazine devoted to literature and public affairs, analyzed the results of a "scientific" survey of San Francisco's charities. This survey, conducted by the Collegiate Alumnae, sought to aid and bolster the social services performed by Collegiate Alumnae members. Her conclusions agreed with those of Gibson and other women who were attempting to rationalize charitable endeavors: experts must administer charities so that they maintained the status quo. College women proved especially adept in learning the principles of this "new charity," but all who were willing to study would soon agree with its fundamental principles. According to Shinn, these were, first, that "drunkenness and laziness are the real causes of all poverty in San Francisco," and, second, that poverty "exists almost entirely among the foreign-born." Poverty could be prevented—but only through reforms that bolstered the social order. Shinn recommended the "toilsome, inch-by-inch improvements" of public institutions, work that she knew women were capably performing in San Francisco and elsewhere.[72]

Although the Pacific Association of Collegiate Alumnae devised a number of innovative schemes to advance women into the workforce, it remained, in the 1880s, distinctly uninterested in women's suffrage. The association's president in 1887, Mary McHenry Keith, a graduate of Hastings Law School who married the noted California landscape artist William Keith, attempted to speak to them about women's enfranchisement. They listened to her, she recalled years later, "with an air of amused indulgence." Nonetheless, the association's interest in public education in general and working conditions for women teachers in particular led it into the San Francisco school board elections of 1886 and 1888. Those steps raised the possibility of cross-class alliances and helped transform the Collegiate Alumnae into the nucleus of an urban women's movement.[73]

Bay Area professional women found the city schools in dire need of reform. San Francisco, in common with other U.S. cities in the late nineteenth century, possessed an inadequate public school system. In 1886 the *San Francisco Chronicle* described conditions in the city's schools: "the dilapidation of our schoolhouses, their crowded conditions, the absence of fresh air in the classrooms, the presence of sickening smells from the sewers and the fact that hundreds of children are allowed to sit day after day in unsafe structures." In addition, and what especially angered the women, the school board managed city schools on the principle of patronage politics. At least every two years teachers had to approach a new board to renew their contracts, forcing them to use a variety of methods to maintain their positions, from persuasion to bribery, circumstances conducive to numerous kinds of scandals.[74]

The women laid the blame for these conditions on the Democratic political machine of Christopher Buckley, the Irish "blind boss of San Francisco." Buckley, who kept his machine in power from 1881 to 1891, followed a policy popular with voters and saw to it that the city maintained low taxes. However, the city grew during the 1880s, which heightened demands for services. New homes were built in the southern and western outlying areas of the city, and homeowners wanted paved streets, gas lines, streetcar service, and so on. To provide these services without raising taxes, Buckley arranged deals with businesses that wanted city contracts; in turn, Buckley gained enough financially to manage the machine (elections were quite expensive) and make himself a wealthy man. The machine viewed the city school system, which employed more people than all other city agencies combined and needed many business services, as yet another means to make money and grease political connections.[75]

For a variety of reasons Buckley's school board seemed politically vulnerable in the 1886 election. When the schools faced a large deficit in 1882, the directors dismissed teachers, reduced salaries, and closed schools. These steps alone angered some voters; in addition, the numerous allegations of graft and corruption against the school board seemed quite persuasive to many. In the 1884 city election not a single Democratic machine candidate was elected to the city school board. The new Republican school board, however, did not improve the quality of education—city Republicans followed the same political principles as Buckley's Democrats. So two years later, in the 1886 election, the schools were once again an issue.[76]

The city elections of 1886 were contested by eleven political parties, including a number of "nonpartisan" reform groups that shared an animosity for Buckley's political machine. Reformers unsuccessfully attempted to build a united reform coalition. The school board race provided a striking example of their failure, remaining a campaign of "nearly eleven separate and distinct tickets." Women took advantage of this chaotic situation to run women for the school board.[77]

The Public School Reform Association, an ad hoc organization formed quickly and solely by women to place women on the school board, developed a slate of six women candidates (the school board had twelve members), four nominated by the Citizens' Independent Convention, a nonpartisan reform party, and two by the Labor Party. The Public School Reform Association then asked other parties to back these candidates. Four of the women candidates, Sarah Hamlin, May Treat, Mary Campbell, and Cordelia Kirkland, received endorsements from five different parties: various independent groups, the Labor Party, and the Prohibitionists. The rest of the slate of women included Mrs. G. K. Phillips, with four endorsements, and Miss K. A. F. Green, with two. The two major parties refused to endorse any of the women candidates. The Prohibitionists supported the Reform Association's candidates plus six temperance women, filling its entire school board slate with women.[78]

The *San Francisco Bulletin,* a reform newspaper and one of the few to mention the women, noted the endorsements collected for the women candidates and stated that "no male candidate has done quite so well." The women's success rested on several factors. The many competing nonpartisan groups could not unite, and the men recognized the destructiveness of their competition. The women gained numerous endorsement because, more than any man, they could successfully claim "true" nonpartisanship and dedication to improving schools.[79]

Yet another factor contributing to the women's success was their leadership. Members of the Pacific Association of Collegiate Alumnae joined the Public School Reform Association and became leaders of the group. Shinn led during the election. In addition, two of the six women proposed for the school board were, like Shinn herself, founders and activists in the Collegiate Alumnae—Sarah Hamlin and May Treat, a writer and doctor of philosophy.[80]

The Public School Reform Association, however, was plagued by organizational, ideological, and strategic difficulties. The Reform Association did not begin campaigning until a week before the election. The women attributed this delay to "difficulties . . . experienced in the preliminary arrangements." Probably those difficulties included deciding who could join the Reform Association. Until a week before elections the Reform Association assiduously avoided the Prohibitionists, although this group filled its school board slate with women. The Reform Association kept its distance from the Prohibitionists in the belief that "for the entering wedge, it would seem unwise to ask to have the whole board consist of women." The Reform Association also worried that the Prohibitionists would antagonize voters.[81]

Whatever decisions were made or difficulties resolved, when the Reform Association began campaigning, it opened its doors to the Prohibitionists and, apparently, everyone else. According to Shinn, the campaign expanded to include women "of all parties and shades of opinion—Catholics, Calvinists, and Agnostics, Republicans, Democrats, Mugwumps and Prohibitionists." Shinn marveled at the level of cooperation achieved between "leaders of society and working-women." This "variety and novelty" was "refreshing," Shinn thought, "to those of us who had known only their own 'social circle.' "[82]

Despite Shinn's upbeat assertion that all types of women joined the Reform Association, it remains unclear whether women teachers and elite women leaders of the Reform Association developed an alliance. On the one hand, the two groups had obvious differences, based on class and ethnic factors. Most San Francisco teachers had been women since at least the 1860s, and by the mid-1880s about half were Irish. Many women teachers, especially the Irish women, who came from the city's working class, had several reasons to support Buckley's Democratic Party. Aside from being Irish himself, Buckley ensured that his party's candidates represented the ethnic diversity of San Francisco much more than the Republicans' candidates did. Buckley's ward clubs played a vital role in working-class communities as social places that provided some employment.[83]

The women teachers, on the other hand, might find other factors more persuasive when choosing whom to support for the school board, issues related to gender or to teaching as a profession. This was exemplified in the campaign of Kate Kennedy, an Irish Catholic teacher in the San Francisco schools who ran for office in the 1886 election. Kennedy, born in Ireland to a middle-class family in 1827, experienced several years of deprivation in New York after her family fled the potato famine. She began teaching in San Francisco in the late 1850s and became a principal in 1867. Paid less than a male principal, she successfully lobbied the 1874 state legislature for a bill guaranteeing women teachers equal pay for equal work. In the 1880s Kennedy also engaged in the labor movement, joining the Knights of Labor and aiding strikes. In 1883 she became a charter member of the Woman's Christian Suffrage Association, whose objectives expressed some of her political goals: the vote, fair employment practices for women, and support of policies "to increase the efficiency of our public schools." The last reflected her deep disapproval of Buckley's treatment of teachers, making their contracts dependent on political whim. In the 1886 election she therefore ran as the Labor Party's candidate for state superintendent of public instruction in opposition to the Buckley machine.[84]

In contrast, elite women emphasized notions of women's traditional role when working to place women on the school board. The Public School Reform Association's campaign themes coincided with Francis Willard's home protection ideology; women could be trusted to "make an earnest effort to lift our schools out of politics, and . . . govern them in the interests of the mothers and little children." Some of the women's opponents replied that they accepted women's abilities in education but not to manage the financial duties of the school board. The women, whose purpose in running for office was partly to remedy the financial rascality of the male school board, responded that the issue was again one of women's morality: "Here lies the whole opposition, women will be too honest."[85]

Despite the claimed alliance between leaders of society and workingwomen, no women were elected to the San Francisco school board in the 1886 election. Nevertheless, women found a silver lining. Women fought "our first great battle in this city and lost—and won," as a San Francisco woman identified only as "L.L." wrote in the *Woman's Journal*. Although all the reform tickets lost in a Democratic sweep, the women received some 3,000 votes more than the rest of the reform candidates. The women took heart from this and immediately began discussing electing women in 1888. L.L. concluded by rejoicing that the movement "constituted a nucleus which shall help to lift women in California to a higher plane of thought and action." Shinn agreed, stating the campaign "has left its friends here hopeful, eager, in excellent cooperation, and ready to push it to a conclusion."[86]

The women entered the 1888 school board election and ran a very different kind of campaign. They did not conduct a last-minute, hurriedly arranged, and thoroughly ignored affair. Instead, the women managed a well-organized campaign; they received an endorsement from the Republicans and recognition from the city's press. The reasons for this transformation were various, but an important factor was women's experience in the election of 1886. Politicians were surprised and impressed by the record of the women candidates and, more important, so were the women. From the 1886 campaign they gained confidence, some political knowledge and skills, and the nucleus of a movement dedicated to expanding women's place in politics.

One reason for the differences between the two campaigns was that in the summer of 1888 San Francisco women organized the Century Club; this new organization of elite women provided crucial support in that fall's school board campaign. Hamlin, founder of the Pacific Association of Collegiate Alumnae, played a key role in the club's creation, as did other alumnae leaders, Caroline Jackson and Dr. Emma Sutro Merritt. Like the Association of Collegiate Alumnae, the club boasted many affluent women; 54 percent of the club's charter members were listed in the city's *Elite Directory*. These women included the club's first president, philanthropist Phoebe Hearst, wife of millionaire senator George Hearst, and Ellen Sargent, a suffragist whose husband was also a U.S. senator.[87]

Women with national reputations as leaders in voluntary social service organizations, such as Dr. Charlotte Brown, founder of the San Francisco Children's Hospital, and Sarah Cooper, who established the city's free kindergarten system for working-class children, also joined the Century Club. These two women came from a flourishing empire of women's benevolent organizations. By the end of the 1870s San Francisco boasted approximately thirty such women's associations: orphanages and child care centers, benevolent societies, homes for the elderly, and five hospitals. As in Los Angeles, women dominated the city's public welfare system through these institutions. Yet, although women such as Sarah Cooper brought to the club an impressive record of public social service, they did not necessarily support women's suffrage. They believed that women's public work simply extended women's domestic responsibilities.[88]

From the very beginning the Century Club promoted women's intellectual advancement and their involvement in public service. The Century Club required its members to attend study groups, encouraged them to present papers, and stated that the club could decide, by majority vote, to engage in reform. The leaders of the Century Club perceived these requirements as a vehicle to expand women's public role. The club membership grew quickly; it began with 111 charter members and almost reached its limit of two hundred by the end of its first year.[89]

During the 1888 school board campaign the Century Club provided leadership, funding, and half the women candidates. The participation of the club resulted from its activist orientation, the still-scandalous conditions of the city's schools, and the direct involvement of several club leaders in the campaign.[90]

The campaign began when several reform parties asked members of the executive committee of the Public School Reform Association to put forward a slate of six women for the school board. Of the six women selected as candidates, two were listed in the city's *Elite Directory,* Sarah Hamlin and Amelia Truesdell. Three were members of the Century Club: Hamlin, Truesdell, and Nellie Weaver. A fourth, Marcelina Jones, served in a variety of organizations managed by elite women, such as the Old People's Home and the Board of Managers of the Women's Hospital. The last two women candidates were known for their temperance activities—Maria Gray was president of the San Francisco Woman's Christian Temperance Union, and Margaret Cook had run for the school board on the Prohibition ticket in 1886. All the candidates had teaching experience, but only Gray and Cook taught in the public school system. The rest taught in private schools or gave private lessons.[91]

The selection of candidates revealed that women had learned several political lessons from the 1886 campaign. From the beginning, organized women presented a unified front, with a single representative slate of candidates. The candidates were chosen for their numerous skills. Two had business experience: Jones, on the board of the Women's Hospital, and Truesdell, who ran a fashionable boarding house. As Mrs. Theall, a suffragist and member of the Public School Reform Association, stated, the candidates included "some of the best educated and the best business women of the city."[92]

By 1888 political elements outside the regular reform community seemed to appreciate the value of women's political strength. That year the local Republican convention nominated the six women candidates as school board directors. The nominations, introduced as a measure for "the protection of our public schools," received little opposition. Most seemed to agree with the delegates who argued that "California cannot remain behind the rest of the Union," which now benefited from women school board members in many places. When the motion to nominate the women passed, the convention gave "three cheers for the ladies," while "the ladies" waved their handkerchiefs from the gallery.[93]

The Republican nomination of the women candidates became "the chief topic of conversation about town," according to the *San Francisco Examiner*. The Democratic paper could not resist adding that the women, while "modestly flattered at their sudden prominence," were nonetheless humbled by the knowledge that their placement on the local Republican ticket meant that they "were for the first time in their lives in questionable company."[94]

The *Argonaut*, a leading conservative journal in San Francisco, printed the rumor that the Republicans had nominated the women "just to beat the Democrats." This seems likely. The Republicans had suffered a great defeat in the last municipal election in 1886, which had made Buckley the most powerful Democrat in the city and the state. Moreover, Republicans faced many of the same problems in 1888 that had led to their defeat two years earlier: internal factionalism; the nativist American Party, which appealed primarily to Republican voters; and Republican inability to duplicate the Democratic clubs that provided immigrants with opportunities for economic mobility and social recognition.[95]

Given the Republicans' many difficult problems, their endorsement of the women candidates served as an expedient, relatively painless method to bolster Republican chances for victory. The women organized, managed, and financed a flourishing grassroots organization based on interclass and interethnic cooperation. The women were also the chief representatives of a popular reform issue that challenged Buckley's machine in its weakest area. Finally, the women candidates received endorsements from other political parties, such as the Prohibitionists and the NonPartisans. In return for these advantages, the Republican Party legitimized the women's campaign, a political bargain that foreshadowed the relationship between progressive Republicans and organized womanhood in the early twentieth century.[96]

The importance of the Republican nomination can be seen in the reaction of the *San Francisco Chronicle*, a Republican paper. Before the GOP convention it published two editorials opposing the nomination of women, arguing that the "chief duties of School Directors are purely of a business nature" for which, of course, women were unfit. But as soon as the party nominated the women, the *Chronicle* faithfully supported its decision. More important, the coverage of the campaign increased and became very favorable. The paper consoled itself that "the ladies nominated are all that the name implies and can in no sense be considered as members of that clamorous class known as the strong-minded"—that is, the candidates were not militant suffragists.[97]

After the Republican nomination the Public School Reform Association (a group of women numbering anywhere from three to less than two thousand) met and announced its reorganization. Henceforth, the campaign, and thus the Reform Association, would be run by the Committee of One Hundred. At this point the influence of the Century Club became quite evident. One third of the members of the Committee of One Hundred were Century Club members. The reorganization meeting itself was presided over by Mary Campbell, vice president of the club. (She had been a school board candidate in 1886.) The next day the president of the club, Phoebe Hearst, headed the campaign contribution list with a $100 donation and a promise to take care of any deficit left after the election. Altogether, nearly half of the Century Club's fifteen officers were active in the school board campaign. Of the four executive officers of the Committee of One Hundred, three belonged to the Century Club, including the president of the committee, Mrs. L. L. Baker.[98]

The Committee of One Hundred moved election headquarters to the "sky-parlors" of the Palace Hotel, a luxury hotel, and began the campaign with great hopes. Its campaign chest had money and more than two thousand voters pledged to support its ticket. The women's prospects seemed so promising that the Democrats approached them to see if they would place three of their candidates on the Democratic ticket "in the hope of averting a clean sweep by the Republicans." However, the women had no intention of becoming token members on the board and insisted upon all six candidates. The Democrats refused, and the women remained without Democratic support.[99]

Despite the short-lived courtship from the Democrats, women claimed that women from "all" sections of the city flocked to join the Reform Association and thus support the women candidates. The only requirements for admission—"earnest aid and hearty sympathy"—encouraged widespread participation. These early successes and seemingly widespread support led to great plans for the future. The Committee of One Hundred was envisioned as "an effective league for future use" that would serve as a watchdog on school board matters, suggest names to fill any vacancies, and plan for the next election.[100]

Despite their optimism and determination, members of the Committee of

One Hundred felt challenged—indeed, overwhelmed—when the Republicans suggested that the women appear "at the polls to distribute tickets and canvass for votes" on election day. This suggestion caused a "sensation of small proportion" within the Reform Association. Never mind that the women would be performing activities seen as masculine; political campaigns in urban centers at the end of the nineteenth century were rough-and-tumble affairs. Elections could be won by the party that distributed the most patronage, passed out the most liquor, and used strong-arm tactics that most effectively intimidated voters.[101]

The Committee of One Hundred considered the Republican proposal and decided it would accept the challenge with certain provisions. The women would participate in a house-to-house canvass, as a few had done in the campaign of 1886. The Reform Association would hold a mass public meeting, although the meeting would be addressed only by gentlemen, as "the propriety of the lady candidates speaking from the platform was not too easily seen." The lady candidates would express their views, however, at informal "special meetings" that would be held for women only. Finally, the committee decided that women would not appear at the polls, stating that they would leave the matter "altogether in the hands of the Republican gentlemen who are exerting themselves to secure fair play for the whole ticket at the polls."[102]

Even so, women did much more than they had planned. An opponent complained that the Reform Association set hundreds of maids and matrons "to canvass from house to house among the homes of poverty and ignorance, the hospitals, sops, refineries and factories, to solicit votes." Women candidates spoke only at meetings for women, all nonvoters, but the speeches were widely reported by the press. The candidates became local celebrities, public people with their portraits and biographies in the newspapers.[103]

The women did not shy away from issues presented by women running for public office. Many voters believed that women could not manage the business affairs of the school board. Women candidates did not hesitate to speak on this point. Marcelina Jones, chosen for her business experience, stated at a meeting of the Reform Association that she had managed several charities and had always found her women coworkers "to be efficient and able to conduct affairs in a business-like, systematic manner." According to the *Examiner*, "a large number of ladies" in the audience agreed with her and offered additional support for this position, giving such examples as widows who successfully managed their husbands' businesses.[104]

Opponents of the women attacked their chief rationale for entering politics, arguing that women's purity would become corrupted by politics. As the

San Francisco Examiner observed, the women's candidacy was "well-meant and courageous, but perhaps in a place like San Francisco it is too courageous." The *Argonaut* agreed: the dirty pool of politics would soon pollute women's moral character. The *Argonaut* was forced to acknowledge, however, that its argument was handicapped by "the high character of the ladies nominated by the Republic convention."[105]

Of all the issues in the campaign, the Public School Reform Association worried most about the allegations that the association was attempting to institutionalize religious intolerance in the public schools. (Some participants in the campaign stated this was an ethnic-religious attack, but most confined their public statements to a discourse on religion.) The rumors were extensive and affected almost all religious groups. "Catholics were told the women directors were pledged to turn out all of Romish faith [*sic*]; the Jews . . . [that] it was a Catholic plot to turn out all Hebrews," while "intense Protestants" were informed it was a "Jesuit intrigue" against them. A Southern Methodist even heard that "Yankee women were going to put out all Southern teachers."[106]

According to the Reform Association, the charges of religious bigotry came from the teachers who were dependent upon Buckley's political machine to maintain their position. The Reform Association claimed that the teachers, fearful of the professional standards that the women candidates would bring to the schools, actively involved themselves in the campaign. They sent home with the schoolchildren a list of candidates said to be "the teachers' choice for school directors"—and it excluded all the women candidates. This "teachers' ring," asserted the Reform Association, this "small knot of unscrupulous women," instigated the smear campaign against the women candidates, alleging they were religious bigots.[107]

Behind these charges and countercharges stood two groups of women with different perspectives regarding politics and teaching, perspectives intertwined with, yet somewhat separate from, ethnicity, religion, and class. Why a significant number of the Irish teachers opposed the Reform Association in 1888 but not in 1886 is unclear; perhaps the longer campaign of 1888 simply gave them more time to organize. The teachers may have been angered because all the women candidates nominated by the Republicans were Protestants—in a city where church-attending Catholics outnumbered their Protestant counterparts by about 5 to 1. Also, two candidates belonged to the WCTU, which only the year before had persuaded the state legislature to require temperance instruction in the public schools, an act interpreted by both sides as a statement of Protestant influence in the schools. Whatever unhappiness the teachers may have had with Buckley's machine, it had hired them and allowed ethnic communities a certain amount of influence in the schools. The teachers may have worried that the women candidates would not grant them as much.[108]

To combat the charges of racial bigotry, the Public School Reform Association of 1888 took steps to emphasize the pluralist nature of the women's reform effort. A day after the women formed the Committee of One Hundred, they announced that the names of committee members would be published in the newspapers "to satisfy the public that all creeds and nationalities are represented." Later in the election the Reform Association put this list of names on a campaign handbill. Mrs. Theall, a Catholic and a suffragist who belonged to the same suffrage organization as Kate Kennedy, sat on the Committee of One Hundred. (Kennedy supported and spoke for the Public School Reform Association.) One of the city's most avid anti-Catholics, Frank Pixley of the *Argonaut,* charged that Theall "pulls the wires and guides the movement." Whether true or not, the women created an organization led by elite but ethnically and religiously diverse women.[109]

The leaders of the Public School Reform Association, however, directly opposed the schoolteachers on other issues. The elite activists—college-educated, professional, or self-taught women—defined professionalism in education differently than did the teachers; the activists stressed expertise and scientific management. The efforts of the Collegiate Alumnae to encourage school boards to hire college women rather than normal school graduates marked an important ideological and class difference. Furthermore, the elite women did not trust the democratic process to place appropriate officials on the school board. The activists saw women's election to the board as only a stopgap measure. They supported the city charter movement, a reform that promised to make city government more efficient and rational by replacing elected officials with appointed experts. Voters rejected the reformers' city charter in 1883 and 1887; the women hoped that their victory would revive the movement.[110]

In 1888 male voters again rejected the women reformers; nevertheless, the women once again claimed to have won a moral victory. Although not one woman was elected, they were competitive, averaging 24,620 votes, while the Democrats, who won all the school board seats but one, averaged 28,140 votes. The women claimed they had scored a victory by creating "the solidarity of women" displayed in the "earnest, absorbed, loving service of all women, largely strangers to each other, who came day by day to sit at the tables in our rooms at the Palace Hotel to direct envelopes and fold ballots, asking no questions as to politics, creed or race." Whether the campaign was representative or not, the women valued the goal of achieving that kind of gender solidarity.[111]

Participation in the school board campaign also developed a commitment to expanding women's public role, partly because the political demands of the campaign compelled women to defend both their right to enter public life and their ability to deal with it competently. Women's new determination to expand their public role expressed itself through building institutions. In the fall of 1888, in the midst of the school board election, women involved in the campaign established a new organization, the Women's Educational and Industrial Union (WEIU), whose goals embodied their new insights regarding women's advancement. The WEIU proposed to unite women of all classes and religions so that women could, through self-help and not benevolent philanthropy, increase their educational and employment opportunities.

There was a direct link between the campaign and the founding of the WEIU. Of the fifteen officers elected for the WEIU, ten were active in the school campaign. The president of the WEIU, Mary Campbell, had been a candidate in 1886 and a member of the Committee of One Hundred in 1888. Nellie Weaver, a candidate in 1888, was a vice president of the WEIU. At the organizational meeting of the WEIU, Adeline Knapp, a journalist who was an active participant in the Public School Reform Association, referred to the problems of the city's schools and asserted, "The women's board must rise and clean out this Aegean [sic] stable." The women responded with "much applause."[112]

WEIU had links to other components of organized womanhood as well. Five of the first fifteen officers of the WEIU belonged to the Century Club and served in the school campaign. These activists included the WEIU's president, Mary Campbell, and suffragist Ellen Sargent. The women saw both the Century Club and the WEIU as means to increase opportunities for public work for women. This relationship in San Francisco between a women's club and the WEIU reflected the national origins of the WEIU. In 1877 the New England Woman's Club helped organize the first WEIU in Boston. Club women in Buffalo organized the second WEIU. The San Francisco WEIU was the sixth such organization in the United States. San Franciscans modeled their organization closely upon its eastern counterparts. Knapp, a leader in the formation of the San Francisco WEIU, had been an active member of the Buffalo WEIU for several years.[113]

The year 1888 was an auspicious one for San Francisco women to form an organization whose purpose was to advance women into the labor market. Many in America's organized womanhood were worried about the effects of industrial capitalism on women's work. Women in Chicago and New York held meetings that year and started creating cross-class organizations as a means to aid paid women workers and especially to improve sweatshops that employed women and children. The International Council of Women, representing fifty-three women's organizations, met in Washington, D.C., in 1888 and announced that its chief goal was "equal wages for equal work." The *San Francisco Chronicle* made such concerns very concrete for its readers when, in February and March 1888, it ran a series of exposés that documented the poor working conditions for women in the city. Such concerns reflected the fact that in San Francisco, as elsewhere in the nation, the number of paid women workers was quickly increasing. In 1880, 35 percent of the city's daughters participated in the paid labor force; by 1890, 50 percent of San Francisco daughters were in the paid workforce.[114]

By the late 1880s a small yet significant number of San Francisco women workers belonged to labor unions, and in February 1888 women workers organized the Ladies' Assembly of the Knights of Labor. In March they held a mass meeting, attended, according to the *San Francisco Chronicle,* by "fully eight hundred intelligent-looking working-girls." The mayor, male labor leaders, women from the Knights of Labor, and suffragist Laura de Force Gordon shared the platform. Gordon called upon all women of the city to organize "on the plans of the Knights of Labor," no doubt referring to the inclusiveness of the Knights, who organized skilled and unskilled workers, men and women, white, black, and brown. Perhaps Gordon was also thinking of the Knights' support for women's rights—in the home, as paid workers, and as citizens.[115]

Mrs. E. C. Williams Patterson, a leader among the city's Knights, shared interests with many of California's organized women; she was from New York State, a Universalist, spiritualist, suffragist, and temperance supporter. Patterson chose to work for the Knights because she saw the rights of labor and the rights of women as intertwined. Moreover, she believed that the Knights permitted her to be "free and frank to avow her belief upon any topic, claiming for her sex equal rights to every opportunity and condemning fearlessly every wrong action which debars her sex of these rights."[116]

But the WEIU ignored the Ladies' Assembly of the Knights of Labor. The Knights sought to empower women workers so they could transform the inequitable system of wage labor; the WEIU sought to improve women's position within that system. WEIU nevertheless held the greatest potential, among all elite women's organizations at the time, of developing a cross-class sisterhood. At the very least, WEIU possessed the potential to become a vehicle of cross-class communication, sensitizing many of its affluent members to the needs of working-class women and the relevant response they could make.

WEIU organizers wanted to develop a cross-class women's organization in which they could support each other's advancement into public life. Adeline Knapp emphasized that the organization was open to any woman who wished to join. "We seek mutual improvement, protection and sympathy," said Knapp, "and we recognize the fact that need and trouble exist among all classes." WEIU president Campbell declared that the "justifying purpose" of the organization was that "all women need each other." Nellie B. Eyster, a WEIU activist and leader in the WCTU, thought it was "impossible for earnest, thoughtful women, representing such different nationalities, experiences, education and aspirations to meet, as they do here, on the common footing of individual desire and social equality, and not evolve *a force*" (her emphasis).[117]

The WEIU understood its mission of improvement to mean that elite women should provide services for less fortunate working-class women. Working women were to be, as the *San Francisco Call* commented, "educationally and industrially uplifted." The San Francisco WEIU offered, for a small fee, classes in dressmaking, millinery, and stenography, while other classes were free, such as those in reading and writing. WEIU officers believed that the cooking classes would best serve WEIU students because they enhanced women's role within the home and trained them to serve as efficient domestic servants. President Campbell, in a comment that reveals much about how elite women viewed the immigrant working class, argued that when the graduates of the class produced meals of "digestible food," the men in their family would be less tempted to drink "adulterated beer."[118]

The benefits of participation within WEIU were different for its middle- and upper-class members. These women predominated as the officers of the organization, gaining important leadership skills and political and administrative experience. In its early years the WEIU achieved several reforms it felt benefited working-class women. The WEIU cooperated with the WCTU on a bill requiring police matrons; it became law in 1889. The WEIU also successfully lobbied for a bill that improved working conditions for saleswomen. The affluent women of WEIU created and managed several services for working-class women: an employment bureau, an underwear department that sold items sewn by impoverished women, and a downtown Women's Lunch Room that served inexpensive wholesome food to working women.[119]

Before the WEIU had much of a chance to develop its potential, it destroyed itself. Although a new WEIU was rebuilt on the ashes of the old, the new organization never possessed even the vision of interclass mutuality of the first and became simply a philanthropy. The disintegration of the WEIU began in the middle of its second year, when eight of its fifteen officers resigned in an internal dispute. The membership dropped from 626 to 396. When Hannah Marks Solomons became president the next year, she took over an organization that was already troubled and her problems only increased. Her administration was, as she readily acknowledged, a "brave struggle against adverse circumstances." Solomons was not a woman to allow adversity to stop her. A Jewish immigrant, she had arrived in California in 1852, her ship passage paid by a suitor she refused to marry after she met him. The man she chose for a husband, Gershom Mendes Seixus Solomons, was active in community affairs but a problem drinker, leaving her with full responsibility for their five children.[120]

One of the "adverse circumstances" Solomons faced at the WEIU was anti-Semitism. Margaret Dean wrote to Louise Sorbier (both were Catholic members of the WEIU) during Solomons's administration that "Our Union is . . . almost deserted by nearly all of its original founders" and "the Jewish element predominates." (Only two officers were Jewish; Solomons served as one of the original officers.) Sorbier became president of the WEIU the next year; she soon charged that Solomons, as chair of the domestic training committee, wasted WEIU funds by carelessly paying the same bills twice. Solomons denied this and demanded that the records be examined by experts—which was done twice, both times clearing her from any charges of mismanagement. However, the new administration refused to vote to accept the final report. Solomons and fourteen other women walked out.[121]

Sorbier then rebuilt the WEIU, but the new organization made no attempt to mitigate its elitist nature. In Sorbier's first year as president (1891–92), the membership went back up to 470. Despite the walkout of so many of the founding members in 1893, Sorbier was still able to raise funds for WEIU. Upper-class Phoebe Hearst promised to mail WEIU a monthly check. The WEIU became increasingly concerned with supplying upper-class families with reliable domestic servants. The organization never had, to quote its first president, Mary Campbell, a "mission to upset things." Yet, if it had maintained its original course, the WEIU would have continued to involve elite women in political efforts to improve working conditions and opportunities for women of the city. Instead, by the 1890s it functioned as little more than an employment bureau for domestics.[122]

The Century Club followed a similar course for similar reasons. In 1888 the

Century Club shared the WEIU's commitment to expanding women's public role. Activists formed the Century Club with the vision of its uniting professional and upper-class women and training them to serve as patrician leaders in community betterment. But the Century Club's first burst of political activity, its leadership in the school campaign, was also its last. The club decided to limit itself to providing an education for its members, a path chosen by many clubs at the time. The Century Club did not explain its decision; perhaps the members found the public attention, especially when it focused on the deep divisions among women and their unexpected defeat, simply too uncomfortable. By 1893 the club by-laws specifically stated that "no demonstration on behalf of any political or religious object shall ever be made by this club; and sectarian doctrines or political partisan preferences shall not be discussed by this club at any regular or special meeting thereof." A women's club dedicated to civic activism, like the Friday Morning Club of Los Angeles, did not develop in San Francisco until after the suffrage defeat of 1896 when suffragist club women created the California Club.[123]

❖

The decline of activism within the Women's Educational and Industrial Union and the Century Club did not mean that San Francisco women no longer had an interest in advancing women's public work. Rather, women formed another organization, the Pacific Coast Woman's Press Association, which became a leader in the California women's movement.

Emelie Tracy V. Swett Parkhurst, a poet and author, called for women to organize the Woman's Press Association in 1890. Married for only a year to banker John W. Parkhurst, she was "connected" with a poetry journal, the *Illustrated Californian*. Aware of the difficulties faced by women writers, she began research about them, learning that of the nine hundred writers and journalists on the West Coast, one third were women. Despite their numbers, women were unorganized, separated by "distance, isolation, and ignorance of each other." Parkhurst, the twenty-seven-year-old daughter of John Swett, a noted educator who had done much to professionalize San Francisco schools, wanted to do the same for women writers. Because she created the Woman's Press Association as a professional organization, she knew it was an entirely different kind of group from the Century Club. The latter, she argued, served "the purely literary woman, with most of whom the use of a pen is a pastime. The proposed . . . [press association], on the other hand, is for workers and for working purposes."[124]

Parkhurst, described as a woman who "lost no opportunity of advancing . . .

[women's] interests and upholding their dignity," created the Pacific Coast Woman's Press Association so that its members could support themselves through professional and political activism. They were participating in a national movement as women writers elsewhere were forming professional organizations. Jane Cunningham Croly, a prominent journalist, helped New York women organize Sorosis, a club for women writers and other professionals in 1868 and, in 1889, the Women's Press Club of New York. The Pacific association modeled its constitution, however, after that of the New England Woman's Press Association. This group, when it formed in 1885, committed itself to professionalism and politics.[125]

The constitutions of both the New England and Pacific Coast Woman's Press Associations resolved "to promote acquaintance and good fellowship among writers and journalists; to elevate the work and workers; and to forward, by concerted action through the Press, such good objects in literary, social, industrial, philanthropic and reformatory lines as may, from time to time, present themselves." During the Pacific Coast Woman's Press Association's first year, the women discussed these goals, interpreting them in a way that reflected and developed the press association's activism.[126]

Members agreed on the importance of promoting "acquaintance and good fellowship," a goal that encouraged a positive group identity and strengthened the group's resolve to seek its own interest. Mary Grace Charlton Edholm, staff member of the *Oakland Tribune* and temperance woman, wrote, in regard to an organizational meeting of the Woman's Press Association, that "Columbus could not have been more happy in discovering America than these women journalists in discovering each other." Sarah Severance, suffrage writer and WCTU member, explained in the *San Francisco Call* why the "loving sympathy" developed in the Woman's Press Association meetings was so important; in that space, a woman's logic "was as much respected as [her] poetry."[127]

According to Eliza D. Keith, an officer of the press association, it was "a society of women, for women, managed by women." Keith stressed that members were expected to judge each other on the basis of "moral and intellectual worth and not social status." The press association, however, made the same kind of racial judgments as did other white organizations. In 1891 the association's board unanimously denied membership to an African American woman, Mrs. R. M. Lockett, because she was too "aggressive" and because her acceptance would supposedly mean the departure of half the members. Association founder Parkhurst defended the action, denying that the board had discriminated on the basis of race. She thus implicitly acknowledged that racism was antagonistic to the press association's goals.[128]

Press association members believed that their second goal, "to elevate the work and the workers," was their most important. But the best means to do so presented a dilemma. Most male journalists, using conventional standards, would count only a few women in San Francisco as their peers. (Although the women opened their association to women on the West Coast, it functioned primarily as a San Francisco organization.) In 1888 the five major city newspapers employed four women on their combined staffs; ten years later the remaining four major dailies employed fourteen. Even using the more liberal census figures, five women journalists lived in the city in 1880, forty-one by 1900. A professional group proposing to represent such small numbers might well wonder how powerful an advocate it could be.[129]

Equally important, most women journalists did a different kind of work than men and were labeled as subordinate workers performing inferior work. Men reported the news; women generally did not. They usually wrote timeless "magazine" articles for the Sunday editions regarding the arts, society, and more general "women's" topics. On the other hand, many middle-class women wrote. They could enlarge the organization. But these workers and their work were even further from fitting a male professional model.[130]

The Pacific Coast Woman's Press Association members decided to define professional work broadly. The crucial qualifying factor for membership was not whether one was employed on a regular or part-time basis, but whether one was, in fact, engaged in serious work. The workers the association was organized to help were those women engaged as writers with any respectable publication or in legitimate literary work. The purpose of this membership policy was to legitimize women's participation in the paid labor force on women's terms. Women were capable of professional work, although their work might be performed differently from men, on a different time schedule, and with different goals.[131]

In 1891 the president of the Woman's Press Association stated that of the 150 members, 40 were "actively engaged in editorial work" and "all" contributed to "many" periodicals. The membership records are lost, but we can examine in detail the career patterns of the women chosen as officers in the first two press association elections, in 1890 and 1891. Association officers were unusually independent. Of the thirteen officers, eleven were married at one time in their life. When they held these offices, however, only six were actually living with spouses. Of the other five "married" women, four were widowed and one, Charlotte Perkins Gilman, was separated from her husband.[132]

Among the entire group of thirteen officers, only four were employed full time as members of the press. Two of the four were reporters: Frances Bagby with the *San Diego Union* and Isabel Raymond of the *Sacramento Record-Union*. The other two were editors or publishers. "Mrs. Sam Davis," wife of the humorist, was the owner of the *Carson Appeal*. Mary Hall-Wood, twice widowed, helped to establish the *Santa Barbara Daily Independent* and served as its editor. Two of the officers, Parkhurst and Eliza Keith, while not employed as full-time members of the press, contributed on what seems to have been a regular basis. (Keith, by no later than 1894, became a member of the staff of the *San Francisco Call*.) Finally, Mary Stanton was unique. She engaged in "scientific" work, writing "a voluminous treatise," *Scientific Physiognomy*.[133]

The other six officers combined their writing with politics, documenting that the association held a broad and activist definition of women's work. Writing was important to them, often serving as an extension of their reform work and, no doubt, as a means of financial support. But writing was a part, not a whole, of their career pattern. Gilman, who moved to Oakland in 1892, wrote and spoke for a number of political causes, including the labor movement, populism, and the fight against the great monopoly of the state, the Southern Pacific Railroad. Sarah Cooper and Kate Douglas Wiggin, known for their work establishing the San Francisco free kindergarten system, wrote about the need for reform and, in Wiggin's case, literary efforts. Finally, Nellie Eyster, president of the press association for its first two years, wrote children's books and served as editor of the northern California WCTU journal, the *Pacific Ensign*.[134]

Members of the Woman's Press Association specifically addressed how much of society believed that women were incapable of professional work and therefore concluded that even if women performed such work, it would be substandard. The women contended that such assumptions were unjust, and now that women had the advantages of education, employment, and organized womanhood, these assumptions would be demonstrated as untrue as well. Agnes Manning, a school principal and officer for WEIU as well as the press association, forcefully argued that the value of women's work had been denied, throughout history, on the basis of sex. Future ages, she prophesied, "will hardly understand how there ever could have been such injustice meted out to any human effort,—*because it was a woman's*" (her emphasis).[135]

Keith, who had written for San Francisco newspapers since the 1870s, often using the pen name Di Vernon, wrote about the attitudes of many male journalists regarding their female colleagues. "It is such an old joke," she sighed, "but to the average newspaper man it is always bright, witty and new to dub a woman who writes a 'blue stocking.' Whatever the word may once have meant, it is now intended as an opprobrious term in ridicule of the pretensions of a woman to literary skill which she does not possess." Keith personally had experienced a varied career. Like so many women, she began paid work as a teacher, but she became an author of stories, poems, and book reviews for literary and religious papers and a journalist. Keith supported the inclusive membership policy of the Woman's Press Association, contending, "there is no sex in brain."[136]

Responses by San Francisco newspapers to the Woman's Press Association showed that male editors and journalists understood that the women's objective was to change public opinion and practices regarding women professionals and their work. But the responses varied immensely from relative approval to deep scorn. At one end of the spectrum the *San Francisco Call,* in an editorial response to the Woman's Press Association's 1891 convention, saw no reason that women could not become men's equal as writers. Furthermore, continued the *Call,* "every woman who is trying to earn her living by her own labor, so as to emancipate herself from the necessity of marrying for a home, is entitled to the respect and kindly consideration of mankind."[137]

The *San Francisco Examiner* stood at the other end of the spectrum. It mocked the women's professionalism, referring to them as "the ladies whose business with journals has been limited to carrying poems to editorial rooms," whose work "has never required them to go to the counting-room for any emolument for their labor." Ambrose Bierce, the brilliant journalist known as "Bitter Bierce," made the most hostile statements in the *Examiner.* He responded to Keith's assertion that "there is no sex in brain" by declaring that "in no respect do men and women differ so widely, so conspicuously, so essentially as in mind." Because he judged the female mind inferior, he found it impossible "to take the [Woman's Press] Association quite as seriously as it takes itself."[138]

Bierce found the association's objective of members aiding each other professionally especially humorous. Although his comments were intended to denigrate the women's professionalism, he provided an accurate analysis of the association's strategy and objectives. According to Bierce, the women's "policy of work" was to make a human ladder for one another. At the top of this ladder each woman could, standing on the shoulders of her sisters, tug at her "little rift in the veil of obscurity," each "showing her funny pansy face at it in turn and executing a comical little mouth for Posterity."[139]

The positions of the *Examiner* and the *Call* regarding women journalists reflected their different market strategies; moreover, those strategies affected their hiring practices. The two distinctive cultures of the *Call* and *Examiner* illuminate the complex labor market faced by women journalists and help explain why the women's first political action was an effort to cleanse sensationalism from the city papers, beginning with a national leader of sensationalism, the *Examiner*.

All city newspapers faced an especially competitive market in the last decades of the nineteenth century. The *Call*, in order to compete, made a series of decisions from the 1870s through the mid-1890s to attract women readers that made it the paper most favorable for women journalists. In the mid-1870s the *Call* began the city's first coverage of local "society"—the teas, receptions, and parties of the wealthy—with the idea that such coverage would encourage elite women to buy the paper. The innovation proved profitable for the paper and for women journalists. By 1888 Frona Eunice Waite served on the *Call*'s editorial staff, a position held at the time by only one other woman in the city; Waite worked as assistant social editor.[140]

The *Call*'s development of a society page illustrated a larger trend; newspapers competed by developing special sections that covered such topics as society, the arts, and "women's interests." The last proved to be one of the most popular, and the *Call*, along with other dailies, began to both give more space to features marked specifically for women and hire more women journalists to write these sections. The *Call*, however, led in both areas. By 1894 it employed twelve women on its staff; at least five belonged to the Woman's Press Association.[141]

Although the women gained "regular" employment, they were restricted, for the most part, to writing essays for the sections that were seen as compatible with their gender. Adeline Knapp, one of the five members of the Woman's Press Association, proved a notable exception; she wrote for the *Call* regarding horses and horse racing. However, a growing number of women wrote about local events, aside from social occasions, because they reported about the women who were engaged in public affairs.[142]

The *Examiner* developed a different means to build circulation and, subsequently, a different employment policy regarding women journalists. William Randolph Hearst, the indulged only child of George and Phoebe Hearst, persuaded his millionaire father to give him the *Examiner* in 1887; ten years later it led the city's newspapers in circulation. The young Hearst did this by using sensationalism to a greater extent than any other local paper. Indeed, the *Examiner* held a national reputation as a pace setter in press sensationalism—stories of the exceptional that triggered the readers' emotions. Reporters made themselves part of the stories they told, the better to develop readers' emotional interests, and if tear-shedding or awe-inspiring stories proved hard to find, reporters created them.[143]

"Annie Laurie," or Winifred Sweet Black Bonfils, aided Hearst in his circulation competition as a sensational reporter. She personally benefited as well, becoming a nationally known reporter so popular at home that when she died in 1935 the San Francisco mayor ordered that her body lie in state in the city hall rotunda. Bonfils began working for the *Examiner* in 1888; a former actress in her twenties, she wrote with a dramatic flair that caught Hearst's attention. He had also noticed "Nellie Bly," or Elizabeth Cochrane, of the *New York World*, who pioneered as the first "stunt girl" reporter. At Hearst's request Bonfils began performing stunts that created stories in which she, as the intrepid "girl reporter," played a leading role. In 1890, in one of her first and most famous stunts, she "collapsed" on a busy San Francisco street in order to expose the city's facilities for the medically indigent. Disguised in shabby clothes, she was medically maltreated and roughly treated. Her report became a sensation, selling papers, advancing her career, and helping to reform the city's medical services.[144]

Bonfils did more than stunts. She worked as an "all-around" reporter, writing on a broad range of local events in the city. She had her own column, located in a prominent place and under her own name. But how much her career opened doors for other women is not as clear as it might seem at first glance. Hearst sold papers on the basis of Bonfils's exceptional case. The *Examiner*, of all the city's dailies, hired the fewest women journalists. During ten of the twelve years between 1888 and 1900, no more than four women served on the *Examiner*'s staff at any one time; usually only two women were on staff at one time. Moreover, while Bonfils broke sex barriers by reporting on local news in her column, Ambrose Bierce in his column attacked, as we saw earlier, the abilities of "most" women journalists to do the same. Hearst cultivated such contradictions at the *Examiner* in an effort to sell papers to as many different interest groups as possible; to attract readers who wanted to follow the exploits of a daring woman reporter, he provided a broad opportunity for the very few.[145]

When Gilman became president of the Pacific Coast Woman's Press Association in 1893, she immediately led it into a political crusade against press sensationalism for numerous political, professional, and personal reasons. Not coincidentally, she led a campaign chiefly directed against the *Examiner*.

Another factor that helps explain the women's campaign against sensationalism was that from the beginning the Woman's Press Association resolved, for its third and final goal, that it would forward "by concerted action through the Press" certain "good objects." However, the association also pledged that it would not, as an organization, endorse suffrage. Many members supported

suffrage. Sarah Severance passed around a suffrage petition at a press association conference and, according to her, nearly every woman there signed it.
Emelie Parkhurst personally approved of suffrage, declaring that "the granting of a citizenship to women will equalize the business relations of women
and men and that will dignify all such relations." But she advised the press
association not to sponsor it. She argued that such a controversial political
step could harm individual members employed by the conservative press and
prove detrimental to the organization as a whole. The membership followed
her advice.[146]

Parkhurst believed that members of the Pacific Coast Woman's Press Association should become involved in politics, as she phrased it, "the absolutely
non-partisan work of Coast advancement." She wanted the women to write
about the "educational, mercantile, industrial, social or scenic conditions of
her particular section of country"; in other words, to boost the West Coast as
an "honorable means to secure an influential standing in the commercial
world." She wrote this kind of story. The press association gained railroad
passes for its March 1891 convention by a "tacit understanding" that all members would write such articles. However, Parkhurst's vision extended far beyond
such a limited cooperation between the press association and railroads.[147]

Parkhurst wanted members involved in all civic improvements, from building parks and libraries to "substantial constructions of permanent highways"
so that women would be respected as writers and as civic activists. She felt the
combination would be mutually beneficial to all involved, women professional writers and their communities. "This is a time," she solemnly declared,
"when the women of the press can make their mark as individuals, as journalists and as an association of public-spirited wielders of the pen, molders of
public opinion and builders of the commonwealth. This cannot be accomplished by the energy and activity of a few members of the Association, but it
can be accomplished by the concentration and determination of all of the
members together." But before Parkhurst could develop fully such long-range
goals of political involvement, she died in childbirth in the spring of 1892.[148]

Her death left the Woman's Press Association adrift. When Gilman became
president in the fall of 1893, she determined that the association would immediately become involved in politics. "We are beginning to get a grasp of the
purpose of this association," she declared in her presidential address. "There
has been a constant steady growth in the feeling of unity; the members are
getting accustomed to working together, but the life of this body must consist
in what it does." Therefore, Gilman announced that "there is a very definite

hope and promise for the year to come that we shall accomplish a large and definite object."[149]

Within a month the Woman's Press Association was involved in a crusade for a "pure" press. The members announced that they were campaigning against sensationalism, and they carefully defined what they meant. They were protesting explicit details regarding sexual and violent crimes in newspapers and attacks on the private lives of individuals. The women called for "objectivity," which they defined as the "clean statement of facts and truth." The women organized the campaign in order to achieve two major goals. They intended to expand women's moral guardianship of the home into the public arena and enhance the professional opportunities for women journalists.[150]

Although the Woman's Press Association created the pure press movement, the press association refrained from taking a formal leading role within the pure press campaign. Few association members became officers of the pure press organization. The press association chose this course of action in part to encourage a large representative women's campaign. The organizational meeting of the pure press movement, called by the press association, was attended by more than one hundred women, representing nearly every women's organization in San Francisco and neighboring Alameda County. The WCTU, which shared a warm relationship with the Woman's Press Association and admired the goals of the pure press campaign, lavishly praised the campaign in temperance papers and contributed many members to the cause.[151]

The press association chose not to lead the campaign for another reason: to prevent any charge that women journalists were conducting it to further a certain paper or their own careers. This decision reflected prudent considerations. The *Call* employed the highest percentage of the association's members; furthermore, the *Call,* in response to the ability of the sensationalist *Examiner* to build such an immense circulation, began labeling and marketing itself as a "family journal." More than one member of the pure press campaign publicly demanded such a newspaper. In addition, as we saw earlier, the *Examiner* publicly attacked the professionalism of the association and its individual members. For example, Bierce wrote that Gilman's poetry was "something to remember on one's deathbed—something to remember and forgive."[152]

The *Examiner* most angered the press association, however, when it printed a story—written by a member of the press association—that attacked the morality of its members. Millionaire reformer Adolph Sutro invited the association to his villa for breakfast after their March 1891 conference. According to the story, the women drank champagne quite liberally; they soon felt "great glee and much playful whooping of it up." A member announced that she was going to kiss Sutro and so should the rest of the association, which they did, and all of which the *Examiner* reported in great detail. Six months later Parkhurst mourned that "the affair at Sutro's, though a very trifling matter, has never been forgotten." The association's long and sensitive memory probably owed much to the story's insinuation that women with public careers could not be trusted to maintain high standards of private morality. Some members of the association thought the woman who wrote the story ought to resign; as Parkhurst concluded, "Women working on good papers think that women who write for blackmail papers should not be members of the association."[153]

For all these reasons, the press association began, but did not lead, the pure press campaign. Women involved in the campaign asserted that it was a spontaneous and democratic movement, yet another reason for the press association to take a back seat. Early in the campaign women even refused to give their names to reporters, stating that "this is not a movement led by Mrs. So and So" and "the women of California have come to feel that they would like to go on record as a whole in this matter." They suggested with a great deal of humor that if someone wished to know who was involved in the movement, that person could read the long list of names on the petition.[154]

At the height of the campaign the pure press organization announced a list of "some" of the officers, a list that included no less than 114 names. This announcement served several political purposes. It gave the pure press organization more structure, and at the same time the very size of the officer list announced the inclusiveness of the campaign. Members of the pure press association nominated Mrs. A. L. Bancroft as president, but they maintained the original commitment for an egalitarian campaign by naming all the other officers vice presidents. The pure press association reinforced the ecumenical nature of the campaign by selecting Jewish women for approximately 5 percent of the officers.[155]

On the other hand, San Francisco's *Elite Directory*, or Blue Book, listed 65 percent of the officers of this "spontaneous, mass movement of women." One third of the officers, including the president, belonged to the Century Club, and 15 percent of these club members were also active in the school board campaigns. The Woman's Press Association openly invited all women and women's organizations to participate in the pure press campaign; nonetheless, it was led—not by a single "Mrs. So and So"—but by a small cohesive group of elite women.[156]

The women of the press association chose three tactics for the pure press campaign: the circulation of petitions that were sent to newspaper editors, a mass meeting, and the dedication of one sermon by the clergy to the issue of purity in the press. These tactics were ones in which women could actively participate or count upon a reliable ally. Women collected signatures for the petitions, and only women could sign them. The purpose of this exclusiveness was to develop gender solidarity and to prevent a male takeover of the campaign. More than three hundred women attended the mass meeting and, with the exception of one or two reporters, no men were present. Only women spoke at the meeting. Because of women's requests, more than five hundred ministers throughout the state pledged to preach on the subject.[157]

The campaign was short but influential. The movement was formally organized on October 24, peaked at the mass meeting held on November 7, and ended on November 24, when the petitions, condemning lurid details in the press and signed by twenty thousand women, were sent to the editors of Bay Area newspapers.[158]

The women began the campaign by emphasizing that they, as women, were the "guardians of family purity"; therefore, they were concerned with the quality of newspapers that came into their homes. The women agonized in particular that the minute details given in reports of "crime, wickedness and sensuality . . . can gratify only prurient and vulgar curiosity, or awaken such curiosity in innocent and inexperienced minds." Many families, they asserted, did not, under these conditions, have a newspaper in their home.[159]

The women held broader objectives. They intended to guard the purity of society as well as the home, establishing a public discourse that supported their sense of morality and made them the public gatekeepers of that morality. They viewed their movement as a method of disciplining and cultivating an unruly and ill-mannered society, particularly the working class. The journal of the Woman's Press Association, the *Impress,* argued that the low level of the press was the result of the preference of the working class for lurid sensationalism, a preference that the newspapers, with their "money-making instinct," attempted to fulfill. The women worried, as they stated in their petition, that "vicious and debasing news . . . has a tendency to lower the tone of thought among the best of our people, and to strengthen the worst instincts among the morally lower classes."[160]

So long as the women restricted themselves to serving as the guardians of morality, both private and public, they received wide support for their efforts. The *Argonaut,* the journal of San Francisco's conservative old guard, believed that it would "be a happy thing for San Francisco if the ladies could . . . exclude offending newspapers from their home." The *Examiner* gave the women its "hearty good wishes" and stated they aimed at a "real evil." Bierce agreed completely with the women's goals of enforcing the morality of the "best of our people." He wrote that if a newspaper editor does "damage or disgust or distress [to] the best people among whom he lives he cannot plead the profit that he makes in gratification of the worst. It is in no way desirable that they be gratified. The women are right."[161]

The women, however, made it clear at their mass meeting that they also saw the pure press movement as a chance to enhance professional opportunities for women journalists; they believed a clean press would mean more news assignments that were "appropriate" for women. Although the women's linkage of morality and women's employment ultimately limited women to certain kinds of reporting, that was not their intent. An editorial in the *Examiner* lampooned the press association for what the paper accurately understood as their objective, increasing women's employment opportunities. The paper sarcastically charged the association with believing that the "refusal of the [newspaper] proprietors hitherto to avail themselves of the pens and the elevating influence of these hundreds of female journalists has had much to do with bringing the newspapers to their deplorable moral and intellectual level." In addition, continued the *Examiner,* the association believed that its members were "prevented from exercising their profession because of the iniquitous conditions under which the newspapers have heretofore been published."[162]

Gilman knew from the beginning that the pure press movement was fated to have only a limited success in changing the newspapers. She argued that the only real hope of achieving a cleaner press was through an economic boycott. Gilman believed such a boycott would be impossible for the women to enforce, however, so long as men were the major subscribers and purchasers of newspapers. This did not daunt or deter her from the pure press movement, for a pure press was not her chief goal.[163]

"The great good" she wished to see accomplished was the effect it would have upon the women themselves. She believed the crusade would reveal "the limitations of mere 'influence' expressed in words, as compared with practical power expressed in money." Most important, Gilman thought that San Francisco women, and in particular its society women, "are not as fully awake to their public duties as those of the older cities of our country and Europe." Thus the chief function of the pure press campaign, as Gilman forthrightly declared, was to teach women that they were "half the public; its affairs are their affairs."[164]

Edna Snell Poulson, an officer of the pure press campaign, believed that the campaign did induce women to become active participants in public affairs.

"Formerly," she commented, "when anything went wrong, women used to get together and discuss it, and all the talk would, perhaps, end in their reading a paper or two. But now," she added jubilantly, "we have gone to work." By going to work in a political campaign, even one as fleeting as the pure press movement, the women made a feminist declaration that they would not limit themselves to the private concerns of domesticity and that they could legitimately participate in paid work.[165]

The pure press campaign served as a steppingstone for San Francisco women into a wider public sphere. It engaged a large group of women, many for the first time, in a small but nonetheless significant political act, the collecting and signing of public petitions. The campaign continued political alliances among women's groups, in particular between the women's clubs and the WCTU, an alliance first developed during the school board campaigns. Finally, the pure press campaign provided further training for and raised expectations of the women who were emerging as the leaders of the as-yet formless women's movement.[166]

Dorcas Spencer wrote in the northern California WCTU journal that a "satisfactory feature of the [pure press] movement is the evidence of a hitherto latent sense of responsibility among women." The pure press movement, by providing an acceptable way for women to participate in politics, built bridges that led to an even greater participation in politics and, slowly, the achievement of more and more political power.[167]

❖

When Spencer praised the pure press campaign in the fall of 1893, she and the rest of the state's organized womanhood had recently finished participating in the efforts of the national women's movement to advance women's work at the World's Columbian Exposition in Chicago. Spencer's enthusiasm for how the pure press movement had encouraged women to become more "responsible" for their public work may well have been generated in part by the women's World Fair experience.

At the fair, which opened its doors in May 1893, California women displayed much of the work they had accomplished during the previous ten years—their organizations, institutions, and efforts in politics and the paid labor force. The women made these displays in order to gain more legitimacy for their increasingly public lives, to push the acceptable boundaries of women's work further yet, and to find remedies for the dire labor situation faced by working-class women. Organized women developed numerous ways to focus public attention on their work at the fair; for example, they created a Woman's Congress at which women explained how advancing women's work advanced national progress.

Deeply impressed with the efficacy of the Woman's Congress, northern California temperance women and members of the Pacific Coast Woman's Press Association created a similar congress in California in 1894. Women from all over the state came to the congress to advance women's work; their cooperative efforts at the congress developed a statewide women's movement. Within a year the congress and the state's organized womanhood were involved in a suffrage campaign. Just as women in the pure press movement found that their efforts to advance women's work were tied to political activism, so many organized women who participated in the congress to increase women's "responsibilities" quickly found themselves suffragists.

2

THE POLITICS OF POLITICS: THE CALIFORNIA WOMEN'S MOVEMENT EMERGES AND CAMPAIGNS FOR WOMEN'S SUFFRAGE, 1893–96

FROM ALL PARTS of the country activists of the late nineteenth-century women's movement—club women, temperance advocates, settlement workers, philanthropists, labor activists, and suffragists—went to Chicago in 1893 for the World's Columbian Exposition, one of the great international expositions of the era. They went to the fair to advance women's public work. These women realized that the fair, which was attracting thousands of visitors and inspiring endless pages of comment, offered an unprecedented opportunity to make their views on women's work known. The activists presented their message but not without opposition from the men who ran the exposition. As a result of their experiences at the fair, many women resolved to work harder to build a movement powerful enough to transform women's work.

California women's participation in the World's Fair proved to be a defining experience for the development of their political consciousness. Returning home from the fair, they created the Woman's Congress, modeled after a similar organization at the fair, with the intention of initiating a statewide women's movement. Partisan political forces, however, soon pushed the congress into becoming a de facto suffrage organization. The strength of the People's Party, the political arm of the populist movement, was growing in California, and it supported giving women the vote. To counter the populists' popularity, the Republicans, the state's dominant party, ensured that the state legislature approved a suffrage referendum that needed ratification by the male electorate in the November 1896 election. When this occurred, the Cal-

ifornia women's movement, which had been moving toward support for suffrage for some time, focused on that goal.

The 1896 campaign presented steep challenges. California and the nation
were in the third year of a deep depression; most regarded the presidential
election of 1896 as a national referendum on the best way to respond to the
tumultuous social upheavals of the Gilded Age—whether to conserve or challenge the social order. Facing an electorate divided over the desirability of
reform, organized women acknowledged that voting represented empowerment for women, a dramatic social change—but vowed that once they gained
their citizenship, they would seek to conserve the social order. Suffrage lost.
Perhaps voters were swayed by the antisuffragists' argument that suffrage represented a radical transformation of power relations between the sexes and
would therefore topple the social order.

Suffragists were disheartened by their loss but began developing a political
but nonpartisan role for women that helped them achieve suffrage fifteen
years later. Organized women took up work that they had promoted during
the campaign, civic activism. They had argued that women citizens, through
such nonpartisan efforts, would further their self-development and societal
evolution. Without the vote but not without hope, women still perceived civic
activism as a means to achieve those goals while paving the way for their
citizenship.

❖

In the late 1880s, as San Francisco women were trying to extend the outreach
of the Women's Educational and Industrial Union (WEIU), the U.S. Congress
and the male managers of the 1893 Columbian Exposition in Chicago were
making decisions about how to organize the upcoming World's Fair. Eastern
organized women lobbied both groups to gain an official role for women at
the exposition, and Congress responded by creating the National Board of
Lady Managers in 1889. The board was composed of two women from each
state and territory plus nine women from Chicago, a total of 115 women. The
male commissioners nominated the board members and tended to select
women more for their relationships with important men than for their leadership within organized womanhood. The choice of Bertha Honoré Palmer as
president of the board rested more on her status as the wife of Chicago real
estate magnate Potter Palmer than on her two decades of membership in
Chicago women's clubs.[1]

Bertha Palmer was in many ways typical of the upper- and middle-class
women who filled the ranks of organized women; any representative list of

prominent women included many organized women. As a consequence, the commissioners—perhaps without realizing it—placed significant numbers of organized women on the National Board of Lady Managers. The board in turn chose to promote a women's agenda at the fair, which, as Palmer frequently announced, provided them with their "great opportunity."[2]

Her speech at the opening of the Woman's Building, which was to be a pavilion of exhibits by and about women, made the front page of the *San Francisco Call* in May 1893. She stated that the grand purpose of the National Board of Lady Managers was "to create, by means of the Exposition, a well defined public sentiment in regard to . . . the propriety of their [women's] becoming not only self-supporting, but able to assist in maintaining their families when necessary." Palmer argued that every woman who presided over a happy home was "fulfilling her highest and truest function." At the same time, however, she understood that the "vast majority" of women had to work outside the home. These women faced a "frightful struggle" as employers used public disapproval of women who worked outside the home to pay them minimal wages and thus maintain them in a perpetual subordinate caste. The public, Palmer believed, lacked a "just and general appreciation" of women's economic position; therefore, informing the public was the work of the National Board of Lady Managers.[3]

Palmer and the board were quite conscious of what they wished to see included in this "well-defined public sentiment." Palmer stated frankly in 1893 that "we have taken advantage of the opportunity presented by the Exposition to bring together such evidences of . . . [women's] skill in the various industries, arts and professions, as may convince the world that ability is not a matter of sex." By demonstrating women's ability, the board intended to prove that women's labor was "a fixed and permanent element and an important factor in the industrial world." Furthermore, the board planned to use this demonstration of women's skills to show that women could profitably receive technical training and gain employment in a variety of new fields.[4]

But, most of all, the board hoped that proving women's ability to work and their permanence in the marketplace would create "a healthy public sentiment . . . which will condemn the disproportionate wages paid men and women for equal services." The board's hope was that its demonstration of women's ability to do equal work would produce equal treatment.[5]

The board voted overwhelmingly at its first meeting in November 1890 that, at the Columbian Exposition, unlike all previous expositions, women's work would be integrated into the other exhibits, competing "without regard to sex distinction." The board worked to see that as many applications from women were accepted as possible, covering "every line of industrial, scientific, and artistic work." The board provided display cases to women who could not afford them. It pressured male managers to assign women's exhibits to satisfactory locations within the principal buildings, rather than relegate them to the far corners. The women did not believe their work was equitably represented, but it was placed on display and it did win awards. For example, Harriet Strong, a southern California club woman and rancher, won a prize for her inventions to aid agricultural irrigation.[6]

In addition, the National Board of Lady Managers built and managed the Woman's Building and used it as place to display exhibits that presented the board's message regarding women's work, not competitive exhibits. The presentation began with the building itself, designed by architect Sophia Gregoria Hayden. The exhibits inside included, and thus honored, the work of the home, work in the paid labor force, and the work of reform by organized womanhood. The building had a scientific kitchen and displays of women scientists. It boasted lavish parlors filled with amateur crafts, such as the California Room, decorated by the board members from California, and galleries crowded with the work of professional women artists. Inside the building were charts that plotted the progress of women wage earners in the industrial workforce and the Organization Room, which displayed the wares of philanthropic and political work.[7]

At the Columbian Exposition organized women also participated in the World's Congress—a convention intended through speeches and debates to display the great ideas of the time. At the two hundred meetings and conventions that comprised the Congress, experts discussed issues believed to be crucial for world progress. Ellen Martin Henrotin, an upper-class Chicago club woman, directed the Women's Branch of the World's Congress Auxiliary, which attempted to gain equal representation for women at the conventions.[8]

Under the watchful eye of Henrotin, women used the World's Congress to advance women's work. They defined women's work broadly. The women's committee for the Government and Law Reform Congress invited as speakers women reformers who were active in such areas as urban civic activism, world peace, and women's suffrage. The committee organized a congress of women lawyers from which emerged the National League of Women Lawyers. Clara Foltz, a California lawyer and suffragist, spoke at two different legal congresses. She returned home filled with enthusiasm, urging "women of the coast to organize" and predicting California women would soon gain the ballot.[9]

The World's Congress began with the Congress of Representative Women, which ran from May 15 to 22, 1893. Although placed within the organizational structure of the World's Congress Auxiliary, the Congress of Representative Women developed independently and held a different political agenda. May Eliza Wright Sewall, a suffragist, managed the Congress of Representative Women. She initially organized it as a convention of the International Council of Women, an umbrella organization of the suffragist movement, and planned to use the congress to enlarge the international council by requiring membership in the latter in order to speak in the former. But the male administrators of the World's Congress and nonsuffragists Palmer and Henrotin disapproved and persuaded her not to do so. Sewall opened the congress to all women's organizations, and 126 participated.[10]

Sewall perceived the congress as a means to promote women's work—and women's suffrage. She believed the suffrage movement had long held both objectives, and she placed the Congress of Representative Women within that movement. According to Sewall, the purpose of the congress was to "commemorate the struggle through which some women (aided by some men) have won for all women the place conceded to them in modern life." "Shall we," she asked, "be willing to see the origin of this great Congress in the little meeting held in Seneca Falls?" Women were discontented, Sewall argued, with positions in society "arbitrarily assigned to them" and dissatisfied "with any conception of themselves . . . which implies their natural, necessary, and, therefore, perpetual subordination to men." The congress was a means through which women could collectively "read their own interpretation of their natures, their own version of their rights, responsibilities, duties, and destiny."[11]

Sewall chose as the official theme of the Congress of Representative Women "the contribution of woman alone to the general progress of society." She picked eight different areas—education, industry, art, philanthropy and charity, moral and social reform, religion, civil law, and government—within which speakers could address women's contributions to progress. In theory, every speech should have demonstrated the advantages of women's public work to society. Sewall believed that organizing the congress in this way would lead women to realize that they possessed the power to change the world. She prophesied: "What such a congress may do for the uplifting of humanity if the women of the world avail themselves of its unique advantages . . . is incalculable. The aid which such a congress will give to the solution of . . . 'The Woman Question,' is equally beyond measure."[12]

Most speeches at the congress were exactly what Sewall had planned: they praised women's public work and linked it to social progress. Kate Tupper

Galpin, the nationally prominent educator from Los Angeles who was a friend of Caroline Severance's and honorary member of the Friday Morning Club, gave such a speech at the congress. In her talk, "The Ethical Influence of Woman in Education," Galpin documented the important role of women teachers in the schools and in society, where teachers and former teachers became "leaders of thought, directors of the great ethical movements of the day, organizers of clubs, classes, societies, and church activities." Some speeches praised the efforts of women's organizations, as did Lily Alice Toomy of California in her talk, "The Organized Work of Catholic Women." Also, many national women's organizations held sessions at the congress and presented similar messages.[13]

California, as a state, participated in the Columbian Exposition, and California women were influenced by this participation. Like other states, California formed a state World's Fair Commission (doing so in 1891), built a state building on the Chicago fairgrounds, and created a state Board of Lady Managers. California women worked hard to bring glory to their state and to honor the work of its women. Their experiences helped build the state women's movement.[14]

California women's prominent role at the fair resulted from the efforts of women at the national level. The National Board of Lady Managers played a key role in encouraging all states to develop official roles for women who worked for the fair. Because of the lady managers' recommendations, the director-general of the fair recommended to state legislatures that women who worked for the fair either become "full members of their respective State Boards" or, if women formed their own state boards, that the women be appropriated a "specific sum" of money to support women's exhibits. The National Board of Lady Managers hoped that women who participated in the state boards would promote the fair and thus bolster the position of the National Board of Lady Managers at the fair. The national board also believed that such participation would enlarge the women's movement and "develop to the fullest extent the resources, attainments and possibilities of the women of every section and State of the Union."[15]

The National Board of Lady Managers played an instrumental role in establishing the California Board of Lady Managers. When Thomas Thompson, secretary of the state World's Fair Commission, suggested in January 1892 that the commission appoint a state Board of Lady Managers, he did so "on the suggestion of Mrs. Potter of Chicago" (he meant Palmer). The California commission divided over whether to appoint such a women's board but decided to do so at its January meeting. Commissioner L. J. Rose explained their actions by declaring, "This exposition has a new, American departure—the recognition of women." Besides, he continued, "nearly every State has given recognition to woman." The state commission was swayed by the official support expressed by the director-general of the exposition for women's participation at the state level. Thus the National Board of Lady Managers influenced the state commission both directly and indirectly.[16]

Within a month the state commission appointed the seven members of the California Board of Lady Managers; although membership in organized womanhood was not a criterion, most California lady managers belonged to women's groups and performed public work. Both Mrs. Edward Owen Smith and Anna Morrison Reed belonged to the Pacific Coast Woman's Press Association and advocated women's rights. Smith was elected president of the state board. Flora Kimball and Virginia Bradley served on school boards; Kimball was also a suffragist. Olive Cole, wife of a former Republican U.S. senator, belonged to the Friday Morning Club of Los Angeles. Ella Sterling Cummins worked as a San Francisco journalist, while Amelia Marsellus was said to always find time for societies "where intellectual advancement and the building up of communities was the watchword."[17]

In 1892 the California Board of Lady Managers visited twenty-seven counties and formed thirty World's Fair Auxiliaries—all to collect exhibits of women's work that would promote the state and show the ability of its women. Board members took both duties seriously. California established an impressive display at the exposition; its state building stood second in size only to the building of host state Illinois. California women placed great faith in what these exhibits would mean for women. Frona Eunice Wait, a journalist for the *San Francisco Call* who served as a California member of the National Board of Lady Managers and thus an ex officio member of the state board, declared, "When the great Fair is over, and we shall be made familiar with the percentage of female labor which entered into all lines of products, . . . the scales of the bread winners will be much more evenly balanced."[18]

"Susan Sunshine," who wrote the women's column for the *Los Angeles Times,* believed that the fair would demonstrate that "men no longer put up bars in the way of her [woman's] progress." But as the state's lady managers struggled to promote women's work at the fair, they learned a different lesson. Some men—including men publicly pledged to support women's efforts at the fair— tried to stop them or, failing that, restrict their efforts. At the fair, as back in California, men, no matter what they said in public, were in no hurry to give up their traditional prerogatives.[19]

A typical example of men's obstructionist tactics came from coastal Ventura

County in southern California. The Ventura County World's Fair Commission (a male group) initially assured the World's Fair Auxiliary in the early part of 1892 that its assistance was needed and granted the group a small amount of money. By August, however, the men had decided that the only examples of women's work that they would accept would be homemade jellies. Pauline Curran, leader of the women's group, attempted to change their minds, assuring them that other counties were displaying women's work. But she lamented in November 1892 that "this World's Fair business in Ventura is uphill work all together since our commissioners told us they did not care for any of women's work." Despite the women's efforts, not a single item from Ventura County was displayed in the Woman's Department of the California Building or in the Woman's Building.[20]

James Phelan, vice president of the California World's Fair Commission, a San Francisco patrician, and a political liberal, also opposed the creation of the state Board of Lady Managers. Once the board was created, he prevented it from receiving a budget. Instead, the women were forced to request money from the men for each project. Throughout the fair Phelan let the lady managers know that he, like the Ventura County Commission, "did not care for any of women's work."[21]

Despite this opposition, the California State Board of Lady Managers achieved much. It created almost as many county organizations as the men. In addition, the *Final Report of the State World's Fair Commission*—rather ironically—praised the women for being "ingenious in devising plans for raising money." Rossiter Johnson, who wrote a four-volume history of the exposition, reported that the California women's state exhibit "was one of the most complete and representative displays of women's work" of any state at the exposition.[22]

Although opposition did not stop the women from fulfilling their fair obligations, it did have an effect on them that was heightened because it was unexpected. When the state World's Fair Commission approved the state Board of Lady Managers, the women believed this implied complete support for their work. In early 1892 the organ of the commission, the *California's Monthly World's Fair Magazine,* published the objectives for state Boards of Lady Managers that the national board had developed: to illustrate "woman's part in developing the natural and material products of her native or adopted State; her influence in its mental and moral advancement, her share in shaping its history." The California lady managers adopted these objectives and assumed the male commissioners would too.[23]

Consequently, when the male commissioners created the state Board of

Lady Managers in January 1892—and immediately sought ways to diminish the women's efforts—the matter became an issue of public debate. The *San Francisco Call* chided Phelan for refusing to grant the women a budget. The *San Francisco Chronicle,* not a friend of women's causes, also commented on the board's problems, observing that it was not appointed until a year after the all-male commission was organized and that the board suffered from a "lack of funds." The women agreed. The lady managers' anger regarding their treatment became public when Flora Kimball, one of two suffragists on the board, spoke out on the subject. "Had the Board of Lady Managers of the California World's Fair Commission been organized a few months earlier," she wrote in the August 1892 issue of the *Illustrated Pacific States,* "or had women been accorded a place on the Commission, as they should have been, the amount of women's work in the state might have been largely increased."[24]

The variety of California women's organizations that participated in the Chicago exposition and took back to their constituencies reports on their experiences added to the fair's significance. The Friday Morning Club of Los Angeles, for example, exhibited a book extolling its activities in the Organization Room of the Woman's Building and sent four delegates who conscientiously reported what they had observed. In addition, the club invited guests to speak on the lessons of the fair, the growth of the women's movement, and the new ideas regarding women's work. Altogether, the club devoted two months' worth of meetings to the fair between the spring of 1892 and the spring of 1893. The discussions had their lighter moments, such as the story of the California woman who thought the fair's greatest exhibit stood in the California Building, the life-size knight on horseback made of prunes. As the club history recounted this incident, it concluded, "*Our* club members absorbed the meaning of that great Fair."[25]

For many women—board members, those who engaged in work for the exposition, women who made the pilgrimage to Chicago or followed the World's Fair events in the press—the fair's meaning was clear: men opposed their advancement. Faced with the ongoing opposition of men in Chicago and in California, the women concluded that they must create a strong women's movement to further their interests. The *Argonaut,* a conservative San Francisco journal, sarcastically underscored that conclusion in October 1893, observing that women working for the fair believed "that but for Men, Woman would have won a splendid, an unclouded triumph at the exposition." The *Argonaut* reached the "melancholy conclusion" that most of those women believed that the end of the exposition meant "the beginning of their work for Woman."[26]

California women quickly fulfilled the *Argonaut*'s prophesy; they created a California Woman's Congress that was part of the 1894 Midwinter International Exposition in San Francisco. The Midwinter Exposition was the brainchild of M. H. de Young of the *San Francisco Chronicle*. He participated, as a vice president, in the Chicago exposition and quickly saw the commercial advantage of holding such a fair in California—especially during the winter. The Midwinter Exposition was hurriedly put together, and congresses were not originally planned. The women independently organized a woman's congress and convinced the men to form the Midwinter Fair Congress, of which the Woman's Congress became a part. The women were largely excluded from speaking at the other congress and were denied membership in the Midwinter Fair Auxiliary, which supervised all the congresses. But the women had complete control of the auxiliary in charge of the Woman's Congress and therefore of the Woman's Congress itself.[27]

❖

The California Woman's Congress played a decisive role in building a state women's movement, a feat made possible by the network of cooperation developed among the organized women. The Pacific Coast Woman's Press Association, prompted by the temperance women of northern California, called an organizing meeting for the summer of 1893 that was attended by at least "twenty women's organizations of San Francisco and adjacent towns." A list of these organizations no longer exists, but one can identify the influential groups in this movement by examining the organizational ties of the members of the executive committee for the Woman's Congress Auxiliary. Among the fifteen women on the committee were several members of the Woman's Press Association, including Sarah Cooper, Charlotte Perkins Gilman, and Ada Van Pelt. Van Pelt also belonged to the WCTU. Leaders of the San Francisco Women's Educational and Industrial Union, such as Louise Sorbier, served on the executive committee of the Woman's Congress. Edna Snell Poulson, an educator, Century Club member, and former officer of the pure press movement, belonged, as did Ellen Sargent, the noted California suffragist.[28]

The Woman's Congress brought together women from both northern and southern California, a pivotal accomplishment, for no other California civic women's group was then functioning as a statewide organization. Although the executive committee of the Woman's Congress Auxiliary was organized in San Francisco and did not include a single woman from southern California, southern California women served as members of the advisory council.

Women from southern California were also invited to sit on the platform during the congress as a gesture of respect. Further, southern California women took an active part in the Woman's Congress, delivering several speeches.[29]

From the very beginning the organizers intended the Woman's Congress to advance women's work. According to Sarah Cooper, when California women organized the Woman's Congress they copied the Congress of Representative Women—Sewall's organization for the Columbian Exposition. The "preliminary addresses" of the two congresses had the same themes and sometimes the same wording. Both were intended to demonstrate women's progress in the public world by discussing, in Sewall's words, "every living question pertaining to the education, employment and advancement of women." Like Sewall, the California women planned for their congress to build a women's movement of activist women "who have attained distinction in any line of worthy activity." The congress would bring them together to give them "the valuable opportunity of meeting each other all at once." The congress would increase communication and cooperation among activist women in California; it would develop a movement.[30]

The women made "woman and the affairs of the world as they affect or are affected by her" the theme of the Woman's Congress; the single most popular subject was careers for women. When the women discussed business, they debated the best ways for a woman to enter business, and when they discussed science, they reviewed careers for women in such diverse fields as medicine and astronomy. When the subject was philanthropy, the women discoursed on the management of philanthropic institutions, and when the topic was religion, they heard about women ministers, nuns, and participants in the Salvation Army.[31]

Helen Stuart Campbell, a new arrival to San Francisco, gave one of the few speeches regarding working-class women, "The General Condition of Working Women in the United States." She represented, however, a significant wing within organized womanhood, those who argued that affluent women must take up the work of changing the conditions that working-class women faced as paid workers. Campbell also served as an object lesson in the various ways that elite women could perform this work. In the 1880s Campbell developed a national reputation as a writer who introduced workers, especially women workers, to affluent readers. She pursued her objectives as a reformer, helping to create the first Bellamy Nationalist Club in Boston during the late 1880s (it was a non-Marxist socialist organization that pushed for the nationalization of public services) and joining the board of directors of the New York City Consumers' League when it was founded in 1891. As a scholar she won an award from the American Economic Association for her monograph, "Women Wage-Earners."[32]

During the congress middle-aged middle-class women sat for a week in rapt attention, listening to the intricate details of careers like Campbell's that most would never enter. The purpose of this discussion of public work was not so much to advance their specific careers or even their daughters'. Rather, the purpose, repeating the lessons of the World's Fair, was to prove that women in general could develop a self-supporting independent life. The discussion at the California Woman's Congress looked forward, imagining a future when women's work would encompass the world, when women could choose their work, and when women's work would be equally rewarded.

The California women's discussion reflected the thoughts expressed two years earlier by Elizabeth Cady Stanton in her famous speech, "The Solitude of Self," which she delivered upon her retirement from the presidency of the suffrage movement in 1892. She argued that women possess a "birthright to self-sovereignty" that they must exercise in order to face life's inevitable challenges. This would enable women to do more; as women gained personal independence, they would expand their abilities. "Nothing strengthens the judgment and quickens the conscience like individual responsibility." Stanton also believed women would evolve as they claimed their public work in an industrial society that was transforming the nature of work. "Machinery has taken the labors of woman as well as man on its tireless shoulders; the loom and the spinning wheel are but dreams of the past; the pen, the brush, the easel, the chisel, have taken their places, while the hopes and ambitions of women are essentially changed."[33]

Women's messages at the congress did not go unchallenged. According to "Annie Laurie" (Winifred Sweet Black Bonfils), the popular *San Francisco Examiner* journalist, every presentation given at the congress had a theme, the idea "that the one thing needful to make this world a Paradise was the emancipation of woman." Bonfils, rejecting this idea, sarcastically reported that the women of the congress saw themselves oppressed by "the Bogie Man, whom the women referred to simply as 'MAN.'" According to Bonfils, the Bogie Man "jumped out of the box" when Ada Bowles, a Universalist minister from Pomona, attempted to explain why so few women were inventors. Bonfils quoted Bowles as saying, "Slaves were never inventors, because slaves never think." Bonfils noted that some of the world's greatest philosophers were slaves. More to the point, she declared she did not believe women were enslaved; therefore, there was no reason for women to be emancipated.[34]

Winifred Bonfils mischaracterized the message of Bowles's address as well as that of the congress. Ada Bowles had emphasized that women had a history of inventions and that as women's education had increased, so had the number of their inventions. As Charlotte Perkins Gilman commented on Bowles's speech, "Inventive genius is not encouraged by irresponsible and subservient positions." Bowles's point was not that slaves never become inventors but that slavery produced too few inventors.[35]

Bonfils also attacked congress speakers for demanding suffrage. According to her, the women of the congress believed that voting would solve all of women's problems, that it contained "some occult power of putting gray matter into sudden operation." Bonfils argued that women did not have the vote because, as a group, they lacked "the brains, the judgement, and the mental balance of a man."[36]

Bonfils was somewhat correct when she charged that the women made the ballot a panacea. Some speakers at the congress, persuaded that women were morally superior to men and therefore possessed nearly infinite powers, argued this. According to Sarah Severance, the suffragist and WCTU activist, "Without women this State would still be a mining camp, the law would be mob law and the chief executive Judge Lynch." Women deserved to vote, Severance concluded, because "of their refining influence." Bonfils, for her part, wondered whether "pioneers of California were such hopelessly iniquitous creatures" and whether "the painted creatures who were here to meet them when they came . . . were of any great benefit to the poor bogie [man]."[37]

The women at the congress did not claim all women or only women were moral. But they argued that because most women served as society's moral guardians, having the vote would enable them to maintain morality more efficiently and thoroughly. In the session of the congress devoted to "Political Ethics," the speakers, many of them members of the Woman's Christian Temperance Union, agreed with the California WCTU president, Beaumelle Sturtevant-Peet, who argued that "it must be the duty of women to enter politics." In the words of Harriet Strong, the daughter of Harriet Strong, the southern California rancher and club woman, "If women believe in peace and not war, justice and not injustice, virtue and not vice, right and not wrong, they must take their part in life."[38]

The roots of this argument were at least one hundred years old and three thousand miles long, tracing to eighteenth-century New England, where women raised patriot sons and moral daughters who would ensure that the ideals of the new Republic survived. This moral work of mother in the home was women's political contribution to their country. California's organized

Directors of the Woman's Congress Association of the Pacific Coast, ca. 1895. Seated, from the left, are Mrs. Garrison Gerst, Ada Van Pelt, Sarah Cooper, and Nellie Blessing Eyster. Standing are Louise A. Sorbier, Mrs. W. E. Hale, Charlotte Perkins Gilman, and Minne V. Gaden. (California Historical Society, Cecile M. Sorbier Estate, FN-26999)

women, like their national counterparts, simply argued that women ought to make their moral work more public and more direct through the vote.[39]

The Woman's Congress took its most important step toward building a woman's movement on nearly the last day of the congress. It reorganized into a permanent organization, the Woman's Congress Association of the Pacific Coast, with the objective of presenting an annual woman's congress. By making the congress permanent, the women made clear their commitment to effecting changes within women's lives. To ensure cooperation between the two regions of the state, Elmira Stephens, president of the Women's Parliament of Southern California, became the vice president at large.[40]

One of the key objectives of the Woman's Congress Association was to build a women's movement. According to the *Impress,* the organ of the Woman's Press Association that also served as the organ of the Woman's Congress Association, the annual congress would awaken "the sense of union among women" and the sense "of our common interests as citizens." The *Impress,* edited by Charlotte Perkins Gilman, believed that women needed these ideas brought to their "repeated consciousness" because they were so closely confined: to one family, one church, one "rigidly defined social circle" within that church. In the words of the *Impress,* "Every form of human activity needs organization, unity, interchange of ideas. No class needs all these more than women."[41]

Before the next woman's congress met in the spring of 1895, the state legislature approved a constitutional amendment granting women the right to vote; it required ratification by the male electorate in the November 1896 election. This development occurred partly because of the growth of the People's (populist) Party in California, which supported women's suffrage. Equally important, the suffrage movement transformed itself; it built bridges to the populists, used better tactics, and expanded to include more women's groups.

One woman and one organization deserve most of the credit for the changes in the suffrage movement: Beaumelle Sturtevant-Peet and the northern California Woman's Christian Temperance Union. As a young girl growing up in Vermont, Sturtevant-Peet had gained two kinds of education: formal training "at one of the best seminaries in Burlington" and an education in social reform from her grandfather, who boycotted products made with slave labor. She became an abolitionist and a suffragist and helped create the Vermont WCTU. Her responsibilities as state temperance organizer frequently took her away from home, but her husband, E. A. Sturtevant, an attorney, always supported her work. After his early death left her a widow with two children, she married E. W. Peet, a widower with two children, and moved to California. Sturtevant-Peet (she always used both husbands' names) soon made a name for herself in the state WCTU because of her charismatic ability to organize people and to shrewdly represent the WCTU at the state legislature. She assumed the presidency in 1891.[42]

She brought to that office a vision of a new society based on cooperation and social justice. In her first presidential address in 1891 she stated what was to be a concern throughout her long presidency (1891-1907), that the "towering wealth of the few endangers rather than promotes the best interests of the masses." Sturtevant-Peet advanced an active and conciliatory position toward immigrants and labor, urging temperance women to work with these groups rather than against them, to organize working women's clubs and establish industrial classes. Under the guidance of Sturtevant-Peet the WCTU resolved in 1892 to work for reforms that would "enable men and not money, to rule the nation" and "insure to the laborer a voice, as well as heart and hand, in our industries."[43]

Sturtevant-Peet actively promoted in California—as Frances Willard did nationally—ties between temperance women and populism. The People's Party of California, created in 1891, represented a coalition of the Farmers' Alliance and Bellamy Nationalists. Both groups shared an anger at monopolies and other "special privileges" within capitalism that denied farmers and workers—the producers—their fair recompense. The People's Party, the political arm of the populist movement, vowed to end such injustice and establish equal rights for all. In language similar to Sturtevant-Peet's, Thomas V. Cator, a Bellamy Nationalist and leader of the People's Party, charged that "those who produce most have least. Those who produce nothing frequently have over-abundance. . . . Labor should be entitled to what it produces."[44]

Temperance women sent a delegate to the convention that created the People's Party of California, and a working relationship quickly developed between the two organizations. Some urban temperance women, such as Sturtevant-Peet, who believed in Christian socialism, seem to have been most closely allied with the Bellamy Nationalist wing of populism. But in rural areas the membership of the Farmers' Alliance and the WCTU often overlapped. In Yolo County, an inland farming region, the Farmers' Alliance and the local WCTU used the same paper, the *Home Alliance,* as their local organ.[45]

The populists proved valuable allies, but allies, although vital for a campaign, are meaningless unless the campaign possesses dedication, energy, and organization. Sturtevant-Peet made the WCTU a more effective political body and directed its energies toward suffrage. Under her direction the WCTU collected twenty-three thousand signatures in favor of legislation granting women the right to vote for school board members—much more than they or the suffragists had ever achieved. When the California legislature enacted a school suffrage bill in 1893, the *Woman's Journal,* the official organ of the National American Woman Suffrage Association, reported that "Mrs. Sturtevant Peet, and her many active helpers, were chiefly instrumental in securing it." (But the women never actually secured it; the governor raised objections that were not settled until after the bill expired.)[46]

During the lobbying for the school suffrage bill, suffragists worked with temperance women as they had for years, but at this legislative session women from other groups joined them, a new development that documented the growth of the state women's movement. The Pacific Association of Collegiate Alumnae voted unanimously to support the bill and sent two delegates to press for it. The Women's Educational and Industrial Union did not endorse suffrage as an organization, but Louise Sorbier, the director, lobbied for the bill. Sarah Cooper, the best-known California woman reformer at the end of the nineteenth century, spoke to the governor personally on behalf of the school suffrage bill. The distance between southern California and Sacramento, the state capital, prevented most southern California women from attending the legislative session. However, the Women's Parliament and the Friday Morning Club telegrammed their support.[47]

The WCTU, in a step that underscored its organizational strength, paid the expenses for three lobbyists in Sacramento: Sturtevant-Peet, Nellie Eyster, and Sarah Severance. They divided the tasks. Severance did most of the writing, filling columns in the Sacramento papers and reporting for the *Pacific Ensign,* the state WCTU paper, and the *Woman's Journal.* Eyster wrote some too (both she and Severance belonged to the Pacific Coast Woman's Press Association), but she and Sturtevant-Peet concentrated on lobbying for the bill. An unsigned article for the *Ensign* that may have been written by Eyster noted that Severance was excellent with the pen but not as a lobbyist. "No stretch of the imagination could picture Sarah Severance . . . [with her] majestic and firm belief in the superiority of . . . [her] sex . . . clinging to the arm of a legislator and pouring into his ear sweet pleasantries."[48]

Severance and Eyster did not demand the school vote for what it could mean for the home or reform, not even for temperance. They demanded school suffrage for what it meant to women. "For our own sake," urged Severance, "say nothing of our duty to others, we should seek freedom." As Eyster wrote, "Voting is power and power always commands respect." The vote would legitimize the public role women had created for themselves and promised an even further expansion of that role. Eyster dreamed of a time when the legislature would be equally divided between the sexes, with each having "equal stake in the country, . . . and equal capacity to judge of the measures." Woman's "life and being expanded," she asserted, "to accord with her changed political conditions." Given that women were asking for a limited extension of the franchise, school suffrage, their sweeping claims seem misplaced. But they saw their request as politically pragmatic. They hoped that the legislature would accept such a small step; if so, they would later work to expand it.[49]

The women's assumptions proved largely accurate; they were able to persuade the state legislature to grant school suffrage. The Republican state senate overwhelmingly favored the bill and passed the legislation easily. Democrats opposed suffrage, and they controlled the state assembly; however, with the vital aid of the populists, the bill squeaked through the assembly. Governor Henry H. Markham declared he was "fully in accord with the purpose and intent of this measure" but said he perceived certain constitutional problems with it. The governor, a Republican, asked Maximilian Popper, chair of the State Democratic Committee (who opposed women's suffrage), to consult a law firm regarding the bill's constitutionality. The firm did not decide until after the bill had expired. This sly political maneuver, a bipartisan pocket veto, left organized women furious.[50]

The women protested that the governor had vetoed the bill not because of any constitutional concerns but to maintain politics as a male arena. As Severance wrote in an angry article—headlined "Tricked! Tricked!"—if the men really believed the bill was unconstitutional, they would have taken it to court. Alice Stone Blackwell, in the *Woman's Journal,* pointed out that seventeen other state legislatures had granted women the right to vote in school board elections, even though their state constitutions also declared that only male citizens could vote. Every court decision regarding such legislative action found it constitutional because school officers were a creation of the legislature. Governor Markham, observed Blackwell, has "the unenviable distinction of being the only Governor who has ever vetoed a school suffrage bill."[51]

The women's near victory, however, said much about the growing viability of suffrage as a political issue, a viability that increased dramatically when the Republican state convention endorsed full women's suffrage in 1894. The Republicans, expecting the populists to play an important role in the upcoming election, hoped to attract their support. Whatever the influence of the suffrage plank, the Republicans won a landslide victory, gaining a majority in the state legislature and winning most state offices. The populists also made gains. The Democrats saw their reform candidate, James Budd, become governor but won little else. The suffragists approached the 1895 state legislature with a great deal of hope; Republicans, who controlled both houses, officially supported suffrage.[52]

But suffragists were not completely optimistic. Rumors circulated in the state's newspapers that although the Republicans had pledged to support women's suffrage during the heat of the campaign, the party opposed it. Democratic papers instigated many of these "rumors." Republicans, in view of their overwhelming election victories, may well have become less willing to support their rather controversial and politically troublesome campaign promise for women's suffrage. The Democrats covered their bets by making political overtures to women, a potentially important bloc of voters. Governor Budd publicly warned the Republicans that they should not send him a suffrage bill unless they wished to see that bill become law.[53]

Organized women conducted an impressive lobbying effort for women's suffrage; according to the *San Jose News,* the Republican endorsement of suffrage became "prominent" after the 1894 election because of the women's efforts. Beaumelle Sturtevant-Peet, Louise Sorbier, and the two noted California women lawyers, Clara Foltz and Laura de Force Gordon, led the lobbying. The last two gave impassioned suffrage speeches before the legislature. The suffragists held mass meetings in Sacramento, the first of which attracted a crowd estimated at a thousand people. For the first time great numbers of women attended the legislative sessions and gave their "hearty applause" to speeches favoring the vote.[54]

Gordon dominated the lobbying process in early 1895. The *Sacramento Bee* gave her speeches and essays extensive coverage; other suffragists said and wrote similar things but none so well. Gordon, a Bellamy socialist who, like so many other state radicals, joined the California People's Party, called for women's enfranchisement in the name of human rights and democracy.[55]

Gordon began by declaring, "There are serious disturbances in the body politic today, and the American woman citizen is becoming alarmed for the safety of the National household." Gordon believed the economic crisis facing the nation, both the deep depression it was experiencing and its structural economic inequalities, was one reason for women's alarm. "Millions of men and women in this land of plenty are reduced to absolute want; while a general cry of 'overproduction' is sounding, there is a vast army of unsheltered, unemployed tramps roaming over the country; a larger army of men, women and children unfed, unclothed, and suffering for want of a little, while thousands have more than they can enjoy."[56]

Gordon thought that citizens should call upon the state to resolve democratically such economic injustice and inefficiency but worried that they could not or would not do so because democracy itself was under attack. Growing numbers of Americans posited that voting was a privilege, not a right. "This is a dangerous proposition," declared Gordon. "It makes it possible to restrict voting to a small number." She developed her point by making a comparison. The same men who deny citizens—who were women—the vote could just as easily "give the gentry the right to vote, and shut out the laboring classes. It is a kind of political bondage." Therefore she denounced those who called for franchise restriction "as dangerous to our country, and a menace to our Republican institutions" and demanded women's enfranchisement on the basis of "human rights." Gordon also believed, although she made it a minor point, that when women gained the ballot, society gained "better laws, better officers and less complaint of corruption."[57]

Under this political pressure Republican legislators sent contradictory messages. The Republican state assembly passed a bill enfranchising women by legislative statute. The state senate, also controlled by Republicans, vetoed the assembly's suffrage bill on the ground that it was unconstitutional. However, as a compromise move, both houses then passed a constitutional amendment in the early winter of 1895, to be decided by the electorate in the 1896 presidential election. The Republicans could now claim to have kept their campaign promise to support women's enfranchisement, but practically they had made its accomplishment extremely difficult.[58]

❖

The passage of the constitutional amendment by the California legislature found the state's organized women, according to suffragist Ellen Sargent, "very much at sea." The chances of winning the campaign were slight: constitutional suffrage amendments were notoriously hard to pass and California suffrage forces were still quite small. Sarah Severance thought the campaign offered "at the most . . . a chance for education." Carrie Chapman Catt, organization committee chair for the National American Woman Suffrage Association (NAWSA), studied the California situation and agreed with Severance— the campaign had only a slight chance of success. Of the thirty-five state suffrage groups that paid dues to NAWSA, California ranked twenty-eighth. California women sent a "pressing request" to Susan B. Anthony, president of NAWSA, asking her to attend the 1895 Woman's Congress in San Francisco that spring. Anthony and Anna Shaw, a suffrage orator and NAWSA's vice president, decided that the congress and suffrage referendum made it an ideal time to visit California.[59]

Charlotte Perkins Gilman, an influential member of the program committee for the 1895 congress, carefully chose "Woman and the Home" as its theme. She hoped this would encourage women to rethink what she labeled the "ethics of woman's work"; she saw the congress as a chance to convert California women to the same message that she had delivered four years earlier in Los Angeles—the evolution of the human race depended on the evolution of women's work. The "one great purpose of these congresses," she wrote in 1895, was to "show to women that it is their world too, and that they need to know and help each other to really do their duty in it."[60]

More specifically, Gilman wanted women to see that their duty included a commitment to change their work from isolated nonspecialized domestic tasks to cooperative specialized civic responsibilities that may or may not include home responsibilities. As she lectured in 1894, "Women need progressive organized industry as much as they need education or food or air—it is a condition of human existence and progression. That they should be deprived of such industry and relegated eternally to the performance of the nutritive

Susan B. Anthony and Anna Shaw in San Diego. After the 1895 Woman's Congress, Anthony and Shaw toured California for suffrage. In this picture the San Diego women's clubs are hosting a "basket dinner" for them at the olive ranch of Flora Kimball. Shaw and Anthony are sitting on the right side of the table, third and fourth from the front. (The Huntington Library, San Marino, California)

and excretory functions of the body politic, and those at the most primitive level, is wrong—grievously wrong to humanity, and to be carefully considered in the ethics of woman's work."[61]

Whatever the general public may have expected the women to say at the congress about "Woman and the Home" in the spring of 1895, suffragists found numerous ways to insist that women could not fulfill their moral obligations unless they transformed the home and women's roles. Speakers who were suffragists agreed that women's first ethical duty was to claim what Elizabeth Cady Stanton called their "birthright to self-sovereignty." As Anna Shaw, who quickly became the favorite speaker of the congress, stated, woman "has always been judged as mother, wife, daughter or sister. . . . Woman has never been permitted to stand alone on the verge of possibility." All the suffragists agreed that the traditional home was the key institution in women's subordination and must therefore be changed. Shaw described the unequal relationship between husband and wife as "oppression"; one rules and the other obeys, a matter of "peace or pieces."[62]

Suffragists called for a "New Home." Alice Moore McComas, a southern California suffragist, observed that although some thought the home should not be altered because of its longevity, the "broad-minded, liberal spirited woman . . . does not recognize man as her head." Sarah Cooper believed the "higher home should be a democracy," for "if there is anything that subverts the higher home it is having a boss in the family." Several thought husbands and wives should share not only decision making but also child-raising tasks. In the ideal home, Shaw thought, the husband and wife were "comrades" and the father, as well as the mother, served as "teacher and comrade of his children." Shaw predicted that "as man and woman grow more alike they will be more like God."[63]

The crucial question for the suffragists was one of means. How could they develop a New Home, New Man, and New Woman? With the vote, they answered. Voting recognized women as independent citizens, not as subordinate family members, and gave women some power to effect the changes they wanted. According to Susan B. Anthony, the suffrage question was whether women would exercise "influence or power." McComas predicted that the end result of women's citizenship would be "more fatherhood in the family and more motherhood in the state."[64]

The great accomplishment of the 1895 congress was that it provided explicit instructions on how middle-aged, middle-class women could achieve their full citizenship—in politics, public work, and the home. Suffragists called for women to support the upcoming state suffrage campaign. Women were also urged to become community activists. On the day the congress discussed "The Home and Sanitation," seven women, six of them physicians, discussed political problems women needed to tackle such as food adulteration and infant mortality. Two women physicians held or had held public office: Dr. Kellogg Lane was the first woman to sit on an American board of health, and Dr. Sarah L. Shirley was the only woman member of the Oakland Board of Health. In her speech, "The City and the Home," Shaw made several suggestions about how women could become involved in municipal housekeeping, from conducting studies of sewage systems to joining the police force—the latter a certain cure, she felt, for vice and corruption.[65]

No doubt the fears of many women in the audience that such political actions were beyond them were dispelled by the extemporaneous speech of Sarah Pratt Carr. She described how she and other women of LeMoore, a small farm town in the San Joaquin Valley, organized a club and "through their united and strenuous efforts" improved the town's public health standards. The "sweet-faced" Carr, whose actions so represented the goals of the congress, became a minor celebrity there.[66]

The speakers at this congress, dedicated to "Woman and the Home," seldom addressed women's paid labor, perhaps because that had been the focus of the previous congress. The speakers did examine women's traditional domestic tasks, which they presented as valuable—and in great need of being performed efficiently and scientifically. As Sturtevant-Peet concluded in her speech, "Our Household Limitations," women were not limited by the home because they could use their brains and appliances to make tasks less onerous. Gilman and Helen Stuart Campbell, whose study of economics included home economics, had studied exactly this problem of women confined to household work. As a result of Gilman and Campbell's intellectual collaboration, some sessions at the congress discussed how women could develop cooperative kitchens. Campbell thought that the 1895 Woman's Congress was an important event in the American home economics movement; the *San Francisco Examiner*'s headlines reported, somewhat prematurely, "THE DOMESTIC KITCHEN DOOMED."[67]

Such arguments made the congress a congenial place for Anthony to strengthen the state suffrage movement. Moreover, the rhetoric, the celebrities in attendance, and the publicity swelled attendance at the congress. All the news stories regarding the congress remarked on the size of the crowds. The congress moved to accommodate them, but the new accommodations, which seated fifteen hundred, quickly proved too small. Hundreds stood and hundreds more were turned away.[68]

Anthony used the congress as an organizing vehicle for suffrage and effectively transferred some of its respectability and popularity to the suffrage campaign. On the day devoted to "The Home and Politics" (suffrage "pure and simple," all agreed), the congress attracted the largest attendance to date, twenty-five hundred. Taking advantage of the growing momentum, organizers officially "adjourned" the congress, only to reconvene the gathering as a meeting of a new organization, the California Suffrage Constitutional Amendment Campaign Association. The officers were also officers of the Woman's Congress, with the single addition of Sarah Cooper's daughter, Harriet Cooper. Seven hundred women were present at this organizing meeting, and when the women met two months later to reorganize the state suffrage association, the members still numbered seven hundred. The increase in membership alone represented progress; the year before, suffrage forces in San Francisco had numbered fewer than two hundred.[69]

Anthony also faced the problem that the northern California suffragists were divided into two factions, between the partisans of Laura de Force Gordon and those of Nellie Holbrook Blinn. Blinn had studied and taught drama in her native Vermont before coming to San Francisco in 1868. Within two years she was teaching elocution at a fashionable seminary and had married a well-known city businessman. Her dramatic performance for a local charity led to a brief career on the stage before she retired to care for an only son. She next became an orator for Republican presidential candidates, first speaking for Rutherford B. Hayes in California in 1876 and then on the national circuit for James A. Garfield in 1880 and James G. Blaine in 1884. When Blinn spoke for suffrage before the California legislature in 1895, she, like Gordon, emphasized the importance of women's self-development but, unlike Gordon, did not go beyond the individual woman to discuss her relation to the social turbulence of the 1890s.[70]

Since July 1894 both Gordon and Blinn had claimed to be president of the California State Woman Suffrage and Educational Association. The chief cause of the debate was not so much the technical question regarding the outcome of the election but the women's different organizational strategies. Blinn's supporters complained that Gordon "talked and talked" rather than organized; as a result, the suffrage movement stayed small and dormant. They told reporters they wanted "a modern worker who does not weary them with ancient history." Gordon publicly labeled the other side "kindergartners," and, more to the point, the divorced attorney and populist orator stated she did not want the work to be managed by "women who had taken it up as a society fad." Gordon had put many hours into suffrage campaigning, but she devoted most of her energies to an individualistic agitation that was typical of antebellum suffrage organizers. She gave speeches and lobbied the state legislature instead of organizing the movement. Anthony faced a dilemma.[71]

Partially to resolve this impasse, in May 1895 Anthony organized the new Campaign Association at the congress, bypassing the embittered state suffrage association. Popular Sarah Cooper was made president of the Campaign Association, while Gordon and Blinn were members with equal standing. Two months later, when Anthony and Shaw helped reorganize the state suffrage association in July 1895, Ellen Sargent, a longtime friend of Anthony's, became the compromise candidate for the presidency. Sargent was the socially prominent and financially secure widow of a former U.S. senator, but she was also a pioneer suffragist. Sargent won the presidency in a landslide victory and Blinn became vice president. Gordon, who announced ahead of time that she would endorse the ticket "provided it is composed of women who are in earnest in the work, instead of society women," accepted the election result. With a unified suffrage organization the women formally launched the campaign in August 1895. The congress, wrote Sarah Severance, "has taken the centre" of organized womanhood and "helped us more than if it had been a suffrage society."[72]

The 1896 suffrage campaign, both in its content and final outcome, was deeply influenced by the depression of the 1890s and the subsequent social and political turmoil. Hard times hit the Golden State in 1893 with great severity. Three years later the state, like the nation, remained in an economic depression. California was second only to Kansas in the number of banks that closed. Seven thousand lost their jobs in San Francisco; fifty thousand lost jobs statewide. The unemployed, labeled "tramps," were driven forcibly from some counties, such as Sacramento, and given minimal social services in others, such as San Francisco, but to all, the tramps symbolized the potential for social anarchy.[73]

In the winter of 1893 and the early months of 1894 the unemployed across the country organized themselves into "industrial armies" and began a march to Washington, D.C., to demand a public works program. Jacob Sechler Coxey, the populist businessman from Ohio who proposed that the government hire the unemployed to build roads, led the most famous contingent, "Coxey's Army," but brigades marched from California. Anna Ferry Smith, an organizer for Bellamy Nationalism and the Farmers' Alliance and a supporter of women's suffrage and temperance, led one of the San Francisco brigades. Parts of Coxey's Army reached Washington, D.C., met with brutal repression, and fell apart. But tramps still walked California roads in 1896. Those both for and against women's suffrage asked what granting women citizenship—a fundamental change in state governance—would mean in a state already in the midst of turmoil.[74]

California populists called for radical changes to end the suffering and to establish justice; they agreed with sister populist Gordon that the "safety of the National household" demanded that the state take actions to make the marketplace democratic. As part of their agenda for expanding democracy, they supported women's suffrage. If the People's Party could benefit from the social disorder, by expanding its farm membership while gaining members of the urban working class, it could provide the bridge to women's citizenship in California just as it had in Colorado, where women won the ballot in 1893. The great Pullman strike of 1894 initially seemed as if it might be the catalyst for just such a victory. The strike began in Chicago and spread across the United States, but no state, with the single exception of Illinois, felt its effect more than California.[75]

In California the Pullman strike quickly became a contest between the Southern Pacific Railroad and the American Railway Union (ARU) because the SP dominated the state's rail system. State farmers, workers, and many of the affluent already detested the Southern Pacific for using its monopolistic powers to gain special, often corrupt, advantages in politics and the marketplace. The behavior of the Southern Pacific during the strike did much to demonstrate the accuracy of its longtime comparison with an octopus as it defeated the ARU through its use of federal courts and troops. Populists, who called for the nationalization of railroads in order to end just such arrogant use of "special privileges," supported the strike, denounced the Southern Pacific, and won in the California gubernatorial election of 1894 their greatest state electoral victory to date.[76]

But the Southern Pacific won victories as well, arguing that whatever mistakes it might have made, it stood for the legitimate American social order. Railroad spokesmen and others committed to the status quo painted the populist demand for government ownership of the railroads as a usurpation of the rights of property rather than a restoration of the rights of the people. Aided by violence at the end of the strike, the SP persuaded many that the farmers' and workers' demands represented anarchy. When Yolo County populists ran jailed ARU strike leader Henry Knox for sheriff in 1894, C. K. McClatchy, editor of the *Sacramento Bee*, sputtered that "the Populists of Yolo county have demonstrated that they have no regard for the law, no veneration for the constitution, no respect for the Flag, and are determined not to pay to common public decency the slightest tribute of consideration." That year marked the peak of populist power in the state; after that the fortunes of the populists, and arguably women's suffrage, slid.[77]

The California suffrage campaign coincided with the 1896 presidential campaign. In this watershed election Americans debated how the nation should respond to disruptions caused most immediately by the depression and more generally by industrialization and economic consolidation. At the heart of the campaign was the question of who should run the country. In the last decades of the nineteenth century, Americans had seen entrepreneurs and financiers build colossal monopolies that invested a few men with great power and fame. Were they heroic captains of industry who built the country or notorious robber barons who stole from the people?

Unbridled capitalism had changed the country in other ways too. Inside the monopolies was a growing middle class of the highly skilled—accountants, managers, and engineers—who put their considerable energies to disciplining industrial workers, pushing them to perform simplified tasks that produced mountains of American goods. Industrial workers saw their numbers increase to one third of the population by the end of the century, but most were not sharing in the prosperity. At the end of the 1880s, before the depression, about 45 percent of industrial workers lived barely above the poverty line, and 40 percent struggled to live below it. Farmers were in a similar plight. They were suffering hard times, and they blamed commodity brokers, railroad corporations, and the financial establishment. During the 1890s depression— the worst for the country until the 1930s—many workers and farmers were destitute and hungry. Should they come together in the People's Party and demand that the government take action on their behalf? Or should these producers trust the captains of industry to build a prosperous, harmonious America for all?[78]

When the depression began, 1 in 3 industrial workers was an immigrant. For many of the native born, the depression threw a glaring spotlight on the faces of these recent arrivals, Slovaks, Italians, and Russian Jews, who seemed menacingly different. The fears provoked by the depression explain the phenomenal growth of the American Protective Association. A small nativist organization in the Midwest in the early 1890s, it blamed Catholics for the steep downturn in the nation's economy and all the subsequent ills the country faced. Papists had weakened the banks, flooded the country with immigrants to take American jobs, and caused strikes—all to undermine America so that Rome could take over. On the strength of these assertions, the APA's membership boomed to half a million by 1894. They were convinced that only Protestants should govern America.[79]

For others, the cause of the depression and its solution were more traditionally and overtly political; the depression had begun under a Democratic president, Cleveland, so the Democrats were at fault and must be turned out of office. So the great political question of the depression became whether the Republicans or the populists would benefit. Unfortunately for the populists, they did not win in the 1894 congressional elections the kind of mandate that they needed to become a major party.[80]

The populists heatedly contested the course they should take. Some argued that they must continue to demand that the federal government take positive measures to restore opportunity for the dispossessed, from enacting the eight-hour day to nationalizing the railroads. Others contended that they could not win a majority with such a platform; therefore, they must concentrate on a single issue that could gather votes, such as their call for "Free Silver." Focusing on this demand—that the federal government increase silver coinage and thus stop the deflation of the depression—seemed the surest path to political victory. The call for silver reduced the sweeping populist agenda for democratic change to an adjustment of the country's money supply. Many on both sides still invested the populists with radical claims and powers, but they had cut out the heart of their radicalism with a silver knife.

Those who saw silver as the means to gain popular support led the party into "fusion" with the Democrats, nominating the Democratic presidential candidate, William Jennings Bryan, as the populist candidate. During the campaign Bryan promoted silver as the people's money that would end the depression and restore opportunity for workers and farmers. He ignored the populists.

In California, as in the nation, the populists fused with the Democratic Party and made this decision from a position of political weakness. The radical populists, who called for a massive shift of power from the "plutocracy" to the people, were heard less and less during the campaign. Most who spoke for reform from the Democratic-populist platform called instead for limited reforms, such as silver.[81]

Conservatives lined up behind the Republicans, who argued that the nation should not respond to the depression and, especially, the social agitation that followed, with reform. Instead, the nation ought to maintain its traditions, such as using the gold standard to guide its financial decisions, as the best means to maintain the social order. The Republicans won the election on the strength of their claim that their candidate, William McKinley, the "Advance Agent of Prosperity," would reestablish social order through a prosperity that would benefit all Americans. The message implicit in the GOP slogan was that prosperity could return only if the government followed conservative economic verities and not an untested program of reform.[82]

The political climate created a major problem for the suffragists: how to present their issue, clearly a major social reform, to an electorate divided about the desirability of reform. Above all, the suffragists, native-born middle-class white women who were chiefly Republican with a significant populist contingent, had to decide what kind of changes they thought their enfranchisement ultimately portended. The political climate of 1896 suggested that they had to choose between a radical restructuring to bring forth a new millennium or the reinforcement of conservative values in order to secure a stable social order. But suffragists attempted to develop other possibilities during the campaign.[83]

❖

In northern California Anthony took over the management of the suffrage campaign in March 1896 at the request of the San Francisco women. She, with the aid of six organizers, set up a series of suffrage conventions planned for every county seat in the state; the objectives were to persuade voters, organize local suffrage groups, and develop a momentum for suffrage that would push the political conventions into endorsing votes for women. The suffrage conventions began in April 1896 in San Diego and ended in northern California a month later, just as the San Francisco Woman's Congress and the state Republican convention were beginning. The suffrage conventions were envisioned as the means to build a mass base for the movement; in each county seat local women would be recruited and left in charge of new or newly revived suffrage organizations. According to almost all reports, the meetings generated large friendly crowds and favorable press coverage. Harriet May Mills, a suffrage organizer from New York who came to California, thought the conventions formed a "triumphal march" across the state.[84]

As part of such a march, made the sweeter by the *San Francisco Call*'s endorsement of suffrage on May 3, the suffragists met with a warm welcome at the Republican state convention on May 5. The Republicans once again added a women's suffrage plank to their platform, just as they had in 1894, and so did the People's and Prohibition parties. The Democrats refused, as they had earlier, but the suffragists were cheered at what they had gained. Alas, the promised support proved ephemeral. The populists, faced with a disintegrating party, fused with the Democrats in August; the Democratic–People's Party did not endorse votes for women.[85]

Moreover, the Republicans began backing away from suffrage. Perhaps, as many suffragists charged, the Republicans did so because of pressure from the state liquor lobby. The lobby, recently reorganized and consolidated into an effective political group, began in 1896 what proved to be a successful campaign against prohibition ordinances. But Republicans had their own reasons for moving away from support for suffrage. They no longer faced a competitive third party that favored votes for women, and in the last few weeks of the election the presidential contest between Bryan and McKinley appeared to be very close in California. At that point Republican support for women's enfranchisement, dwindling since August, collapsed. By the end of the campaign suffragists found it nearly impossible to speak at either the Democratic-populist or Republican rallies. They were on their own.[86]

Suffragists realized one of the most important challenges they faced was winning San Francisco, the eighth-largest city in the nation, the state's population center, and the hub of California financial, commercial, and industrial interests. Organized women found the city's immigrant working-class population the most daunting aspect of the San Francisco campaign. Immigrants or first-generation Americans comprised more than 70 percent of the population. Irish and Germans (Protestants, Catholics, and Jews) formed the two largest groups; Asians (Chinese and Japanese) represented 5 percent of the city's population.[87]

Under Anthony's direction suffragists made only limited attempts to reach the great laboring classes of San Francisco. In the summer of 1896 the state suffrage association hired Naomi Anderson, an African American woman who had actively supported suffrage since 1869, to "work among her own people in the cause of equal rights"; Anderson spoke throughout the state. Carrie Chapman Catt and Anna Shaw, both national suffrage leaders, delivered noontime suffrage speeches at the city's "factories, foundries, and mills"—but not until the last two weeks of the campaign. "A woman long in Chinese mission work" visited the American-born Chinese—those whose birth gave them the right to vote—but this too seems to have been a last-minute arrangement. The suffragists did not perceive the immigrant working class as providing enough political support to make greater effort worthwhile.[88]

A few northern California suffrage leaders had ties to the left and might have made the campaign more inclusive; however, for a variety of reasons they did not work closely with Anthony. Both Laura de Force Gordon and Charlotte Perkins Gilman joined the socialist movement inspired by Edward Bellamy, Nationalism, and both were populists. Both had ties to the labor movement and might have worked to take advantage of the fact that San Francisco labor, in a joint farm-labor conference held in 1894, had declared its support for women's enfranchisement. But both served the movement more as gadflies than as organizers, and Gilman moved to the East in 1895. Finally, as we saw earlier, when Anthony reorganized the state suffrage association, she pushed Gordon out of her ten-year presidency.[89]

The WCTU proved to be a mixed blessing for the suffrage campaign. Sturtevant-Peet and other WCTU women had ties to the populists; moreover, the WCTU was the state's largest member of organized womanhood (six thousand members), the best organized, and the most politically experienced. On the other hand, prohibition was very unpopular in northern California, especially in San Francisco and the wine-growing regions. Anthony therefore asked the WCTU not to become involved in the suffrage campaign as an organization, although individuals were welcome. Despite her request, which temperance women regarded as an indignity, they successfully campaigned for suffrage in rural areas; in some counties the WCTU conducted the work singlehandedly. Near the end of the campaign suffragists revoked their policy of WCTU nonparticipation and officially requested assistance from its members. Suffragists simply could not build an entirely new movement, from the ground up, in such a short time.[90]

Guided by Anthony, northern California suffragists emphasized recruiting wealthy women into leadership roles in the campaign, especially women who worked as hard for philanthropy and civic affairs as they did for glittering receptions—club women, in other words. Lucy Stone and Carrie Chapman Catt had developed this "society plan" in the 1893 Colorado campaign, and suffragists credited it as an important factor in that victory; it gained members with time and money to donate; transformed press reports into favorable, even fawning, pieces; and brought a heady cachet of elite gilt-edged success to the movement. Such a plan seemed well suited for San Francisco. So many society women had attended the 1895 Woman's Congress that the *San Francisco Chronicle* thought it could be mistaken for a "swell reception."[91]

The California society plan, inaugurated in May 1895, consisted of two strategies: recruiting prominent women and then encouraging them to hold "parlor meetings"—preferably in their lavish parlors—to persuade still others in their class or those enamored with the trappings of the upper class to join the suffrage movement. Anthony tried unsuccessfully to convert upper-class Phoebe Hearst and Jane Stanford. But suffragists won Mary Wood Swift, president of the Century Club, widow of the former ambassador to Japan, and an officer of the 1895 Woman's Congress, to the cause. Swift immediately became second vice president of the Campaign Association and held parlor meetings at her home, a house "filled with priceless treasures of art gathered from every part of the world." Anthony used similar methods throughout northern California. When she campaigned in Sausalito, a small town across the bay from San Francisco, she was accompanied by "well-known society people," an effort that led "many prominent ladies" of Sausalito to organize for suffrage.[92]

The elitist campaign did not bring the desired results. The 1896 California suffrage campaign was defeated primarily because it lost in the San Francisco Bay area, the state's population center. Statewide, 137,099 votes were cast against women's enfranchisement and 110,355 in favor, a difference of 26,734.

In San Francisco County voters defeated the amendment by 23,772 votes. Every city assembly district and all precincts voted no; negative votes stood at an overwhelming 74 percent. In Alameda County across the bay, suffrage lost by 3,627, primarily in the cities of Oakland and Alameda. Together, the San Francisco County and Alameda County negative votes totaled 27,399, or 655 votes more than the entire margin of defeat.[93]

When suffragists studied the election results, they concluded that class mattered but not in the way they had anticipated. One suffragist, after comparing the votes of the districts of the "best people" versus those of the "ignorant, the vicious and the foreign born," found that the wealthy wards had returned a higher majority against suffrage than the working-class districts. Anthony, reflecting upon the California campaign at the 1897 National American Woman's Suffrage Association convention, thought that the campaign could have been won "if the slums of San Francisco and Oakland had been . . . organized" with a committee in every precinct. This insight, that the immigrant working class would support women's suffrage, would prove important in the early years of the twentieth century when women began to reorganize the suffrage movement.[94]

National politics also influenced the California suffrage vote. Both San Francisco and Alameda counties voted for the Republican presidential candidate, McKinley. Many of the Bay Area's male voters may have decided for McKinley and against women's suffrage as a means to preserve the status quo. Fearing any change during "hard times," they may have seen no reason to grant a reform that could radically transform gender relations and that was linked to radical reform—populism and Bellamy Nationalism. Southern California provided a backhanded kind of proof for this argument as the region favored women's suffrage and the Democratic-populist candidate, Bryan. Additionally, in Idaho, another western state with women's suffrage on the ballot in 1896, the male electorate voted for Bryan and to enfranchise women.[95]

Los Angeles County provided a bright spot for suffragists. The county, as did all southern California counties except Kern County, returned a majority for women's enfranchisement. Los Angeles voters, however, delivered the largest majority for suffrage—3,596 votes.[96] Some of the Los Angeles suffrage success can be explained by demographics and ideology. Voters there were more inclined to support votes for women: they were white native-born Protestants who favored temperance and Bryan. But this profile of the electorate does not explain all the reasons for the suffrage success in southern California; much of the credit belongs to the Los Angeles women, who ran their own campaign and ran it well. Women in Los Angeles County began precinct organization in April 1894, before the campaign started—a sharp contrast with their northern sisters, who were disorganized and rent by faction long after the campaign began. Some southern organizational efficiency may be related to the match between the populace and organized women. Suffrage cooperation with temperance women, the largest and best-organized women's group to support the vote, occurred to a much greater degree in southern California than it did in San Francisco; temperance women held one third of the seats on the executive board of the Los Angeles County Suffrage Association.[97]

Many Los Angeles suffrage leaders held multiple memberships in a wide spectrum of groups, which enabled them to create a much broader, more harmonious suffrage coalition than the one to the north. As we saw earlier, Caroline Severance helped build an elite liberal salon, establishing a Unitarian church and the Friday Morning Club. These efforts blossomed into the Women's Parliament of Southern California, which in turn became a crucial mechanism for recruiting prominent women to suffrage. Severance, a sympathizer with causes on the left, became a Christian socialist in the 1890s; she worked easily with such suffrage leaders as Mary Garbutt, a temperance advocate, Bellamy Nationalist, populist, and Christian socialist. Margaret Vatel Longley, another suffrage leader, served as the suffrage liaison with the People's Party, writing the suffrage plank at the state party's founding convention of 1891.[98]

Because of this socialist leadership, the Los Angeles suffragists made the "key-note" of the campaign to "reach every voter without regard to race or rank." Despite the suffragists' claim to reach every voter, the women do not seem to have reached—or even tried to reach—Mexican workers. Suffragists may have found it easier to approach the city's white working class than did their San Francisco counterparts because so many Los Angeles workers, especially skilled workers, were white native-born Protestants. Southern California suffragists displayed, however, a long-term interest in conditions faced by white working women; in 1893 suffragists had attempted to improve working conditions for retail clerks. During the 1896 campaign suffragists recruited and organized working-class women, who then spoke for suffrage at "workshops, factories, and railroad stations." Such tactics no doubt contributed to their success.[99]

Suffragists in all parts of the state put forward similar arguments for women's enfranchisement that were much the same as those they had presented at the women's congresses and parliaments during the last several years. When Nellie Holbrook Blinn wrote in 1895, "We protest against the public tyranny of that public sentiment which assigns any arbitrary sphere to woman," she was emphasizing a familiar theme. The franchise would legitimize and expand the public life that women had already created; as an instrument of evolution, the ballot would aid women's individual development and their ability to create a better society. As Blinn explained, "All this unrest and rebellion against the old established abuses among women is simply an effort of nature to improve the race."[100]

An anonymous suffrage pamphlet published in San Francisco most clearly and comprehensively articulated how suffrage would function as the evolutionary tool of human progress. It would do so through empowerment. "When women are a recognized and responsible factor in the commonwealth," argued the unknown pamphleteer, they will grow beyond "narrow and trivial lives" and "develop into a nobler womanhood than the world ever has known." Granted, women were currently engaged in an "immense work . . . in charities and reforms," but they were "shut out from all influence over causes and permitted to deal only with effects." The ballot would enable women to achieve more through its ability to increase their political power. The writer did not shy away from the implications of this last statement, arguing that women, "conscious of their own integrity and strength," were "not afraid to enter politics."[101]

The pamphleteer no doubt meant that women were not afraid to enter the world of elections and legislatures, but increasing numbers of women, including the pamphleteer, saw most women as initially entering politics through a broader (and less controversial) arena—civic activism. The California women's movement had coalesced around the issue of public work in the early 1890s, and many 1896 suffrage meetings continued to highlight the links between women's paid work, as professionals or workers, and their enfranchisement. But this movement of married, middle-class, and middle-aged women always found engaging in public service a particularly hopeful endeavor; they perceived such efforts as filled with the promise of political empowerment and less daunting to take up than work for wages. California women made this promise the implicit theme of the 1895 Woman's Congress, "Woman and the Home," and the explicit theme of the 1896 Congress, "Woman and Government."[102]

The suffragists' declaration that women intended to enter politics, however slowly through nonpartisan activism, represented a potentially radical transformation of the social order—and one that suffragists softened by arguing that women's enfranchisement would, in some way, improve and therefore stabilize society. Anna Shaw's stump speech, "The Fate of Republics," which she delivered throughout the state after the 1895 Woman's Congress, provides an excellent example of one way suffragists made such an argument in the

California campaign and in countless other state campaigns during the last two decades of the nineteenth century.

Shaw pointed out that America in the Gilded Age already was experiencing social turmoil and argued that women's enfranchisement was required to develop and maintain societal peace. She began by asserting that "all the great republics" fell because of "internal strife, begotten of a large warlike population . . . and the growth of licentiousness and intemperance." She next observed that the United States currently suffered from such problems, because of the power of monopolies and government support of gambling and liquor. Only women, Shaw contended, could save the Republic. Her argument rested on gender complementariness and her proof was the westward movement. Men explored and conquered the West, but because women developed homes and thus morality, the West became "civilized." Both tasks were essential. America faced unrest because only men formally participated in politics; to develop a modern social order the country must evolve and grant women full citizenship.[103]

Shaw's argument closely resembled Frances Willard's "Home Protection" campaign for suffrage for many reasons, not least that both sought to develop sweeping arguments for women's citizenship that appealed to a broad audience during a time of bitter social divisions. Both Shaw and Willard contended that women's distinctive moral natures and domestic duties demanded that they participate in public life to represent those interests and to improve the country. They presented such demands as just and expedient while portraying women's duties as domestic and civic. Shaw and Willard presented women's citizenship as a reform that was both deeply conservative—it would preserve the Republic and the home—and quite radical—it would abolish or, at the very least regulate, monopolies and empower women. Both women called for the vote in the name of all women, and both agreed that white native-born Protestant women served as key agents of "civilization."[104]

Suffragists sometimes focused on the last argument: the country needed women such as themselves, white and affluent, as citizens because they would use their votes to maintain a certain kind of order, one with rigid class and racial hierarchies. Immigrants, blacks, and the lower class ("tramps" and the "rabble" vote) all were blamed for the problems of industrializing capitalism. Against these symbols of disorder, suffragists based their plea for enfranchisement on their race and class. White women from the "better, decent classes" could be counted on to bring the proper kind of order to a society threatened with disorder. Eliza Keith, speaking at the 1896 Woman's Congress, predicted that Americans "acting in self-defense will give women the ballot to rescue the Nation from the ignorant foreign voter and the criminal element in our National life." The suffragists refused to speak out against the anti-Catholic American Protective Association (APA). The California APA, organized in San Francisco in the fall of 1893, claimed twelve thousand members within a year. Initially, it supported women's suffrage, in part because the Catholic Church opposed it, and the suffragists hoped to benefit from APA support.[105]

Leaders of the movement, such as Susan B. Anthony, took special care, through actions and speeches, to develop suffragists who were perceived as successful agents of evolutionary change. Anthony found the society plan of recruiting elite women attractive largely because she saw it as a crucial means to achieve this goal. She portrayed women who opposed the ballot as stumbling blocks on the road to progress. Some antisuffragists, Anthony declared, were upper-class women too "devoted to society and selfish ease," whereas others were women with "no life beyond domestic duties." She thought working-class wage-earning women did not support suffrage because they could not spare the time. But, Anthony triumphantly asserted, "every woman of affairs who attempts to accomplish any great work in the world, becomes convinced of the vital need of the ballot."[106]

Anthony felt confident that such women—among her examples were the upper-class club women Bertha Honoré Palmer and Ellen Henrotin, leaders at the 1893 World's Fair—would promote the appropriate kind of social evolution. This is why, at the May 1895 meeting at which suffragists formally made wealthy Mary Wood Swift a suffrage officer, Anthony announced that suffragists "are not trying to revolutionize the world" and denied that they would use the ballot to "overturn existing institutions." Anthony was emphasizing that suffragists were seeking a certain kind of change—a gradual transformation that would nonetheless advance women and, through their public activism, stabilize social relations. The audience applauded her statement. Perhaps the women saw it as a pragmatic statement of the possible, although they might also have been relieved that she was distancing suffrage from radicalism.[107]

Antisuffragists attacked the idea that the enfranchisement of women would secure social order. The *Los Angeles Times* turned the suffrage argument upside down and argued that women's formal entry into public life would bring social disorder. The "Eagle," a *Times* columnist, declared that a suffragist was a "female Debs . . . quite as dangerous to the community in her own artless, fish-wifey way as Debs was in his." (The reference, of course, was to Eugene V. Debs, the leader of the American Railway Union who had been jailed during the Pullman strike.) A *Times* cartoon, on the front page of the paper in June 1895, portrayed the New Woman as a tramp, dressed in trousers and smoking

A NEW DANGER.

When the "new woman" comes in will we have female tramps?

(*Los Angeles Times*, June 11, 1895)

while sitting cross-legged on a fence; everything about this female tramp symbolized a shocking social upheaval. The Eagle took issue with the suffragists'
argument that their race and class justified their enfranchisement. He argued
that the "good woman" would be outvoted by the "Mollies and Marquitas
[*sic*]," that is, Irish and Mexican women, because for every "one good woman"

who voted, "a dozen of the ignorant and vicious class . . . [would] vote against her methods of reform and her clean and decent candidates."[108]

Antisuffragists based most of their opposition to women's enfranchisement, however, on their belief that the social order demanded that women remain in the patriarchal home. H. H. Powers, an economics professor at Stanford University, believed that "social necessity" still demanded that women "shall perpetuate the race under conditions compatible with the social order." These conditions included the "traditional home . . . based on the principle of subordination." Powers was quite explicit that by this he meant that "women must acquiesce" to male authority. Powers argued that patriarchy had developed "a type of woman who acquiesced instinctively, heartily, even craving an opportunity to do so." He acknowledged, "This may all have been very mean and unjust, but it worked."[109]

Dr. Jacob Voorsanger, the liberal rabbi of San Francisco's most socially prominent synagogue, also objected to enfranchising women and for the same reason as Powers. But Voorsanger, the most popular and probably the most effective antisuffrage speaker in the state, cushioned his argument. He argued that if equality meant "mutual recognition of responsibility and of function," the sexes were equal. He thought that women were correct to protest the disrespectful treatment they often received from men. Nonetheless, Voorsanger opposed women's suffrage because he believed that a woman could not be both an "independent factor" and an "actor in the family." As "proof," he argued that as women were becoming more independent and less domestic, the home was deteriorating. The New Woman, Voorsanger warned, was "rampant, anarchistic, and rebellious."[110]

One of the great weaknesses of the 1896 suffrage campaign was that relatively few women were in the paid labor market or engaged in municipal reform; in 1911, when California women finally won the vote, they did so as a movement of working women organized into labor unions and as civic reformers organized into the women's wing of social reform progressivism. But in the 1890s both kinds of women workers were few. Thus it is hard to understand how the suffrage debate evoked so much passion among antisuffragists. One way to gain some insight into the source of this passion is to look at the antisuffrage humor of the campaign because humor, whether in essays, verse, or cartoons, reveals fears.[111]

The theme of the antisuffrage humor was that, as women gained more rights, men would lose their advantage. More than that, men would be at a distinct disadvantage. A California legislator who opposed granting women

(*Los Angeles Times,* May 5, 1895)

the vote best expressed this when he said the vote might be "heaven for the New Woman [but it] would be hell for the old man." In an 1895 *Los Angeles Times* cartoon entitled "The New Woman," two women tower over one very small man. The caption predicts that "if the present process of development keeps up," this would be the norm for the next generation: "We men won't be 'in it.'"[112]

Sometimes the New Woman, with the threat of surpassing men, could appear very menacing. Another cartoon in the *Los Angeles Times* (the *Times* was the only major California paper to use cartoons throughout the campaign to oppose suffrage) lampooned Anna Shaw for announcing at the 1895 Woman's

WHEN ANNA JOINS "DE FOORCE."

Anna C. Shaw wants to be a policeman. We protest, for her first official act will probably be to run in the "Times" artist and the "Eagle bird."

(*Los Angeles Times,* June 18, 1895)

Congress that she thought women should be able to serve on the police force. Shaw appeared in the cartoon as a sexual hybrid, both male and female, and thus unsexed. She towers over the two male figures, the *Times* cartoonist and the *Times* columnist, the Eagle, and is carting them off to jail for their statements against the women's movement. Only two days before the election the hitherto "cautiously friendly" *San Francisco Chronicle* used such "humor" with what suffragists believed was deadly effect, presenting a "huge virago menacing with a club a small man." The diminutive threatened male, the *Chronicle* declared, was "the kind of man that believes in woman suffrage."[113]

Both cartoons portrayed women who sought greater public power, whether as citizens or as paid workers in a "man's job," as menacing men and as ridiculous creatures. The demanding women became absurd—and thus a laughing matter, easily dismissed—because their demands challenged men. The cartoons represented women's desire for more power as a demand to be men, an impossible request that turned them into unsexed beings. In the case of Anna Shaw, the cartoon lampooned her as someone unsexed and politically, perhaps even mentally, unbalanced. In the cartoon she responded emotionally (a stereotypical woman's response) to the *Times's* criticism and abused her position as a police officer by curtailing the right of free speech. The cartoon represented her demands that women be placed in positions of policing the social order as the ridiculous demands of an anarchist who would push men out of their rightful place in the social order as paid workers and as citizens. Women could not be citizens; American society, and with it American rights, could not survive.

Antisuffragists could agree with their opponents, however, that some social change regarding women's role would and should occur. Both the *San Francisco Call,* a paper favorable to women's suffrage, and the *Los Angeles Times* (announcing it had received "considerable criticism" regarding its attitude toward women) printed illustrations and verse of approved and unapproved roles for women; for both papers the acceptable rate of change was quite slow. The domestic woman received the most praise, and the woman who ventured beyond the domestic sphere was reminded, gently by the *Call* and harshly by the *Times,* that she had left her appropriate station in life. The *Times* caricatured the "female athlete" as indistinguishable from the male, as unsexed, whereas the *Call* stated:

> There's a place in the world for her muscle,
> Let her be just as strong as she can,
> If she will only smile like a woman
> And make sunshine in life for some man.

Humor was a socially acceptable way of presenting deep-rooted fears regarding the New Woman while seeking to restrict her at the same time.[114]

The purpose of this humor was best summarized by Ada Van Pelt in her presidential address at the 1895 Pacific Coast Woman's Press Association. Answering humor with humor, she opined that man regarded woman much as he did electricity: "She required certain restrictions or she might become dangerous."[115]

❖

The 1896 suffrage defeat initially affected organized women negatively. Suffrage groups grew smaller or disappeared. But some changed their strategy, chose to win the vote through civic activism, and thus laid the foundation for their eventual victory. One group of San Francisco suffragists provided the most notable example of transformation when they turned their suffrage organization into a women's club dedicated to civic reform, the California Club. They resolved to change public opinion and build a women's movement by first developing women's place in the public sphere. Only after they had accomplished this would they again campaign for the ballot. The California Club became a center of civic reform in San Francisco and the state; it also contributed to the development of a statewide club movement of civic activists. Around 1906 some of these women, as they had all along planned, began working for suffrage.

This movement toward civic activism made women a powerful force in the public sphere and became the organizing theme for the women's movement in the next decade. But the turn to civic reform also strengthened the club women's belief that their progress as women was tied to maintaining the social order, a belief that limited their vision of what they wished to accomplish for women and made developing a coalition with working-class women as difficult as ever.

THE POLITICS OF ALTRUISM: REBUILDING THE CALIFORNIA WOMEN'S MOVEMENT, 1897–1905

FOR SEVERAL YEARS the 1896 suffrage defeat in California devastated the state's suffrage movement. Suffrage organizations lost so many members that they were maintained by skeleton crews of stalwart souls. Other women's groups were only minimally involved in public affairs. Although organized women from around the state had discussed at the California Women's Congresses in the mid-1890s whether to take up urban reform, only a few clubs had taken steps toward doing so by the beginning of the new century. The Women's Congress itself did not live to see that century.

Yet by 1906 organized women—in particular, club women—had enhanced their role in the public sphere and made their movement an influential force in urban public affairs. Club women did not describe their activism as political; instead, they referred to their program as "civic altruism." In part, the women did this because they understood politics to mean partisan activities, and, like many other affluent white Americans of the era, they equated partisanship with corruption. Club women labeled their public deeds as altruistic to separate themselves from corrupt politics, to underscore that they were performing in public the same tasks of moral guardianship that they had previously done in private spaces.

Club women chose the term *civic* to declare that they were building a new public space, a civic arena, in which citizens—women and men—concerned with the public good could build a moral, humane, harmonious America. The women saw themselves as engaged in a dual process, making themselves civic persons—citizens—and creating a better society. The women defined citizens as those who were honest—no partisans allowed—and whose vision was not blinded by narrow opportunistic class interests. The best citizens, in other words, looked very much like the club women—white affluent folks from the "middle classes" who assumed that because they were white and neither extremely rich or poor, they could speak for all.[1]

The women's agenda was connected to their movement in historical time. As we saw in Chapter 2, they had lived through the tumultuous 1890s; they had witnessed the depression, tramps in the streets, and the flowering of radicalism, such as Bellamy's Nationalism, populism, and the great railroad strike of 1894. For a time a significant number of influential women, including leaders of the Woman's Christian Temperance Union, adopted socialist principles and tried to persuade their followers to join them; they envisioned a great movement of men and women that would come together and create the "Cooperative Commonwealth." This proved unsuccessful.

Most organized women did not want social revolution—no matter how peacefully and slowly it was promised to come about. Organized women were deeply distressed about the human suffering, social ills, and urban blight that they saw all around them in an industrializing America; they were equally persuaded that they must make finding the solutions their responsibility, their "work." Therefore they created their program of civic altruism. They made themselves mediators and saw themselves as crossing class lines (but seldom those of race) in order to achieve a more humane social order. As civic workers, they sought to make cities beautiful and the state more responsive to its citizens. Calling themselves "city mothers," they intended to create a civic home that provided services—but not a cooperative commonwealth—for its members.

Pursuing this course, organized women built a loose alliance between the women's club movement and male civic leaders, "city fathers." The groups had similar values. Many of these men worked hard at "improving" their cities, seeking to make them bustling places of business. The men believed, as did the women, that providing efficient public services and an aesthetically pleasing civic environment were steps that boosted their chances for financial success and made other significant contributions to civic life. Both the men and the women proudly saw themselves as "boosters," as people who were building their city and state and who were doing more than that. As westerners they were attempting to fully incorporate their region into the nation and not as some quiet provincial backwash. By engaging in boosterism—supporting activities of great importance to male business elites—women became accepted influential factors in civic life. They were making themselves citizens in their cities and members of the national polity.

Women's enhanced role in public affairs led to the reinvigoration of the suffrage movement. Women were creating a public arena, civics, in which fashionable women served as the citizen builders of a new era of progress. Women gained more chances for meaningful work, more public power, and a heightened sense of themselves as the invincible agents of social evolution. The ranks of organized women, especially club women, swelled. Filled with this heady and growing sense of empowerment, organized women began to demand—in significantly increasing numbers after 1900—their citizenship.

❖

Mary McHenry Keith, suffragist, attorney, and wife of the well-known artist William Keith, later recalled the five to six years after the 1896 suffrage defeat as a time of discouragement and declining enrollments. Many who had entered the suffrage movement "under the stimulus of an exciting campaign . . . could not be persuaded to resume the drudgery of converting the individual voter." Keith herself remained faithful and played an important role in the suffrage revival that started during the first years of the new century. But suffrage statistics support Keith's conclusions: in 1900 only a hundred suffragists remained active in nine organizations in the entire state. Annie L. Corbert, president of the Santa Clara County Equal Suffrage Association, gave a pragmatic but hopeful appraisal of suffrage possibilities in her presidential address of April 1900: "We are simply waiting and watching, and working to strengthen our forces and our cause, so that at the golden moment we may be ready to spring into place."[2]

The California Woman's Congress, which did so much to build the women's movement in the 1890s in general and suffrage in particular, held its last meeting in 1898. The cause of its death is unclear; perhaps the congress was simply too closely identified with the now unpopular suffrage movement or perhaps it could not continue long after its intellectual leader, Charlotte Perkins Gilman, moved out of state. What is clear is that women lost the only statewide organization that brought women from many different groups together. But the debate about the proper public role for women in a rapidly industrializing America continued.[3]

In particular, leaders in the WCTU continued to believe that industrial capitalism was transforming America into a society that was so deeply and permanently unequal that neither social justice nor democratic politics would survive. Beaumelle Sturtevant-Peet, president of the northern California

WCTU, had spent the 1890s supporting the populists and denouncing the power of monopoly. She did not change and neither did Mary Garbutt, a southern California temperance leader who participated in Bellamy's Nationalism and populism during the 1890s. Both continued to believe, as Garbutt warned in 1904, that "the concentration of wealth in the hands of a few, the increasing army of the unemployed . . . are all portents of great social changes which must be disastrous in their results unless the Christian and moral citizens are aroused to their duty."[4]

Sturtevant-Peet, Garbutt, and other temperance women who shared their political analysis agreed that the solution was to create a cooperative commonwealth, a democratic egalitarian society without classes. Most temperance women spoke vaguely about the cooperative commonwealth, particularly about how power would be shared and among whom. But a significant number of the temperance leaders specifically declared that they were socialists. As Dorcas Spencer, the northern California temperance woman who led the 1880s temperance education campaign, observed in 1900, *Christian socialism* was a term in which one word would suffice "as in 'final ultimatum'—one word conveying all sense of both." These temperance socialists believed the cooperative commonwealth would arrive through peaceful reforms, a process of gradual evolution; therefore they sought to create an activist state, one that would end monopolies, the liquor trade, prostitution—and grant women's suffrage.[5]

Because temperance leaders could not achieve their goals without rank-and-file support, the leaders attempted to persuade the members to work for the cooperative commonwealth. But most WCTU women did not work actively for socialism. As long as Sturtevant-Peet remained president of the northern state organization (and she held the office until 1907), its members endorsed her resolutions, which made the same fiery attacks upon capitalism that they had in the 1890s. Both the northern and southern California WCTUs had declared that they stood for a living wage and an eight-hour day. But most temperance members did not follow the radical ideas of their militant leaders with radical actions. If they did work to resolve the labor problem (not a popular concern at the grassroots), they generally engaged in palliative activities that focused on providing alternatives for supposed working-class vice, such as coffeehouses (seen as a substitute for the saloon), or means for individual mobility, such as vocational training (usually "domestic science" classes).[6]

Nevertheless, both Garbutt, in charge of labor activities for the southern California WCTU, and her northern counterpart, Mae M. Whitman, sought

to create a broad coalition of temperance women, labor activists, and reformers that supported the cooperative commonwealth. They urged temperance women to educate themselves about the country's political economy,
suggesting reading lists that included treatises ranging in theme from socialism to labor unions to middle-class reform campaigns. Second, both Whitman and Garbutt hoped that after temperance women read about these various groups, they would form coalitions with them. Because Sturtevant-Peet
shared Garbutt's conviction that temperance women ought to give themselves
a more comprehensive, less provincial political education and build a broader
political alliance, she created the Congress of Reforms in 1900, a WCTU convention that would invite guests from other organizations.[7]

The northern California WCTU began hosting the Congress of Reforms
every summer at the coastal resort town of Pacific Grove, next to Monterey.
Sturtevant-Peet wanted to make the congress a place of debate and dialogue
between temperance women and representatives, men and women, from a
wide spectrum of political and social reform movements. Each group could
meet and learn about the other. Within a year the 1901 congress had achieved
remarkable success as well as controversy. Many reformers invited to the 1901
congress were radicals, such as Rev. J. Stitt Wilson, a socialist, who spoke on
Christian socialism. Other speeches, all given by "experts," included "Public Ownership," "Labor Unions," and "The Evolution of Industrial Life." A
few temperance leaders wrote enthusiastic articles for the *Pacific Ensign,* the
northern California WCTU organ, about this congress.[8]

The evidence, however, suggests that most temperance women were not
ready for a radical restructuring of society. All subsequent Congresses of Reform differed substantially from the congress of 1901. WCTU leaders never
again invited so many radicals to one congress. Some were still invited, such as
socialist Jack London, who spoke on the tramp problem in 1902, but radicals
never again dominated the program. Sturtevant-Peet carefully explained the
objectives for the congresses in her opening remarks at the 1902 congress, and
her points seem quite clearly to have been her response to internal criticism.
She began by contending that "as we progress we must see that the temperance reform is complex in its relationship to other reforms." Attempting to
justify the predominance of radical speakers at the previous congress, she
argued that "in order to get the best results we must touch every spring of
action." To underscore her contention that temperance would progress in
alliance with radical reform, she added, "Bigotry is a barrier to progress." She
concluded rather defensively, "We are not here to adopt new reforms, but to

consider them. This is not a delegated body; no business is transacted during the session . . . but we may discuss questions and take with us what we please and apply as we may."[9]

The year 1902 was a watershed for temperance women. Some, such as Mary Garbutt, became socialists. In 1902 she served as both the vice president of the Woman's National Socialist Union and president of the California Woman's Socialist Union, groups that she helped organize in 1901 and 1902, respectively. Socialist women saw themselves as agents who would transform the larger women's movement. They would recruit working-class women into the movement and teach organized women that their goals for women's advancement and social justice could never be achieved without creating the cooperative commonwealth. By 1906 socialist women would be influential within the suffrage movement. Garbutt continued as a WCTU leader, always working to convert her temperance sisters to a wider, deeper sympathy with labor. But the lack of enthusiasm from the WCTU membership meant that the torch for the cooperative commonwealth had passed from temperance hands to those of socialist women.[10]

❖

Among those attending the 1902 Congress of Reforms was Dr. Dorothea Moore, representing the newly formed California Federation of Women's Clubs. She asked temperance women to support the women's proposed legislation for a juvenile court system. Moore's request was a turning point for California's organized womanhood. During the Gilded Age the WCTU had dominated the legislative efforts of the state women's movement, lobbying for temperance, suffrage, and "social purity," that is, laws regarding sexual mores. Temperance women would continue working for these campaigns, but women's clubs soon would dominate women's civic work. And white affluent club women would choose a distinctly different path from that taken by temperance and socialist women.[11]

Much of the women's club movement was hostile to socialism. The political development of Mrs. Lou V. Chapin, a member of the Los Angeles Ebell Club, illustrates this point clearly. In the late 1890s the Ebell Club took a step that many other women's clubs took—it broadened its traditional examination of the arts to include studies of current social issues. Chapin led a study group in an investigation of the American political economy. She concluded that American society was basically sound. At the April 1899 session of the Woman's Parliament of Southern California, the regional group of organized women formed in 1892, she "decried the socialistic tendencies of the day, and held

Edward Bellamy as responsible for much of the dissatisfaction with existing conditions."[12]

Chapin's views did not go unchallenged. Especially in California, many women had been converted to socialism through Bellamy's novel, *Looking Backward*. California had about 40 percent of all the Bellamy socialist, or Nationalist, clubs in the United States. California women belonged to those clubs and served as officers; moreover, many other women were sympathetic to socialism. After Chapin's attack on Bellamy, Helen Elliott Bandini of Pasadena stood up, defended socialism, and "urged all women to throw their weight against any movement which should bring labor and capital into conflict."[13]

Such a diplomatic action, seeking social peace and accommodation, typified much of Bandini's life. Her father, Dr. Elliott, pioneered in southern California in the early 1870s, helping to establish the "Indiana Colony"; this Anglo Protestant settlement of midwesterners developed into the staunchly Protestant town of Pasadena by the mid-1880s. She married Arturo Bandini, a member of a prominent *Californio* family. Elites from these two groups, the former Mexican citizens of California and Anglo Americans, often intermarried, but an Anglo groom nearly always married a Californio bride. Helen Elliott made an unusual decision when she chose to marry Arturo Bandini. In 1902 she lived in Pasadena with her husband and two sons (both of whom spoke Spanish), where she studied the Southwest and spoke out for Indian rights. Six years later she published the *History of California* in which she documented Anglo injustices against Californios. But she implied that such wrongs were more understandable when committed against the "lower class [Californios] many who were part Indian, who would lie, steal, or if they had an opportunity murder" and less so when the victims were members of the elites, "men of education, brave, hardy members of good Spanish families." Helen Elliott Bandini was an awkward diplomat at the California crossroads of ethnicity and class.[14]

But many organized women agreed with her 1902 call for women to serve as mediators across class lines, a position that organized women proclaimed frequently during the 1890s, from the 1893 Columbian Exposition in Chicago to the subsequent California Congresses. In 1898 the General Federation of Women's Clubs, the national organization of clubs, created its Committee on Industrial Problems Affecting Women and Children. The resolution that created the committee declared that "right and justice demand that women of larger opportunities should stand for the toilers who cannot help themselves." Women of social position should engage in social work that would achieve social justice and social peace.[15]

The Committee on Industrial Problems sent a circular to all the clubs in the General Federation, calling women to work and explaining why such actions were crucial for them as women and as citizens. The circular explained that although industrial capitalism had brought prosperity to some, such as the club women, it meant great suffering to many others. Ominous problems of social upheaval and perhaps even revolution lay ahead. The first circular, sent soon after the 1898 Convention of the General Federation of Women's Clubs in Denver, described an America in which the poor, forced into a desperate struggle, were replacing their moral standards with amoral behavior that they hoped would enable them to survive. The circular warned that "women cannot ignore the disastrous effect of such [moral] displacement upon their own sex or upon their children." A woman must take up reform in order to "insure a safe and positive future for her children."[16]

Perhaps influenced by these warnings, the Ebell Club and other Los Angeles women's clubs formed the Los Angeles Civic League in the fall of 1899. When Chapin spoke to the 1900 Woman's Parliament, she explained why the clubs had created the Civic League. Women's clubs knew they must reach out "to help those who can not help themselves, to mold public opinion, to take an active part in the world's great work of righting the disinherited." The audience applauded. Perhaps conscious that this sounded much like Bandini's call for class mediation and quite unlike Chapin's earlier denial of serious social problems, Chapin went on to declare that while "all of us have a great fear of being considered radical," such a fear in this case was baseless. She contended, "The great power that is everywhere inherent in the woman's club . . . lies in the ability to so harmonize the radical conservative, and radical progressive, and create a unity resulting in progress." Chapin felt comfortable asking club women to serve as class mediators because she felt certain that as elite women they would strive for social peace and reform, not revolution.[17]

Chapin and others saw the Los Angeles Civic League as a means of building a women's reform vehicle for the city. Clara Burdette, also a member of the Los Angeles Ebell Club, created the California Federation of Women's Clubs in January 1900 in order to build a statewide women's reform organization.

Burdette's ultimate success probably surprised no one who knew her; she had long demonstrated the ability, ambition, and organizational skills necessary to achieve such a goal. Born in 1855 in New York State as Clara Bradley, she worked her way through Syracuse University. In 1876 she graduated and married Nathaniel Milman Wheeler, a former student at Syracuse, who was developing a career in education in Wisconsin. In the mid-1880s they moved to Los Angeles in the hope of curing his tuberculosis. But he died in 1886,

Clara Burdette (The Huntington Library, San Marino, California)

leaving her alone with a young son. She pursued a variety of low-paying jobs, including one secured for her by organized women in 1887, managing the Woman's Exchange at the Flower Festival Home. In 1890 she married "Colonel" Presley C. Baker (he had served in the Confederate army), an immensely wealthy older man who had retired to the fashionable town of Pasadena. He died in 1893, leaving her once again emotionally bereft but this time a widow of great wealth. Six years later she married Robert Burdette, a humorist and journalist.[18]

Clara Burdette's second husband, Colonel Baker, had asked her not to engage in club life, and she did not during their brief marriage. After his death, however, she became a charter member of the Ebell Club, and for the rest of her life she served as a leader of clubs, charities, and civic groups. In Sunny Crest, the handsome Pasadena mansion bequeathed her by Baker, she held forth in a salon of "bright and busy people . . . a brilliant circle of authors, teachers, travelers, musicians, [and] artists." Years later Burdette recalled that she was initially content in the early 1890s to simply participate in the "serious study programs" and social life of organized womanhood, but soon she was asking "to what end, if we do not reach out into the community and unite our strength for some betterment?"[19]

Burdette decided that "the answer" was that women should become civic activists and in the late 1890s took an important step toward facilitating her vision. She began attempting to organize a state federation of clubs, partly as a means of converting other women to public service. May Wright Sewall's speech before the Congress of Representative Women at the Chicago World's Fair had emphasized the relationship between women's power and their organizational solidarity; this had persuaded Burdette that women needed federation to enhance their effectiveness as activists. January 1900 marked her crucial first step: club women assembled in Los Angeles to consider forming a federation. In her opening address Burdette acknowledged that most did not want to be civic activists or, as she phrased it, "the much-needed City Mothers have not been wooed and won yet." Therefore Burdette urged not only club federation but women's commitment to civic reform.[20]

Burdette, like Chapin, based part of her call for women's activism on the state of American society: "We are confronted by conditions, not theories, and conditions that have never before existed. The question is not, 'Shall we meet them?' but 'How?' for meet them we must." Mrs. Isidor Lowenburg, president of the Philomath Club, a club of Jewish women in San Francisco, agreed. "Against the widening of the gulf between the rich and the poor . . . society should array the forces that make for progress." But, Lowenburg felt compelled to add, "few of us would like to see Bellamy's theories prevail in legislation."[21]

Burdette's response to this perceived social crisis was to call on women to become city mothers; she was asking them to become a powerful force in the public arena based on their traditional roles at home. She explicitly connected federation to empowerment. She informed women that "there is as much difference between unorganized and organized effort, as there is between the power of a handful of [gun] powder scattered loosely on the floor, and that of the same amount compressed into the chamber of a gun." Burdette wanted women to pull the trigger so they could use that force to take women's values from the home into society. She succinctly summarized these ideas in her 1902 "Club Creed," which declared: "Home must always be the center, but not the limit, of woman's life." Burdette envisioned city mothers as engaging in a policy of separate but equal: they would expand and empower women's sphere in politics.[22]

Burdette did not call women's public activism "political" in either her 1900 address or in the speech she made as president of the federation at its first convention two years later. She claimed that city mothers must fulfill civic obligations, meaning nonpartisan public acts of "social service"; to her, the federation represented "organized altruism." Burdette envisioned women's civic duties as overlapping a significant sector of male civic responsibilities, from education to civil service, and she believed that women's duties would expand. In both speeches Burdette urged women to take up certain public endeavors that would encourage them to do more. She included areas of reform in which organized women held a relatively long record of activism— such as placing women on school boards—as well as new frontiers of womanly public work—such as civil service and slum prevention. She placed all this within the context of "an inevitable process of evolution" and warned women that "if they insist in lingering lovingly in the traditions and customs of the past . . . they will have to step aside, and watch the world go by."[23]

Many women determined that they would take a step toward making their place in the world. Accepting Clara Burdette's advice, women representing forty clubs with a combined membership of 6,000 formed a state federation. In comparison, the combined membership of the northern and southern California WCTU organizations also totaled 6,000 in 1900. But as the number of women connected with the club federation increased, the number affiliated with the WCTU declined. By 1902 the federation reported 7,000 members, whereas WCTU membership had dropped to approximately 5,600. Although the temperance groups soon began a slow but steady growth, reaching 7,000 members in 1905, the federated clubs' membership that year stood at 10,765. Moreover, this pattern, with the clubs as the largest segment of the women's movement and temperance women as the second largest, continued for the rest of the decade. What made these women's clubs increasingly popular in the early twentieth century as they stood ready to propel women into civic life?[24]

Around the turn of the century, memberships in women's clubs became a symbol of elite status. Newspapers made lists of the "fashionable clubs." By definition these clubs were filled with affluent women, but the term *fashionable* implied something more: popularity and desirability. As clubs became popular, the nature of club life changed, as the history of the Friday Morning Club of Los Angeles illustrates. Caroline Severance, the noted club woman and reformer from Boston, established the club in 1891 with twenty members. The club's membership expanded to two hundred members during the first year, but club life changed more slowly. For a decade the Friday Morning Club held meetings in rented rooms and served lemonade and cookies. Club members presented most of the papers.[25]

In 1900 the four hundred members of the Friday Morning Club moved into their own clubhouse, a Mission-style building that reporters and members referred to as "magnificent" and "imposing." Every month the club would cater a luncheon, hold a tea, and occasionally sponsor lavish entertainments, complete with a string ensemble. The fashionable activities underscored and deepened the elite nature of club life and may partly explain the continued popularity of the club, which had more than nine hundred members by 1906. Perhaps because of its size, outside speakers gave most of the talks. Only at the club's monthly luncheon could members participate in public discussions, usually about books.[26]

The Friday Morning Club's building symbolized the growing stature and changing nature of the club movement and, indeed, of organized womanhood. Club women across the nation began building their own clubhouses in the 1890s; a writer for *Harper's Bazaar* in 1908 found seventy such clubhouses across the nation. (The writer did not include remodeled houses or rented quarters.) The reporter declared that club building proliferated in certain states; California had eleven clubhouses, or 10 percent of the national total, and was prominently featured. In addition to the Friday Morning Club's house, valued at $30,000, the *Harper's Bazaar* reporter particularly praised the "Spanish Renaissance" clubhouse of Clara Burdette's club, the Los Angeles Ebell Club, valued at $20,000. Burdette, who built the clubhouse at her own expense in 1897, was probably pleased with the praise, although many Los Angeles women felt it resembled a Greek temple.[27]

The women's clubhouses provided a protected interior social space that facilitated the objectives of its members, whether study, reform, sociability, or all three. Clubhouses also represented much more. They stood as solid, expensive, and aesthetically pleasing testimonials to the inextricable link between gender and elite class standing in the world of women's clubs during the progressive era. Club members proudly emphasized that the clubhouses demonstrated women's business acumen; the cost of the buildings underlined that

To build their permanent clubhouse, women of the Friday Morning Club formed a corpo-
ration, the Woman's Club House Association. That's why the name on the Friday Morning Club building is the Woman's Club House. (The Huntington Library, San Marino,
California)

they exercised their financial skills in an environment of wealth. The buildings were expensive because the women used them to make an aesthetic
statement—the buildings were what would be expected of ladies of culture—
and because they provided spaces for libraries, auditoriums, meeting rooms,
and banquet halls, places of women's work.[28]

Most of all, clubhouses made a statement, to members and to society, that
women's clubs had arrived. They were now an established part of upper- and
especially upper-middle-class society. In its editions of January 1, 1900, the *Los
Angeles Times* provided a summary of the city, meant to boost its accomplishments at home and abroad. The *Times,* a fierce opponent of women's suffrage,
included in its survey something that was becoming common on such lists,
detailed descriptions of women's clubs, complete with a sketch of the reception hall of the Friday Morning Club.[29]

Club women limited membership in these lavish clubhouses to whites, an-

other declaration of their elite identity. Because a significant number of leading women, such as Clara Burdette, intended to make the clubs centers of
civic activism—and soon succeeded—their restrictive membership policy
did more than make the clubs an exclusive social group. The club women,
through policies that were overt and covert, formal and informal, were announcing that some women—white and financially secure—were capable of
civic leadership and other women were not. When the women created membership policies for their private clubs, they were also making political decisions that shaped organized womanhood and influenced society's notions
regarding women, race, class, and politics.[30]

Individuals in and out of the club movement publicly debated the implications of these decisions. In the summer of 1902 the reporter for the women's
club section of the *Los Angeles Capital* began the column by asking, "Is club
life breaking down the class barriers of modern society?" According to the
paper, "the society woman is taking up club life," but "club life is not, and
cannot be, as exclusive as society." For clubs to flourish the society woman
must "recognize brains and admirable womanly traits, no matter if the pos-
sessor is not, strictly speaking, in her set." On the other hand, a restricted
membership policy empowered the clubs. Recognizing this, club leaders were
"willing to risk much that no objectionable element might be introduced," a
policy that could enable the clubs to "bring about the establishment of an
intellectual aristocracy that shall be more pronounced in its exclusiveness
than the one which is fed now by wealth and family standing." This was why,
the journalist concluded, the white women excluded African American wom-
en from the national organization of clubs, the General Federation of Wom-
en's Clubs.[31]

Members of the General Federation formally voted to exclude African
American women at their 1902 convention in Los Angeles. The incident that
led to this decision had occurred two years earlier, at the Milwaukee convention in 1900. Josephine Ruffin, an African American woman, had attempted
to claim her seat as a representative of a black women's club, Boston's New Era
Club, but the federation revoked the club's federation membership on a tech-
nicality. The incident sparked a debate of "intense feeling" at Milwaukee. The
president of the General Federation, Rebecca Douglas Lowe of Georgia, refused to allow the issue of admitting black women's clubs to come to the floor,
which meant that the question would most likely be settled at the federation's
next biennial convention.[32]

California women, representing a state federation only months old, came
to Milwaukee to ask that the next biennial be in Los Angeles. They won their

bid. The press printed rumors that the federation had chosen the western location because it believed—or hoped—that Ruffin could not afford to travel so far. Whether true or not, the rumor documented the intense feelings aroused in Milwaukee, an intensity that continued, by all accounts, for the next two years.[33]

Leading California women took vigorous steps to ensure first that women committed themselves to a policy of racial exclusion and, second, that they made this decision smoothly and without incident. Clara Burdette placed herself in charge of ensuring both. She began in California. Under her leadership the state federation convention, meeting in early February 1902, agreed, by a vote of 129 to 9, to send its delegates to the General Federation convention "uninstructed," that is, without a specific charge on how to vote regarding African American women. According to the *Los Angeles Times*, although this resolution contained no reference to "the color question," the vote was "generally understood" to be about race. Why Burdette chose this particular course is not clear. Most women agreed with her; club membership must remain white. Perhaps Burdette found the minority who opposed her simply too militant and boisterous to risk giving them ammunition.[34]

San Francisco club women in particular complained about Burdette's tactics at the state convention; they charged that Burdette had "railroad[ed] it [her motion] through before it had been discussed." Laura Lovell White, founder of San Francisco's California Club and candidate for the presidency of the state federation, withdrew her name from the ticket in order to protest Burdette's actions.[35]

Burdette also took actions on the national level during the same month. She called for a special conference of General Federation leaders so that they could hammer out an agreement regarding the admission of black women's clubs before the upcoming biennial meeting. At the February conference, held in Boston, Burdette successfully "counseled letting the Southern [white] women handle that question in their own way," which meant excluding African American women.[36]

Burdette offered this advice because she, like many other whites at this time, saw herself as part of the generation that had finally buried the animosities of the Civil War and achieved national white unity. Club women also perceived their General Federation of Clubs as both reflecting and building white unity and thus white dominance. Because the General Federation gained strength from its national white inclusiveness, it could not sacrifice that strength for racial equality. As Mrs. George W. Bunnell, self-identified as a "Southern woman" and president of the Oakland Woman's Club, declared, "It is not what's right, but what's expedient. If the colored women's clubs were to be taken into the federation, almost every club of white women in the South would leave it. I don't see why there should be any question of it." Burdette may have held yet another, more personal reason for her actions to unite white women; she very much wanted to be elected president of the General Federation of Women's Clubs at the Los Angeles convention.[37]

Burdette's efforts failed to win her the presidency; women elected her vice president of the General Federation of Women's Clubs. The *Los Angeles Express* declared that Burdette was so deeply disappointed that she became deathly ill. Burdette actually remained quite alive—whatever her disappointments—and local women rallied publicly to her defense. Journalists hinted at several reasons for her loss of the highest office; one of them, women intimated, was her "railroading" through the state convention her position regarding black clubs. But the new president of the General Federation, Mrs. Dimies T. S. Denison of New York, endorsed the exclusion of African American women, as did an overwhelming number of delegates. Most likely, Burdette lost the office because of the assertive manner in which she pursued it, as evidenced in the methods she used to gain a whites-only federation, and not because of her white supremacist objective.[38]

When women debated what newspaper reports referred to as "the color question" at the convention of the General Federation of Women's Clubs, they framed their debate as an argument about the best means of social evolution. "This is not a question of color," asserted Mrs. Gallagher of Ohio. "It is a question of an embryonic race, not yet strong enough to stand with us. . . . If we admit them to associations with us, they will lose their power of independent development and become merely followers of the whites." The audience gave Gallagher "tremendous applause." Of all the speakers who responded to Gallagher, Jane Addams, the nationally famous settlement worker from Chicago's Hull House, received the most attention.[39]

Addams both challenged the racism of Gallagher's remarks and, to some degree, accepted the racial hierarchy implicit within her evolutionary argument. "I think," Addams stated, "that we all feel that this is a discussion of the color question." She continued, "There are those of us who hold that . . . it lies with the stronger peoples to stand with the weaker, and aid them in their development." According to the *Los Angeles Times,* Addams felt and spoke "with a deep conviction that drew respectful attention, although it failed to convince the house."[40]

Within the small group of white California women who supported Addams, Mabel Craft most eloquently expressed their principles. Craft's parents brought her to California from Illinois as a child, enabling her as a young adult to take advantage of some of the opportunities provided California women—opportunities that organized womanhood had helped make possible. Craft was graduated from the University of California at Berkeley at the top of her class in 1892 and next attended Hastings Law School. After graduation in 1895 she chose journalism as her career, seeing it as a vocation that provided women with the greatest chance for success. She became the Sunday editor of the *San Francisco Chronicle* in late 1899 at the age of twenty-seven.[41]

During the debates about a racially restrictive membership policy, the *San Francisco Examiner* described Mabel Craft as "a young woman of advanced ideas . . . the leader of the liberalists among local women." Craft, a member of the San Francisco Forum, a women's club, proclaimed that "the color line is drawn by prejudice" and that she could not "reconcile this prejudice with twentieth century logic or our boasted progress in civilization." Craft applied her own logic to the argument being waged within the federation about admitting African American women. She stated the same position as Addams but with less diplomacy and more heated passion: "Our motto is 'service' and if we cannot find it in our hearts to do what we can to help the colored women, why, we had better break up our Federation."[42]

California women did not break up their federation; they reinforced the color line. Although some women justified drawing the national line by arguing that it gave states greater freedom to draw the line where they wished, the California Federation of Women's Clubs did not accept black women. African American women therefore built a separate state club movement and a successful one, despite the adverse conditions they faced. Racism blocked their opportunities for education and employment. Furthermore, only a few African Americans lived in California; as late as 1900 their numbers stood at eleven thousand. But black Californians, men and women, worked at creating institutions—building churches, schools, self-help groups, and fraternal organizations. In 1899 black Baptist women in Oakland began another kind of endeavor when they created the first black women's club in the state, the Fanny Jackson Coppin Club, dedicated to the study of culture and community improvement.[43]

African American women soon established other clubs and in 1906 formed the State Federation of Colored Women's Clubs, which joined the National Association of Colored Women in 1908. The California women resolved—as did other African American women across the nation—"to do some monumental work of interest to the race." In Los Angeles the Sojourner Truth Club, created in 1904 at the African Methodist Church, determined to build a "home for self-sustaining women." In 1909 the Art and Industrial Club of Oakland celebrated the opening of its new Woman's Exchange and sent invitations to various white women's clubs. Some mailed back greetings. But Mrs. James B. Hume, president of the white state federation, and her secretary attended. Seven years after white women debated whether they were strengthening a color line, two white women felt able—briefly—to cross it.[44]

California women reinforced another color line at the 1902 club biennial, that between white American nationalists and the Mexican population of Los Angeles. Club women celebrated the conquering American military forces that about fifty years earlier had defeated Mexico, taken California (along with several other Mexican provinces), and incorporated all the spoils into the United States. By celebrating the war, the women declared themselves patriots of white America. The United States was correct in appropriating Mexican land because this meant the victory of "civilization" over "barbarism," of an advanced "white" race over those backward races, Indian and Mexican, who stood in the way of Manifest Destiny. When Ione Cowles, the Los Angeles woman who served as president of the local biennial board, welcomed women from across the nation to California, she asked the audience to venerate the moment when the American flagship *Savannah* "hoisted the American ensign over the long-desired territory of California." Club women responded, according to the *Los Angeles Times,* with hearty applause.[45]

A few days later club women once again valorized the American fulfillment of its Manifest Destiny over Mexico. In the parade for the city's annual Fiesta de las Flores (a different event than the flower festival), the president of the General Federation, Rebecca Douglas Lowe of Georgia, rode in a carriage covered with roses and pink satin ribbons. She was accompanied by Elizabeth Frémont, the daughter of John C. Frémont, who had encouraged Euro-American settlers in California to revolt against Mexico before the United States declared war on Mexico; in this revolt, later labeled the Bear Flag Rebellion, white Californians committed numerous atrocities upon Californios, soldiers, and civilians. Nonetheless, many Americans revered John Frémont as a dashing standard-bearer for the wave of American imperialism that swept through much of America after the Spanish-American War of 1898.[46]

Members of the former ruling class of Mexican California, the ranchers who once owned vast empires of land, traditionally participated in the Fiesta de las Flores. But in 1902 "Spanish American ladies"—as the press always referred to the female members of the ranchero families in regard to this incident—threatened to boycott the fiesta because of a statement by Caroline

Severance. Ironically, Severance made this statement as she was trying to defend her acquiescence to the clubs' whites-only policy.

Severance, a former abolitionist who was now in her eighties, felt compelled to defend herself, acknowledging that her own daughter thought she "might be called a backslider from [her] past position on the question of the freedom of the slave." Severance believed that white women needed to be "educated to the point of drawing the line of social fellowship at education, character and good breeding" rather than at race. But until all white women were so educated, Severance concluded, it would be unfair and unwise to insist that clubs practice racial equality. Most important, Severance believed, an attempt to admit black women would jeopardize the fellowship between the northern and southern white clubs. At the conclusion of her disingenuous argument, Severance declared herself "amazed at the illogical position of Americans of culture and broad views, who can draw the line at color, in the case of our own southern blacks, while receiving socially representatives of other dark races, Spanish, Italian, East Indian, etc., and giving them national recognition and honors."[47]

The Californio women protested the last statement; they perceived Severance as drawing the color line around them as a "dark" and thus a "not white" race. In the minor brouhaha that followed Severance's statement, both those who attacked and defended Severance categorized the descendants of the Californio elite in the same way—as holding an intermediate racial position. They were not white, as were Anglo-Saxons, but neither were they dark in the same sense as working-class Mexicans, Indians, or African Americans. Mexican elites were characterized as "Spanish," a less dominant member of the European family than sturdy Anglo-Saxons but still part of the white family. This characterization reflected the racial line drawn more than fifty years earlier, during the Anglo-American conquest of Mexican California. The Americans chose to perceive the Mexican elites as Spanish largely because the Mexicans' wealth and political circumstances enabled them to demand an enfranchised citizenship.[48]

Those involved in the 1902 brouhaha, however, did not mention past history but contemporary racial boundaries. Like Severance, they deplored the color line and, like her, they strengthened it. The *Los Angeles Times* found the color line "absurd at best" but especially as used by Severance; "if there is a difference between the Anglo-Saxon and the negro there is manifestly a similar difference between the Spaniard and the negro." A few days later club woman Helen Densmore defended Severance in a letter to the editor of the

Times; according to Densmore, the possibility never occurred to Severance that the Californio women "could take umbrage at what she said, or that they could be placed in the same class with the negroes." Despite all the heat of this debate, all agreed. Female members of the Mexican elite were white; they were Spanish American ladies, not Mexican women.[49]

As white women they could and did belong to white women's clubs, a status that confirmed the elite status of the clubs and of whiteness. Florence Dodson Schoneman—daughter of a San Pedro developer, James Hilsey Dodson, and of Rudecinda Sepulveda Dodson, who came from a prominent Californio family—joined the Order of the Native Daughters of the Golden West. This patriotic mutual benefit society limited its membership to white women born in California; members dedicated themselves to venerating the memory of white pioneers in California. Schoneman, along with Mrs. Reginaldo del Valle, the wife of a second-generation ranchero who became an attorney and successful politician, also belonged to Los Angeles women's clubs. As a *Los Angeles Times* journalist enthused in a report on the city's clubs in January 1920, both were "modern women *yet* each descended from the oldest, most aristocratic Spanish families. They give a touch and color to club work that no other section of the country possesses" (emphasis added). As Spanish American ladies they contributed the right touch of color.[50]

Because the Californio women could contribute an elite tie to the past, the *Los Angeles Times* wanted them to continue their participation in the city's Fiesta de las Flores in 1902. Those who did march in the parade demonstrated the growing ties between the women's club movement and male elites. During the parade some of "the most prominent men of the city" rode next to the women's carriage. The Los Angeles Chamber of Commerce, Board of Trade, and the Merchants and Manufacturers' Association all had backed bringing the General Federation's convention to the city; visions of thousands of well-heeled club women in the city made the businessmen most enthusiastic. They donated $2,000, which paid for a little less than half of the biennial's expenses.[51]

The Merchants and Manufacturers' Association assured the General Federation that the date of the Fiesta de las Flores would be changed to accommodate the organization. Why not? The Merchants and Manufacturers' Association had created the ersatz Spanish fiesta in 1894 to increase tourism. The fiesta, a collage of borrowed celebrations, reflected the male boosters' single-minded intent to promote the region. The fiesta included a carnival (borrowed from the New Orleans Mardi Gras) and a floral parade (borrowed from the defunct Flower Festival Society). Those who marched in the parade presented another collage, the boosterism and idealized imagery of contemporary Los Angeles; the parade included caballeros—the Californio gentry on horseback—entries by Anglo Protestants from schools and clubs and, from the small Chinatown of Los Angeles, a Chinese dragon. The Merchants and Manufacturers' Association proudly informed the club women that such a fiesta "with its local color, its rare pageants, its barbaric Chinese features" could not "be produced in any other section of the United States."[52]

When the women met in Los Angeles in 1902, the campaign to boost the city by linking it to a mythical history of Spanish romance was in full swing. Charles Fletcher Lummis, Los Angeles booster, journalist, and reformer, led the campaign; city entrepreneurs financed it and women played a prominent role. As editor of the *Land of Sunshine* (later called *Out West*), a journal initially subsidized by the Los Angeles Chamber of Commerce, Lummis promoted southern California as a place of perfect, health-giving weather and a picturesque Spanish past. In 1895 he both began the *Land of Sunshine* and started the Landmarks League; its main objective was to preserve the Spanish missions. Organized women wrote for the *Land of Sunshine* and joined the Landmarks League. Some did both. When Charlotte Perkins Gilman lived in Pasadena, she was a staff writer and a member of the Landmarks League.[53]

Lummis and organized women had a mix of motives as they wrote about and attempted to preserve relics of California history. Transplanted from the East, they sought to come to terms with an unknown place and make it their own. They shared a certainty that they were living healthy, productive lives in southern California; the sunshine did not—as many feared at the time—dissipate the Anglo Saxon. Gilman, who recovered much of her emotional and physical health in Pasadena, wrote a testimonial for Lummis in *Out West* in which she praised the healing qualities of California. Such "proof" of Anglo adaptability meant much to Lummis, who thought that southern California ought to become "the new Eden of the Saxon homeseeker."[54]

Such messages were intended to challenge the view of many easterners who, during the 1870s and much of the 1880s, found California, like the rest of the Far West, an embarrassment; the West, even more than the rest of America, lacked the history, art—the civilization—of Europe. Boosters for California and its early resort hotels swore that the state resembled Europe, especially Italy; boosters kept quiet about the missions because so many Americans found them primitive and crude and therefore uninteresting, at best. Grace Ellery Channing, a friend of Gilman's and, like her, a transplanted New Englander who regained her health in southern California, maintained some of this early disinterest in western culture. Channing wrote for *Out West*, becoming an associate editor in 1898, and she joined the Landmarks League, thus supporting the rebuilding of the missions. But she advised eastern settlers in Los Angeles to adapt to the region by using not Indian or Spanish or Mexican models but an Italian one.[55]

Lummis made himself the national leader of a movement that promoted the Southwest and its history—especially its Spanish history—as a point of pride for the West and the United States. Lummis contended that if the United States made the Spanish past its own, Americans could fully assimilate the romantic but doomed "white" Spanish empire into the vigorous regime of American imperialism. By attempting to save the "past"—the missions and the few remnants of "mission Indians"—the Anglos could inherit the romance; by maintaining a silence regarding Mexican achievements (and the Mexicans living in the city), Anglos consolidated their conquest and domination. Lummis frequently declared that redeeming the missions constituted an act of patriotism because it made the West part of the national body; apparently agreeing, women's patriotic organizations, such as the Order of the Native Daughters of the Golden West and the Daughters of the American Revolution, joined the Landmarks League.[56]

Lummis, some concerned local women, and Los Angeles city fathers all joined together to persuade women at the 1902 biennial to restore the King's Highway—El Camino Real—which once connected all the missions. Lummis contributed by speaking at the biennial—one of the few men invited to do so. He published, in the issue of Out West that greeted women when they came to the City of Angels, Auguste Wey's article promoting El Camino Real. Both Lummis and Wey emphasized that rebuilding El Camino Real would bring to the state both a most utilitarian gain—a needed, improved road—and beauty, art, and history. Restoring El Camino Real meant increased tourism to the missions, which meant more money to restore the missions. Expanding tourism brought more dollars for local businesses, while those making this modern pilgrimage would find personal, higher rewards.[57]

Those who participated in the El Camino Real project saw themselves as patriots, as benefactors of the arts, and loyal regional boosters. That was exactly why, declared Lummis, he addressed women, the guardians of civic virtue. "Just as 3600 years ago the women kept alive the sacred flame of Vesta," he said, "so it is the women today who are keeping alive the flame of thought— it is the women who care. We men are too busy, and therefore, stupid; for to be too busy to live aright is stupidity."[58]

Club women found this call attractive—just as they had before Lummis made his appeal for El Camino Real. Anne B. Pitcher, a Pasadena club woman and ardent student of California history and art, and Tessie Kelso, the Los Angeles city librarian, had organized the Society for the Preservation of the Missions in the 1890s. They traveled "in a springless heavy farm wagon, from Mission to Mission, photographing and sketching and securing such data as was procurable and that would form the basis of a series of lectures." In the lectures, illustrated by lantern slides made by Kelso, they emphasized the duty of the audience to restore the decaying historical landmarks. From the beginning Pitcher advocated reconstructing El Camino Real as part of the project of preserving the missions. Lummis built his Landmarks League upon the work of these women, as he publicly acknowledged.[59]

At the 1902 biennial, Pitcher, with the aid of city fathers, put together an El Camino Real exhibit. Both she and the men saw the project as boosting the region, which made it a civic project. The Los Angeles Chamber of Commerce gave Pitcher permanent space for the exhibit in its assembly room. She invited the Los Angeles Board of Supervisors to be the first to view the exhibit; they had paid for part of its cost.[60]

Visitors to the exhibit saw little regarding a road, noted a *Los Angeles Times* reporter in a complimentary account; instead, they gazed upon "objects" that were intended to convey the national and cultural significance of the art and history of old California as well as its exotic nature. One table featured Helen Jackson's *Ramona,* the 1884 book about star-crossed lovers that did much to popularize the mission myth. Visitors could pick up leaflets (and copies of *Out West*) that suggested tours to the missions. They could watch "a Mexican" carving leather or view statues of saints made by "a Los Angeles Indian"—the reporter did not provide the artists' names, even though the account named many of the club women who helped Pitcher. Finally, the exhibit included an "oriental corner, a collection of historic embroiders and drawn work, oriental art, music, pictures and curios."[61]

The women probably included this "oriental corner" in an exhibit entitled El Camino Real for the same reason that the merchants and manufacturers labeled their parade La Fiesta de las Flores and placed in it a Chinese dragon as well as caballeros. The boosters, men and women, saw the Mexican and Chinese communities in California as similar; they were an exotic people who had once challenged or troubled Anglo dominance but were now defeated. Both had therefore become picturesque; both were relics from the past. Those who created the El Camino Real exhibit presented California history as the story of white American conquest and progress; they celebrated the might of the American nation that had conquered Mexico and restricted Chinese immigration. They were patriotic citizens who were engaging in that great issue of western politics, boosterism.[62]

Pitcher and the other women involved also saw themselves as benefactors of the arts or, more precisely, of western art. Pitcher invited Mrs. Albert H. Brockway of Brooklyn, New York, the chair of the art committee for the General Federation of Women's Clubs, to be an honored guest at a reception at the exhibit; together they consulted "as to the best means of interchanging eastern and western art." Western women could now serve as conservators of regional "art" because these relics, reinterpreted by Lummis and club women as markers of Manifest Destiny, illuminated the American mission and thus spoke to all citizens.[63]

California women enthusiastically supported the idea of developing a romantic regional history. The state Federation of Women's Clubs had formed a committee dedicated to California history and landmarks a few months before the 1902 biennial; Mrs. A. S. C. Forbes, a Los Angeles woman, became chair. The following year Forbes asked women to join in the work of restoring El Camino Real. They helped locate the road and marked it with mission bell guideposts. Various leagues of men and women and the automobile clubs worked with the women; eventually, auto clubs took over the responsibility for maintaining the bells.[64]

Year after year club officers reported the popularity of the Committee of California History and Landmarks. They saw its work, according to Mrs. A. Osborne of the San Francisco District, as an act of "pure patriotism." They were making themselves patriots by declaring themselves capable of shaping American history. Club women's support for the history and landmarks committee reflected their growing interest in becoming civic activists. In 1903 the president of the California Federation of Women's Clubs, Mary Darling, commented on the increase in civic activism within the federation, the first president to do so. According to Darling, the federation was "largely composed of literary clubs, and yet, without neglecting any of the purposes for which they were organized, nearly all participate in some outside altruistic work."[65]

❖

From different kinds of reports in which women counted their activities in individualistic ways it is clear that by 1906 a significant number of clubs were engaged in a small, tentative movement into public life. If a club woman entered civic affairs, she most commonly served as a volunteer for the public schools; planting trees and other efforts to create a "City Beautiful" came in second. On the other hand, a few leading clubs, such as the California Club in San Francisco and the Civic League in Los Angeles, had become fully committed to civic affairs; many of their projects were quite ambitious. But the leading clubs shared with the less active a great interest in creating the City Beautiful, from planting trees to building parks.[66]

California clubs' interest in the City Beautiful movement was shared with other women in the early years of the century. After reading the state reports in 1906, Kate Cassatt MacKnight, the chair of the Civic Committee for the General Federation of Clubs, concluded that "the City Beautiful appeals to the largest number of clubs." When historian Mary Beard wrote *Women's Work in Municipalities* in 1915, she wanted women to be involved in city planning, which she saw as "the climax of municipal endeavor." But, she acknowledged, "the movement for municipal beauty has been the strongest phase of city planning up to the present time and the element that has appealed to women's civic leagues in their early days very strongly."[67]

City Beautiful, a national movement, conformed with organized women's concept of civic activism. City Beautiful activists, firm believers in the power of the environment to shape society, felt certain that civic beauty could transform political and social life, creating a harmonious, cooperative, and contented society. In addition, a city's beauty would boost its growth, attracting new businesses and citizens; promote tourism; and, finally, all these would increase real estate values. Advocates of City Beautiful, men and women, were white upper-middle-class professionals and businessmen and their wives; they believed that creating harmony within a society deeply divided by class and racial hierarchies served the public good.[68]

The City Beautiful movement presented several different ways this urban transformation ought to be done; its different perspectives represented the smaller movements that merged into the larger one. Some, such as the American Park and Outdoor Art Association (1897), promised good results if a city provided places of contemplation, such as parks. Women who wanted to participate were placed in auxiliaries. Urban improvement associations, which formed the National League of Improvement Associations in 1900, soon renamed the American League for Civic Improvement, argued that a beautiful city possessed an efficient sewage system (and other mundane city services) as well as landscaped boulevards. Women joined improvement clubs with men or formed their own.[69]

In 1904 the American Park and Outdoor Art Association and the American League for Civic Improvement formally merged, creating the American Civic Association, although their approaches to the City Beautiful movement had informally merged earlier. City Beautiful advocates, aware of what vast changes they were demanding, now recommended that cities rely on expert city planners. These experts designed all the components of the plan, from landscaping to plumbing; they rebuilt the entire city into a place of order. The power of urban governments to impose this orderliness was celebrated at magnificent civic centers. Women, often organized into separate groups, could aid through fund-raising efforts, such as campaigns to sell bonds.[70]

Mary Beard explained the popularity of the City Beautiful movement among women by arguing that "it is a most legitimate object of civic endeavor and it is comparatively easy of accomplishment where it touches no vital economic interests." California women stressed the importance of engaging in a "civic endeavor"; when they described their urban reforms, however, they used the words *civic* and *altruism* interchangeably. Mrs. F. W. Gorham, a San Francisco club woman, declared in 1906 that "to make towns and villages more beautiful, more inviting to the casual visitor, to take a lively interest in educational affairs—this is a legitimate field for the exercise of that high altruism which desires the greatest good for the greatest numbers." When Darling, as president of the California Federation of Women's Clubs, announced in 1904 that women were engaging in more civic efforts, she declared that "nearly all [California clubs] participate in some outside altruistic work." MacKnight, chair of the General Federation's Civic Committee, reported the term civic was "generally used by the clubs all over the country to indicate any altruistic work performed by the club as a whole."[71]

Women wanted to do much more than altruistic good works. By emphasizing that they were working on behalf of the public good, they would highlight what they believed was a corollary, that the public good depended on women's actions.

Mary Beard said that the City Beautiful movement was popular among women for another reason: it was "comparatively easy of accomplishment where it touches no vital economic interests." Beard made an understatement. Club women conflated City Beautiful altruism with boosterism; their civic activism served the public good as an investment, or "improvement," to use their term, that would bring material returns as well as more ethereal ones. When Mrs. Conde-Hamlin, president of the Civic League of St. Paul, Minnesota, spoke to Los Angeles women in May 1902 to persuade them to form an outdoor art league, she entitled her speech "The Commercial Value of Civic Beauty." Los Angeles women formed the league. Gorham, in her report about San Francisco clubs, explained how such civic efforts improved a town: "A well kept park imparts a dignity and respectability to a town, and stands as ever present evidence of local pride and civic enterprise."[72]

❖

The experiences of two clubs, the California Club of San Francisco and the Civic League of Los Angeles, are good examples of how women perceived their civic activism, engaged in it, and were affected by it. Neither was typical, but both were influential, affecting other women's clubs and their respective cities. Club members sought to boost their cities by enhancing them aesthetically and by providing social services, such as juvenile courts and playgrounds, that promoted order, unity, and civic enterprise. In the name of altruism and as city mothers they sought to re-form society in a way that would simultaneously boost their interests as white elites and as women.

A small group of San Francisco suffragists created the California Club in 1897 with the specific intention of making it serve as a suffrage vanguard within the women's movement. After the 1896 defeat, members of the Political Equality Club for the city's 41st assembly district held a series of meetings in which they debated what their next step should be. They concluded that creating a civic club would be the best way to rebuild the suffrage movement. They reasoned that such a club, if not organized under the suffrage flag, could pull together a large number of women who were interested in public affairs, although perhaps not in agitating for the vote. This kind of club, they were confident, would teach other women the value of the ballot. Mrs. J. W. Orr, a suffragist and member of the new club, summarized its organizing principle in a speech she gave in May 1898: "Nothing so reveals the possibilities of our sex to our sex as [our] concerted action."[73]

Laura Lovell White, a banker's wife and president of the Political Equality Club, held the preliminary organizational meeting for the new civic club at her home in late December 1897; only twenty-five women appeared on that cold and rainy evening. But those present formed a club and elected Lovell White president. By the spring of 1898 four hundred women belonged to the California Club, making it one of the largest in the state. All stood for increasing women's civic service; some intended to achieve political equality. In Orr's 1898 speech, in which she discussed women's urban civic activism, she concluded with a statement meant to predict—and influence—the future: "The club [referring to all women's clubs] must be ever more and more responsive to social needs as it grows more powerful, and grow into a higher and clearer conception of its duties both socially and civilly; for, desired or dreaded, women in America are proceeding straight to the inevitable goal of the largest social and political responsibility."[74]

Just how the California Club intended to respond to social needs is demonstrated in its campaigns to save San Francisco's Telegraph Hill and a grove of sequoias in the western Sierra. In January 1900 Telegraph Hill and the working-class Italian homes built on it were in danger of collapsing. Each time a contracting firm hauled away rocks from the hill to use as quarry for building material, the hill grew smaller and the foundations of the homes on the hill less secure. City hall refused to listen to the complaints of the Italian homeowners. The California Club sent a message of solidarity to the homeowners' association, drafted a protest resolution for the Board of Supervisors, visited the park commissioners, and sought an attorney to win an injunction against the contracting company. These efforts proved effective; the California Club saved Telegraph Hill.[75]

Catherine Hittell, chair of the California Club's civic section, wrote for the *San Francisco Examiner* an explanation of why the club decided to save Telegraph Hill. She began by placing the club's action within the context of civic activism: "This movement [saving Telegraph Hill] gives proof of the growth of civic pride, and civic pride makes cities great." For Hittell, civic pride meant saving Telegraph Hill because of its historic significance, "its possibilities as an ornament to the city"—she thought a protected and improved Telegraph Hill could become the most beautiful urban hill in the world—and, of course, the matter of justice for the homeowners on the hill. In all these actions women intended to create a city both more beautiful and with a more unified civic consciousness. They placed their economic boosterism in the framework of public good for all.[76]

The California Club engaged in other efforts that placed it squarely within the City Beautiful movement. Laura Lovell White underscored this when in 1902 she and a small but "earnest" band of members—about thirty women— established the California Outdoor Art League, a local auxiliary of the American Park and Outdoor Art Association. Although "active membership" was limited to this small cadre, women who were interested in the work and willing to pay dues but unable to give fully of their time could join as associate members, as could men. The league resolved "to preserve the natural attractions of localities . . . to advance the interests of forestry" and, in summary, "to promote all work relating to the artistic and industrial development of California."[77]

Members of the Outdoor Art League had already gone to work to save

Telegraph Hill, but forming the league seems to have encouraged their attention to numerous urban projects. They landscaped schoolyards; advocated for the restoration of San Francisco's Mission Dolores; "secured the care and cleaning of the ocean front"; and fought to retain street flower markets. But the campaign of the Outdoor Art League–California Club (they merged after a few years) that gained national attention was its effort to save the Calaveras Grove. This stand of Sierra redwoods, or *Sequoiadendron giganteum*, grew in the Stanislaus watershed of the western Sierra; today the trees are part of Calaveras Big Trees State Park. Like the campaign for Telegraph Hill, it began in January 1900. On that date Mrs. D. J. Murphy "heard casually at a reception . . . that the Calaveras grove had been bonded to a lumber firm." She immediately notified her club, the California Club, and its campaign began at once.[78]

The club, with Lovell White still serving as president, developed a comprehensive strategy. It decided, first, that the grove would best be protected as a national park. To secure the legislation necessary, Lovell White asked the club's vice president, Mrs. A. D. Sharon, who, serendipitously, was already in Washington, D.C., to lobby for a bill that authorized the federal government's purchase of the Calaveras Grove. To aid passage of the bill the club resolved to "put in circulation hundreds of petitions"—sending them to every organization in the state. By the end of February club member Mrs. J. W. Orr reported that about forty organizations, representing twenty thousand people, had endorsed the California Club's resolution regarding the big trees.[79]

In March President William McKinley signed a bill that supposedly would save the trees; the gold pen he used to sign the bill was given to the California Club in recognition of its efforts. Unfortunately, although the bill authorized purchase of the land, it did not provide money for the purchase. The California Club, led by Lovell White, would struggle nine more years until it won national legislation it believed was strong enough to save the trees.[80]

The Calaveras Grove campaign provided the California Club with an opportunity to enhance its political relationship with San Francisco's male establishment. The *San Francisco Examiner* gave the California Club's initial campaign to save the Calaveras Grove, which lasted from January through March 1900, intense coverage. This coverage demonstrated that the California Club did not stand alone in its campaign to save the big trees. The *Examiner* wanted to save the trees, as did the city's mayor, the Irish millionaire reformer James Duval Phelan, and many of the city's male civic organizations: the Chamber of Commerce, Merchants' Association, Bohemian Club, Pacific

Union Club, and the Native Sons of the Golden West. The "socially prominent" California Club, as it was frequently referred to in the city's press, led a campaign that was backed by male elites.[81]

The California Club, the *Examiner,* and Mayor Phelan all put forward the same argument for saving the Calaveras Grove, and it rested on motivations quite similar to those of the reformers in southern California, men and women, who worked to save the missions and El Camino Real. The forests of big trees created natural cathedrals that lent dignity to a region once scorned for its lack of shrines; given the monumental aspects of the sequoias, many would benefit from pilgrimages to the sacred groves. As the California Club observed, the age of the trees, estimated at six thousand years, and great size, some more than twelve feet in diameter, meant that they were a "great natural attraction." According to Phelan, the big trees created a "wonderland" or, said the *Examiner,* "a wonderful heritage of nature." Such an attraction meant, according to the club and Phelan, who used exactly the same phrase, "thousands of tourists." One tree, thought the *Examiner,* brought more tourists than the Eiffel Tower; of course, this was "thousands of tourists." As Murphy of the California Club pointedly argued, the living trees made more money for the state than they would as lumber.[82]

The women's club, the mayor, and the newspaper agreed that the destruction of such a heritage would bring "disgrace upon California," as the club wrote in its resolution. The *Examiner* concurred that it would be a "reproach" against the state. Destruction would be a "crime in eyes of the world" because the world, explained Phelan, has "a proprietary feeling concerning the wonders of the world." As the *Examiner* posed the question, "If Americans owned the pyramids, would they quarry them?" All three worried about that answer. However, the *Examiner* went to the greatest lengths in contrasting mercenary, short-sighted Americans to Europeans, who had the aesthetic and commercial vision to appreciate and market such attractions. If the sequoias grew in France or Germany, the paper assured its readers, the big trees would never be destroyed.

This melodrama of "Woodman Spare That Tree!"—a phrase that the *Examiner* used in its headlines—culminated with wrapping the trees with patriotism and/or spiritual values. Saving the sequoias was patriotic; destroying them was treason or sacrilege or both. Murphy of the California Club refused to believe that any "Californian was so disloyal to the state" as to permit such destruction. Phelan agreed: such destruction would show Californians "unworthy of our heritage if we allowed such vandalism." The *Examiner* was certain: "California was not the kind of state to permit such sacrilege." Preserving the trees meant preserving a public heritage from the vandalism of unrestrained commercial greed; it also meant using the trees for tourism.

The ties between the club movement and civic boosterism thus gave organized women more public exposure, gained more acceptance for women's public activism, and helped build a loose coalition between the women and male civic leaders. These men supported the women because they too sought to create the City Beautiful. Most notably, Phelan, mayor since 1897, had led a host of male civic organizations in the 1890s and during the early years of the new century in a movement to transform San Francisco. They wanted it to become the commercial and military center of the American Pacific empire, an imperial city. To make this possible the men planned a city of magnificent public spaces and efficient services. All these "improvements" cost money. Phelan, his fellow reformers, and the *San Francisco Examiner* began in the late 1880s to refer to those who were willing to raise taxes for these improvements as "progressives"; those who remained tied to the traditional city policy of low taxes were far back in the evolutionary cycle, back in the "silurian" age of "slime and ooze."[83]

The members of the California Club and the city fathers who believed in the City Beautiful movement continued to work together to bring progress to San Francisco. In 1903 Catherine Hittell explained to the San Francisco Merchants' Association, a leading group in the effort to make the city beautiful, why men should support city bonds for the latest project of the California Club, building a park on Telegraph Hill. She began her speech by predicting that world power was shifting to the Pacific and that San Francisco would become the leading city of this new empire, surpassing New York. She argued that voting for the bonds would show the "world that we have confidence in the destiny of our queen city"; furthermore, the bonds would provide a measure of justice for the impoverished homeowners that the California Club had taken under its maternal wing. She denigrated those who refused to support the bonds as "silurians."[84]

The following year, 1904, San Francisco businessmen created the Association for the Improvement and Adornment of San Francisco; Phelan served as president. Although some men, such as Phelan, adamantly opposed women's suffrage, the Outdoor Art League—the City Beautiful arm of the California Club—belonged to the association. The women had achieved a place in the civic arena as people who worked altruistically for the public good.[85]

Women in the Los Angeles Civic League, the state's other major urban civic women's organization (which became the Civic Federation in 1903), had a similar experience. They too organized an outdoor art league in 1902. Under the leadership of Arabella Rodman, they held an Arbor Day celebration the following year that became an annual city event. The women planted trees in city parks; they invited male organizations to serve as co-contributors and thus presumably also as appreciative colleagues. Those invited included the Chamber of Commerce, Merchants and Manufacturers' Association, the city's Park Commission, and the mayor. Women organized the volunteer gift giving that male leaders often applauded and nearly always accepted, even when, as in the case of the editors of the *Los Angeles Times,* they satirized the women's actions.[86]

The *Times,* reporting in the fall of 1904 on the Civic Federation's annual meeting, splashed across the front page cartoons and a lengthy article that ridiculed the women for planning "some magical civic heaven where there is naught of trash nor even the slightest hint of orange peel." The *Times* wanted the reader to laugh at women who saw their small objectives, such as clean streets, as a component of a "civic heaven"—or, more to the point, as a factor that mattered in civic affairs. As part of the same comic routine, the paper noted that these "daintily clad and high-bred women" intended to banish "immoral" billboards and "spooning" in the park. Nonetheless the *Times* supported many of the women's objectives—how could it oppose a Los Angeles that boasted streets cleaner than any eastern city's? Furthermore, although its humor was meant to marginalize the women, its emphasis on their elite status and conventional femininity signaled the *Times*'s resigned acceptance of their civic participation.[87]

Despite the satire, the women successfully pursued many of their projects, such as their campaign against "unsightly" billboards. The women perceived them as an immoral, aesthetic, and economic blight on their community. In 1907 a city judge accepted parts of local legislation promoted by the women: billboards could be taxed, and immoral billboards could be outlawed, but the billboards themselves remained otherwise unregulated.[88]

After the women found themselves stymied by the judge's decision, they called upon various male groups that boosted the city, such as the Chamber of Commerce, the Municipal League, and the Merchants and Manufacturers' Association. The women asked them to join in the campaign, by writing advertisers and asking them to voluntarily not use "country billboards" to advertise their wares. The men agreed and collected favorable endorsements, which were published in the *Los Angeles Express* in April 1908. As in the San Francisco effort to save the Calaveras Grove, the local press, in this case the *Express,* and the male civic leaders joined the women of the Civic Federation to put forward a united argument against billboards. Mrs. J. F. Kanst, chair of the billboard committee of the Civic Federation, no doubt expressed all their sentiments when she said billboards must be regulated because "scenery is an asset of the city's prosperity."[89]

❖

In accordance with the women's concept of civic activism and their efforts to enter the public sphere more fully, women, in common with many other advocates of the City Beautiful, believed that improving a city also meant ensuring that it provided efficient social services. California women worked especially hard, and were nationally known, for juvenile courts and playgrounds. These reforms stemmed from a common belief that elite women could mediate social problems through the use of scientifically informed social services managed by experts. Club women were quite successful in ensuring that these experts included women, often club women.

Settlement houses in New York, Chicago, and Boston pioneered in establishing playgrounds in the 1890s. Playgrounds offered urban children something more than space to play; playgrounds meant "directed play" under the direction of professional recreational leaders who would teach immigrant working-class children the skills and values deemed necessary to make them good citizens. After the industrial Northeast and Chicago, the other center of the playground movement in this country was California; playgrounds thrived there because of club women.[90]

California reformers, men and women, shared with eastern reformers a faith in the transformative power of playgrounds; Arabella Rodman affirmed that "directed play affords the best opportunity and method of developing manners, morals and citizenship." Supporters of playgrounds frequently claimed that they reduced juvenile crime, which meant, according to the *Pacific Outlook,* the southern California progressive organ, that "as a money-saving enterprise, playgrounds have proved to be more than satisfactory." In addition, playgrounds were touted as a means to teach the work ethic, to decrease the number of dependents demanding public charity. Finally, playgrounds developed good citizens. As Bessie D. Stoddart, a Los Angeles settlement worker, described the reformers' objective: "On the playground fair play must be constantly practiced, self-control constantly maintained. This is the very essence of democracy. For to know how to associate, how to co-operate with one's fellows is the foundation of our national form of government."[91]

Men and women reformers agreed on the importance of playgrounds, but women led the campaign to develop them. In Los Angeles the College Settlement—a settlement house created in 1894 by the local branch of the Associa-

tion of Collegiate Alumnae—began agitating for playgrounds in 1897. The
Civic Federation, led by Rodman, joined the campaign in 1904 and persuaded
the city council to create a playground commission. The five seats on the
commission were allocated by sex: three for men, two for women. Rodman
became president of the commission and Bessie Stoddart, of the College Settlement, its secretary.[92]

By 1911 the city playground commission, with Rodman and Stoddart still
serving as president and secretary, respectively, managed six permanent and
seven vacation playgrounds that were visited annually by 365,000 children.
But the reputation of the city's playgrounds rested on more than numbers. As
Stoddart wrote in 1910 for the *Annals of the American Academy of Political and
Social Science,* the playgrounds were best described as "recreative centers"
because they offered so many of the services generally provided by settlements. Playground directors (a man and a woman, usually married) lived at
the parks, just as residents lived in the settlement, the better to provide continual service and influence for good. Playground clubhouses were places for
lectures, plays, and music. A librarian told stories at the playgrounds and a
nurse set up a clinic.[93]

Women in San Francisco and Oakland followed a similar path in establishing playgrounds. The California Club opened a public playground in San
Francisco in 1898, the first on the West Coast, and managed it for three years
as an "experiment" in the hope that the city would take it over. But the city
seems to have ignored the lesson. Around 1904 the Pacific Association of
Collegiate Alumnae asked the San Francisco Council of Women, composed
of thirty-three clubs, "to work for socialization of public school properties
and the establishment of school playgrounds." They hoped to turn each public school into a minisettlement house that provided numerous services, including playgrounds, a vision quite similar to the one being followed in Los
Angeles.[94]

Within a few years San Francisco women had made progress in establishing
playgrounds. The Council of Women created a school playground in 1906 in
a tenement school district under the supervision of Emma L. Noonan, a
teacher in the school and member of the Collegiate Alumnae. The following year the Outdoor Art League, now a committee of the California Club,
managed a political campaign, asking city voters to support bonds to build
playgrounds and to form a commission to manage those playgrounds. The
women, under the direction of Laura Lovell White, drafted the measures,
persuaded political parties in the city to support it, and campaigned vigorously for its passage. The women's measures won and, among their rewards,

women became members of the playground commission. They had, like the women in Los Angeles, mandated seats by sex: two of the seven commissioners had to be women. Lovell White, named to the commission in 1908, remained there until 1912.[95]

Across the bay in Oakland the playground campaign gave women the chance to expand their public role even further. In June 1908, six months after Lovell White and one other member of the California Club took their seats on the San Francisco Playground Commission, the Oakland City Council created a playground commission; its ordinance mandated that a majority, three of its five members, be women. The commission was charged with investigating playgrounds and reporting to the council and mayor on the advisability of establishing city playgrounds. All three women members, Cora Jones, Alice Bunnell, and Ethel Moore, were club women who were already involved in managing a playground, created by the Oakland Woman's Club in 1899 and supported by that club until 1909. As Cora Jones reported to the California Federation of Women's Clubs in 1910, the Oakland Playground Commission owed its existence to the club women's success in the playground campaign.[96]

The California system of juvenile courts also owed its existence to club women, most of all to Dorothea Rhodes Lummis Moore, a woman who impressed everyone as an exceptionally talented, unconventional person. Olive Percival, a member of the Friday Morning Club, wrote on her 1908 club program that she found Moore "a born anarchist[,] a wit and fine critic of the arts and, of life." Clara Burdette, who described few other people in her 1951 autobiography, characterized Moore—who was not an ideological anarchist—as a person "with a piquant, original mind of her own." The writer Mary Austin, who disliked many, admired and felt drawn to Moore.[97]

Dorothea Moore made several crucial decisions in her early adulthood that made her distinctive. She entered medical school at Boston University. In 1880, when she was a twenty-year-old medical student, she secretly married Charles Fletcher Lummis, then a junior at Harvard. Mary Austin, who despised Lummis, charged that they kept the marriage a secret because Lummis was enmeshed in a paternity suit with another women; this was most likely true, given that Lummis later recognized this daughter. Lummis flunked out of Harvard the following year, and Dorothea's parents gave him a job on the family farm in Ohio's Scioto Valley. While she finished medical school in Boston, he moved from farming to editing the *Scioto Gazette*. He acquired a position at the *Los Angeles Times* through stunt journalism—walking from Ohio to California in 1884. The following year she joined him in Los Angeles. She set up a flourishing practice, held numerous positions in local medical societies, served as drama and music editor for the *Times*, joined many women's groups—including the Pacific Coast Woman's Press Association—and founded the local Society for the Prevention of Cruelty to Children.[98]

After ten years of marriage Charles sought a divorce. Dorothea granted it, maintained friendly relations with Lummis and his new woman friend, who married the next year (relations that therefore inspired malicious gossip, according to Austin), and went on with her life. She married Ernest Carroll Moore, whose long career in education spanned service as superintendent of Los Angeles city schools to provost of the University of California at Los Angeles. In the late 1890s she decided to spend some time at Hull House, Jane Addams's Chicago settlement house, and this led to her involvement in the juvenile court movement.[99]

Settlement workers at Hull House and members of the Chicago Woman's Club established the first juvenile court in the nation in 1899. Moore participated in that campaign, which involved lobbying the state legislature to pass enabling legislation and then establishing a juvenile court in Chicago. The settlement workers and women who supported juvenile courts argued that youths could be rehabilitated if they were removed from the adult criminal system and placed in courts that specialized in transforming young people. After Moore arrived in San Francisco, she led the California Club in the same crusade. The women went to the city's police courts and compiled a record based on 175 cases of delinquent juveniles that Moore felt demonstrated the need for a juvenile court. In 1901 she presented the state legislature with a juvenile court bill supported by the California Club, but the bill failed to pass.[100]

When Dorothea Moore began her campaign for the juvenile court legislation the second time, in 1902, she did so as the chair of the California Federation of Women's Clubs' Civic Committee. Moreover, she did much to broaden the campaign—especially among those she considered the interested public. She distributed copies of the bill written in lay terms, held conferences with relevant professionals, spoke at the WCTU Congress of Reform in 1902, spoke at individual clubs such as the Friday Morning Club, and spoke to suffragists. Club women, temperance women, and suffragists all resolved to support juvenile court legislation and saw the bill pass the legislature in 1903.[101]

The passage of the juvenile court bill gave women the opportunity to again expand their public role—this time as paid professionals. The state law allowed juvenile courts to be established but did not provide funding for probation officers. This represented a potential defeat for the juvenile court reformers. Probation officers were charged with much of the responsibility for rehabilitation: they evaluated the environments of youths charged with crimes to determine the cause of their delinquency and thus created the supposedly scientific data that would allow the court to choose the appropriate course of action. If youths were placed on probation, the officers would monitor their behavior. Club women initially provided funding for probation officers in San Francisco and Los Angeles. The women soon demanded, and achieved, the hiring of women as the probation officers who dealt with delinquent girls.[102]

Club women well understood the importance of these various campaigns in expanding their public role and making them accepted, valued participants in civic affairs. Dorothea Moore asserted in 1906, "In every [California] town and city the [women's] clubs have now an acknowledged position for which they no longer need to fight and which they must now merely keep fresh and confident with ever more and wiser effort." This "acknowledged position"— that women had fought for and won—was that society recognized women as legitimate members of the civic sphere, as those who worked to maintain order and build harmony. Other club women agreed with Moore. In 1905 Mrs. W. H. Lawson of the northern district of the California Federation of Women's Clubs reported that "it is a common occurrence for municipal authorities to seek the co-operation of these clubs in every public enterprise." The following year Mrs. E. B. Scott of the southern district of the federation gave the same assessment: "Our clubs have become such a moral and intellectual force that their co-operation is sought in many enterprises that aim to upbuild the community and to alleviate much of the suffering of humanity."[103]

❖

Club women's entrance into civic service helped reinvigorate the state's suffrage movement, which had lapsed after the 1896 defeat; however, it was temperance women who had taken the first major step toward reviving suffrage. In 1898 Beaumelle Sturtevant-Peet, thinking aloud in her presidential address, asked what could be done to keep alive the interest in suffrage. She recommended that the WCTU "do something" at the next state legislative session; "if nothing more," the WCTU could ask for school suffrage. Sturtevant-Peet probably hesitated about recommending school suffrage because suffragists tended to view such partial steps as humiliating, that is, as actions that mocked women's right to full citizenship. But Sturtevant-Peet and Sarah Severance saw the matter differently.[104]

They saw such a small step as the catalyst the movement needed; a victory, even a partial one, could rally women and inspire them to do more. As Severance argued, "Many of us think that agitation must be continuous, that work for statutory suffrage educates Legislators and paves the way for full suffrage." Temperance women therefore placed a school suffrage bill before the 1899 state legislature—just as they had in 1893—and, once again, came maddeningly close to victory. The legislature overwhelmingly approved the bill—but Governor Henry T. Gage vetoed it. Nonetheless, in making the attempt the women gained more than they lost. Major newspapers, such as the *Sacramento Bee* and the *San Jose Mercury,* took the opportunity to endorse school suffrage—and equal suffrage. Moreover, Governor Gage could not veto the advances women were making in public life. By 1900, although women still could not vote for school board members, they were serving on school boards in almost every county.[105]

Three years after Gage vetoed the WCTU's school suffrage bill, he felt personally obliged to welcome women gathered in Los Angeles for the 1902 club biennial and to endorse their advancement into public life. He, like so many others in this era, celebrated women's achievements by collapsing them into a story of social evolution; his endorsement of "progress" therefore muted the story of women's struggles on their own behalf. Yet his presence and publicly stated approval of women's civic endeavors underscored the strength of their movement and their success in creating a new civic role for women. The governor observed that while "feudal laws and customs and narrow views of modern society" once restricted women, "this industrial and mechanical age requires the refining and educating work of woman. She needs a wider scope for the exercise of her influence for good. Her assistance is needed in the solving of the sociological problems that vex and perplex the statesmen of the times."[106]

Mayor M. P. Snyder of Los Angeles shared the platform with the governor at the biennial, and he gave a remarkably similar speech. He too noted past—and thus unfair—restrictions on women and rejoiced that men and women now jointly participated in the march of progress. He perceived the convention as "a monument to the laudable ambition of woman to secure a place in worldly affairs, where she can be a powerful factor in making mankind better." The politicians certainly told the exceptionally large audience of women what they wanted to hear; the two public figures also expressed sentiments being put forward by leading newspapers. A 1902 editorial in the *San Francisco Chronicle* praised women's clubs for doing much "in forming public opinion and molding legislation for good and necessary ends." The *San Francisco Examiner* concurred, giving its opinion in a series of editorials from late

1901 to 1903 with such titles as "Women in American Politics: A Pleasing Supposition" and "Women's Clubs Are Good Things."[107]

Although the *Examiner* took pains to differentiate suffrage from the civic activities it approved for women, such as instigating the cleaning of city streets and strengthening public schools, suffragists took heart from the growing public approval for women's civic activism and the near victory for school suffrage in 1899 and began to rebuild their organizations. Mary Wood Swift, president of the northern California suffrage association, traveled to Los Angeles in November 1900 and persuaded women there to revive their expired suffrage league. The Los Angeles suffragists chose for their first formal political act to personally thank the southern California members of the state legislature who supported the 1899 school suffrage bill.[108]

Northern California women also began reorganizing in the fall of 1900. Mary McHenry Keith restarted Berkeley's lapsed Political Equality League, and it grew slowly but steadily. Two women came to the September meeting, forty in November; two years later, 115 belonged to the league. At the 1901 northern California state suffrage convention, the women proudly announced that their membership had grown 100 percent over the last year. Because the suffragists had lost members every year since 1896, this 1901 achievement marked a watershed, as substantiated most immediately by the 1902 suffrage convention: forty-four delegates attended in 1901; one hundred came the next year representing sixteen suffrage clubs.[109]

Ellen Clark Sargent, a San Francisco suffragist, took actions that helped develop these numbers. A pioneer in the state suffrage movement, she sat quietly in the Century Club for years. She did not challenge the club's 1893 ruling that called for silence regarding votes for women in the club, nor did she do anything outside the club after the 1896 campaign that brought undue public attention to her suffrage activities. But starting in the fall of 1899, she began to wage an individual yet very public campaign for the ballot. She attempted to register to vote in September 1899. Refused that right because she was not a male citizen, she nonetheless later went to the voting polls and demanded to vote. She was once again refused on the same ground.[110]

Sargent, undaunted, continued her methodical campaign. At the beginning of 1900 she, the wealthy widow of a former U.S. senator, received the tax assessment for her property. She paid the tax and, defended by her son, George Sargent, a San Francisco attorney, filed suit to reclaim it, charging that because she had been denied the right to vote, she could not legally be taxed. She lost the case. But she and the movement gained much publicity and, more important, a sense of momentum. Energized suffragists enthusiastically made "Taxation Without Representation Is Tyranny" the theme of the 1901 convention. Everything about the bustling 1901 convention declared that the women again saw victory on the horizon—from their larger numbers and their warm reception for Ellen Sargent to their numerous calls for direct political action. Speakers urged each woman to file a protest on "every occasion when called upon to pay taxes."[111]

A year later Los Angeles suffragists demonstrated for their rights, largely because socialist women provided the catalyst. Thirty-five women formed the Woman's Socialist League of Los Angeles in the fall of 1901; it quickly became the state's largest urban organization of socialist women. They also soon established themselves, in greater numbers than socialist women did elsewhere in the state, as a significant presence within the city's suffrage movement. Socialist women instigated the suffragists' first militant action in the new century; in August 1902 they asked temperance women and suffragists to join them in a protest meeting at city hall. Fifty women, armed with the U.S. Constitution, demanded to be registered as American citizens. Like Sargent, they were denied that right and, like their northern California counterparts, continued to organize in order to achieve their rights.[112]

Suffragists at the early conventions of the new century frequently made careful distinctions between their call for women to work for political equality and women's participation in partisan politics. At the 1901 state convention Mrs. Benjamin Fay Mills, a Christian socialist whose husband was a noted speaker for Christian socialism, asserted that "the new woman should have the obligations of the ballot"; however, she continued, "I hope that they [women] will not get into politics, as it is not what they should be in until there is something in it more worthy of right-thinking, progressive people."[113]

Mills clearly shared, as did many other suffragists, the women's distinction between civic reform and politics. When Clara Burdette addressed California club women at the first state conference of the California Federation of Women's Clubs in February 1902, she reiterated that distinction. She stressed that even if women sought the vote, she fervently hoped that "by all that is womanly within[,] you continue to paint on your banners 'keep out of politics.'" When suffragists met in the fall of that year, they differed from Burdette by arguing that women ought to seek formal political equality. But suffragists generally did not address or left quite vague whether and how women should enter partisan politics; instead, suffragists found numerous ways to demonstrate how the vote empowered women in their newly expanded yet still restricted public space, the civic sphere. At the 1902 northern California suffrage conference Dorothea Moore called for women to serve in municipal offices as well as to work for the juvenile court system. Moore emphasized that women who held these civic offices would do so as altruistic public servants, not as politicians.[114]

The *San Francisco Examiner* declared that the 1902 meeting made evident that "the [state] suffrage movement is making great progress." In the months that followed the leaders of the National American Woman Suffrage Association (NAWSA) agreed; as Henry Blackwell editorialized in the 1903 *Woman's Journal,* they had always predicted that California would see the next suffrage victory because the 1896 defeat had been so close. National leaders were especially heartened by the promising situation in California because the years after 1896 saw a great drop in the national fortunes of the suffrage movement; after the 1896 victory in Idaho, women would not win another state victory until Washington State in 1910. During these "doldrums" years, as a historian later labeled them, suffragists searched for ways to build membership, funding, and hope. Because California seemed auspicious, in the early months of 1904 NAWSA sent Gail Laughlin, a suffrage organizer, from New York to what everyone hoped would be the golden state.[115]

Laughlin helped create new suffrage clubs, rebuild the old ones, and unify the two separate state organizations of northern and southern California. Her achievements documented her skills, those of the California women, and the changing political environment in the state. The women merged their regional groups in 1904, incorporating themselves as the California Equal Suffrage Association. They held their convention in Los Angeles to celebrate and cement their achievement; "several hundred assertive-appearing women" attended, according to the not-so-friendly *Los Angeles Times.* Laughlin reported fifty-two new suffrage clubs and a membership that had more than doubled during the past year. Los Angeles women declared they were better prepared for a suffrage victory than they had been in 1896; they had already organized almost every ward in the city.[116]

Such portents of success served as a catalyst at the convention. When the state treasurer, Clara M. Schlingheyde, made her plea for donations, she argued that although the organization urgently needed $300 that was already past due, it required much more if the women hoped to win. "How much do you want?" asked a delegate. Schlingheyde replied, "If you want an answer, I'll say we want every cent we can get." According to the *Times,* her reply "brought down the house." Mary McHenry Keith, affluent wife of artist William Keith, pledged $500, the single largest pledge.[117]

But Amanda Way's contribution also gained notice and, to many of the delegates, represented much that they valued about organized womanhood. A pioneer member of the Indiana Colony that settled Pasadena, a Quaker who now lived in Whittier, and a suffrage humorist, Way held up a ten-dollar gold piece. She said, "I have nobody to depend on and nothing to live on—only what Uncle Sam gives me for helping to take care of the soldiers during the war—$12.50 a month. I will give this." Following her offering, donations poured in from all over the floor, and the final count of pledges totaled more than $1,100. In California, at least, suffragists had expectations.[118]

Laughlin helped build those anticipations. She is a "unique character," judged the *Times*, "who grows an inch every time she emphasizes a word." Laughlin had demonstrated her uniqueness at twelve: she vowed to "study the law and dedicate my entire life to the freeing of women and establishing their proper place in this 'man's world.'" Her decision no doubt reflected both her admiration for her mother, whom she described as "an able, courageous, independent self-reliant woman," and the difficulties both faced during her childhood. Laughlin's father, an iron worker, had died in 1871 when she was three, leaving her mother with seven children. Her mother responded by creating a "household of equals." Every child had responsibilities; the boys' work included tasks inside the house, and the girls' chores included some outside.[119]

Guided by such values, Laughlin worked hard to achieve her early objectives. She graduated from the Portland, Maine, high school in 1886 at the top of her class. She worked for four years as a clerk, saving her money for college, until she was able to attend Wellesley College. Graduating in 1894, she worked for two years before she could begin law school at Cornell University. After graduation in 1898, her funds depleted, she worked part time before she could open a law office in New York City in 1900. She spent the next two years as an expert agent for the U.S. Industrial Commission; her work included investigating the conditions of domestic service. She documented how servants, whose ranks were filled with rural, immigrant, and black women, received few dollars and unending, unreasonable demands. When her term with the commission was over, she gave up her law practice and became a full-time organizer for the National American Woman Suffrage Association.[120]

In California Laughlin chose to build the suffrage movement—at least in part—by appealing to club women. When she arrived in San Francisco, she spoke at clubs, including those at which discussion of suffrage was held taboo. By the summer of 1904, after Los Angeles suffragists had benefited from Laughlin's efforts, suffrage leaders in Los Angeles reported that many well-known club women, who had previously held aloof from the movement, were pledging their support. Laughlin might have decided on this course of action after talking with Carrie Chapman Catt, who became the NAWSA president in 1900. Catt immediately began to urge suffragists to develop an outreach strategy to tap prominent individuals and organizations, chiefly "society women"; in 1904 Catt persuaded NAWSA to adopt the "society plan," a formal statement of the strategy the organization had been following for the past four years.[121]

On the other hand, Laughlin may well have heard from California suffragists about the partial efficacy of such a strategy. California women had practiced a society plan in the 1896 campaign, recruiting upper-class women into their ranks and holding parlor meetings at their lavish homes. Although they had lost, many of these wealthy women remained suffragists, and in particular the 1901 northern California convention, dedicated to "Taxation Without Representation Is Tyranny," bears their mark. Women with property, such as Ellen Sargent, would find such a slogan compelling, and the *San Francisco Examiner* commented that many women at the conference "represent large landed interests." Mrs. Edward Owen Smith of San Jose, the former president of the California Board of Lady Managers, boasted at the 1901 convention that she had organized the Tax Paying League with six women who paid taxes on property valued at $1 million.[122]

Some California suffragists, however, did not want to commit themselves only to a society plan; these suffragists believed that they must also persuade and organize working-class women. Socialists, who led this dialogue, emphasized when they spoke to suffragists the ways that enfranchisement would empower working women. At the 1902 northern California state suffrage convention Villa Reynolds, a delegate from the newly organized California Woman's Socialist Union, declared that "the common people would not get anything until they voted for the election of those who were pledged in their interests." The following year G. B. Benham, president of the San Francisco Labor Council, addressed the 1903 northern state convention; the suffragists discussed at the same convention the need to "earnestly" seek labor's support. However, they failed to earnestly do so until 1906.[123]

The women probably decided to seek a broader coalition in 1906 because they had failed to persuade state legislators to grant women the vote during the 1905 legislative session. The suffragists attempted to persuade the legislators by presenting them with a petition "signed by 15,000 of California's best citizens," a list that included political leaders, college presidents, and the entire state teachers' association. Not coincidentally, the suffragists had decided not to try other means to expand their movement; they sought neither the active support of working women, nor did they ask the WCTU to work with them.[124]

Temperance women engaged in the campaign as individuals but chose not to enter the battle as an organization. Sarah Severance, the northern California temperance leader in charge of suffrage, explained that they made this decision partly because suffragists did not want them and partly because they felt the 1905 political situation presented an impossible challenge. One party, the Republicans, reigned supreme and faced no significant challenge from the Democrats or a third party; therefore, the Republicans felt no need to form alliances with any new groups. The temperance women's analysis included optimism, however. They were waiting for the appropriate time; at that point, they would launch their forces and win.[125]

Suffragists too remained hopeful. They too looked to the future and believed that through the continued expansion of women's public role their movement would continue its dynamic growth. As national suffrage leader Anna Howard Shaw wrote to California suffragist Mary Keith in 1905, months after the California women failed to win the ballot, "the good news comes from California that enthusiasm is growing among you." Suffrage leaders quite consciously tried to link their movement to the women's club movement as a way to ensure that suffrage would continue to attract followers. After the 1905 defeat the state suffrage organization sent a letter to every suffrage club that advised: "Hold your clubs together by work not immediately pertaining to suffrage. Take up civic work. Make your clubs improvement clubs in every sense of the term."[126]

Mary Keith, taking this advice quite seriously, led the Berkeley suffrage club into an alliance with the city's Chamber of Commerce. As she saw it, they could work together for the "health, beauty and general prosperity of the city." From 1906 onward, in city after city, organized women and city fathers began building alliances with each other. Men and women created progressivism in this coalition; support for women's suffrage blossomed within their ranks. Progressives played an important role in winning suffrage but, as we shall see, so did the labor movement.[127]

4

THE POLITICS OF GOOD GOVERNMENT: THE CALIFORNIA WOMEN'S MOVEMENT HELPS BUILD PROGRESSIVISM AND WINS SUFFRAGE, 1906–11

AFTER 1906 affluent men and women reformers began working together as political allies in San Francisco and Los Angeles. Earlier, the women had persuaded men to support their various urban reform projects, such as juvenile courts and playgrounds, but both men and women saw these as civic—not political—efforts. The reformers joined forces in the political but nonpartisan good government movement, an urban forerunner of progressivism that promised to end corruption in city government. This alliance helped make possible the 1911 suffrage victory. After the men accepted the women as political allies, the male reformers as a group—eventually—supported women's suffrage. Many organized women, especially club women, who generally entered the alliance with male progressives as civic activists but not as suffragists, subsequently perceived themselves as political activists, became suffragists, and dedicated themselves to winning the vote.

Good government men in both San Francisco and Los Angeles began achieving notable successes in their campaign for a moral polity in 1906. Many suffragists wished to forge an alliance with these men whose goals were so similar to their own. But most organized women, who were not suffragists, found it too daunting in 1906 to cross the line from civic to nonpartisan political activism. The latter, with its concern for building a political movement that elected candidates, looked quite like the politics that ladies avoided. But women did cross that line—over the bridge of moral nonpartisanship.

A few men in the 1906 good government movement welcomed women as members, but most men were either reluctant or resistant. Nonetheless, before the end of 1909 men in the good government movements in San Francisco and Los Angeles accepted the women who, in growing numbers, wanted to be political allies.

This evolution of political identity occurred in similar political situations and as part of the same political process in both cities. First, the changes developed fastest when the male good government force seemed very likely to lose. At that political moment, when the male reformers deeply feared losing, they decided to open the door of political recognition for women civic activists. They believed that the women could be the key to victory; these elite women simultaneously reinforced the good government movement's claim of morality and its understanding of morality in class terms—these men and women saw themselves as holding down the middle, somewhere between the corruption of great wealth and the "barbarism" of the laboring class.

This alliance says much about how these men and women defined their gender, class, and political roles and it gave rise to progressive support for women's suffrage. The men presented themselves not as class-bound politicians but as the nonpolitical moral force of "good" government. Their enemies denigrated their nonpartisanship and crusading fervor by attacking their manhood, deriding them as effeminate "goo goos." But when the men faced defeat, they turned to the members of their class who were seen as even more moral and nonpolitical—women. Enfranchising such an ally made political sense.

Women in the good government movement identified themselves as suffragists who were also progressives. They felt that progressivism and suffrage were inextricable: progressivism made women's suffrage possible (at the very least, a progressive state government placed a suffrage amendment before the state electorate), and women's political participation made the good government movement viable by making its tenets of morality and nonpartisanship credible. Josefa Tolhurst, a prominent Los Angeles suffragist, club woman, and progressive, put it this way: "Suffragists [are] . . . standing for the ideas which have brought about insurgency, in line with the progressive and the patriotic."[1]

Thus women progressives participated in two overlapping but sometimes conflicting political coalitions, good government and women's suffrage. In joining good government coalitions, they participated in a business and professional men's movement that looked upon labor parties with great suspicion, as sources of divisive class politics that quickly degenerated into sources of political corruption. But as members of the suffrage movement, the women believed that victory depended on winning at least some of labor's votes. Beginning in 1906 elite suffragists began to make serious attempts to build an alliance with trade union women, efforts that were not always harmonious but were successful enough to win the vote in 1911.

The women put together a broad suffrage umbrella that encompassed groups that sought the vote as a means to advance their "special interests." Insurgent Republican women assured their male counterparts that women's enfranchisement would advance progressivism; women labor activists argued that the vote would protect the interests of working women—and the working class in general. But women also sought ways to speak together as women and, following the precedent of the women's movement during the Gilded Age, they explored ways to define women's work that could represent all women. Unlike their predecessors, suffragists of the early twentieth century were quite clear about how women's work was related to women's demands on the state. Women progressives took up this dialogue and placed their view of the state, gender, and class at the forefront of the women's movement.

❖

In 1906 male reformers were making progress with their program for "good government" in San Francisco and Los Angeles. They presented themselves as moral crusaders who were battling the evils of machine politics, a corrupt system of urban influence peddling. In this script public utility corporations—streetcar lines, water companies, and so on—bribed city officials in order to win city contracts and various other illegal considerations. Purveyors of vices that city laws prohibited or attempted to regulate—prostitution, gambling, and saloons—also used bribes to protect their businesses. As the reformers saw it, these practices meant higher city taxes, poor municipal services, and the flourishing of urban vice. Nonetheless, the machine stayed in power through the clout of its corporate supporters and the loyalty of working-class voters, a loyalty greased with patronage. In contrast, good government reformers claimed they stood for morality and efficiency in government.[2]

In the fall of 1906 the San Francisco reformers gained indictments of city officials in the Union Labor Party on charges that involved the acceptance of bribes from brothels and utility companies. The reformers believed that the trials were a start toward dismantling a corrupt political machine, and they promised to bring still more indictments against the corporate participants. In San Francisco and across the nation, many understood the graft trials as a morality play whose heroes were nonpartisan men who generally came from and spoke for the "middle" class.[3]

Dr. Edward Robeson Taylor—physician, poet, attorney, and dean of the Hastings College of Law—in sum, an accomplished member of the city's elite—ran as the good government candidate for mayor in the fall of 1907 and won, at least in part because public support for the graft trials was at an all-time high. His predecessor, Eugene Schmitz, had been jailed in the summer of 1907 on corruption charges; the San Francisco Board of Supervisors had appointed Taylor mayor on July 16, an action challenged by Schmitz but upheld by the state Supreme Court a month later. After Taylor was elected in his own right, he attempted to underscore the good government triumph as a moral victory. He did so by crediting women—widely perceived as the moral guardians of society—for the success of the good government forces. According to Taylor, "Back of the forces of good government in the campaign were for the first time in the history of the city arrayed a great majority of the women of the city. They seemed to realize, in greater measure even than did the men, the real significance of the contest, and to them must be attributed in great measure the victory achieved."[4]

Taylor's comments can be interpreted in at least two ways. On the one hand, he clearly preferred the women who privately supported his campaign through the traditional means of moral influence. He probably also meant to signal his appreciation to suffragists. According to newspaper accounts, club women were among his campaign workers. Fearing a backlash, male politicians who supported Taylor had "pleaded with the clubwomen not to try to help." But the women replied that "they were going to crusade in behalf of Taylor whether Taylor or his friends objected or not."[5]

Whatever Taylor's preferences about women in politics, he nominated California Club members Laura Lovell White and Mrs. L. A. Hayward to the city's Playground Commission in January 1908. His nominations acknowledged the pioneering work of Lovell White and the California Club that had established the city's first playground in 1898.

His nominations also reflected Lovell White's more recent civic activism. In the 1907 city elections she had led the California Club's Outdoor Art League in a campaign for a city playground commission with stipulations that two of the seven commission seats must be held by women. The women drafted the amendment, persuaded all political parties to make it a plank in their platforms, and campaigned vigorously in the election. They leafleted every polling place, and the more daring targeted streetcars. One particularly daring woman made a speech in a streetcar on behalf of playgrounds.[6]

Because the playground amendment ran well in all city wards, winning by the same percentage in wealthy and impoverished districts, Taylor's nominations can also be seen as a reflection of the city's approval of women's role as civic activists. Yet the very nature of the 1907 playground campaign, with its open, even militant politicking, and with its demand for an official role for women in city government, marked a change in women's public role. Women's volunteer work was becoming institutionalized, part of the city's services; clearly, voters would soon have to decide whether the volunteers should be accepted as full citizens. Suffragist Lovell White, in the aftermath of the 1907 campaign, pointedly informed a *San Francisco Call* reporter that women could have achieved playgrounds much more efficiently had they been enfranchised.[7]

San Francisco women soon took advantage of these victories to become an even greater part of the city's political structure. In the early months of 1908 the California Club led San Francisco women in the battle to end bubonic plague in the city, the "war on rats." In this campaign, closely identified as part of Mayor Taylor's good government administration, women gained a quasi-institutionalized public position that identified them as official good government volunteers. In August 1907 city physicians had diagnosed patients as suffering from bubonic plague, and scientists agreed that rats must be eradicated in order to end the spread of the disease. San Francisco's rats had proliferated since the 1906 earthquake. But the Schmitz administration was too busy, first with rebuilding after the earthquake and then with the prosecution in the graft trials to do much about the rats. Even Schmitz's health inspector had been forced to resign in the wake of the corruption revelations.[8]

When Taylor the physician had taken control of city government in July, he had placed experts, both local and federal, in charge of the campaign against the plague. The epidemic peaked in September 1907 and the incidence of new cases started to fall; by January 1908 Taylor's administration faced the problem of waging a vigorous, ongoing, and thus expensive "war against rats" with a public that believed the crisis had passed. In response to the rat problem, prominent businessmen organized the Citizens' Health Committee, a bureaucratic yet voluntary means to protect the city's health—and reputation. Leaders of the city's various business sectors were placed in charge of ridding their areas of rats.[9]

In this spirit of organized compartmentalization, members of the Citizens' Health Committee met with women of the California Club in February and asked them to enlist the city's housewives in the war on rats. The women formed the Women's Auxiliary Committee, which quickly became the Women's Sanitation Committee. The California Club brought sixty women's groups into the campaign, including suffragists. The women carried the war against rats into homes, restaurants, and schools—and women in places across the bay, such as Berkeley, took up the war in their neighborhoods too. Men frequently praised women's efforts; the Citizens' Health Committee declared that its decision to enlist women had been "its greatest step forward." One newspaper account stated that the "best assurance San Francisco has that there will be no plague is the activity the women are taking to clean up the city." After city officials declared victory over the rats in the fall of 1908, the women transformed their sanitation committee into the Women's Public Health Association.[10]

Women's political status was, however, still precarious. Despite their immediate response to the war against rats, the male reformers did not immediately turn to women when the good government campaign faced a series of setbacks in the same period. San Francisco's upper class had cheered when officials of the Union Labor Party were prosecuted, but when powerful business leaders such as Patrick Calhoun, president of the United Railroads of San Francisco, a streetcar company, were also indicted and brought to trial, many leading citizens turned against the reformers and their legal crusade. Reformers worried that the combined enmity of the city's elite and its labor unions could defeat the good government candidates in the regular 1909 election.[11]

To gain more public support for the trials and for the good government movement, the male reformers organized the Citizens' League of Justice in the spring of 1908. The league presented its support for prosecution as an ethical position that all good men must support. Theodore Roosevelt, the popular former president who exemplified for many Americans the best of noble, virile manhood, wrote an open letter to support the league; he proclaimed the political necessity for male bonding among good men. "It is profoundly un-American," declared Roosevelt, "and, in a social sense, profoundly immoral, to stand for or against a given man . . . because he does or does not belong to a labor union or does or does not represent the big business interests. In their essence, down at the foundation of things, the ties that are all important are those that knit honest men, brave men, square-dealing men, together." As the men in the Citizens' League of Justice announced in an open letter, "San Francisco must assert its manhood."[12]

Ironically—or predictably—in order to assert their manhood, the men of the Citizens' League of Justice recruited women in the fall of 1908 as auxiliary members. The men's reasons were pragmatic. They believed that the courtrooms were being packed by people sympathetic to the defense, "paid thugs" who might sway the jurors. But the male reformers, "clerks and professional and small business men," could not leave their businesses to come to court. So they recruited women.[13]

The men intended that the women would restrict themselves to this minor supplementary role and that the women would do so through a women's auxiliary that was clearly subordinate to the men's organization. The men called an organizational meeting for the women's auxiliary on September 17, 1908; Elizabeth Gerberding, club woman, suffragist, and widow of a prominent city businessman, was elected president of the Woman's Branch of the Citizens' League of Justice. Suffragists, including Ellen Sargent, joined the league, as did women from the California Club, such as Catherine Hittell, who had long been active in civic reform. Additionally, women from the Century Club, despite its extended abstention from civic affairs, became committed league members. Day after day Gerberding led these women—wearing their league buttons—into the courtroom. Much of the response was hostile, even personally vindictive. But they attended the trial, according to Gerberding, in order to "encourage justice by our presence."[14]

In her writings Gerberding proclaimed a wider political role for women than serving as silent benchwarmers during the trials. She described women's role as one of teaching morality, not simply to guilty individuals but to the classes she felt they represented—workers and upper-class businessmen. She believed that women must reconstruct American society. Gerberding described meeting a newsboy who refused to accept her judgment that Abraham Ruef, the political manager of the Union Labor Party, "should be punished." "Not on your life!" the boy answered. "He's a wise guy!" Gerberding reported that she left this encounter feeling "like a mother in the nation." It is telling that in her only explicit portrayal of workers she presented the working class as children needing the maternal nation to teach them civic morality.[15]

Gerberding spent much more time attacking the moral lapses of what she referred to as "the upper class" and the steps women should take to remedy them. Although most of the city's upper class believed that streetcar magnate Patrick Calhoun was guilty of bribery, they nonetheless attempted to protect him. Gerberding confided, "I found men and women of my closest acquaintance virtual anarchists—and without the anarchist's excuse of injustice and oppression."

Gerberding wrote that the experience of sitting in the courtroom for months taught the women the source of this upper-class anarchy; upper-class men compartmentalized "home morals" and "business morals." Unlike the newsboy, they, as adults, knew morality, but they limited its practice to a small sphere, the home. The solution, Gerberding believed, rested with women, who must take home morality into the public arena. The reason for Gerberding's concentration on the upper class becomes clear: male elites were unfit to rule alone. Only with women's aid could a new moral political culture be constructed that deserved public power.

Under the spell of dramatic events male good government reformers soon came to agree with Gerberding. In November 1908, after the women had been attending the trial for only a few weeks, they witnessed the courtroom shooting of prosecutor Francis Heney. Some assisted the wounded man. Women attended the mass meeting held by the men the following night and, nine days after the shooting, the Woman's Branch called a mass meeting of women. According to the *San Francisco Bulletin,* an avid sponsor of the graft trials, "More than one thousand women, including most of the intellectuals, and many from well-to-do families . . . pledge[d] themselves by speeches and by formal resolutions unanimously carried to stand by the Prosecution."[16]

Walter MacArthur, one of the few city labor leaders who supported the prosecution, demonstrated the centrality of women to the good government movement when he declared at the women's mass meeting, "The world gets its morals from its mothers." Enthused at the idea of women's bringing morality into politics, women flocked into the Woman's Branch, doubling its membership to two thousand. The women soon devised a plan to put their moral power into action: they would boycott all city tradesmen who refused to support the graft prosecution. The *San Francisco Call* commented that "when the women engage in public action to express a sense of wrong and take measures for its abatement . . . [they provide] eloquent proof of a moral awakening in the community."[17]

In the aftermath of the mass meetings the Citizens' League of Justice began transforming itself into a national organization that accepted women as full members with equal voting rights. Gerberding became a member of the Committee of Fifty, the governing committee of what became the National League of Justice in the spring of 1909.[18]

The recognition of the role women were playing in politics came from their political activism and the moral authority that they shared with the reform movement. An editorial cartoon in the *San Francisco Bulletin,* published in the spring of 1909, leaves no doubt that male reformers understood the women's contribution. Columbia, a majestic woman, sits on a platform inscribed "National League of Justice." In her lap rests the book of good government. Sitting at her feet and studying the book are an affluent man and woman.

(*San Francisco Bulletin,* April 24, 1909)

Columbia is twice as large as her students, who are presented as equals. The cartoon's caption reads "Co-Education."[19]

The cartoon presents the league as apolitical. Members of the league sought only "good government": they did not seek partisan gain. Part of the proof offered in the cartoon is the utter lack of partisan political methods. League members were not shown marching in a boisterous, emotional midnight torch parade—or any of the other political acts associated with masculinity, partisanship, and participation by the lower classes in the nineteenth century. Instead, the league members quietly gained an "education," the better to become experts who will lead the masses into good government. The other evidence that they meant their campaign to truly be apolitical lies in the caption of "Co-education": who could doubt that women would maintain the good in good government?[20]

Women's entrance into the Los Angeles good government movement followed a similar but somewhat different route. By the end of 1906 that city's male good government movement had, like the San Francisco movement, attracted national attention. The Los Angeles reformers entered a nonpartisan ticket in the 1906 city election, although, given the overwhelming Republican membership of the good government organization, they were best seen as reforming, or "insurgent," Republicans. They intended to cleanse the GOP of its corrupt and servile relationship with the Southern Pacific Railroad. Reformers had been angry about this relationship for some time, but their feelings were particularly intense in the fall of 1906 after the *San Francisco Call* printed an exposé, complete with photograph, that documented how the railroad, aided by thousands of dollars in bribe money, had controlled the Republican state convention. The railroad worked at maintaining the same kind of relationship with the Democratic Party, so the reformers sought to make their organization nonpartisan, a force dedicated to business principles and scrupulous honesty. The Los Angeles reformers' nonpartisanship did not extend to the Public Ownership Party, a socialist-labor coalition that called for municipal ownership of city utilities. The good government men attacked the Public Ownership Party, labeling it—without any proof—as the Los Angeles counterpart of San Francisco's corrupt Union Labor Party.[21]

In the 1906 election, contested by four major parties—the Democrats, the Republicans, the Non-Partisan Committee of One Hundred (the formal name of the organization of insurgent Republicans), and the Public Ownership Party—the Democratic candidate, Arthur C. Harper, won the mayoralty. But good government candidates won numerous other offices. The delighted reformers began building a permanent reform organization, the Los Angeles City Club, and increasing their strength in the Municipal League, a civic organization of businessmen and male professionals. This served them well when Mayor Harper, charged with corruption and facing a recall, resigned from office in March 1909. In the special election held that month for a new mayor, George Alexander, the candidate of a good government coalition, faced socialist Fred Wheeler. Alexander won by only 1,600 votes. He assumed office in April but faced election again in that fall.[22]

Thus male reformers in Los Angeles were in a difficult position in the spring of 1909. To their right were conservative Republicans who angrily charged that the reformers' defection from the Republican Party had nearly permitted the socialists to win the mayoral election. The conservatives, led by Harrison Gray Otis of the *Los Angeles Times,* portrayed this desertion in terms of gender. In Otis's newspaper the good government forces became "goo goos" whose weakness almost allowed the victory of the "labor thugs." To the left of the reformers stood the nearly victorious socialist-labor movement. The reformers identified themselves as "businessmen who are interested in good government," and animosity between the good government men and labor ran deep.[23]

At this crucial moment male reformers rediscovered the importance of giving women the vote. Meyer Lissner, an attorney whose real estate investments allowed him to devote himself full time to politics and thus become the best progressive political organizer in southern California, publicly, although not enthusiastically, supported giving women the vote. He revived the support for women's enfranchisement that good government reformers had voiced in 1907 when they formed their state organization, the League of Lincoln-Roosevelt Republic Clubs (hereafter the Lincoln-Roosevelt League). Two years later Lissner's weak endorsement came as a challenge to women. They could and must win the ballot on their own, Lissner said, because men were "too busy with the distinctly masculine concerns of government to take up arms in the cause of women's suffrage."[24]

Another reformer, Charles Dwight Willard, chose this time to urge the reformers to go beyond the political reforms of good government and take up social reformation, an endeavor in which women had traditionally played an important, albeit buried, role. Willard first acknowledged that social problems were daunting and that something must be done, echoing what leading club women had said when they founded the state Federation of Women's Clubs back in 1900. Agreeing further with many women, Willard did not believe socialism was the answer—he thought the revolutionary step of giving workers control over the means of production would collapse the social order. He did not think individual actions to rescue individuals was the answer either. Instead, the "rational social reformer: the man or woman who is striving to establish the normal" should "tackle the job piecemeal and by degrees"; such reformers would slowly and minimally increase the power of the state until just enough social services were in place to prevent social problems from occurring. Most organized women agreed.[25]

Reformers, Willard asserted, have "a program just as the socialist has," and

Willard presented that program—a list of reforms. He posited that reformers should first address the "simple, uncontested issues of sanitation, honest taxation, good government, decent housing, control of liquor traffic, juvenile court, child labor legislation, playgrounds and pure food laws." Women were involved in almost all these issues and had achieved some enviable successes, such as the creation of juvenile courts and the building of playgrounds. In the case of housing, Willard, as executive secretary of the Municipal League, had worked with the women of the College Settlement to create the Los Angeles Housing Commission in 1906.[26]

When Los Angeles's organized women thought of what step, if any, to take in the upcoming city elections of 1909, they drew upon memories of several projects in which they had cooperated with the men of the Municipal League and good government movement. In 1909 two women were among the seven members of the city's Housing Commission, which had one woman housing inspector. The Municipal League was also one of the booster organizations that had worked with club women especially closely in 1907–8 to rid Los Angeles of billboards. In the summer of 1908 a large coalition of reformers—temperance women, club women, various churches, and the Municipal League—had begun pushing for a city ordinance to regulate dance halls, prohibiting, among other things, unaccompanied minors from frequenting dance halls. The coalition worked for the ordinance until it passed in 1909.[27]

Whether or not Lissner and Willard meant to invite women to publicly campaign for good government in return for support for social reform that included women's suffrage, the women took action that seems to have been based on such an understanding. During the final months of the insurgents' 1909 campaign for mayor, the Political Equality League, a local women's suffrage organization, made what the *Los Angeles Herald* labeled its "formal entry into Los Angeles politics" and did so simultaneously for suffrage and the cause of good government.[28]

The Political Equality League had taken this step in stages. First, the members invited reform candidates to speak. During his visit in November 1909, a month before the election, Mayor George Alexander declared, "I am unequivocally in favor of political equality . . . [and] I believe that the agitation for suffrage will in time bring the same results that the agitation for good government has brought." According to the newspaper account, the league members gave him a "rising vote of endorsement, both of his conduct as mayor and for his re-election to the office."[29]

Then, only four days before the municipal election, the Political Equality

League, which now boasted a thousand women pledged to suffrage, held a rally dedicated to equal enfranchisement and good government. According to the *Los Angeles Herald,* all the speakers at the rally were supporters of the good government movement; the *Herald* felt that in the upcoming election "there can be little doubt on which side the influence of these thousand women will be thrown." Speaker after speaker linked suffrage and good government. Suffragist Margaret La Grange declared that "it was the duty of women to go into politics and help break the hold of men, machines and bosses who control public offices for private gain and to the detriment of all the people."[30]

After the election, a clean sweep for the good government forces, Ella Giles Ruddy, president of the Political Equality League, jubilantly informed Caroline Severance, the noted club woman and suffragist who at eighty-nine served as honorary league president: "*Our* ticket has triumphed" (emphasis added). Ruddy no doubt meant the ticket championed by the Political Equality League, and she may also have meant the ticket that she and her friend Severance supported (Severance had been writing favorably about good government reform for more than a year). Ruddy continued, "I am not the only woman who feels, as a member of the Political Equality League, that we have at least done *all we could do* to bring about this splendid result. . . . The men we wanted to vote for (but couldn't) telephone us now thanking us for [the] help" (emphasis hers).[31]

But linking suffrage and good government was not equally successful everywhere. While Los Angeles women became a recognized part of the good government movement by supporting a winning ticket in 1909, San Francisco women had supported a good government campaign that lost that year. Nonetheless, the women gained recognition as the political allies of male reformers. The movement of San Francisco women from the National League of Justice to the California Women's Heney Club provides the most direct evidence that members of the league, men and women, had changed their views regarding women's activism in politics.

This transformation occurred when, once again, the reformers faced a crisis. While Francis Heney recovered from his gunshot wound, Hiram W. Johnson and Matt I. Sullivan, two reform-minded attorneys, continued the graft prosecution but with little to show for their efforts. The reformers wanted to convict the business leaders whose bribery had corrupted the political system, but the 1908 trial of Patrick Calhoun ended in a typical manner—with a hung jury. In the 1909 city elections (San Francisco held municipal elections every two years), reformers wanted to reelect Heney as district attorney to ensure that the prosecutions would continue. The good government forces had reason to worry. In the campaign they faced a reinvigorated Union Labor Party and aroused businessmen; both shared a deep animosity toward the trials. Heney, who barely won the Democratic nomination, depended on the reformers for support. His opponent, Charles M. Ficket, who promised to end the trials, ran on both the Republican and Union Labor Party tickets.[32]

To bolster support for Heney, two thousand women from the League of Justice transformed themselves into the Women's Heney Club, a nonpartisan but very political organization. Elizabeth Gerberding, who became president of the Women's Heney Club, had started working for just such a move months earlier. She justified women's entrance into politics by arguing that "while the League of Justice is nonpolitical, its members must perforce be interested in politics. It is essential that upright honest men be elected to office." In pursuit of the "nonpolitical" objective of aiding Heney's election, the women held a few mass events and numerous "home meetings"; the women especially emphasized the latter, a strategy that replicated the parlor meetings of the 1896 suffrage campaign.[33]

Male reformers praised the women's decision to formally enter the Heney campaign; the *San Francisco Bulletin* delightedly declared in June 1909 that the "voice of two thousand women cannot pass unheeded even if they can not vote." Male members of the League of Justice enthusiastically supported the women, a marked contrast to their reluctance to see women campaign for Mayor Taylor just two years earlier. An anonymous male reformer wrote, "We have organized as our fighting weapon of the League, the California Women's Heney Club to supplement the Men's Heney Club." He acknowledged, "Ordinarily a women's campaign is not of much account in politics, but the opinion of the men here is, that at this juncture a women's campaign can be of very great service." This appraisal rested on the assumption that because "the issue is so clearly a moral one," a women's campaign could "be an effective means of doing at least a part of the work."[34]

Just as male support for women in good government politics expanded during the Heney campaign, so too did the number of women willing to commit themselves to good government politics. Although the state suffrage organization refused to endorse Heney because it wished to maintain its tradition of nonpartisanship, Lillian Harris Coffin, a leading San Francisco suffragist, publicly endorsed him at the beginning of October. She was no doubt partly persuaded to do so because thousands of women now belonged to the Bay Area's good government movement, whereas only hundreds in the area supported suffrage. About ten days after Coffin's endorsement the northern California WCTU announced its support for Heney and good government.

Two years earlier the temperance women had removed their fiery president of seventeen years, Beaumelle Sturtevant-Peet, from the organization's highest office. (She lobbied the state legislature for the temperance women for many more years.)[35]

Exactly why the WCTU retired Sturtevant-Peet can only be inferred from the records, which never directly address the issue. Most likely, the organization felt her radical politics no longer reflected WCTU policy. In 1906, Sturtevant-Peet's last uncontested year in office, she continued her vigorous attack against capitalism's oppression of workers, pointedly complaining in her presidential address that labor received only twenty cents for every dollar it produced. Temperance women at the 1906 WCTU conference endorsed a resolution that recognized the "right of all organized labor to claim a fair percentage of the wealth they create," but membership dropped in 1906 and again in 1907.[36]

The WCTU elected Sara Dorr as president in 1907; thereafter, temperance women endorsed good government reform, not working-class insurgency. (Sturtevant-Peet, in her 1907 farewell speech, supported Francis Heney's prosecutions; she also reminded her temperance sisters that the work of the WCTU "has been"—she used the past tense—the attempt "to give full economic expression to Christian ideals in the government of State and nation.") At the 1908 WCTU Congress of Reforms, temperance women promised to boycott newspapers that supported the position of the Union Labor Party in the graft trials. Under Dorr's presidency membership shot up in 1908 and again in 1909. Marie Snooks, an officer of the Women's Heney Club, visited the WCTU's fall convention in 1909, seeking and receiving its endorsement of Heney. In her presidential address that year Dorr put forward that "what is needed now in California is all who are interested in good government to unite."[37]

Heney lost the 1909 election in a landslide. Earlier, during the exciting spring of 1909, the National League of Justice had expanded to Los Angeles, building an organization that included women and electing them as officers; however, statewide the league fell apart soon after the failed Heney campaign. But the league contributed to the development of an important cadre of people, men and women, who played a pivotal role in the development of progressivism. Furthermore, women's participation in the league built a close relationship between the good government movement and much of organized womanhood and increased the politicization of many organized women. In Berkeley women placed their own candidate on the 1909 good government slate, running Elinor Carlisle for a seat on the school board, and won. Carlisle, a teacher, club woman, and suffragist, campaigned with the active support of the city's women's movement.[38]

Although the National League of Justice collapsed, the state organization of good government men, the Lincoln-Roosevelt League, remained active and vital. Male Republican reformers had organized the league in 1907 to destroy the machine that controlled state politics; above all else, these reformers intended to crush the political arms of the Southern Pacific Railroad. They hoped to smash the machine by first cleansing the Republican Party. The men had put the league together in the spring and fall of 1907 with the expectation that they would gain control of the state Republican convention in the fall of 1908. They failed. The *San Francisco Call,* a paper firmly dedicated to the Lincoln-Roosevelt League, declared in screaming headlines that the defeat of the reformers meant that the Southern Pacific's machine still controlled the Republican Party.[39]

California suffragists made their most militant demand for the ballot to date at the 1908 state political conventions, Republican and Democratic; like the male reformers (upon whom the women had placed much of their hopes), they won headlines but not a political victory. Behind the women's dramatic 1908 tactics stood decades of organizing, but, especially in northern California, the women's strategies and track record had begun to change significantly two years earlier. One woman claimed and deserved much of the credit.

❖

Lillian Harris Coffin, chair of the civic section of the California Club, had chosen 1905 as the year to abandon the club's indirect method of acquiring the vote through civic action. She declared that she "grew into a suffragist in the California Club, that it was in the club that her interest was aroused in juvenile courts, child labor and the duties of a citizen," but that she felt now was the time to take "direct action" for suffrage. Coffin began developing what she later called the "political" strategy: women must organize themselves, down to the precinct level like a political party, and they must engage in continuous political actions. Most important, they must secure suffrage endorsements from political parties and other groups, especially labor organizations. In 1906 she helped create a central committee for the California Equal Suffrage Association (as the state organization had renamed itself in 1904) and the Equal Suffrage League of San Francisco; the latter was dedicated to "gain[ing] converts to equal suffrage among wage earners."[40]

Coffin's insights, combined with her organizing skills, did much to transform the California suffrage movement. Her political vision extended no further than making women part of the political system, but she understood that system and knew how to shrewdly manipulate it in order to win the vote. Perhaps because she was a former opera singer, now married to a San Francisco businessman, she emphasized the importance of suffragists staying in the headlines, of projecting an image of themselves as affluent and feminine women (whose working-class allies were junior colleagues), and, most of all, of being willing to wield power as prescribed by the rules of realpolitik. The *Los Angeles Herald* described her as "vivacious, keen of wit, and a brilliant speaker," a woman who "doesn't scorn beautiful and becoming raiment." She described herself, years later, as a woman who had political power and was willing to use it.[41]

Coffin triumphantly announced her political strategy at the October 1906 suffrage convention, but suffrage successes, also proclaimed at the convention, demonstrated that suffragists had been following this strategy for months. Chief among these was that suffrage leaders had obtained endorsements from all the state's political parties but one, the Republicans. This achievement electrified the convention. Coffin, chair of the suffragists' state central committee, committed them to further organized action; she intended that the committee would function like a state central committee in a political party, organizing the state by counties. Coffin and other San Francisco suffragists achieved all this despite the 1906 earthquake and fire that destroyed much of the city, including the homes and businesses of some suffragists.[42]

The beleaguered suffragists liked to emphasize that they had collected endorsements from five political parties—the Socialist Party, Union Labor Party, Prohibition Party, Independent League, and the Democratic Party. These endorsements represented traditional patterns of political support in several ways. In the 1896 campaign California women had received support from the People's Party (populists), Socialist Labor Party, labor groups, the Prohibition Party, and the Republican Party. State populism perished after that election, but when the California socialists reorganized in 1902, they pulled together former populists, members of the Socialist Labor Party, and various other radicals to form the California branch of the Socialist Party of America. Both the national and state organizations continuously placed a women's suffrage plank in their platforms as a statement of their commitment to full democracy.[43]

The endorsements by the newly created Independent League and the state Democratic Party represented both old political patterns and new possibilities. William Randolph Hearst, the newspaper magnate, created the Independent League to serve his political ambitions; nonetheless, in 1906 the league ran as a reform party—as did the Democratic Party. Following the path blazed by the populists, both parties vowed to expand democracy, pledging support to a variety of measures, such as the direct primary and, of course, votes for women. Both also ran as parties of middle-class reform, attacking the political power of corporate capitalism and organized labor. In California this meant campaigning against the Southern Pacific Railroad and the Union Labor Party of San Francisco. Democratic gubernatorial candidate Theodore Bell nearly won by running such a campaign; a victory by a party formally pledged to women's suffrage would have presented possibilities that suffragists had not seen in California for a decade.[44]

Despite—or perhaps because of—the Democratic Party's narrow defeat, the 1907 state legislature came within two votes of passing a constitutional amendment for women's suffrage. Suffragists were disappointed, yet they had decided ahead of time to continue working if they lost. In 1907 suffragists could point to important gains regarding one of their 1906 objectives, the courting of club women. Katherine Reed Balentine, editor of the short-lived California suffrage paper *Yellow Ribbon*, wrote in the November 1906 issue that she hoped to eventually send the journal to women who were not suffragists, especially to club women engaged in civic work, because she thought they would demand the ballot as soon as they "discover the powerlessness of the nonvoter." Balentine also thought that some club women who had once worked for the ballot had "gone into other club work," mainly because lately "there has been very little to do along suffrage lines. But now the situation has changed, and there is plenty of active and practical work to be done. We are at the commencement of what, we hope, will be the greatest Equal Suffrage campaign in the history of California."[45]

Several women's clubs responded by endorsing the 1907 suffrage amendment to the state constitution; all had either supported suffrage in the past or had a significant number of members who had done so. These endorsements represented the awakening of suffrage friends; all agreed with Balentine—that this time they would win. The California Club of San Francisco was among those that endorsed the suffrage amendment—"not surprising," noted the *Woman's Journal*, "for it was founded by suffragists, all its presidents and most of its officers have been suffragists." In Los Angeles the Friday Morning Club and the Woman's Press Club (the local descendent of the Pacific Coast Woman's Press Association) also endorsed the 1907 suffrage amendment. Suffragists felt certain that all this marked the beginning of a groundswell for suffrage within the club movement; as one suffragist asserted, "Suffrage sentiment is increasing through the medium of women's clubs much more rapidly than its opponents realize."[46]

Among suffragists, support for good government reform was rapidly increasing too, as were a desire to be politically active and a keen sense that such activism could well serve both the good government and suffrage movements. Many suffragists were persuaded, just as were men of their class, that city bosses were running a corrupt system, granting—for a substantial price and at immense cost to the good of the city—favors to big business and organized vice. Suffragists such as Mary Keith often assumed that enfranchising women, society's moral guardians, would "largely overcome the corrupt influence of money." Keith attempted to prove her point—and highlight the political usefulness of women's vote for reform—by arguing in the fall of 1907 that "the corporations, banks, railroads, liquor dealers' associations and the like, are all opposed to woman's suffrage because they . . . are not sure [women] will vote obediently to the dictates of party bosses." When suffragists met for their yearly convention in October 1907, they resolved to support "good government" although not a specific candidate.[47]

Keith soon took steps to facilitate an alliance between those interested in civic reform and organized women. In January 1908 (when Mayor Taylor appointed two women to the San Francisco playground commission) Keith informed the newly established Berkeley Chamber of Commerce that "you can never be a progressive city to the utmost possible limit, until the men and women in it consolidate in the work of municipal reform"—and she made it quite clear that men and women could not consolidate if women could not use the ballot to speak for themselves. Although Keith's proposal initially "aroused protest and trouble" in the chamber, by the fall of 1908 the chamber had resolved to support women's suffrage. No doubt the chamber was at least partly persuaded because of the activism of women like Keith in campaigns that both men and women regarded as progressive, such as the war on rats in Berkeley.[48]

Suffragists were hard at work in other cities too. It was in the fall of 1907 that some San Francisco suffragist club women were actively campaigning for Taylor and six months later that they helped him reduce the city's rodent population. Activists perceived both actions as part of good government concerns or nonpartisan politics. In February 1908 the *Los Angeles Express*, a paper that campaigned for good government reform, printed an article headlined "San Francisco Women Enter Political Arena"; the article linked women's politicking for Taylor with the war on rats and for morality.[49]

Suffragists marching to the state Republican convention in Oakland, August 1908. Lillian Harris Coffin is at left. California women later used this picture for suffrage postcards. (The Huntington Library, San Marino, California)

Mary Keith believed that working for good government was a profitable way for women to spend their time; she asserted in the spring of 1908 that "equal suffrage has been advanced 50 per cent since the women organized to help the men drive out the rats." Many concurred that the suffrage movement underwent significant changes that year; it became larger and grew more militant, the latter evidenced by the suffragists' 1908 decision to demonstrate at the Republican and Democratic state conventions. How much these changes were related to women's participation in the good government movement is a moot point, although surely there was some relationship; more important, when the suffragists decided to march at the conventions, they did so as an independent movement and as a movement tied in various ways to urban reform. The women, dressed in white, marched two by two into the Democratic convention in September, and the Democrats endorsed women's suffrage because they remained, as they were in 1906, a party of reform.[50]

Two hundred women, "handsomely gowned and bonneted" and wearing yellow suffrage ribbons, had marched in pairs into the Republican convention a month earlier but with opposite results. Just as the Lincoln-Roosevelt League, the state organization of mostly male Republican reformers, was defeated at this convention, so too was women's suffrage. When the men voted to thank the women for their attendance rather than at least explain their negative decision, the women demonstrated their anger by hissing and hooting. One quick-thinking suffragist, Agnes Pease, shouted in response, "We don't want your thanks—we want justice." The women left the convention defeated but invigorated, declaring that their militancy was winning them new supporters and giving greater resolve to the older rank-and-file.[51]

In late August 1908 the *San Francisco Call* published an editorial cartoon about the fate of reform at the Republican convention that, like Mary Keith's political analysis, merged women's suffrage with the struggles of male reformers for good government. In the cartoon William F. Herrin, chief counsel for the Southern Pacific Railroad, a man used by the reformers as a symbol of the Southern Pacific machine, controls the ballot box of the Republican Party. The state of California, presented as a majestic woman wearing a helmet, stands next to the ballot box watching Herrin, but she is unable to stop him because her hands are shackled. "You do your business, I'll do mine," growls Herrin to California, a common refrain used by men to justify restricting women to the private sphere while they controlled the public. The meaning of the cartoon becomes even more significant when one sees the caption: "The Suffragette."[52]

The parallels between this cartoon and the "Co-education" cartoon, about ten months later, by the *San Francisco Bulletin,* another paper dedicated to reform, are significant. Both present women's political activism as a nonpartisan moral reform that will develop good government. In this sense, both cartoons argue that male reformers should support women in politics for reasons of political expediency. The *Call,* for example, in its coverage of the 1908 Republican convention, linked women's suffrage and opposition to racetrack gambling. The *Call* thought both issues were "conspicuous by their absence from the party platform," which machine control of the convention had ensured. Temperance and club women supported progressives at the 1909 state legislature in formal opposition to racetrack gambling. Their combined effort paid off; that year male progressives pushed through a bill that prohibited gambling at racetracks.[53]

But the *Call*'s "Suffragette" cartoon conveyed yet another message. By conflating the state of California with the cause of suffrage, by presenting them together in the body of one woman whose hands are chained, the image vividly calls for freedom—for the state and for women, and it was a call that went beyond expediency to justice. In the upcoming suffrage campaigns, reformers, women and men, used both arguments, expediency and justice, to bolster support for women's suffrage; nonetheless, when reformers, women

The Suffragette

(*San Francisco Call,* August 29, 1908)

or men, declared that they believed in the justice of enfranchising women, they were expressing a deeper commitment to suffrage and the need to change women's position in politics from expedient ally to citizen with the right to participate in public decisions.

Although women reformers in the suffrage movement and male progressives were of the same class and shared ideologies, ideological and structural obstacles impeded the formation of a formal alliance so long as women could not vote. When the state suffrage convention met in the fall of 1909, Coffin urged the delegates to endorse Francis Heney for San Francisco district attorney; she argued that because progressives were likely to win the gubernatorial and state legislative elections the next year, they would repay suffragists by endorsing the vote for women. The convention refused. The suffragists also refused to endorse the National League of Justice. In both cases the women were expressing the traditional suffrage position, that the ballot was best attained by remaining independent of any single party or candidate in a partisan race and by seeking endorsement for suffrage from all parties.[54]

Suffragists refused to openly endorse progressive Republicans in 1909 in order to maintain the broad coalition of women's groups they believed they needed to win the vote. By 1909 the suffrage umbrella stretched from socialists to the Catholic Ladies' Aid Society. The suffragists had little to gain from supporting the progressives and much to lose, given their already close ties to Republican insurgency. Speakers at the 1909 suffrage convention included male progressives, such as Franklin Hichborn, a leader in San Francisco's National League of Justice; Marie Snooks, from the Berkeley branch of the League of Justice; and Elinor Carlisle, who had just won a seat on the Berkeley Board of Education on the good government ticket.[55]

More than personal links connected the two movements, for by 1909 most suffragists held the conviction that Mary McHenry Keith had expressed two years earlier, that both their movement and insurgency stood together for "civic righteousness." To prove this point suffragists commonly used Keith's technique, observing that the two movements shared enemies. Because reform stood for "civic righteousness," its opponents, all those who greased machine politics, represented political wickedness. When California suffragists explained why the 1909 state legislature refused to send women's enfranchisement to the electorate, they argued that "the same forces for evil, working against civic righteousness in our cities and towns, were working against us."[56]

When the progressives finally gained control of the Republican Party, the long-standing working relationship between the male and female reformers paid off for the women. In the spring of 1910 the progressive candidate, Hiram Johnson, began campaigning for the governorship. In August he won the Republican primary, a victory that allowed the progressives to take over the state party in September. When the reformers wrote the party platform that year, they had to decide whether their platform would include a suffrage plank. Some progressives, such as Johnson, deeply opposed enfranchising women; nonetheless, the party accepted a suffrage plank, albeit number sixteen in a platform of seventeen resolutions. Johnson remained silent about women's suffrage throughout the campaign.[57]

Supporting women's suffrage did not come easy for many male reformers. The *California Weekly*, the San Francisco organ of progressivism, responded to the reformers' endorsement of women's suffrage with the acknowledgment that "down deep most men at once favor women's suffrage and fear it." The *Weekly*'s coverage of women's place in American society during its first two years of publication, 1909 and 1910, reflected this ambivalence. It reported favorably on women's municipal housekeeping, admired women's intelligence, and acknowledged that women were already deeply involved in public life. Yet the *California Weekly* felt that women's immediate demand for full citizenship was unwise; the paper clung to the notion of politics as a masculine endeavor. Men voted, held office, engaged in partisan politics with other men because men were citizens; they stood at the head of their households, and from that position of power they spoke for all the female members of their family.[58]

Hiram Johnson's 1910 gubernatorial campaign documents how men, including male progressives, understood politics as a male arena, a place for men to prove their manhood. During the campaign male contemporaries wrote him words of encouragement in terms of masculinity. Men congratulated him for having waged "a clean, manly campaign" and for "the magnificent tribute to your glorious manhood paid by the patriotic manhood of California" because "the manhood of California is on trial." Johnson himself defined insurgency as "the struggle of free men to begin self-government against the special interests." He waged his struggle by promising to kick the Southern Pacific Railroad out of California politics, a manly deed, and asked his listeners whether they were man enough to join him in the "bully fight." If so, they would all march under the flag of Theodore Roosevelt, "the man who typifies American virility, American courage, American manhood, American conscience."[59]

Given that Johnson collapsed masculinity and politics, it is no wonder he privately agonized about granting women their citizenship. "The more I think of the situation with regard to woman's suffrage," he wrote political activist Meyer Lissner, "the more I think [this is] . . . something that will ultimately destroy us." Johnson probably meant that women's enfranchisement would destroy the popularity of progressivism among male voters. But he may have meant as well that women's citizenship would destroy the traditional role of men in politics, their ability to be men in the public arena. Johnson did feel that before women could become full citizens, progressives would need to educate them, just as they had previously educated men, overcoming "their [women's] selfishness and their ignorance, and their cupidity."[60]

Despite their misgivings, when the progressives won control of state government with Johnson's election as governor in 1910, they approved a constitutional amendment for women's suffrage that would be placed before the voters in October 1911. Putting aside his personal opposition to giving women the vote, Governor Johnson stressed the importance of keeping campaign promises and that, in approving the amendment, legislators were not endorsing women's enfranchisement; they were simply allowing the male electorate to decide the issue.[61]

Yet progressives endorsed women's suffrage. They did so because large numbers, men and women, felt they shared many of the same values. Both endorsed measures to expand democracy, such as "direct legislation"—the initiative, referendum, and the recall; the prosuffrage progressives, men and women, placed granting the vote to women in this category. Both suffragists and progressives opposed machine politics, arguing that corrupt politics blocked the voice of the people. As Lissner wrote Johnson in the summer of 1910, why not support the suffragists? They're antimachine. Elizabeth Lowe Watson, president of the state suffrage organization, made the same point when she wrote Johnson that fall. Why not speak for suffrage? "The women had worked very hard in the primaries for the liberal candidates, for while we are non-partisan we have used our influence in favor of the anti-machine candidates."[62]

❖

But the women's alliance with insurgency carried a risk. Suffragists agreed that they had lost in 1896 because they had failed to win working-class immigrant votes in San Francisco. How would they now persuade these men, who saw their interests as different from those of the progressives, to approve a state constitutional amendment that would enfranchise women? Johnson, who had lived in San Francisco for years and had served as an attorney for several unions, won by only a narrow margin in San Francisco in 1910. Throughout the campaign Johnson felt compelled to explain that when he proclaimed himself against the party bosses of the machine, he meant vice interests, not honest working men. But in the context of San Francisco politics, many in the labor movement felt that attacks on "the machine," whether they came from men or women, were simply a smoke screen to cover an assault on labor's ability to organize the workforce and to represent itself in politics.[63]

San Francisco workers consistently supported the Union Labor Party, awarding it pluralities in working-class neighborhoods from 1901 through 1911, because they saw it as speaking for labor and thus maintaining labor's right to speak for itself. Workers had created the Union Labor Party in response to the violent waterfront strike of 1901 in which teamsters, sailors, and longshoremen had confronted the Employers' Association. Because the Employers' Association refused to negotiate with unions—and openly announced that its long-term objective was to end collective bargaining—the strike triggered a public debate about whether business had the right to set public policy unilaterally. When Mayor James Phelan allowed city police to assist strikebreakers, the debate became even angrier as workers decided that an Irish Democratic mayor, leading a reform coalition formally dedicated to equality, could not be trusted to represent them.[64]

That was why labor movement activists had created the Union Labor Party. Although two Republicans, attorney Abraham Ruef and musician Eugene E. Schmitz, quickly became major powers within the party, serving as its unofficial manager and mayoral candidate, respectively, labor identified the party with the interests of labor. In one fundamental way and only in this way, the party directly served the interest of labor: it insisted that the city's police force remain neutral during strikes. Otherwise, Ruef and Schmitz presided over a party that built a cross-class coalition, practiced fiscal conservatism, and stayed within the accepted limits of political corruption. After the Union Labor Party's landslide victory of 1905, it exceeded those limits and lost the 1907 election to the nonpartisan forces of good government. But the Union Labor Party, under new labor leadership, was swept back into power in 1909. Supporters included businessmen who were tired of antigraft proceedings and workers who had decided that the reformers were crusading less for good government and more against the democratic rights and political power of organized labor.[65]

Given these multiple meanings of *antimachine*, how could suffragists, so closely identified with the good government movement, especially after its endorsement of Heney, hope to win San Francisco's labor vote for suffrage? Labor was a bloc everyone believed was crucial for victory—and California suffragists had worried about winning labor's vote much earlier. At the 1906 state suffrage convention the women discussed how to develop a coalition with working-class women; at the 1907 convention suffragists resolved to seek the support of wage-earning women and the labor movement. LuLu Pile Little, a Los Angeles suffragist and socialist, held meetings with women union members in 1906 in order to build such a coalition. Radical suffragists—union women and socialists—praised her efforts and held them up as a model.[66]

Little's politicking represented the relatively harmonious cross-class relations within the organized womanhood of Los Angeles. A significant number of its leaders were socialist. The city's relatively weak labor movement had built an alliance with socialists in 1902 that lasted for the next ten years. Socialist women, such as Little, with ties to both labor and organized womanhood, committed themselves to expanding both socialism and the women's movement. They wanted socialist analysis to include issues of gender and the women's movement to include a class analysis. Their "dual commitments," to borrow the phrase used by historian Sherry Katz, put them in the vanguard of two fronts; much of the success of Los Angeles's suffragists in winning the city's labor vote belongs to the efforts of the socialist women.[67]

In San Francisco suffrage gained much from women trade unionists who were committed to expanding the rights of workers and women. The city's labor movement had experienced hard times during the 1890s, when a depression and an antiunion drive by employers destroyed many unions, including the Knights of Labor, which had sought to organize women in the late 1880s. But at the turn of the century, trade union membership increased at the astounding rate of 500 percent. The San Francisco Labor Council encouraged the organization of trades that included high numbers of women, such as restaurant workers, launderers, and factory workers. By 1910, 7.6 percent of the city's wage-earning women belonged to unions, compared to the national average of 1.5 percent. San Francisco women trade unionists contributed to their locals, helped wage the anti-Asian campaign that white workers saw as crucial to their interests, and filled positions in city, state, and national labor groups. Their public activism soon led many of them to support suffrage.[68]

Elite suffragist Lillian Coffin, seeing the possibilities of a cross-class suffrage alliance, had organized the San Francisco Equal Suffrage League in 1906 in order to achieve this objective. The league initially prospered, gaining male and female members from the working class and winning suffrage endorsements from city unions and the Union Labor Party. But cross-class relations within the league quickly deteriorated. Union women were deeply disappointed by the suffragists' refusal to support the bitter streetcar strike of 1907. Suffragists probably refused both because of their ambivalent feelings regarding unions and because they saw the strike as related to the ongoing battle between the Union Labor Party and good government reform. Elite and working-class women were pulled in different political directions in that contest. In the fall election of 1907 working-class women supported the Union Labor Party candidate for mayor, P. H. McCarthy, not the good government candidate favored by the club women, Edward Taylor.[69]

Trade union women activists formed their own, separate suffrage organization, the San Francisco Wage Earners' Suffrage League, on September 22, 1908—five days after the club women formed the Woman's Branch of the Citizens' League of Justice. The labor activists made explicit the separate nature of their efforts. At their organizing meeting they announced that their objectives included creating better conditions for working women and promoting "the suffrage idea, although the league will be in no way connected with the women's suffrage organization."[70]

Despite the rebuff by trade union women, middle-class suffragists continued their efforts to build a broad coalition in favor of women's enfranchisement. At the 1908 state suffrage convention, presided over by Coffin, delegates stated that although they "well understood" that the Wage Earners' Suffrage League "did not care to affiliate" with them, they nonetheless invited its members to speak. The state association, having resolved in 1906 and more emphatically in 1907 to establish cross-class suffrage alliances, hoped to establish closer relations between the two groups. Instead, the 1908 convention saw an explosion of pent-up feelings. [71]

It resulted from the labor women's deep suspicion of the middle-class suffragists. Minna O'Donnell, a member of the women's auxiliary of the typographical union and president of the Wage Earners' Suffrage League, addressed the state suffrage convention; she declared that an alliance between the two was "out of the question" because the two groups of women wanted the ballot for "very different reasons. Our idea is self-protection; you want it to use for some one else," a reference to the way club women tied their demand for the vote to social improvement. When O'Donnell finished, Coffin "immediately rose to say with great warmth that the women present were heartily in sympathy with the wage earning women." O'Donnell retorted that the state suffragists "had no conception of the meaning of the word wage earning." The convention audience broke apart, with little groups debating the issue. The four or five trade union women present "stuck firmly to their ground, asserting over and over that the [state] league was not in sympathy with them and . . . merely wished to gain their added strength of members."[72]

Despite this rather fundamental ideological split, elite and working-class suffragists presented a united front at the 1909 session of the state legislature. The San Francisco Wage Earners' Suffrage League campaigned as a separate organization and as part of a broader suffrage coalition. The union women did so without publicizing any of their grievances with the affluent suffragists. As Louise LaRue, a labor activist from the Waitresses' Union, explained, the labor women believed that class tensions among the suffragists should not prevent them from winning the vote, an instrument they intended to use to protect and promote their own interests, as women and as workers.[73]

The suffragists were especially eager to present a united front in 1911—when they were as close to winning the vote as any time since 1895. Along with backing suffrage at the 1911 legislature, trade union women lobbied for an eight-hour day for women workers. A few union women had already achieved an eight-hour day, but they vividly remembered working a fourteen- to sixteen-hour day at the beginning of the century. How women's organizations lined up on this issue shows how united—and divided—the California women's movement was just as it was beginning its great push to achieve women's citizenship.[74]

❖

Frances Nacke Noel, a Los Angeles labor activist, socialist, and suffragist, did the most to make the eight-hour day for women a leading issue in California. She brought to her task a broad vision of what she wanted women to achieve—economic, political, and social rights—as well as a deep trust that women would accomplish these objectives through a cross-class movement. Her confidence in women's ability to build such a movement grew from her experiences in crossing class and geographical borders. Born in Germany in 1873, one of six children in the comfortable home of a factory superintendent, she immigrated to the United States in 1893. A year later she began her westward trek across the country, moving to Chicago, Denver, and, in 1898, Los Angeles, where she quickly became a fixture in socialist and suffrage circles. She supported herself in various ways, opening a German kindergarten in Denver and later working as a governess and waitress. In 1902 she married Primrose D. Noel, a small businessman who shared her middle-class background, commitment to socialism, and the raising of their only child.[75]

In 1907 Frances Noel took her first direct step toward making the eight-hour day a reality in California when she joined a Los Angeles affiliate of the Woman's International Union Label League. Usually, these leagues were filled with female relatives of union men and were concerned with ensuring that union members purchased only union-made goods. By 1909 Noel had transformed the league in California into a state organization that crusaded to gain for women workers the vote, more unionization, and the eight-hour day. That same year the league presented a resolution for the eight-hour day to the California State Federation of Labor; the federation put the eight-hour day on its list of demands for the 1911 state legislature.[76]

San Francisco activists from the Woman's International Union Label League, who were much closer to Sacramento than their southern California counterparts, traveled to the state capitol to lobby for the eight-hour day. They went with great hopes. With Johnson ensconced in the governor's office, progressives controlled state government. Although the insurgents had not put the eight-hour day into their 1910 party platform, progressives tended to favor "protective" labor legislation—measures they felt shielded workers as individuals from hazardous conditions—over legislation that aided union organization. Not all progressives agreed to support the eight-hour day. Lillian Coffin, among others, argued for a nine-hour day, and some thought the entire notion too radical. Nonetheless, union women persuaded the progressives to adopt and pass the eight-hour bill.[77]

While the Woman's International Union Label League deserves the most credit for passage of the eight-hour day, it did not act alone. When the league sought backing from the State Federation of Labor, it promised to also ask other women's organizations for their support. Both state branches of the Woman's Christian Temperance Union endorsed the bill. Some temperance leaders had worked hard for many years to foster this kind of legislation. Although Beaumelle Sturtevant-Peet was no longer president of the northern branch, her legacy continued: a year earlier the women had resolved to work for a "just, living wage for women," a more radical measure than the eight-hour day. Mary Garbutt, who chaired the southern California WCTU's labor department from 1906 to 1915, organized countless events to educate Los Angeles temperance women regarding labor issues.[78]

Garbutt, seeking to enlarge and strengthen the solidarity of the Los Angeles women's movement on labor issues, urged temperance women to support the city's Consumers' League, an organization dominated by club women. They had organized it in 1902, after Florence Kelley and Jane Addams, the noted settlement workers, made an appeal for club women to form consumers' leagues at the General Federation of Women's Clubs' conference in Los Angeles that year. The Consumers' League investigated labor conditions for women and children and granted factories the right to use the "Consumers' White Label" if conditions were decent. The Los Angeles club women first collected labor statistics, in the belief that this was the necessary precursor for success; in 1906 they turned to direct action and achieved shorter hours for department store clerks, a largely female workforce. The Los Angeles Consumers' League endorsed the eight-hour day for women workers in 1911.[79]

San Francisco women, despite the clashes between elite and working-class suffragists, also developed a coalition of women's groups in favor of the eight-hour day, a network that included the Catholic Humane Society and the Bay Federation of Mothers' Clubs. The women had put together a similar coalition the previous year when the Women's International Union Label League had successfully lobbied for a woman factory inspector. League activist Hannah Mahoney Nolan, a leader in the laundry workers' union, asked forty-four women's groups to support the measure and they did, without exception.[80]

❖

The cross-class coalitions that developed from the eight-hour-day campaign served organized women well when they lobbied for the suffrage amendment. When organized women in California began working for the vote in 1911, their movement was a fluid, heterogenous collection of groups that formed shifting coalitions. Organized womanhood was also a relatively stable, united movement. Elite women could join forces with working-class women to endorse a labor issue, such as the eight-hour day, if that issue seemed to protect the rights of women as individuals and not as members of an economic class. Elite and working-class women demanded suffrage, on the other hand, because it was an individual right that allowed them to pursue their own class interests.

Their coalitions were much in evidence in January 1911 when suffragists spoke before the state legislature, demanding that the legislators send a suffrage amendment to the male electorate. Seven women spoke for suffrage. They included trade unionists Louise LaRue and Maud Younger; members of the Pacific Association of Collegiate Alumnae, such as Ethel Moore of Oakland, a leader in the state playground movement; and several suffragist club women known also for their involvement with progressivism, such as Coffin, Gerberding, and Tolhurst. Three speakers emphasized the relation of the vote to women's work, using the same broad definition of work as the suffragists in the 1890s, whereas the other four addressed "political" issues related to women's enfranchisement. Together, they presented a message of diversity and unity. They said that all women, through private and public work, made positive contributions to American society but the lack of full citizenship unfairly and unwisely weakened those women and limited their work.[81]

Soon after the legislature agreed in February 1911 to put enfranchisement on the fall ballot, suffragists began organizing for the campaign in earnest. They sought to make their organizational structure replicate their understanding of how their movement functioned best: a wide umbrella that included a diverse collection of white women's organizations. In March, Elizabeth Lowe Watson, president of the state suffrage organization, specifically invited groups that were not affiliated with the state suffrage association, such as "the Socialists and the Women's Labor Unions," to coordinate their activities with the state association at the beginning of the campaign. Suffragists subsequently organized Central Suffrage Committees in Los Angeles and San Francisco that managed their respective urban and regional campaigns. Both committees functioned as clearinghouses with delegates from various groups: temperance women, club women, union activists, and socialists.[82]

With their organizational structure in place, the cross-class alliance for women's suffrage required but two more ingredients: the largest member of the state women's movement, the California Federation of Women's Clubs, needed to endorse women's suffrage and signal that it favored legislation supported by women in the labor movement. Up to that point the federation had remained silent about the eight-hour day. When the federation opened its yearly convention in May 1911, suffragist club women stood prepared, with long hours of organizing and lobbying behind them, to convert their organization into a suffrage stronghold. By an overwhelming majority the club women endorsed enfranchising women. In their suffrage resolution the women made clear their commitment to a wide range of issues in public life; they argued that women should vote because they were "vitally interested in all questions relating to the social, industrial and political status of women." Because of these commitments and probably also because doing so would be useful in the upcoming suffrage campaign, club women also passed a resolution in favor of the "living wage" for working women—a remarkable turnabout. In addition, club women created the Department of Industrial and Social Conditions; Beaumelle Sturtevant-Peet served as its first chair.[83]

When suffragists campaigned for the vote, they did so in a movement of many groups sheltered under one umbrella. This type of organization encouraged both unified heterogeneous campaigns and separate homogeneous ones. Such campaigning influenced the participants and their audiences in two different ways. Women left the campaign with a heightened awareness of themselves as female members of various groups and an increased feminist consciousness of themselves as women, as a group denied basic rights, such as the vote, because they were women living in a society dominated by men.[84]

The second Los Angeles Political Equality League provides an excellent example of how partisan politics reflected and influenced women's perceptions of themselves as women, as elites, and as progressives. In 1909 the first Political Equality League, under the leadership of Ella Ruddy, had championed George Alexander for mayor. In 1910 John Braly, a retired banker and millionaire, organized the second Political Equality League as the male suffrage arm of Republican insurgency. That year his league played a vital role in putting a women's suffrage plank in the Republican Party's platform and boasted that all state legislators elected from the nine southern California counties promised to send suffrage to the electorate. Braly had justified forming his league by declaring that the first league was "discouraged and dispirited"; whatever his reasons, Ruddy continued to lead a very much alive, indeed militant, league for the rest of the campaign. Braly quickly opened his league to women; by February 1911 women progressives had taken control. Grace Simons, a Smith College graduate, club woman, and reformer, became president; Braly became president emeritus.[85]

Braly openly claimed that his league was successful at least in part because it especially targeted affluent individuals and courted them—thanks to Braly's largesse—with opulent lobbying tactics. All accounts of the league verify his description. Male league members, "representative and influential men," came from the professions, "bankers, judges, educators, ministers and doctors," whereas the women were "prominent in club and charitable work."[86]

To impress state legislators with the importance of endorsing suffrage, Braly's league held a banquet in December 1910—after the election and before the legislators assembled in Sacramento. At the banquet they were treated, according to the *Los Angeles Express,* to "three hours of lavish entertainment and able oratory." Present at the banquet, asserted Braly, were "nearly 300 of the elite of Los Angeles." Men and women members of the league provided the able oratory; Josefa Tolhurst, club woman and progressive, served as presiding official. She had served in other public roles; after suffragists aided good government mayoral candidate George Alexander in the 1909 election, he appointed her to the board of the city's public library.[87]

At the banquet Mayor Alexander "was brought to the fore as 'a living sign and symbol of good government' "; no one mentioned, as a socialist had two months earlier at the state suffrage convention, Alexander's draconian anti-picketing legislation (discussed shortly). Given the male progressives' support for women's suffrage, and women's participation in the league as progressives and suffragists, the step the women took at the end of 1911—forming an explicitly partisan organization—was the logical completion of a process long underway.[88]

When the women suffragists took over the leadership of Braly's Political Equality League, they made it clear that they intended to continue its specialized political tactics; they would organize a particular target group and lobby its constituency in order to win the vote. Early in the campaign the league formally identified itself as "largely composed of club women and women of leisure" who intend "to do quiet, dignified educational work." As late as August 1911, as the suffrage amendment campaign shifted into high gear, the league called a "mass" meeting: a tea party at the Italian gardens of Mrs. John D. Hooker. More than one thousand women attended what the *Los*

Angeles Times referred to as "the brilliant gathering . . . resplendent with the creme de la creme of Los Angeles."[89]

Los Angeles trade union and socialist women waged the same kind of specialized campaign. They organized into specialized groups, forming, for example, the Los Angeles Wage Earners' Suffrage League, a group of socialist women and wives of trade union men. They made themselves responsible for speaking to their constituent groups and used tactics developed in their communities; in this case, this meant using the "militant" tactics developed by women in labor strikes and radical demonstrations—they would speak to the general public to highlight their demand for equality in the public arena.[90]

Militant tactics were tied to class. Labor women had experience with such tactics because they represented a traditional means for the working classes to make their voices heard. Middle-class progressives, on the other hand, found such tactics beneath them. When Ella Giles Ruddy, a suffrage leader active in Alexander's 1909 mayoral campaign, argued in the summer of 1911 that suffragists ought to start holding open-air meetings, she defended this by declaring, "There is a prospect of many new workers who have been enthused by the idea of what may turn out to be useful 'slumming.' "[91]

Given such differing perceptions of militancy, it was working-class women who, through the Los Angeles Wage Earners' Suffrage League, initiated the suffragists' first open-air meetings, held in the city's parks in July 1911. Such tactics were seen as militant because women were engaging in public politics and perhaps illegal actions as well, because a city ordinance held it illegal to give political speeches in the parks. To overcome the law the women sang suffrage songs and passed out donuts. Around the donuts they tied the slogan "Votes for Women," a political expression that Los Angeles courts found permissible in the parks. Mainstream suffragists quickly began passing out donuts in the parks too, documenting at least one advantage of a broad coalition: effective tactics can be easily shared.[92]

In San Francisco the College Equal Suffrage League, filled with college graduates and professional women, dominated the suffrage coalition. Boston suffragist Maud Wood Park, one of the founders of the national College Equal Suffrage League in 1906, helped organize the College Equal Suffrage League of Northern California in 1908. Park, with the able assistance of Mary Keith, easily established chapters at the University of California at Berkeley and at Stanford University. Following the precedent of the national College Equal Suffrage League, the California league began by declaring its allegiance to women, progress, and prosperity. National suffragists, such as Park, perceived the College League as a new kind of society plan. The league would recruit

affluent women who were young and well educated, teach them how to become activists, and use their activism as a symbol of a transformed suffrage
movement that was on the cutting edge of fashionable change.[93]

San Francisco members of the College Equal Suffrage League excelled above
all at advertising, and what they advertised most was themselves. Mabel Craft
Deering, the journalist who had protested the racial exclusiveness of club
women and who later married attorney Frank Deering, described the members in two contrasting ways. According to Deering, who was a Berkeley graduate and league director, members were "the graduates of Eastern women's
colleges and members of the most exclusive California families" who had
"distributed literature at public meetings, . . . spoken from automobiles in
every district of the city, . . . [and] addressed the factory workers at the noon
day hour." As college women militants, they could cross the boundaries that
had once restricted respectable women and speak for all women. They re-
affirmed the lines of class, always wearing expensive formal dresses for their
public appearances, and they sought to use their privileges to break down the
tyrannies that oppressed women. League activist Louise Herrick Wall drove
out to neighboring rural Contra Costa County in a large automobile with
other league members and spoke to groups of country women. As the league's
history later described the event, " 'You, also, are real,' we cried. 'What you
think counts, but it must count for more,' and then would come on her [a
rural woman's] face that look of half-incredulous hope."[94]

At the end of the suffrage amendment campaign, when the College League
began planning the last mass meeting—a ritualized political ceremony intended to remind and summarize for voters the meaning of the suffrage
movement in the countdown before election—league members "agreed that
the mass meeting should be representative of every sort of suffrage organization." Therefore, although the league organized and paid for the meeting, it
placed on the platform representatives from the entire spectrum of the suffrage coalition. Speakers included—in addition to mainstream suffragists and
Charles Aked, a popular Protestant minister—labor leader John Nolan, Rabbi
Martin Meyer, Illinois factory inspector Helen Todd, and J. Stitt Wilson, "the
most prominent Socialist of the State." The overflow crowd of six thousand
saw a women's movement of diverse groups forming a united front.[95]

Suffragists themselves reflected on the meaning of the new public ways they
had chosen to present themselves to a mass audience, "advertising" the suffrage message through the use of mass events, billboards, contests, store win-
dow displays, pageants, parades, and plays, to name only some. Genevieve
Allen, chair of the advertising committee of the College Equal Suffrage League,

wrote that "as a woman looks at the crude portrait of her son, spread on the hoardings of a city in his first political campaign, and realizes that those things that she has pondered in her heart are at last posted for the world's appraisal, so the suffragist, in fear and elation, rejoiced in her posters with a double sense of creator and spectator." Just as the billboards reinforced a legitimate public identity for suffragists, so too did mass meetings and public demonstrations.[96]

Along with visual presentations of their unity, suffragists developed a consensus regarding women's right to citizenship and—to a more limited extent—women's work. Suffragists believed in their democratic right to vote; in claiming that right, they also claimed their right to individuality. Club woman Fannie Lyne Black wrote, "A fundamental principle of democracy is the right of every adult individual to the expression of the personal will." Rev. Wiley J. Phillips told temperance women that he believed in woman's "inherent, her divine right, to express her will and serve her own and her country's interests at the ballot box."[97]

Although white suffragists of all classes claimed the vote as a democratic right for women, they sought to limit that right selectively. College women demonstrated this when they called for the vote in the name of justice and because "the FOREIGN ELEMENT in the vote would be MODIFIED" (emphasis in original). Maud Younger, a San Francisco labor activist, believed wage-earning women should have the vote as their democratic right—and as a tool to use against the Chinese. Younger expressed the position of almost all the state's organized labor, which frequently presented its organizing as a drive to push Asians, both Chinese and Japanese, out of the labor market.[98]

This attitude, however, did not stop white suffragists from courting the minority and immigrant vote or women from those communities—often affluent women—from campaigning for the vote. Maria Lopez, the president of a college women's suffrage organization in southern California and schoolteacher, spoke in favor of suffrage to Mexicans in the Los Angeles Plaza. In San Francisco elite Italian women of the Vittoria Colonna Club, founded by physician Mariana Bertola, worked for the vote. African American women in the Bay Area also formed a suffrage league.[99]

But many of the native-born white suffragists, the dominant group within the movement, felt ambiguous about this outreach to immigrant voters. Irish Catholic suffragist Mary Keith declared in 1908, "We should keep steadily before our minds the fact that Americanism is a question of principle, of purpose, of idealism of character, that it is not a matter of birth, place, creed, or line of descent." But in 1911, two days after the state's male voters approved the suffrage amendment to the state constitution, when she witnessed San Francisco Italians celebrating Columbus Day, she acknowledged she was pleased that suffragists would "no longer be obliged to solicit the votes of the large foreign population of San Francisco . . . distributing tracts printed in nearly every language under the sun, including even those in the Chinese language."[100]

Although women demanded enfranchisement as their democratic right, they placed even greater emphasis on another argument. They posited that because industrial capitalism had transformed women's work, making it more public, women must therefore have greater political rights that addressed their changed situation. In the September 1911 issue of *Federation Courier*, the journal of the California Federation of Women's Clubs, club woman Fannie Lyne Black wrote, "Women are demanding the ballot as a right . . . and as a legitimate recognition of the service and responsibility in the world of affairs in which the natural evolution of society has forced them."[101]

Countless suffragists agreed with Black; "evolution" or "progress" (what socialists labeled capitalism) pushed women into public life. Industrial capitalism changed women's work in two ways. First, it so dramatically changed women's household work that women could no longer perform their domestic tasks without calling upon government. California suffragists distributed Jane Addams's famous argument on this point, that women could keep their homes safe and healthy only with the vote. To be a housekeeper one must become a municipal housekeeper. California women made the same point in a variety of ways, including in a series of slides that they showed in nickelodeons, theaters, and wherever else suffragists could set up a screen. One set of slides argued that "If Politics is in Baby's food"—in this case, dependent on the milk inspector—"Why Should not Mother be in Politics?"[102]

Capitalism also moved women's household production to the factory; women who followed their work as it left the home needed the vote to protect themselves in the marketplace. The women showed a set of suffrage slides that began with a picture of a woman at a spinning wheel; it bore the legend, "The old way,—industry in the home." Pictures of women wage earners followed, from factory workers to teachers, and the set ended with the statement, "Industry has been taken out of the home into Shops, Factories, Stores and Professions, which are regulated by Law, therefore women workers should have the protection of the Ballot."[103]

Much of this narrative on the evolution of women's work should sound familiar; organized women of the late nineteenth century used it to encourage women of their generation to claim their rights to a public life. Socialists first developed these ideas, but temperance and club women quickly adopted them; Frances Willard and Charlotte Perkins Gilman served as conduits between socialism and their respective movements. The narrative's political strengths were many. It cut to the heart of the antisuffrage argument that women could not be full citizens because they were dependent family members. Its inclusive description of women's work held the potential for uniting women of many walks of life in a movement that demanded their rights in recognition of their economic contributions.[104]

The suffrage float in the San Francisco's Labor Day Parade presented this message of unity based on the commonality of women's work: all women work, all deserve and require the ballot. The San Francisco Wage Earners' Suffrage League planned to make the float but ran out of time and money so it appealed to the College Equal Suffrage League, which supplied both. The float presented a range of women workers: the mother at home, college-trained professionals, factory workers. Each was portrayed by an actual representative of that group. Above them on the float stood two other women: "California" demanding the vote from "Justice."[105]

The narrative of women's economic evolution usually left untouched how wives dependent on husbands could or should be independent; nonetheless, Katherine Philips Edson, a Los Angeles club woman, declared that women's financial dependency was "the determining factor in women's subjection." When she married, in 1890 at age twenty, she had fully intended to make her marriage an economic partnership. She and her husband, Charles Farwell Edson, dreamed of European opera careers; they met at a music conservatory in Chicago where he taught and she had enrolled as a student. To finance their dream they joined his family's ranch in Antelope Valley, California, but the ranch failed. They moved to Los Angeles at the turn of the century. He became a music teacher and promoter of the fine arts; she joined the Friday Morning Club. Very quickly she became a club leader who dramatically expanded women's role in civic affairs; most notably, in 1909 she led the "pure milk" campaign that sought to ensure that commercial milk was free of bovine tuberculosis, a potentially lethal menace for infants. But she did not receive wages for her work.[106]

In 1911, during the suffrage amendment campaign, Katherine Edson was particularly concerned with developing a justification for the civic activism of women like herself, wives who were financially supported by their husbands. Motherhood, she observed in various public speeches during the suffrage amendment campaign, was "a most splendid profession for any one wishing

Katherine Philips Edson (Department of Special Collections, Charles E. Young Research Library, University of California at Los Angeles)

to specialize in it, but unfortunately economic conditions over which we have no control are such as to necessitate small families." (By 1905 Edson had three children.) She next wrote, "How can one strong mature woman spend all her time specializing of a few children who do grow up?"—but she crossed that line out.[107]

To justify women's civic activism to the electorate, Edson focused on how women's activism made crucial contributions to the country and improved women who, if they stayed home, would become "lazy, frivolous and sensual." Through the work of civic reform, women and the country would both evolve for the better, a popular point made by many suffragists in their speeches. Grace Simons, for example, declared that "the world needs women's influence in public affairs, and women need the influence of a larger world."[108]

Some suffragists discussed in their public writings and speeches the kind of society women needed in order to become fully equal citizens. Socialists most forcefully and fully argued that political equality was not enough. "We stand for the ballot, but we stand for far more," stated socialist activist Ethel Whitehead. Socialists stood for a state-controlled economy that would be directed by an empowered, fully enfranchised citizenry.[109]

Grace Simons and Katherine Edson, two prominent Los Angeles suffragists—both were officers in the city's Political Equality League—agreed that political freedom for women was not enough. As progressive Republicans, not socialists, they did not believe in the cooperative commonwealth that made the state owner and manager of the economy. But they did feel strongly that democracy meant, in Simons's words from a campaign leaflet, "equality of opportunity, for everyone to be born in decent, wholesome surroundings with sufficient food and clothing and an American free chance for an education . . . an opportunity, not to escape work, but to discover and to undertake that which he can do best." As Edson asked rhetorically in her suffrage speech, "Does America exist for the exploitation of its people for the sake of enriching a few or does it exist to give the many an equal opportunity for life, liberty and the pursuit of happiness?"[110]

As the United States developed into an industrial nation, its problems were compounded, both women argued, because they were perceived only from the viewpoint of industry, of the businessman—with the emphasis on "man." Both felt—and made clear in their campaign rhetoric—America could become a full democracy only if the government made social justice one of its responsibilities, and both believed that the success of this venture required women's full citizenship. Edson and Simons stood with Jane Addams: woman's traditional concerns for the welfare of her family and community could be upheld only if she entered politics to do battle against unrestrained male materialism.[111]

Many socialist women believed this last point too, but the women progressives opined that women should create social services rather than a cooperative commonwealth. Simons and Edson spoke specifically of such state services as protective labor legislation for women and children wage workers. Edson called equal wages for equal work the best protection of the home; Simons declared in a leaflet that "personal welfare is now being considered a legitimate object of government." Not all women progressives took the same

stance for regulated capitalism. Both Coffin and Lovell White of San Francisco seemed content with a democracy that was much more limited to political rights, and during the campaign both felt most comfortable discussing
women's advancement in the paid labor force in terms of individual elite
women.[112]

California women who stood under the suffrage umbrella of 1911 nonetheless agreed on some basic principles. Women were individuals with the rights
of full citizenship. This had always been true, but the changes in women's
work made it easier now to understand why they needed to exercise those
rights. As women made more and more contributions in the public sphere,
they needed to be able to call upon the state to ensure that those contributions
were fairly rewarded. At the heart of the consensus of the women's movement
of the progressive era was the belief that although political rights were important, political freedom would never be enough to ensure women's equality.

❖

When male voters went to the polls for the special election on October 10,
1911, they rendered judgment on twenty-three measures; along with women's
suffrage, voters decided the fate of such issues as public utility regulation and
direct legislation. Reformers saw these as issues that defined the progressive
government. Women's suffrage passed but only by the smallest of margins.
Californians cast 246,487 votes regarding suffrage; the measure won by only
3,587, a margin of less than 2 percent. Yet, as testimony to the level of heated
emotional controversy regarding women's citizenship, more people voted regarding suffrage than they did for any of the other twenty-two issues. Gender
mattered.[113]

Participants at the time (and historians since) believed the election statistics
demonstrated that class mattered as well. Just as in 1896, suffrage carried in
Los Angeles and almost all the rural counties and lost in San Francisco, albeit
by a much smaller margin. The Los Angeles socialist-labor coalition claimed
credit for winning women's suffrage, and even the conservative *Los Angeles
Times* agreed. These appraisals rested on an election analysis that reported
working-class districts as returning a larger majority in favor of suffrage than
wealthy districts.[114]

San Francisco voters followed a similar pattern. Working-class districts reported the highest percentage of affirmative votes for suffrage (40 to 42 percent), and professional and middle-class districts came next (about 37 percent), whereas upper-class Pacific Heights reported only 32 percent in favor of
giving women the ballot. The waterfront, home of sailors and the raucous

Barbary Coast, came in at the bottom, with 24 percent. Mabel Craft Deering interpreted these numbers as proof of machine politics. Just as city "aristocrats" and the "riffraff" of the Tenderloin districts voted for corrupt politicians, the better to gain corrupt privileges, so they voted against women's suffrage, because they dreaded women's moral vote.[115]

Deering was also implying that the men between the aristocrats and riffraff—professionals and respectable workers—voted for good government and women's suffrage because they believed in morality and practiced civic righteousness. Deering was expressing what many other suffrage progressives felt: people like themselves—white, native born, and middle class—represented America's best hope for civic improvement. Mary Roberts Coolidge, who like Deering was an activist in the College Equal Suffrage League, also linked class and suffrage support, but she did so more explicitly. Coolidge contended that the most votes for women's enfranchisement came from "the comfortable, hard-working American middle class and in the upper organized laboring group." However, she felt that the middle-class men, the "tradesmen, clerks, subordinates of various kinds," possessed "to a greater extent than any other single group the American sense of fair play and the more generous attitude toward women." Such men, she added, were "almost wholly American born." Linking support for suffrage with assimilation, she observed that the skilled unionized workers who supported suffrage were "much Americanized," but workers opposed to suffrage were "less American, usually foreign born."[116]

Although women progressives had developed by the end of the campaign a sharply defined sense of themselves that tied together their gender, race, class, and reform politics, they continued to stress that the suffrage movement stood open to all women. Los Angeles suffragists, at a victory celebration held soon after women won the vote, emphasized that women had managed and won the campaign as women, not as members of an economic class or political party. Grace Simons thought the campaign proved that "women have learned to work harmoniously side by side," whereas Katherine Edson announced that "class distinctions have gone down and a real democracy is here." Yet, as we have seen, during the campaign they did indeed demand citizenship as women and as members of a specific class or party. Now that they were citizens, women who could vote, how would they use it?[117]

❖

This question became profoundly important in the Los Angeles mayoral elections of December 1911. Good government mayor George Alexander faced socialist Job Harriman in a runoff election. Behind Harriman stood the city's labor movement, in the middle of an intense campaign to establish organized labor as a vital force in the city known nationwide as the leader of the anti-union or open-shop campaign. Behind Alexander stood good government reformers and their former opposition—conservatives. The reformers' new allies included their chief conservative nemesis, Harrison Gray Otis of the *Los Angeles Times*, who had decried the reformers as goo goos. Reformers, conservatives, businessmen, professionals—all united to prevent a socialist victory in Los Angeles.[118]

"In no other city," wrote historian George Mowry, "were class lines so deeply and clearly drawn." He placed most of the blame for this on Otis. A Los Angeles real estate speculator as well as a newspaper publisher, Otis accepted the common business assumption that the city's commercial growth depended on low wages, and he waged an uncommonly determined and ruthless battle against organized labor. He turned the Merchants and Manufacturers' Association into a labor-fighting machine that hired its own police to break strikes, ensured that businesses that showed a willingness to negotiate with labor failed to qualify for bank loans, and collaborated closely with city government, including the police, to make sure that strikes were broken. When the Los Angeles growth rate clearly surpassed San Francisco's in 1910, Otis claimed the credit belonged to his union-busting open-shop policy, although many other factors, such as the inexpensive energy and land available in Los Angeles, were probably more important.[119]

Los Angeles labor determined in 1910 to end the open shop locally. That summer the city experienced the largest strike in its history. Most metal workers walked out; they were joined by men in the leather trades, brewery workers, Mexican streetcar workers, and others. Alexander's good government administration responded by passing an antipicketing law that prohibited all picketing, no matter how peaceful, a law written by the Merchants and Manufacturers' Association. The strike kept going, but hundreds of workers were sent to jail as violators of the antipicketing law. On October 1, 1910, a bomb exploded in the *Los Angles Times* building, killing twenty-one men and wounding several others. Harrison Gray Otis immediately blamed labor, and in the spring of 1911 two trade unionists, the McNamara brothers, John and James, were charged with the crime. The labor movement across the nation denounced the charges as a malicious falsehood, designed to discredit labor.[120]

This wave of aroused militant labor gave socialist Job Harriman a plurality in the November primary election, 44 percent of the vote. Harriman began campaigning for the runoff election scheduled for December 5 as the likely winner over incumbent Alexander, the good government candidate. The socialist-labor alliance looked forward to victory in December, but only days before the election the McNamara brothers confessed their guilt. Alexander won easily.[121]

The *California Outlook*, the state's progressive organ, editorialized that "we are convinced that good government would have triumphed just the same if the women had not had votes, if the McNamaras had not confessed and if it had rained pitchforks on Tuesday" (election day). The *Outlook*'s editorial, "The Nightmare That Passed," continued, saying that, nonetheless, "it would be difficult to imagine a more complete vindication of the woman suffrage idea than this election has afforded." The journal judged the women progressives' political work to be "historic" and "of heroic proportions" and, as a final tribute in what the *Outlook* deemed its highest praise, it declared that "the oldest political experts among the men looked on in astonishment and admiration." By closely examining the 1911 mayoral campaign we can see how once again a political crisis enabled women progressives to transform themselves politically. The women expanded their political activism, built a "nonpartisan" but highly political organization, gained more political power, and began to tentatively identify themselves as politicized citizens.[122]

During the campaign both sides looked to women, enfranchised that October, as a crucial factor in the December election. Local socialist women, aided by Charlotte Perkins Gilman, worked hard and effectively to register women in the working-class wards. The *Los Angeles Times,* the one leading newspaper of the state that stood adamantly against women's suffrage, began pleading with women to register to vote—against the socialists. According to Mabel Craft Deering, "The humor of the situation"—of the *Times* "on its knees to the women whom it had abused for years—was so pungent that many who had worked themselves to the bone for suffrage said that it more than repaid them."[123]

Despite their earlier cooperation with socialists, the elite women of the Political Equality League reorganized as the Woman's Progressive League. Following the pattern set by their male counterparts, the women labeled the league as a nonpartisan organization dedicated to the reelection of the good government slate. They quickly began registering women only in the wards that gave a majority to Alexander in the primary election, setting up registration booths in department stores, banks, and churches. After registering thousands of women within a few days, the league ran a well-organized, innovative—militant—campaign. Members went door to door, set up noon talks for working women, and led a pro-Alexander demonstration that used the American flag as its icon. The women filled a long line of cars with five thousand American flags and gave them away until, declared the *Los Angeles Express*, "business blocks, homes and automobiles" were covered with the red, white, and blue of "civic righteousness." The women also developed "afternoon teas" and "voting schools" as popular campaign strategies. With four to five hundred automobiles at their disposal, they conducted a successful get-out-the-vote campaign on election day.[124]

Josefa Tolhurst, the Los Angeles club woman, suffragist, and progressive, made most of the league's key addresses. No doubt other league members chose her because of her "enviable reputation as a public speaker and considerable diplomatic power." She had developed these skills in the Friday Morning Club, where she served as president for five years and became known as the "most tactful and gracious" of club presidents. Club member Olive Percival wrote in her scrapbook that Tolhurst "was the best presiding officer known. Elegantly tailored, alert, amiable, witty, with marvelous (non-maudlin) impromptu!"[125]

Percival also repeated the gossip that Tolhurst's "speech before the state senate won the suffrage for California women," a comment that underscored Tolhurst's abilities as speaker, suffragist, and politician. During the campaign to get the state legislature to pass a suffrage amendment, Tolhurst had expressed a powerful argument for the vote that collapsed women's enfranchisement, progressivism, and democracy. She described antisuffragists as "reactionary, un-American, advocating class legislation and special privilege, scoffing at democracy." Suffragists, on the other hand, pleaded "for the divine right of the individual to self-government, standing for the ideas which have brought about insurgency, in line with the progressive and the patriotic." Tolhurst brought this argument and her considerable skills to Alexander's good government campaign for mayor.[126]

When Tolhurst rose to deliver her first major speech for Alexander, "the audience greeted her," according to the *Los Angeles Times,* "with a warmth of applause that was like a shower of red rose leaves at her feet." She stated in this and subsequent speeches that she deeply admired the theory of socialism and the socialist candidates; she made no personal attacks against any of them. Harriman's platform was only modestly to the left of the good government forces and would seemingly be attractive to the women progressives. He promised to immediately end the antipicketing ordinance, to expand municipal ownership somewhat more than good government had done, to increase funding for playgrounds, and so on. Tolhurst, however, did not debate Harriman's platform; she made other arguments.[127]

Tolhurst contended that "Good Government stands for nearly all of the

Socialist ideals and the Socialists who are in good faith with their cause can better serve it by voting for those who can put these principles into practice than by casting their ballots to install an administration which could not be effective." Socialists could not enact their principles because they would ruin the city's credit ratings, and this would allow an "evil combination of influences"—large capitalists and vice interests—to take over the city. Indeed, Tolhurst alleged that these groups were backing the socialists in order to achieve two antireform objectives. "The very rich know that the election of the socialists would . . . [destroy] the city's credit [so] that they can delay and perhaps defeat the municipal ownership of power and light." Additionally, "lesser business men join in this conspiracy from the erroneous impression that a wide open town is good for business."[128]

Tolhurst warned that "such a combination [large capital and vice interests] so demoralized San Francisco that its assets were fed to political vultures," a reference to the corrupt influence peddling of Ruef and Schmitz under the Union Labor Party. She did not, however, provide any proof of such corruption in the Los Angeles socialist-labor slate and acknowledged that "Job Harriman might repudiate these elements." She made her case through guilt by alleged association, saying that the same kind of powers that played such a vital role in creating and maintaining a machine in San Francisco were secretly supporting the Los Angeles socialists. Male members of the good government forces explicitly argued that Harriman's sympathy with labor—his commitment, just like the Union Labor Party's, to command the police to neutrality during a strike—would be a key factor in destroying Los Angeles; however, the women never developed—at least publicly—that part of the San Francisco analogy.[129]

Members of the pro-Alexander Woman's Progressive League instead emphasized the "morality" of good government, defining it as honesty and dedication to prosperity. As Maria Lopez, the suffragist, explained to an African American audience, she saw "the whole issue of this campaign as one of bread and butter for the whole people," and she failed "to see how it can help the wage-earner to frighten away the investor." Tolhurst praised Alexander for his "decent and economic government," warning that "it would be very unwise to surrender the services of an experienced, true man like Alexander." Caroline Severance, the city's most noted socialist club woman, chose to emphasize the last point when she declared publicly for good government: "I do not believe in changing horses in mid-stream. I endorse heartily the program of our Good Government administration and rejoice in the active work of our

Woman's Progressive League." The *Los Angeles Express* quoted her in a front-page story.[130]

The Women Wage Earners' Alexander Club, a group of women workers probably organized by the Woman's Progressive League, agreed with Severance's definition of good government morality but gave a more comprehensive reason for its decision to support Alexander. Iva LeClaire, stenographer for an insurance company and president of this club of several hundred "teachers, stenographers, saleswomen, telephone operators, [and] clerks," explained its position at its first large meeting, held in late November 1911. "We believe the Good Government ticket is not a class ticket"; in other words, the Alexander Club supported the ticket because it "represents all of the people."[131]

LeClaire understood this representation of all classes without class conflict to be the heart of Christian socialism—an ideology she stated that the Women Wage Earners' Alexander Club supported. LeClaire contended that the local socialist ticket repudiated community representation through its "class discrimination"—its voice for labor. LeClaire agreed with Tolhurst: good government delivered as much "socialism" or labor representation as the city's social order and credit rating could withstand.[132]

Women in the good government movement often mentioned the diverse backgrounds of the women who participated in it; members understood this as a significant part of their political identity. They felt that diversity justified their claim to represent "all of the people" and confirmed the sectarian narrowness of their opponents. Jeanette Converse of the Woman's Progressive League insisted, "Too much emphasis cannot be placed upon this catholicity of our membership. . . . It has not been a campaign of society women alone, but has embraced a broad sisterhood of women appreciative of their enfranchisement." When the *Los Angeles Times* editorially assessed the forces aligned for Alexander, the paper observed that the Woman's Progressive League provided a "bulwark of strength" for the campaign; nonetheless, the members of the league "cannot be coolly claimed in a body by the Good Government organization, for the League embraces women of wide and varying views on general, political and civic questions." The "broad sisterhood" that composed the league strengthened it in politics but also made it not quite a part of traditional politics.[133]

Activists in the pro-Alexander Woman's Progressive League saw themselves in but not of politics for another reason: they belonged to a nonpartisan movement specifically organized to advance good government. As league member Mrs. C. H. Kysor explained, "This organization is not a matter of class, or a matter of selfishness, but purely one of judgment and good citizenship. We have been charged with being partisan, but we have acted only within sound reason." Nancy T. Craig, a good government candidate for the board of education, described the predicted victory for Alexander as a "victory for civic righteousness." As women, as members of the good government movement, they saw themselves crusading in politics for principled objectives; they believed they did not seek partisan advantage and that they would not become part of any political corruption.[134]

During the campaign the Woman's Progressive League announced that it was becoming a permanent organization; the women hoped to become a power in politics. Buoyed by their success in the campaign and their numbers, which quickly grew into the thousands (reports varied from two to four thousand), the women aimed to make the league a vehicle "through which they intelligently may participate in all matters of government." The league would not become a political party but an instrument that would enable women to represent themselves more forcefully in politics. As Martha Nelson McCan, a leader in the league, explained, "We do not want to run things nor to start a new party, but simply to educate the women of the State in citizenship and to protect our interests." To that end, the women developed three long-range political objectives for the league; in addition to providing political education, the league would initiate legislation, especially for women and children, and decide whether to support candidates proposed by other organizations. The league would operate in politics, but it would remain, according to McCan, "a distinctive woman's organization which is nonpartisan."[135]

As McCan's statements reveal, she—and most women in the league—felt ambiguous about defining the league as political. Her statements swing between declarations that committed the league to acquiring and using power and, in the next breath, declarations that denied or softened any such claim. She announced that women did not even "*want* to run things," but she also described the league's goals as becoming powerful enough to "*compel* such legislation as is vital to the women and children of California" (emphasis added). The league would gain its power by organizing women in a most political manner: its state board would serve as a central committee, coordinating women's actions in every district. McCan described the league as a nonpartisan group dedicated to representing the interests of all women. She also issued a warning about the ability of the league to defend its agenda: "No party backed by men or women will ever again succeed in this State unless its platform and its candidates stand for what is wise and healthful." McCan felt confident that the league would know what was wise and healthful; league women were "going to stand together for everything progressive and good." United by their ideology, they could make political decisions wisely.[136]

The Woman's Progressive League intended to become a power within progressivism, but its ability to do so was partly dependent upon its relations with the men who dominated the movement. During the 1911 mayoral campaign good government men urgently called for the women's help, happily worked with the women (for the most part), and subsequently praised the women's achievement. Yet women gained little in the way of more substantial awards for their efforts. An article in the *Federation Courier,* the state's club journal, which wholeheartedly supported the good government forces, pointedly observed that "while the Socialist ticket names several women on the school board, as in previous years, the Good Government ticket has but one." Nancy Craig, the suffragist, Friday Morning Club member, and (widowed) owner of a grocery business, won her seat, along with the rest of the slate, but her victory did not represent a political innovation in 1911.[137]

Male progressives placed another member of the Woman's Progressive League in political office, but they did so in a process that documented male resistance to women's political power as well as male recognition of women's strength. Governor Hiram Johnson nominated Carrie P. Bryant, "one of the leading spirits in the Woman's Progressive League," to the state Board of Charities and Corrections, a significant but not daring political step. When Meyer Lissner, the good government activist who led the coalition of reformers and conservatives for Alexander, asked the governor to nominate Bryant, Lissner felt compelled to assure Johnson that she did "not come under the genus 'militant suffragette.'" Lissner added that he thought the league "will be very helpful to us in our state politics." Women progressives subsequently became a vital part of the state Progressive Party but only through continual struggle.[138]

Women progressives saw themselves as mediators who worked for a social peace favorable to all women; as good women they could do this without prejudice, uniting women on the bias of morality. Women progressives worked hard and relatively successfully to achieve women's citizenship, help develop a broad coalition within the women's movement, and successfully lobby for laws that most organized women felt were in women's interests. At the same time, as workers for good government, their definitions of women's interests were inextricably tied to their partisan and class identities. During the final days of the 1911 suffrage campaign Josefa Tolhurst declared that women represented "the one element which may make capital and labor co-operate to bring peace out of the conditions that now exist." A month later, serving as the chief representative of women progressives, she remained silent on an issue at the core of the campaign, the good government antipicketing ordinance.[139]

❖

In December 1911, a month after the women's suffrage victory, the aging suffragist and temperance worker Sarah Severance wrote to the aging suffragist and club woman Caroline Severance (no relation) to express her thoughts about the suffrage campaign and women's political future. Sarah Severance professed her "faith in women . . . and great hope for the future"; she wanted—and expected—women to continue campaigning for women-related reforms. She also thought the progressive Republicans "did well by us, and deserve to rule while they behave."[140]

Her qualified commitment to the progressive Republicans and expectation that women would continue their own movement and political agenda expressed what women progressives meant when they said they were nonpartisan. The women saw themselves as allies of male progressives, but the women believed their alliance rested on nothing less than red, white, and blue civic righteousness. If the men proved disappointing, the women still had their own movement, organized womanhood, whose independence and strength flowed from its ability to organize large numbers of women, a "broad sisterhood," into a single cohesive political body. Women progressives sought diversity within their movement and sought to contain it. They wanted working-class women who followed their leadership. They led a movement that was neither nonpartisan nor an egalitarian sisterhood. But within that movement women were beginning to struggle with the political possibilities of formal citizenship.

EPILOGUE:
THE POLITICS OF WOMEN'S CITIZENSHIP

CALIFORNIA WOMEN pursued citizenship to make themselves powerful. As they struggled to make their voices heard in the public arena, they changed their lives and created new definitions of the appropriate relationship between women and power. They created these new understandings by borrowing from older notions of gender, power, and politics. Women became citizens who sought power but only, they declared, for the public good. They engaged in politics but only for nonpartisan goals. They developed an ideological agenda but only for civic righteousness. Such a borrowing from the old to create the new does not document any particular weakness in women and their movement; it verifies the way all social movements create meaning.

California women's enfranchisement changed the political landscape of national suffrage, California politics, and the state's organized womanhood. Because of the California victory both suffragists and antisuffragists rethought their respective national campaign strategies. Both sides agreed that progressivism had helped California women gain the ballot. Some suffragists found the western relationship between suffrage and progressivism significant for additional reasons. It confirmed their belief that women progressives would take women into politics and that most Americans would accept these actions because the women were making the social order more humane and democratic and thus more stable. Women in California found that citizenship did not give them political power but that they could use it to gain more power. They attempted to do so in two different arenas, within organized womanhood and within partisan politics. Such a strategy enabled them to achieve a remarkable slate of legislative victories during the 1913 session of the legislature, both because the women had put together a highly representative, nonpartisan women's political lobby and because so much of organized womanhood overlapped with the party in power, progressive Republicans. Although the political power of the women's movement subsequently declined—as social movements always do—it left behind numerous legacies. Perhaps the greatest was the much larger number of women who saw themselves as citizens.

❖

National observers of the suffrage movement, those who supported votes for women and those who did not, agreed that the victory in California marked a turning point in the campaign to enfranchise women. Antisuffragists had become worried when women in Washington State won the vote in 1910, after a fourteen-year stretch of suffrage defeats. But when women in the much more populous state of California gained their enfranchisement the following year, the alarmed antisuffragists decided that they must unify their various state societies into one national organization. A few weeks after the California victory, they formed the National Association Opposed to Woman Suffrage.[1]

Suffragists perceived California as a turning point too; however, they debated which strategy they should use to best take advantage of the new situation. Some, particularly the leadership of the National American Woman Suffrage Association (NAWSA), felt that the California victory, like the one in Washington the previous year, demonstrated the validity of struggling for the vote state by state. But other activists read the two victories differently. They argued for a new emphasis on securing an amendment to the U.S. Constitution. Women voters in the six western states—California and Washington as well as Wyoming (1869), Utah (1870), Colorado (1893), and Idaho (1896)—represented a political resource that could make a significant difference in achieving women's national enfranchisement, thanks in part to the large number of voters in California. Reflecting the changing, albeit still controversial, sentiment within the organization, in 1910 NAWSA created the Congressional Committee to push for a federal amendment. In 1912 suffragist Alice Paul took over the committee. Energized by her radicalizing experience in Britain, the 1911 California win, and the subsequent western suffrage victories that brought the number of suffrage states up to nine by 1913 (with the 1912 wins in Arizona, Oregon, and Kansas), Paul called upon women voters in the

West to vote as a bloc for women's suffrage. Her call transformed the women's movement and helped make the suffrage amendment, the Susan B. Anthony Amendment, as it was known, part of the U.S. Constitution in 1920.[2]

National suffragists read the California victory in yet another way: they interpreted it as a victory of women progressives. Alice Stone Blackwell, editor of the *Woman's Journal*, the national organ of NAWSA, began her column of October 21, 1911, by crowing, "The victory in California was a victory for the Progressives all along the line." Blackwell and others were pleased with this connection for several reasons. It meant that women had a political ally—and one that was developing a national movement—that would support women's suffrage nationally. Also, the woman progressive represented the good woman of the respectable middle classes—Blackwell placed her between "intelligent greed and unintelligent ignorance"—and the woman progressive engaged in acceptable public work, what Blackwell called "human-welfare" activism. As that kind of activist, she could share the concerns of women socialists and labor unionists about conditions for working women, build alliances with them, and reform the workplace—and thus defuse the kind of social upheavals that had shaken the country during the 1880s and 1890s. The woman progressive seemed the ideal resolution of the tension between women who were demanding changes in the social order—their citizenship and the right to public work—and the highly effective charge that such changes would destroy the social order.[3]

Blackwell described a political situation that was clearly, simply, and deeply divided: the "forces of monopoly and special privilege" were on one side, whereas suffragists and progressives, the joint forces of civic righteousness, stood on the other. But California politics were, as we saw during the suffrage campaign, much more complex, and they remained so after women gained the vote. Women suffragists who were progressives sought to become a recognized part of the progressive wing of the Republican Party, but they also sought to keep organized womanhood formally separate from partisan groups. Women in Los Angeles formed the Woman's Progressive League to help George Alexander win the 1911 mayoral campaign; only a few months later, in the early months of 1912, the women remade the league into a women's nonpartisan civic group, the Southern California Civic League. By the end of the year representatives from all the state's major parties, including the socialists, sat on the league's board of directors. Organized womanhood and progressivism were tied together by numerous links—sometimes the two movements overlapped—but they were not synonymous.[4]

In 1912 organized women in California took another step to make their movement politically powerful yet free from partisan entanglements. They created the California Women's Legislative Council to lobby the state legislature for measures deemed in women's interests. The state Federation of Women's Clubs, the largest state women's organization, led the efforts to organize the council and remained its major voice. Nonetheless, under the council umbrella, along with club women and temperance women, stood trade union and professional women's organizations, partisan women's groups—Democrats, progressive Republicans, and socialists—and African American women, represented by the San Francisco Colored Women's Non-Partisan League. The Legislative Council's heterogenous composition was clear evidence that organized women had resolved to continue the practice of increasing women's power through a policy of political inclusion.[5]

On the opening morning of the 1913 session of the California Legislature, its first meeting after women gained the ballot, each assemblyman and senator found on his desk a card entitled the "First Legislative Platform of the Women's Legislative Council of California." The card listed seventeen bills the 100,000 women of the council wanted them to enact. Most bills fit into four categories: women's legal rights, women's "work," social legislation focused on women and children, and general social welfare legislation.[6]

The state legislature approved eleven of the bills on the women's list, putting California in national headlines as a state favorable to legislation championed by the women's movement. California was one of the first states to pass a mothers' pension law (welfare benefits for indigent women with children) and to pass a minimum-wage bill for women; its eight-hour law for women, passed in 1911 and strengthened in 1913, set a national record for effectiveness. Women also gained teachers' pensions, joint guardianship of children, the Red Light Abatement and Injunction Act (legislation designed to make it easier to eliminate prostitution), the raising of the legal age of consent, a state training school for delinquent girls, and more.[7]

Several factors account for their legislative success. Behind the California Women's Legislative Council stood vast numbers of women committed to engaging in nonpartisan politics in the name of all women. The council effectively lobbied the state legislators as the political arm of what seemed in 1913 to be a very large special interest group—perhaps half the electorate. Some male legislators, believing (or fearing?) that they were witnessing the formation of a "woman's bloc," supported women's measures. At the same time, the women succeeded by capitalizing on their political alliances. Progressive Republicans, who were then close to the peak of their political power, backed many bills on the council's list, such as the proposal for a minimum wage. Women activists who were progressive Republicans worked with male progressives to write some bills, but others originated within the women's movement. Two separate yet somewhat overlapping movements, organized women and progressivism, through highly political relationships that were both partisan and nonpartisan, made possible the women's 1913 legislative victories.[8]

Organized women's close ties to progressive Republicans also go far in explaining women's lackluster performance during the 1915, 1917, and 1919 sessions of the legislature. (The California Legislature then met every two years.) The California Women's Legislative Council lobbied during all these sessions but restricted its agenda to winning the right of women to serve on juries (defeated in 1915, approved in 1917), amending community property laws, and seeking uncontroversial social welfare legislation. The women demanded less mostly because the party that had supported their reforms, the progressive Republicans, had suffered many defeats in the 1914 election, and its leaders concluded that they no longer should or would push for reform. The curtailment of women's activism also developed from the fragmentation of organized womanhood. Activists did not find another issue that united them as suffrage once had, but they confronted many issues that divided them, from minimum wage legislation to arguments about the role of the United States in World War I. Organized womanhood experienced this slump in political achievements because, like all social movements, it was linked to the wider world of reform and politics.[9]

❖

When California women won the vote, they achieved a monumental victory; they enhanced the legal definition of their citizenship. But they did not become full citizens; they did not gain the same amount of political power as men. To become equal citizens they needed a movement that continued to move with the same speed and strength that it had before their enfranchisement. As historian Ellen DuBois argues, "The vote did not have the inherent capacity to emancipate women as individuals. . . . Like all institutional reforms, it required an active social movement to give it meaning and make it real."[10]

California women's greatest achievement was that at the beginning of the twentieth century, they created such a movement. This enabled them to transform the meaning of citizenship, politics, and public space, of womanhood and women's work. Believing in a womanhood, they struggled to advance women's interests; believing in the importance of meaningful work for each individual woman, they struggled to legitimize and institutionalize such work for all women. They gained power because of their ability to envision themselves as a womanhood and because they could see within that vision a means to empower themselves as women.

NOTES

INTRODUCTION

1. For additional information about the importance of California to the national suffrage movement, see Steven M. Buechler, *The Transformation of the Woman Suffrage Movement: The Case of Illinois, 1850–1920* (New Brunswick, N.J.: Rutgers University Press, 1986), 14–15; Mari Jo Buhle, *Women and American Socialism, 1870–1920* (Urbana: University of Illinois Press, 1981), 230; Nancy F. Cott, *The Grounding of Modern Feminism* (New Haven, Conn.: Yale University Press, 1987), 27–28; Eleanor Flexner, *Century of Struggle: The Woman's Rights Movement in the United States,* rev. ed. (Cambridge, Mass.: Harvard University Press, 1975), 265.

2. See A.S.B. [Alice Stone Blackwell], "Our New Star," *Woman's Journal* 42 (Oct. 21, 1911): 332. For examples of eastern suffragists who were exalting over the California victory—as they counted electoral votes—see "Another Star Now Added to Suffrage Flag," *Woman's Journal* 42 (Oct. 14, 1911): 321, and "Our Biggest Star," *Woman's Journal* 42 (Nov. 11, 1911): 356. For the importance of the West in winning the national suffrage victory, see David Morgan, *Suffragists and Democrats: The Politics of Woman Suffrage in America* (East Lansing: Michigan State University Press, 1972).

3. For definitions of politics see Louise A. Tilly and Patricia Gurin, "Women, Politics, and Change," in *Women, Politics, and Change,* ed. Louise A. Tilly and Patricia Gurin (New York: Russell Sage Foundation, 1990), 3–32; Sandra Morgen and Ann Bookman, "Rethinking Women and Politics: An Introductory Essay," in *Women and the Politics of Empowerment,* ed. Ann Bookman and Sandra Morgen (Philadelphia: Temple University Press, 1988), 3–29; Paula Baker, "The Domestication of Politics: Women and American Political Society, 1780–1920," *American Historical Review* 89 (June 1984): 620–47, and *The Moral Frameworks of Public Life: Gender, Politics, and the*

State in Rural New York, 1870–1930 (Oxford: Oxford University Press, 1991). For discussions of political culture, see also Thomas Bender, "Wholes and Parts: The Need for Synthesis in American History," *Journal of American History* 73 (June 1986): 120–36, esp. 126, 131, 135; Stephen Weld, *The Concept of Political Culture* (New York: St. Martin's, 1993), esp. 152–58.

4. On the paradox of change see Joan Wallach Scott, *Only Paradoxes to Offer: French Feminists and the Rights of Man* (Cambridge, Mass.: Harvard University Press, 1996); Sidney Tarrow, "Mentalities, Political Cultures, and Collective Action Frames: Constructing Meanings Through Action," in *Frontiers in Social Movement Theory*, ed. Aldon D. Morris and Carol McClurg Mueller (New Haven, Conn.: Yale University Press, 1992), 174–202.

5. Anne Firor Scott developed the model for a history of the women's movement that told the story of its many different participants; see *The Southern Lady: From Pedestal to Politics, 1830–1930* (Chicago: University of Chicago Press, 1970). For a discussion of the relationship between collective identity and feminism, see Gerda Lerner, *The Creation of Patriarchy* (Oxford: Oxford University Press, 1986), 231–43. For other histories that understand politics as the struggle to "reconstitute society and social relations," see Lynn Hunt, *Politics, Culture, and Class in the French Revolution* (Berkeley: University of California Press, 1984), esp. 12 and 72 (quote at p. 12); Lawrence Goodwyn, *The Populist Moment: A Short History of the Agrarian Revolt in America* (Oxford: Oxford University Press, 1978), esp. 293, 295–96.

6. For an insightful discussion of the meaning of a woman's—as opposed to women's—movement, see Cott, *Grounding of Modern Feminism*, 6, 16–19. For other discussions of the meaning of "woman," see Elizabeth V. Spelman, *Inessential Woman: Problems of Exclusion in Feminist Thought* (Boston: Beacon, 1988), x, 11–13, 162–67, 171–77, and Denise Riley, *"Am I That Name?": Feminism and the Category of "Women" in History* (Minneapolis: University of Minnesota Press, 1988).

7. For other histories that study the relationship of women's "work" and political activism of the progressive-era women's movement, see Robyn Muncy, *Creating a Female Dominion in American Reform, 1890–1935* (Oxford: Oxford University Press, 1991); Kathryn Kish Sklar, *Florence Kelley and the Nation's Work: The Rise of Women's Political Culture, 1830–1900* (New Haven, Conn.: Yale University Press, 1995); and Elizabeth Hayes Turner, *Women, Culture, and Community: Religion and Reform in Galveston, 1880–1920* (Oxford: Oxford University Press, 1997).

8. For definitions of citizenship that relate it to gender, see Linda K. Kerber, *Women of the Republic: Intellect and Ideology in Revolutionary America* (Chapel Hill: University of North Carolina Press, 1980), 8–9, 11–12, 36, 119–20, 132–36, 269, 284–85; Gwendolyn Mink, "The Lady and the Tramp: Gender, Race, and the Origins of the American Welfare State," in *Women, the State, and Welfare*, ed. Linda Gordon (Madison: University of Wisconsin, 1990), 92–122, esp. 93–95; Cott, *Grounding of Modern Feminism*, 117–19; Marilyn Lake, "Between Old Worlds and New: Feminist Citizenship, Nation, and Race—the Destabilization of Identity," in *Suffrage and Beyond: Interna-*

tional Feminist Perspectives, ed. Caroline Daley and Melanie Nolan (New York: New York University Press, 1994), 277–94. T. H. Marshall developed the notion of three types of citizenship rights although I, following Sklar, substitute "economic" for his category of "social." See T. H. Marshall and Tom Bottomore, *Citizenship and Social Class* (London: Pluto Press, 1992), 3–51; Sklar, *Florence Kelley,* 321–22 n. 14. For the argument that the vote represented women's autonomous personhood and thus their independent citizenship, see Ellen DuBois, "The Radicalism of the Woman's Suffrage Movement: Notes Toward the Reconstruction of Nineteenth-Century Feminism," *Feminist Studies* 3 (Fall 1975): 63–71.

9. S. Sara Monoson, "The Lady and the Tiger: Women's Electoral Activism in New York City Before Suffrage," *Journal of Women's History* 2 (Fall 1990): 100–35; Melanie Gustafson, "Partisan Women in the Progressive Era: The Struggle for Inclusion in American Political Parties," *Journal of Women's History* 9 (Summer 1997): 8–30.

10. Michael L. Goldberg, "Non-Partisan and All-Partisan: Rethinking Woman Suffrage and Party Politics in Gilded Age Kansas," *Western Historical Quarterly* 25 (Spring 1994): 21–44; for a thoughtful discussion of the relationship between women's history and western history, see Peggy Pascoe, "Western Women at the Cultural Crossroads," in *Trails: Toward a New Western History,* ed. Patricia Nelson Limerick, Clyde A. Milner II, and Charles E. Rankin (Lawrence: University of Kansas Press, 1991), 40–58.

CHAPTER 1: THE POLITICS OF WOMEN'S WORK

1. Gordon is quoted in Elizabeth Cady Stanton, Susan B. Anthony, and Matilda Joslyn Gage, *History of Woman Suffrage,* vol. 3 (Rochester, N.Y.: Charles Mann, 1887), 753; Edward T. James, Janet Wilson James, and Paul S. Boyer, *Notable American Women, 1607–1950,* vol. 2 (Cambridge, Mass.: Harvard University Press, 1971), 68–69; for the importance of spiritualism to the early California women's movement, see Robert J. Chandler, "In the Van: Spiritualists as Catalysts for the California Women's Suffrage Movement," *California History* 73 (Fall 1994): 188–201, 252–54.

2. Philip J. Ethington, *The Public City: The Political Construction of Urban Life in San Francisco, 1850–1900* (Cambridge, U.K.: Cambridge University Press, 1994), 209–16; Gordon is quoted in Chandler, "In the Van," 195. For two discussions of the national movement during this era that include its relationship with women in the West, see Ellen Carol DuBois, *Feminism and Suffrage: The Emergence of an Independent Women's Movement in America, 1848–1869* (Ithaca, N.Y.: Cornell University Press, 1978), 189–202, and Suzanne M. Marilley, *Woman Suffrage and the Origins of Liberal Feminism in the United States, 1820–1920* (Cambridge, Mass.: Harvard University Press, 1996), 66–99.

3. Barbara Allen Babcock, "Clara Shortridge Foltz: 'First Woman,'" *Arizona Law Review* 30 (1988): 673–717, esp. 677–78 n. 15; DuBois, *Feminism and Suffrage,* 200–201.

4. Chandler, "In the Van," 201; Ethington, *Public City,* 215; Sherilyn Cox Bennion, *Equal to the Occasion: Women Editors of the Nineteenth-Century West* (Reno: Univer-

sity of Nevada Press, 1990), 57–62; for a glimpse of Gordon's view of the dissension, see Ruth Barnes Moynihan, *Rebel for Rights: Abigail Scott Duniway* (New Haven, Conn.: Yale University Press, 1983), 86.

5. "The Case in California," *Woman's Journal* 5 (Jan. 10, 1874): 11; Mary J. Collins, "Woman Suffrage in California," *Woman's Journal* 5 (Jan. 24, 1874): 32; Mary F. Snow, "Progress in California," *Woman's Journal* 5 (Mar. 14, 1874): 84; "Women on the School Board in California," *Woman's Journal* 5 (Apr. 4, 1874): 107; Stanton, Anthony, and Gage, *History of Woman Suffrage*, 3: 757, 765–66; Babcock, "Clara Shortridge Foltz," 681–83; for Knox Goodrich's obituary, see "In Memoriam," *Woman's Journal* 34 (Nov. 28, 1903): 381.

6. Susan [?], "Progress in California," *Woman's Journal* 5 (Jan. 31, 1874): 39; "American Woman Suffrage Association Proceedings, California Report," *Woman's Journal* 5 (Oct. 24, 1874): 343; "Letter from California," *Woman's Journal* 11 (Feb. 21, 1880): 64; Sarah Knox Goodrich, "American Woman Suffrage Association Proceedings, San Jose, California Report," *Woman's Journal* 13 (Sept. 30, 1882): 307.

7. Babcock, "Clara Shortridge Foltz," 685–86, 695–715; James, James, and Boyer, *Notable American Women*, vol. 1, 641–43; see also Barbara Allen Babcock, "Reconstructing the Person: The Case of Clara Shortridge Foltz," *biography* 12 (Winter 1989): 5–16; Ethington, *Public City*, 213, 216.

8. Snow is quoted in "American Woman Suffrage Association Proceedings, California Report," *Woman's Journal* 9 (Nov. 30, 1878): 382; Mrs. Fannie Wood, "American Woman Suffrage Association Proceedings, California Report," *Woman's Journal* 17 (Nov. 20, 1886): 370; Ethington, *Public City*, 326–27, 331.

9. Elizabeth A. Kingsbury, "Woman Suffrage in California," *Woman's Journal* 18 (Sept. 3, 1887): 282; for more information regarding Kingsbury, see Sherry J. Katz, "Dual Commitments: Feminism, Socialism, and Women's Political Activism in California, 1890–1920" (Ph.D. diss., University of California at Los Angeles, 1991), 66–67.

10. Knox Goodrich, "American Woman Suffrage Association Proceedings," 307.

11. Bennion, *Equal to the Occasion*, 59–62; Nancy Ann Yamane, "Women, Power, and the Press: The Case of San Francisco, 1868 to 1896" (Ph.D. diss., University of California at Los Angeles, 1995), 288–90. For more information regarding Pitts Stevens, see *San Francisco Call*, Nov. 1, 1891.

12. Suzanne M. Marilley, "Frances Willard and the Feminism of Fear," *Feminist Studies* 19 (Spring 1993): 123–46; Barbara Leslie Epstein, *The Politics of Domesticity: Women, Evangelism, and Temperance in Nineteenth-Century America* (Middletown, Conn.: Wesleyan University Press, 1981), 115–16; Ruth Bordin, *Woman and Temperance: The Quest for Power and Liberty, 1873–1900* (Philadelphia: Temple University Press, 1981), 118–20, 135, 131–32; Mari Jo Buhle, *Women and American Socialism, 1870–1920* (Urbana: University of Illinois Press, 1981), 60–70; DuBois, *Feminism and Suffrage*, 50, 182; Jack S. Blocker Jr., *American Temperance Movements: Cycles of Reform* (Boston: Twayne, 1989), 79–85.

13. Suzanne Lebsock, "Women and American Politics, 1880–1920," in *Women, Politics, and Change,* ed. Louise A. Tilly and Patricia Gurin (New York: Russell Sage Foundation, 1990), 35–62, esp. 38–41. For discussions of women's moral influence, see Nancy F. Cott, *The Bonds of Womanhood: "Woman's Sphere" in New England, 1780–1835* (New Haven, Conn.: Yale University Press, 1977), and Peggy Pascoe, *Relations of Rescue: The Search for Female Moral Authority in the American West, 1874–1939* (Oxford: Oxford University Press, 1990).

14. Material quoted appears in California WCTU, *Yearbook 1880* (Petaluma, Calif.: Courier, 1880), 3. See also California WCTU, *Yearbook 1883* (San Francisco: Winterburn, 1883), 6–8; Dorcas James Spencer, *A History of Woman's Christian Temperance Union of Northern and Central California* (Oakland, Calif.: West Coast Printing, 1913?), 16–18, 23–24, 32; Mary Alderman Garbutt, *Victories of Four Decades: A History of the Woman's Christian Temperance Union of Southern California, 1883–1924* (Los Angeles: Woman's Christian Temperance Union of Southern California, 1924), 15–16.

15. Material quoted appears in California WCTU, *Yearbook 1881* (San Francisco: Winterburn, 1881), 33–35. See also California WCTU, *Yearbook 1884* (Oakland, Calif.: Tribune Steam Printing, 1884), 50–58; California WCTU, *Yearbook 1885* (Oakland, Calif.: Oakland Evening Tribune, 1885), 53–69; California WCTU, *Yearbook 1889* (San Francisco: Bacon and Book and Job Printers, 1889), 39, 53–63; Spencer, *History,* 111; Garbutt, *Victories of Four Decades,* 108.

16. Frank Browne is quoted in California WCTU, *Yearbook 1881,* 10–13. See also Frances E. Willard and Mary A. Livermore, eds., *Portraits and Biographies of Prominent American Women,* vol. 1 (New York: Crowell and Kirkpatrick, 1901), 131–32; California WCTU, *Yearbook 1886* (Oakland, Calif.: Oakland Evening Tribune, 1886), 43.

17. Material quoted appears in California WCTU, *Yearbook 1880,* 6–7, 14–15. See also Spencer, *History,* 23–24.

18. Willard and Livermore, *Portraits and Biographies,* vol. 1, 131–32; Pascoe, *Relations of Rescue,* 11; Bennion, *Equal to the Occasion,* 46–49. For further information regarding women's activism in religious associations, see Anne Firor Scott, *Natural Allies: Women's Associations in American History* (Urbana: University of Illinois Press, 1991), 85–110.

19. Norton Mezvinsky, "The White-Ribboned Reform, 1874–1920" (Ph.D. diss., University of Wisconsin, 1959), 147–49; Norton Mezvinsky, "Scientific Temperance Instruction in the Schools," *History of Education Quarterly* 1 (Mar. 1961): 48–49; Gilman Ostrander, "The Prohibition Movement in California, 1848–1933" (Ph.D. diss., University of California at Berkeley, 1954), 60–61; Spencer, *History,* 138–39; Bordin, *Woman and Temperance,* 135–39; Blocker, *American Temperance Movements,* 82.

20. Material quoted appears in California WCTU, *Yearbook 1884,* 21. See also Marilley, "Francis Willard," 130–33; Lebsock, "Women and American Politics," 41.

21. Frances E. Willard, "Scientific Temperance Instruction in the Public Schools," *Arena* 12 (Mar. 1895): 16.

22. California WCTU, *Yearbook 1880*, 15; California WCTU, *Yearbook 1881*, 14–16, 18–26, 35–36, 43–44; California WCTU, *Yearbook 1882* (Oakland, Calif.: Tribune Steam Printing, 1882), 18–21, 22–23; Spencer, *History*, 24–25, 39–40.

23. Material quoted appears in California WCTU, *Yearbook 1883*, 9–13. See also California WCTU, *Yearbook 1880*, 3, 7–10, 14; California WCTU, *Yearbook 1881*, 14–16.

24. California WCTU, *Yearbook 1884*, 31–36, 72–79; *San Francisco Chronicle*, Oct. 18, 1888; Spencer, *History*, 36–37.

25. California WCTU, *Yearbook 1885*, 82–87; California WCTU, *Yearbook 1886*, 18, 25–27, 43, 51, 82–87; Spencer, *History*, 24–25, 39–40; Garbutt, *Victories of Four Decades*, 118–21.

26. As quoted in California WCTU, *Yearbook 1886*, 25–27, 30.

27. *San Jose Report*, May 29, 1895; Mary McHenry Keith, "Personal Reminiscences," n.d., Keith-McHenry-Pond Family Papers, Bancroft Library, University of California at Berkeley. See also "Sarah M. Severance," *Pacific Ensign* 6 (Apr. 30, 1896): 2; Augusta C. Bainbridge, "Sarah M. Severance," *Pacific Ensign* 15 (Sept. 21, 1905): 1, 6; Spencer, *History*, 126; *San Francisco Call*, Apr. 17, 1896; *Gilroy Advocate*, Mar. 9, 1928; S. [Sarah] M. Severance, "A Word from California," *Woman's Journal* 17 (July 3, 1886): 210.

28. The resolution appears in California WCTU, *Yearbook 1886*, 43, 69–70. See also Spencer, *History*, 35–36, 138–39; California WCTU, *Yearbook 1889*, 94–95; Severance, "Word from California," 210.

29. Spencer, *History*, 9–15; see also Ostrander, "Prohibition Movement," 39–58.

30. Spencer, *History*, 43–45. See also California WCTU, *Yearbook 1887* (Oakland, Calif.: Oakland Evening Tribune, 1887), 107–11, 44; Mezvinsky, "White-Ribboned Reform," 155, 161–62, 154; *San Francisco Call*, Feb. 8, 10, and 11, 1887; *Sacramento Bee*, Feb. 10, 1887.

31. Material quoted appears in California WCTU, *Yearbook 1888* (Woodland, Calif.: Pacific Press, 1888), 35–36. Specifically, the northern California WCTU had 1,257 members in 1887 and 3,321 in 1888. The southern California WCTU had 1,400 members in 1888. California WCTU, *Yearbook 1893* (San Francisco: Brunt, 1893), 83; California WCTU, *Yearbook 1889*, 35–36, 46–48; Mary E. Garbutt, "Historical Sketch of the Woman's Christian Temperance Union of Southern California, 1883–1908," leaflet, WCTU Archives of Southern California, WCTU, Los Angeles.

32. Dorcas J. Spencer, "The Corresponding Secretary," *Pharos* 4 (Nov. 1889): 7.

33. Quoted in California WCTU, *Yearbook 1889*, 39; Nancy F. Cott, *The Grounding of Modern Feminism* (New Haven, Conn.: Yale University Press, 1987), 18–20.

34. Gordon is described in California WCTU, *Yearbook 1889*, 113–14 (see also 53–55 and 140–41). See also Elisabeth A. Kingsbury, "American Woman Suffrage Association Proceedings, California Report," *Woman's Journal* 19 (Dec. 29, 1888): 414; Sarah M. Severance, "American Woman Suffrage Association Proceedings, California Report," *Woman's Journal* 20 (Jan. 19, 1889): 18; Emma Harriman, "Good Work in Southern California," *Woman's Journal* 20 (Feb. 9, 1889): 42; M.E.G., "Los Angeles Woman Suf-

frage Club," *Woman's Journal* 20 (Mar. 9, 1889): 75; Elizabeth A. Kingsbury, "California Moving for Suffrage," *Woman's Journal* 20 (Mar. 16, 1889): 85; Laura de Force Gordon, "School Suffrage Postponed in California," *Woman's Journal* 20 (May 4, 1889): 138; Alice Moore McComas, "Woman Suffrage in California," *Woman's Journal* 20 (Aug. 3, 1889): 248; Sarah M. Severance, "The Suffrage Work in California," *Woman's Journal* 20 (Sept. 14, 1889): 290. For the relationship between temperance forces and suffragists in the West, see Buhle, *Women and American Socialism,* 62–63; Bordin, *Woman and Temperance,* 118–20, 135.

35. Ella Giles Ruddy, ed., *The Mother of Clubs: Caroline M. Seymour Severance* (Los Angeles: Baumgardt, 1906), 24, 44, 50; Mrs. William A. Spalding, "Madame Severance and the First Women's Club of Los Angeles—1878," Oct. 1935, unpublished paper bound in "How Firm a Foundation" Collection, Friday Morning Club Archives, Friday Morning Club, Los Angeles; Mrs. M. Burton Williamson, *Ladies' Clubs and Societies in Los Angeles in 1892, Reported for the Historical Society of Southern California, March 1892* (Los Angeles: Elmer R. King, 1925), 22–23; untitled speech by Caroline Severance, 1904, Caroline Severance Collection (hereafter, Severance Collection), Huntington Library, San Marino, Calif.; Sara Marie Stanley, "Caroline M. Severance: Feminist and Reformer, 1820–1914" (senior thesis, Scripps College, Claremont, Calif., 1978), 50–58, 84–85; Karen J. Blair, *The Clubwoman as Feminist: True Womanhood Redefined, 1868–1914* (New York: Homes and Meier, 1980), 34–35; Julia Sprague, *A History of the New England Women's Club* (Boston: Lee and Shepard, 1894), 8; Buhle, *Women and American Socialism,* 57–58; see also John A. Garraty, ed., *American National Biography* (Oxford: Oxford University Press, 1999).

36. The *Los Angeles Herald* is cited in Spalding, "Madame Severance." See also Blair, *Clubwoman as Feminist,* 34; Stanley, "Caroline M. Severance," 81; *San Francisco Call,* June 8, 1896.

37. Spalding, "Madame Severance." See also Blair, *Clubwoman as Feminist,* 34; Stanley, "Caroline M. Severance," 80–83, 90–91; *San Francisco Call,* June 8, 1896; Los Angeles Woman's Club, Constitution and By-Laws, Severance Collection; *Los Angeles Herald,* Sept. 18, 1886; John D. K. Perry, *A History of the First Unitarian Church of Los Angeles, California, 1877–1937* (Los Angeles, 1937), 5–17; Buhle, *Women and American Socialism,* 77–78; Ruddy, *Mother of Clubs,* 64–67, 90–94.

38. Williamson, *Ladies' Clubs,* 24–28; Los Angeles Woman's Club, Constitution and By-Laws, 3; Ruddy, *Mother of Clubs,* 44, 46, 50; Los Angeles Woman's Club, Minutes, Jan. 15–Mar. 7, Apr. 3, and Oct. 31, 1885, Severance Collection; Los Angeles Free Kindergarten Association, Severance Collection.

39. Material quoted appears in "The Need of a Woman's Home," otherwise unidentified news clipping, Flower Festival Society Collection, Huntington Library, Los Angeles. See also Los Angeles Woman's Club, Minutes, Mar. 7, 1885, Severance Collection; Harris Newmark, *Sixty Years in Southern California, 1853–1913* (New York: Knickerbocker, 1916), 555–56.

40. Barbara Laslett, "Women's Work in Late-Nineteenth-Century Los Angeles:

Class, Gender, and the Culture of New Womanhood," *Continuity and Change* 5 (1990): 417–41, esp. 424, 431–32, 435.

41. Alice Kessler-Harris, *Out to Work: A History of Wage-Earning Women in the United States* (Oxford: Oxford University Press, 1982), 108–41; Kathryn Kish Sklar, *Florence Kelley and the Nation's Work: The Rise of Women's Political Culture* (New Haven, Conn.: Yale University Press, 1995), 71; Joseph A. Hill, *Women in Gainful Occupations, 1870–1920* (Washington, D.C.: GPO, 1929), 19, 30–31; Buhle, *Women and American Socialism,* 55–66; Joanne J. Meyerowitz, *Women Adrift: Independent Wage Earners in Chicago, 1880–1930* (Chicago: University of Chicago Press, 1988), 43–68; Scott, *Natural Allies,* 85–110.

42. Gayle Gullett, "Feminism, Politics, and Voluntary Groups: Organized Womanhood in California, 1886–1896 (Ph.D. diss., University of California at Riverside, 1983), 22–26; see also Gloria Ricci Lothrop, "Strength Made Stronger: The Role of Women in Southern California Philanthropy," *Southern California Quarterly* 71 (1989): 143–94.

43. Los Angeles Woman's Club, Minutes, Apr. 3, 1885, Severance Collection; Williamson, *Ladies' Clubs,* 25–26, 43; Jessie Benton Fremont, *Far-West Sketches* (Boston: Lothrop, 1890), 40–41; Jane Apostol, "They Said It with Flowers: The Los Angeles Flower Festival Society," *Southern California Quarterly* 62 (Spring 1980): 68–70; *Los Angeles Herald,* Mar. 2 and Oct. 23, 1887.

44. Material quoted comes from the Flower Festival Society's leaflet, *Woman's Exchange of the Flower Festival Society,* Flower Festival Society Collection, Huntington Library. See also Apostol, "They Said It with Flowers," 70; from Flower Festival Society Collection, Huntington Library: "Need of a Woman's Home"; Flower Festival Society, Constitution and By-Laws; Boarding Home of the Flower Festival Society, Rules and Regulations. Also see *Los Angeles Herald,* Oct. 23, 1887 and Nov. 16 and June 10, 1888. At the end of the nineteenth century, the Flower Festival Society gave its home to the Salvation Army. See "The Depot Work of the W.C.T.U.," *White Ribbon* 11 (Oct. 1899): 3.

45. Material quoted appears in *Los Angeles Herald,* Mar. 2, 1886. See also the edition of June 10, 1888; Mary Barnes Widney, "To the Members of the Flower Festival Society," 1–10, unpublished speech, Flower Festival Society Collection; Apostol, "They Said It with Flowers," 70.

46. For the leaders' views on poor working conditions, see *Los Angeles Herald,* June 10, 1888; Widney is quoted in Apostol, "They Said It with Flowers," 70–71.

47. *Los Angeles Herald,* Oct. 23, 1887; Boarding Home of the Flower Festival Society, Rules and Regulations, Flower Festival Society Collection. See also Apostol, "They Said It with Flowers," 70–71.

48. Williamson, *Ladies' Clubs,* 44–49; *Los Angeles Herald,* Apr. 23, 1887; Glen S. Dumke, *The Boom of the Eighties in Southern California* (San Marino, Calif.: Huntington Library, 1944), 9. The *Herald* stated that the profit for 1887 was $7,500, but Williamson claims it was $7,000.

49. Apostol, "They Said It with Flowers," 68–73; *Los Angeles Herald,* Apr. 13, 1887, Dec. 3, 1886, Apr. 24, 1887.

50. For quotes by and about Widney see *Los Angeles Herald,* Apr. 11, 1886; *Los Angeles Herald,* Sept. 18, 1886; Widney, "To the Members of the Flower Festival Society," 1–10. For information regarding Widney's husband, see Remi Nadeau, *Los Angeles: From Mission to Modern City* (New York: Longman, Green, 1960), 59–60, 66, 68–69, 73.

51. Jane E. Collier, "Early Club Life in Los Angeles," *Historical Society of Southern California Quarterly* 4 (1899): 221; "The Friday Morning Club," *Land of Sunshine* 5 (Aug. 1896): 133; Spalding, "Madame Severance"; Gregory H. Singleton, "Religion in the City of Angels: American Protestant Culture and Urbanization, Los Angeles, 1850–1930" (Ph.D. diss., University of California at Los Angeles, 1976), 67–68.

52. The Severance quote appears in her untitled paper, June 30, 1899, Friday Morning Club Collection, Special Collections, University of California at Los Angeles; Alice Marian Chapman, "Madame Severance—The Founder of Women's Clubs" (master's thesis, University of Southern California, 1930); Mrs. Henry Christian Crowther, *High Lights: The Friday Morning Club, 1891–1939* (Los Angeles: Quill, 1939), 13–14; Willard and Livermore, *Portraits and Biographies,* vol. 2, 551–52; Charter Member List, Friday Morning Club Archives, Friday Morning Club, Los Angeles; Singleton, "Religion in the City of Angeles," 67–68.

53. Ruddy, *Mother of Clubs,* 24, 44; Crowther, *High Lights,* 13–16; *Los Angeles Times,* Aug. 2–8, 1891. For the *Los Angeles Times's* opinion regarding politics in the schools, see esp. the front-page cartoon of Aug. 5, 1891.

54. For material quoted see *Los Angeles Times,* Aug. 2, 1891, as well as the editions of Aug. 8 and Oct. 24. On October 24, the *Los Angeles Times* reported that twelve teachers were returned to their positions, but Crowther says that thirteen were eventually restored to their posts. Crowther, *High Lights,* 15–16; Emma Harriman, "School of Methods at Long Beach," *Woman's Journal* 22 (Aug. 22, 1891): 274.

55. *Los Angeles Times,* Aug. 2, Aug. 6, Aug. 8, Aug. 15, Aug. 18, Sept. 12, Sept. 23–29, and Oct. 14, 1891, and June 28, 1892; Margaret Minot Fette, "Friday Morning Club of Los Angeles," 1893?, Friday Morning Club Archives; Emma Harriman, "Southern California Notes," *Woman's Journal* 22 (Oct. 17, 1891): 332; Friday Morning Club, Minutes, July 1, 1892, Friday Morning Club Archives.

56. Friday Morning Club, Minutes, June 24, July 1, July 8, Oct. 28, Nov. 4, 1892, and Feb. 24 and Apr. 7, 1893; the material quoted is from Dec. 1, 1893; *Los Angeles Times,* June 13, June 16, July 9, Sept. 12, and Dec. 10, 1892; Fette, "Friday Morning Club," 7. Regarding Galpin's campaign, see Friday Morning Club, Minutes, Apr. 20 and 27, and June 16, 22, and 27, 1894; *Los Angeles Times,* Sept. 5–Nov. 4, 1894; regarding Galpin, see "The Woman's Parliament of Southern California," *Land of Sunshine* 8 (May 1898): 284–89, esp. 286, and Willard and Livermore, *Portraits and Biographies,* vol. 1, 311.

57. Friday Morning Club, Minutes, 1891–1895, esp. June 10 and 17, 1892, Mar. 24, 1893, Nov. 10 and 24, 1893, Oct. 5 and 12, 1894, Mar. 8, 1895, and Apr. 26, 1895; Laslett, "Women's Work," 431–32, 435.

58. For quoted material see Charlotte Perkins Gilman, "Our Place Today," in *Char-*

lotte Perkins Gilman: A Nonfiction Reader, ed. Larry Ceplair (New York: Columbia University Press, 1991), 53–61; Gail Bederman, *Manliness and Civilization: A Cultural History of Gender and Race in the United States, 1880–1917* (Chicago: University of Chicago Press, 1995), 130. Gilman spoke to the Friday Morning Club during its first six months; her talk was entitled "Our Excessive Femininity." See Williamson, *Ladies' Clubs*, 80–81.

59. For material quoted see Gilman, "Our Place Today," 53–61, esp. 61, and Friday Morning Club, Minutes, Apr. 26, 1895, 119–20. See also Bederman, *Manliness and Civilization*, 121–69. Women in the national women's movement usually perceived the "New Woman" in the same elitist manner. See Sara Hunter Graham, *Woman Suffrage and the New Democracy* (New Haven, Conn.: Yale University Press, 1996), 28–30.

60. Material quoted appears in *Woman's Parliament of Southern California: A Magazine of Papers Read at the Woman's Parliament Held at Los Angeles, California, November 15–16, 1892*, vol. 1 (Los Angeles, n.d.), 1; *Los Angeles Times*, Oct. 11, and Feb. 16, 1893. The parliament invited women to join from the following counties: San Diego, San Bernardino, Orange, Los Angeles, Ventura, Santa Barbara, and (later) Riverside.

61. Material quoted appears in *Los Angeles Times*, Feb. 12 and 16, 1893. See also *Woman's Parliament of Southern California*, 1–2; *Los Angeles Times*, Nov. 16, 1892, and Oct. 11, 1893; Garbutt, *Victories of Four Decades*, 41–42.

62. Unfortunately, lists of the organizations that sent delegates and of the individuals who attended the parliament have not been preserved. A careful reading of the newspaper accounts of the three sessions of the parliament from the fall of 1892 to the fall of 1893 produced a general impression of the organizations that sent delegates. Many delegates belonged to several groups; the percentages given reflect the organization each delegate officially represented at the parliament. *Woman's Parliament of Southern California*, 2; Williamson, *Ladies' Clubs*, 30; *Los Angeles Times*, Feb. 12 and 16, 1893, Nov. 11 and 16, 1892, and Oct. 11–12, 1893; Mary S. Gibson, *A Record of Twenty-five Years of the California Federation of Women's Clubs, 1900–1925* (California Federation of Women's Clubs, 1927), 4.

63. *Woman's Parliament of Southern California*, 3–4, 8–14; *Los Angeles Times*, Nov. 11, 15, and 16, 1892, and Feb. 16, 12, and 17, and Oct. 11 and 12, 1893; Garbutt, *Victories of Four Decades*, 100; Margaret M. Fette, "Woman's Parliament in Southern California," *Woman's Journal* 26 (Nov. 16, 1895): 368.

64. Mary S. Gibson, "Reform in Philanthropists," in *Woman's Parliament of Southern California*, 7–14.

65. Ibid.; Lori D. Ginzburg, *Women and the Work of Benevolence: Morality, Politics, and Class in the Nineteenth-Century United States* (New Haven, Conn.: Yale University Press, 1990), 174–213, esp. 197–98; Friday Morning Club, *Mary S. Gibson: Pioneer Memorial, Los Angeles, California, 1930, Presented by "The Friday Morning Club" to Mrs. Gibson's Friends and Co-Workers, in Grateful Appreciation* (Los Angeles, 1930), 1–2, 33; Reda Davis, *California Women: A Guide to Their Politics, 1885–1911* (San Francisco: California Scene, 1967), 153–54; Judith Raftery, "Los Angeles Clubwomen and

Progressive Reform," in *California Progressivism Revisited,* ed. William Deverell and Tom Sitton (Berkeley: University of California Press, 1994), 153.

66. For material quoted see Gibson, "Reform in Philanthropists," 16, 14; *Los Angeles Times,* Nov. 16, 1892, and Feb. 17, 1893. See also *Los Angeles Times,* Apr. 6, 1892; Susan B. Anthony and Ida Husted Harper, *History of Woman's Suffrage,* vol. 4 (Indianapolis, Ind.: Hollenbeck, 1902), 495; Perry, *History of the First Unitarian Church,* 8; *White Ribbon* 5 (Mar. 1893): 2.

67. Material quoted appears in Mary Lynde Craig, *Is Legislation Needed for Women? An Address . . . Read Before the Women's Parliament of Southern California,* 2d ed. (Redlands, Calif.: Citrograph Power Press, 1894), 5. See also Anthony and Harper, *History of Woman Suffrage,* vol. 4, 495. For information regarding McComas, see Willard and Livermore, *Portraits and Biographies,* vol. 2, 483–84, and "A Gifted California Woman," *Woman's Journal* 25 (Oct. 27, 1894): 338.

68. For material quoted see Caroline Cooke Jackson, Katherine Chandler, and Elisie Wenzelburger Graupner, *A Sketch of the History of the Association of Collegiate Alumnae California Branch, 1886–1911* (San Francisco: Paul Elder, 1911), 2–5, 8. The Pacific Association of Collegiate Alumnae later became the San Francisco Bay Branch of the American Association of University Women. Marion Talbot and Lois Kimball Mathews Rosenberry, *The History of the American Association of University Women, 1881–1931* (Boston: Houghton Mifflin, 1931), 100, 65–71; Pacific Association of Collegiate Alumnae, "Sketch of the Pacific Association of Collegiate Alumnae," San Francisco, 1892, 2–5; William L. O'Neill, *Everyone Was Brave: A History of Feminism in America* (Chicago: Quadrangle, 1969), 79. The National Association of Collegiate Alumnae accepted the Pacific Association of Collegiate Alumnae as its third branch in March 1886.

69. The description of the Collegiate Alumnae's membership is based on the only pre-1906 membership list that survived the earthquake (Pacific Association of Collegiate Alumnae, "Sketch," 2–5); Jackson, Chandler, and Graupner, *Sketch,* 2–10. Regarding standards of admission into the city's elite, see Peter Decker, *Fortunes and Failures: White-Collar Mobility in Nineteenth-Century San Francisco* (Cambridge, Mass.: Harvard University Press, 1978), 232–35, and Gunther Barth, "Metropolism and Urban Elites in the Far West," in *The Age of Industrialism in America: Essays in Social Structure and Cultural Values,* ed. Frederic Cople Jaher (New York: Free Press, 1968), 158–87.

70. Jackson, Chandler, and Graupner, *Sketch,* 13–14, 19, 4, 8–10, 36–37; Talbot and Rosenberry, *History of the AAUW,* 100–102, 210–11, 220; *San Francisco Call,* Feb. 14, 1890.

71. American Association of University Women, "Outline of the History of the San Francisco Bay Branch, 1886–1930," v; Talbot and Rosenberry, *History of the AAUW,* 101. Caroline Jackson was consistently listed in the San Francisco Blue Book as an individual, not with a family.

72. Milicent Shinn, "Poverty and Charity in San Francisco I," *Overland Monthly* 14

(Nov. 1899): 536, 538, 541; see also Shinn, "Poverty and Charity in San Francisco II," *Overland Monthly* 14 (Dec. 1899): 586–92; Ginzburg, *Women and the Work of Benevolence*, 174–213.

73. Pacific Association of Collegiate Alumnae, "Sketch," 7; Keith's recollection appears in Mary McHenry Keith, undated, untitled manuscript, Keith-McHenry-Pond Family Papers.

74. *San Francisco Chronicle,* Oct. 24 and Sept. 8, 1886; William A. Bullough, *The Blind Boss and His City: Christopher Augustine Buckley and Nineteenth-Century San Francisco* (Berkeley: University of California Press, 1979), 130–32, 148–50; Ethington, *Public City,* 332–33.

75. Ethington, *Public City,* 289–301; William Issel and Robert W. Cherny, *San Francisco, 1865–1932: Politics, Power, and Urban Development* (Berkeley: University of California Press, 1986), 130–34; Bullough, *Blind Boss,* 130–32, 148–49.

76. Bullough, *Blind Boss,* 130–32, 148–50, 221; Issel and Cherny, *San Francisco,* 132–34.

77. Material quoted appears in *San Francisco Bulletin,* Oct. 21, 1886. See also *San Francisco Chronicle,* Oct. 16 and 27, 1886; L.L., "Women's Campaign in San Francisco," *Woman's Journal* 17 (Nov. 20, 1886): 376; Bullough, *Blind Boss,* 167–68; M. [Milicent] W. Shinn, "Women as School-Directors," *Overland Monthly* 8 (Dec. 1886): 632; M., "The San Francisco School Board," *Woman's Journal* 17 (Nov. 6, 1886): 359.

78. *San Francisco Bulletin,* Oct. 21, 1886; *San Francisco Chronicle,* Oct. 16 and 27, 1886; L.L., "Women's Campaign," 376. Sarah Hamlin, May Treat, Mary Campbell, and Cordelia Kirkland were endorsed by the Independent Republicans, Citizen's Independents, the Committee of Two Hundred, the Labor Party, and the Prohibition Party. Mrs. G. K. Phillips was endorsed by Citizen's Independents, the Committee of Two Hundred and the Labor and Prohibition parties, and Miss Green by Citizen's Independents and the Committee of Two Hundred.

79. *San Francisco Bulletin,* Oct. 21, 1886.

80. Ibid.; Shinn, "Women as School-Directors," 632; "San Francisco School Board," 359; *San Francisco Chronicle,* Oct. 16 and 27, 1886. The Pacific Association of Collegiate Alumnae may well have participated in the election as an organization, as well as contributing leaders; however, the records are too scanty to verify this.

81. *San Francisco Bulletin,* Oct. 21 and 27, 1886; *San Francisco Chronicle,* Oct. 6, 9, and 10, 1886. Material quoted appears in L.L., "Women's Campaign," 376.

82. Shinn, "Women as School-Directors," 632; L.L., "Women's Campaign," 376.

83. Ethington, *Public City,* 332, 334–35; Ira Katznelson and Margaret Weir, *Schooling for All: Class, Race, and the Decline of the Democratic Ideal* (New York: Basic, 1985), 65–68, 90, 108; Issel and Cherny, *San Francisco,* 104.

84. James, James, and Boyer, *Notable American Women,* vol. 2, 328–29; Ethington, *Public City,* 333–35; material quoted appears in A.S.B. [Alice Stone Blackwell], "Woman's Christian Suffrage Society," *Woman's Journal* 14 (Oct. 13, 1883): 321; "Woman's

Christian Suffrage Association of California," *Woman's Journal* 14 (Dec. 29, 1883): 417; Catherine Ann Curry, "Three Irish Women and Social Action in San Francisco: Mother Teresa Comerford, Mother Baptist Russell, and Kate Kennedy," *Journal of the West* 31 (1992): 66–72, esp. 70–72.

85. Material quoted appears in L.L., "Women's Campaign," 376, and "San Francisco School Board," 359. See also *San Francisco Bulletin,* Oct. 28, 1886.

86. L.L., "Women's Campaign," 376; R. Hal Williams, *The Democratic Party and California Politics, 1880–1896* (Palo Alto, Calif.: Stanford University Press, 1973), 104–107; *San Francisco Chronicle,* Nov. 6, 1886, and Oct. 18, 1888; M. W. Shinn, "Women on School Boards," *Overland Monthly* 12 (Nov. 1888): 547–54, esp. 552; "Women on San Francisco School Board," *Woman's Journal* 19 (Dec. 8, 1888): 392; Shinn is quoted in Shinn, "Women as School-Directors," 633.

87. Jane Cunningham Croly, *The History of the Woman's Club Movement in America* (New York: Henry G. Allen, 1898), 249, 251; Pacific Association of Collegiate Alumnae, "Sketch"; Jackson, Chandler, and Graupner, *Sketch,* 2–5; Century Club, *Twenty-fourth Annual Report* (San Francisco, 1910), 46–47, 74–75.

88. Gullett, "Feminism, Politics, and Voluntary Groups," 16–27; Ethington, *Public City,* 331–32.

89. Croly, *History of the Woman's Club Movement,* 249–51; Blair, *Clubwoman as Feminist,* 25–29, 31–38; Shinn, "Women as School-Directors," 629–32; "Mrs. Howe in California," *Woman's Journal* 19 (July 21, 1888): 227; Century Club, Constitution and By-Laws, Bancroft Library, University of California at Berkeley, 3, 8, 18, 20–21; Century Club, *Twenty-fourth Annual Report,* 74–75.

90. Century Club, *Twenty-fourth Annual Report,* 47, 74–75; *San Francisco Chronicle,* Oct. 19 and 27, 1888; Bullough, *Blind Boss,* 190; *San Francisco Examiner,* Oct. 30, 1888.

91. "Women School Directors in San Francisco," *Woman's Journal* 19 (Nov. 10, 1888): 358; *San Francisco Chronicle,* Oct. 6, 11, 13, 17, and 18, and Nov. 2, 1888; *San Francisco Examiner,* Oct. 15, 17, 18, and 31, 1888.

92. Ibid. Theall is quoted in *San Francisco Examiner,* Oct. 17, 1888.

93. Material quoted appears in Shinn, "Women on School Boards," 552, and *San Francisco Chronicle,* Oct. 16, 1888. See also "Women on San Francisco School Board," *Woman's Journal* 19 (Dec. 8, 1888): 392, and the *Chronicle,* Oct. 11, 1888.

94. *San Francisco Examiner,* Oct. 17, 1888.

95. *Argonaut* 23 (Nov. 5, 1888): 3; Williams, *Democratic Party,* 104–107; *Argonaut* 23 (Oct. 22, 1888): 2; *San Francisco Chronicle,* Oct. 20, 1888; "Women on San Francisco School Board," 392; Bullough, *Blind Boss,* 112–14, 167–81, 183, 203–204.

96. *San Francisco Examiner,* Oct. 21, 1888; *San Francisco Chronicle,* Oct. 20, 1888.

97. *San Francisco Chronicle,* Oct. 14 and 16, 1888.

98. *San Francisco Chronicle,* Oct. 17–20, 1888; "Women School Directors in San Francisco," 358; *San Francisco Examiner,* Oct. 19, 1888.

99. For material quoted see *San Francisco Chronicle,* Oct. 18, 1888. See also *Chroni-*

cle, Oct. 19, 1888; *San Francisco Examiner,* Oct. 30–31, 1888; "Women on the San Francisco School Board," 392.

100. For material quoted see *San Francisco Chronicle,* Oct. 19, and Shinn, "Women on School Boards," 554. See also *Chronicle,* Oct. 18, 1888; *San Francisco Examiner,* Oct. 30–31, 1888; "Women on the San Francisco School Board," 392.

101. Material quoted appears in *San Francisco Chronicle,* Oct. 19, 1888. See also *Chronicle,* Oct. 20, 1888; Robert M. Fogelson, *Big-City Police* (Cambridge, Mass.: Harvard University Press, 1977), 13–39; Alexander Callow, "San Francisco's Blind Boss," *Pacific Historical Review* 42 (Aug. 1956): 267.

102. For material quoted see *San Francisco Chronicle,* Oct. 20, 1888. See also *Chronicle,* Oct. 19, 1888.

103. *Argonaut* 23 (Nov. 19, 1888): 3.

104. *San Francisco Examiner,* Oct. 17, 1888. Also see the *Examiner* for Oct. 18, and 31, 1888.

105. *San Francisco Examiner,* Oct. 14, 1888; *Argonaut* 23 (Oct. 22, 1888): 3.

106. The rumors are described in "Women on the San Francisco School Board," 392. See also *San Francisco Chronicle,* Oct. 27, 1888; Shinn, "Women on School Boards," 554; Bullough, *Blind Boss,* 170.

107. Material quoted appears in *San Francisco Chronicle,* Nov. 4, 1888, and "Women on the San Francisco School Board," 392. See also Bullough, *Blind Boss,* 122, 131; *Chronicle,* Oct. 20, 1888; Shinn, "Women on the School Boards," 554. For a defense of the teachers' positions, see *Argonaut* 23 (Nov. 19, 1888): 3, and *San Francisco Chronicle,* Oct. 27, 1888.

108. Mrs. Pescia, wife of a city supervisor, stated that although she supported the women candidates, it was a mistake not to nominate a single Catholic woman. (No Jewish woman was nominated, either.) Pescia felt the Republicans were to blame for this error, but the evidence is simply too scanty to determine the extent to which the Republicans and the Reform Association each were to blame. *San Francisco Examiner,* Oct. 17, 1888; Bullough, *Blind Boss,* 204–205, 93, 169–70; *San Francisco Chronicle,* Oct. 20, 1888; *Argonaut* 23 (Oct. 29, 1888): 1; *Argonaut* 23 (Oct. 22, 1888): 3; *Argonaut* 23 (Nov. 12, 1888): 2–3; Katznelson and Weir, *Schooling for All,* 66, 90, 107–108; Issel and Cherny, *San Francisco,* 56, 144; David B. Tyack, *The One Best System: A History of American Urban Education* (Cambridge, Mass.: Harvard University Press, 1974), 104–106; Janet A. Nolan, "Irish-American Teachers and the Struggle over American Urban Public Education, 1890–1920: A Preliminary Look," *Records of the American Catholic Historical Society* 103 (1992): 13–22.

109. Material quoted appears in *San Francisco Chronicle,* Oct. 18, 1888, and *Argonaut* 23 (Oct. 29, 1888): 1. See also Bullough, *Blind Boss,* 204–205, 93, 169–70; *Chronicle,* Oct. 20, and 27–28, 1888; *Argonaut* 23 (Oct. 22, 1888): 3; *Argonaut* 23 (Nov. 12, 1888): 2–3; "Women on the San Francisco School Board," 392; Shinn, "Women on School Boards," 554. For information regarding Kate Kennedy see *San Francisco Examiner,*

Oct. 26, 1888. Mrs. Theall was also listed as Mrs. S. M. Theall and L. M. Theall. See "Woman's Christian Suffrage Association of California," *Woman's Journal* 14 (Dec. 29, 1883): 417; L. M. Theall, "Defeated by Fraud in California," *Woman's Journal* 16 (Apr. 4, 1885): 112; Sarah Knox Goodrich, "California Report," *Woman's Journal* 16 (Nov. 28, 1885): 378.

110. Shinn, "Women on School Boards," 554; Bullough, *Blind Boss,* 186–88, 257–58; Jackson, Chandler, and Graupner, *Sketch,* 22–23; Tyack, *One Best System,* 160–67.

111. "Women on the San Francisco School Board," 392.

112. Buhle, *Women and American Socialism,* 58–59; Knapp is quoted in *San Francisco Chronicle,* Oct. 14, 1888; WEIU, *Sixth Annual Report* (San Francisco: Murdock, 1894), 5.

113. WEIU, *First Annual Report* (San Francisco: Murdock, 1889), 1–7; Buhle, *Women and American Socialism,* 58–59; Blair, *Clubwoman as Feminist,* 73–91; Brenda K. Shelton, *Reformers in Search of Yesterday: Buffalo in the 1890s* (Albany: State University of New York Press, 1976), 21–22; *San Francisco Examiner,* Oct. 14, 1888.

114. Buhle, *Women and American Socialism,* 53–69; Scott, *Natural Allies,* 160–62; Sklar, *Florence Kelley,* 146–47; *San Francisco Chronicle,* Feb. 2–Mar. 15, 1888. By 1890 almost 22 percent of all women in the city worked for wages; see Susan Englander, *Class Conflict and Coalition in the California Woman Suffrage Movement, 1907–1912: The San Francisco Wage Earners' Suffrage League* (Lewiston, N.Y.: Edwin Mellen Press, 1992), 26–27.

115. *San Francisco Chronicle,* Feb. 25, and Mar. 11 and 15, 1888; "Women's Work in California," *Woman's Journal* 19 (Mar. 17, 1888): 84; Reda Davis, *California Women: A Guide to Their Politics, 1885–1911* (San Francisco: California Scene, 1967), 24–44. Gordon is quoted in Ethington, *Public City,* 329. Susan Levine, "Labor's True Woman: Domesticity and Equal Rights in the Knights of Labor," *Journal of American History* 70 (1983): 323–39. The San Francisco Knights' Assembly, as the local chapter of the Knights of Labor was known, lasted until 1892. See Rebecca J. Mead, "Trade Unionism and Political Activity Among San Francisco Wage-Earning Women, 1900–1922" (master's thesis, San Francisco State University, 1991), 38.

116. Levine, "Labor's True Woman," 336–37.

117. Knapp is quoted in *San Francisco Chronicle,* Oct. 14, 1888; Campbell is quoted in WEIU, *First Annual Report,* 5–7; Eyster is quoted in WEIU, *Second Annual Report* (San Francisco: Murdock, 1890), 18–19. See also *Chronicle,* Oct. 11, 1888; WEIU, *Third Annual Report* (San Francisco: Brent, 1891), 14.

118. *San Francisco Call,* May 7, 1893; Campbell is quoted in WEIU, *First Annual Report,* 8–9 (see also 18–21). The San Francisco WEIU grew quickly, as did its eastern chapters. The San Francisco group began with seventy-eight members in October 1888 and boasted 430 members by the time of the first report in May 1889. A year later it had 626 members; see *San Francisco Chronicle,* Oct. 14, 1888; WEIU, *First Annual Report,* 14, and *Second Annual Report,* 11–12.

119. Blair, *Clubwoman as Feminist*, 73–74, 90–91; WEIU, *First Annual Report*, 27, 32, 29–31, 11–13; WEIU, *Second Annual Report*, 21–22, 33–34; WEIU, *Third Annual Report*, 32–33.

120. Hannah Marks Solomons is quoted in WEIU, *Third Annual Report*, 12–14 (see also 16, 18, 32–33). See also WEIU, *Fourth Annual Report* (San Francisco: Bancroft, 1893), 15–16, 13–14; Irene Narell, *Our City: The Jews of San Francisco* (San Diego: Howell-North Books, 1981), 394.

121. Deane to Sorbier, Feb. 20, 1891, Louise Sorbier Collection (hereafter Sorbier Collection), California Historical Society, San Francisco; WEIU, *First Annual Report*, 10; WEIU, *Third Annual Report*, 19–20; *San Francisco Call*, May 7 and 10, 1893.

122. Campbell is quoted in WEIU, *First Annual Report*, 8–9. See also Hearst to Sorbier, Dec. 30, 1893, Sorbier Collection; WEIU, *Fourth Annual Report*, 15–16; WEIU, *Sixth Annual Report*, 21; Davis, *California Women*, 44.

123. Selina Solomons, *How We Won the Vote in California: A True Story of the Campaign of 1911* (San Francisco: New Woman Publishing, 1912), 1; Century Club, *Twenty-fourth Annual Report*, 47–58; *San Francisco Call*, May 7, 1893. The Century Club by-laws are quoted in Alexandra Marie Nickliss, "Phoebe Apperson Hearst: The Most Powerful Woman in California" (Ph.D. diss., University of California at Davis, 1994), 128–29; for a discussion of the importance of education to women's clubs, see Scott, *Natural Allies*, 111–21.

124. For material quoted see Croly, *History of the Woman's Club Movement*, 253, and *San Francisco Call*, May 16, 1890. See also Clara Spalding Brown, "PCWPA," *Woman's Journal* 22 (Apr. 18, 1891): 128; Charlotte Perkins Gilman, *The Living of Charlotte Perkins Gilman: An Autobiography* (New York: Harper and Row, 1975), 130; *Call*, Sept. 28, 1890, and Mar. 15 and 17, 1891; Abbie E. Krebs, ed., *La Copa de Oro: A Collection of California Poems, Sketches, and Stories by the Members of the Pacific Association of the Woman's Press Association* (San Francisco, 1905), 113; Willard and Livermore, *Portraits and Biographies*, vol. 2, 558; Tyack, *One Best System*, 98; *Woman's Journal* 23 (June 18, 1892): 199.

125. Parkhurst is described in "Emily Tracy Y. Parkhurst," *Woman's Journal* 23 (June 18, 1892): 199; M.G.C. [Mary Grace Charlton] Edholm, "Pacific Coast Woman's Press Association," *Woman's Journal* 21 (Oct. 11, 1890): 322; *Impress* 1 (Mar. 1894): 5; *San Francisco Call*, Nov. 25, 1890; *San Francisco Examiner*, Sept. 27, 1891; Krebs, *La Copa*, 113; Susan E. Dickinson, "Women Journalists in America," in *The National Exposition Souvenir: What America Owes to Women*, ed. Lydia Hold Farmer (New York: Moulton, 1893), 210–11; Belle Grant Armstrong, "The New England Woman's Press Association—Report," in *The World's Congress of Representative Women: A Historical Resume for Popular Circulation of the World's Congress of Representative Women, Convened in Chicago on May 15, and Adjourned on May 22, 1893, Under the Auspices of the Woman's Branch of the World's Congress Auxiliary*, vol. 2, ed. May Wright Sewall (Chicago: Rand, McNally, 1894), 806–10; Yamane, "Women, Power, and the Press," 214.

126. Material quoted appears in Krebs, *La Copa,* 113. See also Armstrong, "New England Woman's Press Association," 807.

127. Material quoted appears in Edholm, "Pacific Coast Woman's Press Association," 322, and *San Francisco Call,* May 1, 1891. See also *Call,* Sept. 28, 1890, and Mar. 17, 1891; Yamane, "Women, Power, and the Press," 233.

128. *San Francisco Examiner,* Sept. 27, 1891; Parkhurst to Severance, Dec. 9, 1891, Severance Collection.

129. Yamane, "Women, Power, and the Press," 54, 229.

130. Ibid., 214–18, 227–31.

131. *San Francisco Call,* Mar. 17, 1891, May 16, 1890, and Sept. 24, 1891; Croly, *History of the Woman's Club Movement,* 253.

132. Croly, *History of the Woman's Club Movement,* 253; *San Francisco Call,* May 16, 1890, and Sept. 24, 1891. I dropped five officers because information about them was not available. *San Francisco Call,* Sept. 28, 1890, and Mar. 15, 1891; Willard and Livermore, *Portraits and Biographies,* vol. 1, 206–207, 281–82, and vol. 2, 431, 558, 796; James, James, and Boyer, *Notable American Women,* vol. 1, 380–82, and vol. 2, 38–42, and vol. 3, 605–607; Jane Apostol, "Jeanne Carr: One Woman and Sunshine," *American West* 15 (July–Aug. 1978): 28–33, 62–63; Krebs, *La Copa,* 113–18; Clare O. Southard, "The Pacific Coast Woman's Press Association," *Club Life* 2 (Apr. 1904): 5; Clare O. Southard, "P.C.W.P.A.," *Club Life* 3 (Dec. 1904): 7; *Pacific Ensign* 2 (Apr. 28, 1892): 4; Yamane, "Women, Power, and the Press," 260–61.

133. Ibid.

134. Ibid. For information regarding Gilman's reform accomplishments in the Bay Area during these years, see Ethington, *Public City,* 355–59; Mary A. Hill, *Charlotte Perkins Gilman: The Making of a Radical Feminist, 1860–1896* (Philadelphia: Temple University Press, 1980), 167–258; Ann J. Lane, *To Herland and Beyond: The Life and Work of Charlotte Perkins Gilman* (New York: Meridian, 1991), 158–81; and Ceplair, *Charlotte Perkins Gilman,* 37–43. For more information regarding Cooper and Wiggin, see Carol Marie Roland, "The California Kindergarten Movement: A Study in Class and Social Feminism" (Ph.D. diss., University of California at Riverside, 1980), 129–71.

135. Agnes M. Manning, *Because It Was a Woman's: A Paper Read Before the Woman's Press Association, March 1891* (San Francisco: Thomas, 1891), 12–13, 22–24; *San Francisco Call,* Mar. 19, 1891.

136. *San Francisco Examiner,* Sept. 27, 1891. For information regarding Keith, see F.M.A., "Women of the Press," *Woman's Journal* 25 (June 23, 1894): 194; Davis, *California Women,* 158; Willard and Livermore, *Portraits and Biographies,* vol. 2, 430–31; Yamane, "Women, Power, and the Press," 183, 261, 304–305.

137. *San Francisco Call,* Mar. 18, 1891.

138. *San Francisco Examiner,* Sept. 23, 1891 (see also Mar. 17). According to Emelie Parkhurst, the eastern press denounced the *Examiner* "in unequivocal terms for its unmannerly attacks" on the press association. See Parkhurst to Severance, Nov. 6,

1891, Severance Collection. Bierce is quoted in Lawrence J. Oliver and Gary Scharnhorst, "Charlotte Perkins Gilman Versus Ambrose Bierce: The Literary Politics of Gender in Fin-de-Siècle California," *Journal of the West* 32 (July 1993): 52–60, esp. 52, 55.

139. *San Francisco Examiner,* Sept. 20, 1891.

140. Yamane, "Women, Power, and the Press," 105, 152–67.

141. Ibid., 260–61.

142. Ibid., 154, 159–68, 227–32, 260–61; regarding Knapp, see also *Woman's Journal* 23 (July 16, 1892): 227.

143. Yamane, "Women, Power, and the Press," 178–79; Ethington, *Public City,* 308–19.

144. James, James, and Boyer, *Notable American Women,* vol. 3, 154–56; W. A. Swanberg, *Citizen Hearst: A Biography of William Randolph Hearst* (New York: Scribner, 1961), 69–87; Isabel Ross, *Ladies of the Press: The Story of Women in Journalism by an Insider* (New York: Harper and Row, 1936), 14–17; Yamane, "Women, Power, and the Press," 180–81, 196–200.

145. Yamane, "Women, Power, and the Press," 180–81, 200–209, 251–60; Ethington, *Public City,* 317–19.

146. Material quoted appears in *San Francisco Call,* May 15, 1891. See also the editions of Mar. 17–18 and May 1, 1891.

147. Parkhurst in form letter intended only for members of the Pacific Coast Woman's Press Association, n.d., Severance Collection; Gilman, *Living of Charlotte Perkins Gilman,* 130; Ceplair, *Charlotte Perkins Gilman,* 37.

148. Parkhurst, form letter; for obituaries of Parkhurst, see "Emily Tracy Y. Parkhurst," 199, and *Pacific Ensign* 2 (Apr. 28, 1892): 4.

149. Gilman is quoted in *San Francisco Call,* Sept. 21, 1893; see also the edition of Sept. 23, 1893, and Krebs, *La Copa,* 113–14.

150. *San Francisco Call,* Oct. 25, 1893; Yamane, "Women, Power, and the Press," 239–40.

151. *San Francisco Call,* Nov. 7, 1893, Oct. 25–26, 1893; *San Francisco Examiner,* Nov. 7, 1893; A.S.B. [Alice Stone Blackwell], "Women and Press Reform," *Woman's Journal* 25 (Jan. 13, 1894): 12–13; *Pacific Ensign* 3 (Nov. 30, 1893): 4; *San Francisco Examiner,* Nov. 8, 1893; *Pacific Ensign* 3 (Oct. 5, 1893): 4; "Demand for a Purer Press," *Pacific Ensign* 3 (Nov. 2, 1893): 4; D.J.S. [Dorcas J. Spencer], "Women's Press Petitions," *Pacific Ensign* 3 (Nov. 16, 1893): 4.

152. Yamane, "Women, Power, and the Press," 260; *San Francisco Call,* Nov. 7, 1893. Bierce is quoted in *San Francisco Examiner,* Sept. 20, 1891.

153. The story about the Sutro breakfast appeared in *San Francisco Examiner,* Mar. 26, 1891; Parkhurst was quoted in *San Francisco Examiner,* Sept. 22, 1891. For Sarah Severance's account of the breakfast, see *San Francisco Call,* May 1, 1891.

154. Material quoted appears in *San Francisco Call,* Oct. 26, 1893 (see also Nov. 3, 1893). See also *San Francisco Examiner,* Oct. 31, 1893.

155. *San Francisco Call*, Oct. 26, and Nov. 7, 1893.

156. *San Francisco Call*, Nov. 7, 1893.

157. *San Francisco Call*, Oct. 28 and 31, and Nov. 1, 3, and 7, 1893; *San Francisco Examiner*, Oct. 27 and 31, and Nov. 7, 1893. For the list of ministers who gave a "pure press" sermon in San Francisco and Alameda counties, see *San Francisco Call*, Nov. 24, 1893.

158. Blackwell, "Women and Press Reform," 12–13; *Nation* 57 (Nov. 30, 1893): 402–403.

159. For material quoted see *San Francisco Call*, Oct. 25, 1893. See also the edition of Oct. 26, 1893.

160. *San Francisco Examiner*, Nov. 5, 1893; *Argonaut* 33 (Nov. 6, 1893): 2; *San Francisco Call*, Nov. 2, 1893. The *Impress* is quoted in Blackwell, "Women and Press Reform," 12–13. The petition is quoted in the *San Francisco Call*, Oct. 25, 1893.

161. *Argonaut* 33 (Nov. 5, 1893): 2; for quotes from the *San Francisco Examiner* editorial, see Oct. 29, 1893; Bierce's column appears in the *Examiner* of Nov. 5, 1893. See also the *Examiner* for Nov. 8, 1893.

162. *San Francisco Call*, Mar. 17, 1891; *San Francisco Examiner*, Nov. 8, 1893.

163. *San Francisco Call*, Nov. 12, 1893.

164. Gilman is quoted in *San Francisco Call*, Nov. 12, 1893.

165. *San Francisco Call*, Nov. 3, 1893.

166. *San Francisco Call*, Nov. 3 and Oct. 31, 1893; *San Francisco Examiner*, Oct. 31, 1893.

167. D.J.S. [Dorcas J. Spencer], "Women's Press Petitions," 4.

CHAPTER 2: THE POLITICS OF POLITICS

1. Gayle Gullett, " 'Our Great Opportunity': Organized Women Advance Women's Work at the World's Columbian Exposition of 1893," *Illinois Historical Journal* 87 (Winter 1994): 259–76, esp. 261; Jeanne Madeline Weimann, *The Fair Women* (Chicago: Academy Chicago, 1981), 4, 26–36.

2. Gullett, " 'Our Great Opportunity,' " 261.

3. Bertha Potter Palmer is quoted in "Address Delivered by Mrs. Potter Palmer," in *The Congress of Women Held in the Woman's Building, World's Columbian Exposition, Chicago, U.S.A., 1893*, ed. Mary Kavanaugh Oldham Eagle (Chicago: W. B. Conkey, 1894), 26, 28; *San Francisco Call*, May 2, 1893.

4. Palmer, "Address," 28; "Exhibits by Women," leaflet, 1–7, Cornelius Cole Collection (hereafter Cole Collection), Special Collection, University of California at Los Angeles; "Prospectus: Board of Lady Managers of the World's Columbian Commission, Chicago, U.S.A., 1893," *California's Monthly World's Fair Magazine* 1 (Feb. 1892): 20.

5. "Exhibits by Women," 3–4.

6. Material quoted appears in "Exhibits by Women," 1–3, Cole Collection. See also

Gullett, " 'Our Great Opportunity,' " 272–73; Rossiter Johnson, ed., *A History of the World's Columbian Exposition Held in Chicago in 1893*, vols. 1 and 3 (New York: Appleton, 1897–98), 196–201, 206–207, 452–53, 472, 474–75; "Lady Managers Columbian Exposition," *Woman's Journal* 22 (Aug. 8, 1891): 258; Palmer, "Woman's Part," 124–27; "Mrs. H. W. R. Strong, President of the Business League," *Business Folio* 1 (Jan. 1895): 2.

7. Gullett, " 'Our Great Opportunity,' " 264; Palmer, "Address," 26; Johnson, *History of the World's Columbian Exposition,* vol. 1, 244–46; *Final Report of the California World's Fair Commission* (Sacramento: California State Printing Office, 1894), 85–86.

8. Gullett, " 'Our Great Opportunity,' " 262.

9. Ibid., 264; "Government and Law Reform," *Woman's Journal* 23 (June 18, 1892): 198; "The Modern Portias," *Woman's Journal* 24 (Aug. 12, 1893): 249. Foltz is quoted in *Pacific Ensign* 3 (June 9, 1893): 4. Her speech to the convention of woman lawyers was entitled "Evolution of Law," and she spoke on "Public Defenders" to the Congress on Jurisprudence and Law Reform.

10. Gullett, " 'Our Great Opportunity,' " 263.

11. Johnson, *History of the World's Columbian Exposition*, vol. 4, 20–21. The Sewall quotes can be found in May Wright Sewall, ed., *The World's Congress of Representative Women: A Historical Resume for Popular Circulation of the World's Congress of Representative Women, Convened in Chicago on May 15, and Adjourned on May 22, 1893, Under the Auspices of the Woman's Branch of the World's Congress Auxiliary*, vol. 1 (Chicago: Rand, 1893), 2–4, 43.

12. Gullett, " 'Our Great Opportunity,' " 265.

13. Material quoted appears in Sewall, *World's Congress of Representative Women,* vol. 1, 107–14 (see also xix–xx, 2–4, 60–64, 77, 221–28, 260–67). See also Friday Morning Club, Minutes, June 1894, Friday Morning Club Archives, Friday Morning Club, Los Angeles; "A Model Election Canvass," *Woman's Journal* 25 (July 28, 1894): 240; F.M.A., "Reverend Florence E. Kollock," *Woman's Journal* 23 (Feb. 20, 1892): 65.

14. "California at the Fair," *World's Columbian Exposition Illustrated* 1 (May 1891): 16.

15. Johnson, *History of the World's Columbian Exposition*, vol. 1, 208; "Prospectus," 18.

16. For quotes see *San Francisco Call,* Jan. 15, 1892, and "Hon. L. J. Rose: He Explains the Expenses of the Fair Commission," *California's Monthly World's Fair Magazine* 1 (Feb. 1892): 6–9. See also the *Call*, Jan. 14, 1892; Johnson, *History of the World's Columbian Exposition,* vol. 1, 208; H.B.B., "The World's Suffrage Congress," *Woman's Journal* 24 (Aug. 19, 1893): 261.

17. Material quoted appears in "California Board of Lady Managers," *California's Monthly World's Fair Magazine* 1 (May 1892): 39. See also "Board of Lady Managers," *California's Monthly World's Fair Magazine* 1 (Jan. 1892): 47; "State Board of Lady Managers," *California's Monthly World's Fair Magazine* 1 (Feb. 1892): 64; Ella Sterling Cummins, "A Literary Exhibit," *California's Monthly World's Fair Magazine* 1 (Apr. 1892): 52–53; *San Francisco Call*, Mar. 18, 1891, Feb. 13, 1892, and Sept. 5, 1894; "First

Semi-Annual Convention of the Pacific Coast Woman's Press Association," Mar. 16, 17, and 18, 1891, Bancroft Library, University of California at Berkeley; Abbie E. Krebs, ed., *La Copa de Oro: A Collection of California Poems, Sketches, and Stories by the Members of the Pacific Coast Woman's Press Association* (San Francisco, 1905), 115; E.C.S., "In Memoriam: Mrs. E. O. Smith," *Woman's Journal* 35 (Sept. 10, 1904): 293; for information regarding Anna Morrison Reed, see Robert J. Chandler, "In the Van: Spiritualists as Catalysts for the California Women's Suffrage Movement," *California History* 73 (Fall 1994): 196.

18. Frona Eunice Wait, "Woman's Exhibit in Chicago," *California's Monthly World's Fair Magazine* 1 (Feb. 1892): 69–71. See also "Board of Lady Managers," 47; "To the Ladies of the Seventh Congressional District" from Flora M. Kimball, Cole Collection; *Final Report*, 59; "By-Laws of the Board of Lady Managers of the California World's Fair Commission," Cole Collection; David F. Burg, *Chicago's White City of 1893* (Lexington: University Press of Kentucky, 1976), 150–51. Burg believes the California building was the "most successful of all the state buildings, and in fact one of the best structures at the fair."

19. *Los Angeles Times*, Oct. 4, 1891.

20. Curran is quoted in Curran to Olive Cole, Nov. 24, 1892, Cole Collection. See also Curran to Cole, Aug. 25, Sept. 26, and Dec. 7, 1892, Cole Collection; *Final Report*, 171–73, 208.

21. News clippings, Cole Collection; "Roster of California National and State Commissioners," *California's Monthly World's Fair Magazine* 1 (Feb. 1892): 73; *San Francisco Call*, Jan. 14–16, 1892; "May Session of the California Board of Lady Managers," *California's Monthly World's Fair Magazine* 1 (May 1892): 81–83; Thomas Thompson to Olive Cole, Dec. 6, 1892; Mrs. E. O. Smith to Olive Cole, Feb. 8, 1893, and Dec. 28, 1892, all in the Cole Collection.

22. *Final Report*, 59–60 (see also 10, 25–26, 44, 56); Johnson, *History of the World's Columbian Exposition*, vol. 3, 472, 474–75.

23. For the objectives see "Prospectus," 18. See also "Hon. L. J. Rose," 6–9; *Final Report*, 11.

24. F.M.K. [Flora M. Kimball], "Woman's Endeavor for the Fair," *Illustrated Pacific States* 16 (Aug. 1892): 4; news clipping, "For the World's Fair," *San Francisco Chronicle*, Cole Collection, scrapbook 6. See also *San Francisco Call*, Jan. 16, 1892.

25. For the Friday Morning Club history see Mrs. Henry Christian Crowther, *High Lights: The Friday Morning Club, 1891–1939* (Los Angeles: Bundy Quill and Press, 1939), 17. See also Johnson, *History of the World's Columbian Exposition*, vol. 1, 242–44; Friday Morning Club, Minutes, Feb. 12, June 3, and Nov. 11, 1892, and Apr. 28, 1893, Friday Morning Club Archives, Friday Morning Club, Los Angeles; *Final Report*, 31.

26. *Argonaut* 33 (Oct. 30, 1893): 2.

27. "The Official Guide to the California Midwinter Exposition," San Francisco, 1894, 13, 19, 149; news clippings, Louise Sorbier Collection, California Historical Society, San Francisco; "The Midwinter Fair Congress," San Francisco, Mar. 23, 1894,

California Historical Society; D.J.S. [Dorcas J. Spencer], "A Bit of History," *Pacific Ensign* 5 (May 16, 1895): 3; *San Francisco Call,* Dec. 20, 1893; see also Philip J. Ethington, *The Public City: The Political Construction of Urban Life in San Francisco, 1850–1900* (Cambridge, U.K.: Cambridge University Press, 1994), 359–60.

28. Material quoted appears in F.M.A., "Woman's Congress at Midwinter Fair," *Woman's Journal* 25 (Apr. 28, 1894): 132. See also Spencer, "Bit of History," 3; "A California Midwinter Fair," *Woman's Journal* 24 (Sept. 2, 1893): 276; news clippings, Sorbier Collection; Frances E. Willard and Mary A. Livermore, eds., *Portraits and Biographies of Prominent American Women,* vol. 1 (New York: Crowell and Kirkpatrick, 1901), 170–71; *San Francisco Call,* May 1 and 3, 1894, and June 4, 1895.

29. Rose L. Ellerbe, *History of the Southern California Woman's Press Club, 1894–1929* (Los Angeles, 1930), 9–11; *San Francisco Call,* May 1–7, 1894; Clara Bradley Burdette, *The Answer to "Clara, What Are You Going to Do with Your Life?": Memoirs of Clara Bradley Burdette* (Pasadena, Calif.: Clara Vista Press, 1951), 157–58.

30. For material quoted see Sewall, *World's Congress of Representative Women,* vol. 1, 60–64; "Preliminary Address of the Managing Board of the Woman's Congress Auxiliary to the Midwinter Fair, to Be Held at San Francisco, California, 1894," Susan B. Anthony Scrapbooks, 1848–1900, Scrapbook 24, microfilm, Research Library, Stanford University, Palo Alto, Calif.; "Value of Women's Congresses," *Woman's Journal* 25 (Jan. 6, 1894): 8. See also *San Francisco Call,* June 4, 1895; "Woman's Congress Association of the Pacific Coast," *Impress* (Dec. 1, 1894): 7.

31. *San Francisco Call,* May 1–7, 1894; *San Francisco Examiner,* May 1–7, 1894.

32. Ethington, *Public City,* 356–60. For more information regarding Campbell, see Kathryn Kish Sklar, *Florence Kelley and the Nation's Work: The Rise of Women's Political Culture* (New Haven, Conn.: Yale University Press, 1995), 122, 143–45; Edward T. James, Janet Wilson James, and Paul S. Boyer, *Notable American Women, 1607–1950,* vol. 1 (Cambridge, Mass.: Harvard University Press), 280–81.

33. Susan B. Anthony and Ida Husted Harper, *The History of Woman Suffrage,* vol. 4 (Indianapolis, Ind.: Hollenbeck, 1902), 189–91; Ellen Carol DuBois, ed., *The Elizabeth Cady Stanton-Susan B. Anthony Reader: Correspondence, Writings, Speeches,* rev. ed. (Boston: Northeastern University Press, 1992). I want to thank Melanie Gustafson for suggesting that I make this comparison of Elizabeth Cady Stanton and the California Woman's Congress.

34. *San Francisco Examiner,* May 6, 1894; "Reverend Ada C. Bowles," *Woman's Journal* 25 (Apr. 7, 1894): 111.

35. Gilman is quoted in *San Francisco Call,* May 2, 1894. See also *San Francisco Examiner,* May 2, 1894.

36. For Bonfils quotes see *San Francisco Examiner,* May 6, 1894. See also the *Examiner* for May 3, 1894, and *San Francisco Call,* May 3, 1894.

37. *San Francisco Examiner,* May 3 and 6, 1894. See also *San Francisco Call,* May 3, 1894.

38. *San Francisco Call*, May 3, 1894; *San Francisco Examiner*, May 3, 1894.

39. Linda K. Kerber, *Women of the Republic: Intellect and Ideology in Revolutionary America* (Chapel Hill: University of North Carolina Press, 1980); Mary P. Ryan, *Cradle of the Middle Class: The Family in Oneida County, New York, 1790–1865* (Cambridge, U.K.: Cambridge University Press, 1981); Christine Stansell, *City of Women: Sex and Class in New York, 1789–1860* (Urbana: University of Illinois Press, 1987); Peggy Pascoe, *Relations of Rescue: The Search for Female Moral Authority in the American West, 1874–1939* (Oxford: Oxford University Press, 1990).

40. *San Francisco Call*, May 6, 1894; Helen Campbell, "Pacific Coast Women's Congress," *Woman's Journal* 26 (June 22, 1895): 194.

41. "Woman's Congress Association of the Pacific Coast," *Impress*, 7.

42. Material quoted is from "Mrs. Sturtevant-Peet," *Pacific Ensign* 6 (Apr. 30, 1896): 1. See also Clara C. Chapin, ed., *Thumbnail Sketches of White Ribbon Women* (Chicago: Woman's Temperance Publishing, 1895), 27; Dorcas James Spencer, *A History of the Woman's Christian Temperance Union of Northern and Central California* (Oakland, Calif.: West Coast Printing, 1913?), 30–38, 46–47, 59–60, 111–12; D.J.S. [Dorcas J. Spencer], "Beaumelle Sturtevant-Peet," *Pacific Ensign* 14 (Apr. 21, 1904): 1–2; Alida C. Avery, "Central California Letter," *Woman's Journal* 26 (Dec. 28, 1895): 415.

43. Material quoted is from California WCTU, *Yearbook 1891* (San Francisco: Herald of Trade Publishing, 1891), 54–56, and California WCTU, *Yearbook 1892* (Woodland, Calif.: Lee and Warren, 1892), 58. See also Mari Jo Buhle, *Women and American Socialism, 1870–1920* (Urbana: University of Illinois Press, 1981), 60–66; California WCTU, *Yearbook 1892*, 65–69; California WCTU, *Yearbook 1893* (San Francisco: Brunt, 1893), 70–71.

44. Robert C. McMath Jr., *American Populism: A Social History, 1877–1898* (New York: Hill and Wang, 1993), 118–20, 50–82; Cator is quoted in John T. McGreevy, "Farmers, Nationalists, and the Origins of California Populism," *Pacific Historical Review* 58 (1989): 479.

45. Margaret V. Longley, "People's Party in California," *Woman's Journal* 22 (Nov. 14, 1891): 370; R. Hal Williams, *The Democratic Party and California Politics, 1880–1896* (Palo Alto, Calif.: Stanford University Press, 1973), 137–39; Ralph Edward Shaffer, "Radicalism in California, 1869–1929" (Ph.D. diss., University of California at Berkeley, 1962), 113–14; Michael Paul Rogin and John L. Shover, *Political Change in California: Critical Elections and Social Movements, 1890–1966* (Westport, Conn.: Greenwood, 1970), 9; Jack S. Blocker, "The Politics of Reform: Populists, Prohibition, and Woman Suffrage, 1891–1892," *Historian* 34 (Aug. 1972): 614–32; California WCTU, *Yearbook 1891*, 110–11; California WCTU, *Yearbook 1892*, 115.

46. "Franchise Notes," *Woman's Journal* 24 (Apr. 8, 1893): 106. See also California WCTU, *Yearbook 1892*, 65–69; S. M. Severance, "The Removal," *Pacific Ensign* 2 (Aug. 11, 1892): 3; California WCTU, *Yearbook 1893*, 117; S. M. Severance, "Chico," *Pacific Ensign* 2 (Sept. 8, 1892): 2; A.B., "Peep at the Capital," *Pacific Ensign* 3 (Feb. 9,

1893): 4; B.S.P. [Beaumelle Sturtevant-Peet], "From the State President," *Pacific Ensign* 3 (Mar. 9, 1893): 2; S. M. Severance, *Pacific Ensign* 3 (Feb. 23, 1893): 2; S. M. Severance, "Legislative Franchise Annals," *Pacific Ensign* 3 (Mar. 30, 1893): 6.

47. "Encouragement," *Pacific Ensign* 3 (Mar. 30, 1893): 6; "Souvenirs," *Pacific Ensign* 3 (Mar. 30, 1893): 5; S. M. Severance, "Introductions," *Pacific Ensign* 3 (Mar. 30, 1893): 5; *San Francisco Chronicle,* Oct. 17, 1888; *San Francisco Examiner,* Oct. 17, 1888.

48. "Notes Taken at Sacramento," *Pacific Ensign* 3 (Mar. 9, 1893): 2. See also S. M. Severance, *Pacific Ensign* 3 (Feb. 23, 1893): 2; Severance, "Introductions," 5; Beaumelle Sturtevant-Peet, "From the State President," *Pacific Ensign* 3 (Mar. 30, 1893): 5–6.

49. Severance, "Removal," 3; *Sacramento Bee,* Feb. 13 and 16, 1893. See also the *Bee* for Jan. 28 and Feb. 13–15, 1893, and California WCTU, *Yearbook 1892,* 65–69.

50. The women actually lobbied for two suffrage bills, one for school suffrage and the other for municipal suffrage, but only the school suffrage bill passed. Markham is quoted in A.S.B. [Alice Stone Blackwell], "The California Veto," *Woman's Journal* 24 (Apr. 22, 1893): 124. See also *Sacramento Bee,* Feb. 6, 1893; *Pacific Ensign* 3 (Mar. 23, 1893): 4; California WCTU, *Yearbook 1893,* 72; Severance, "Legislative Franchise Annals," 3–4; "School Bill," *Pacific Ensign* 3 (Mar. 30, 1893): 1; *San Francisco Call,* Mar. 17, 1893; Sarah M. Severance, "Tricked! Tricked!" *Pacific Ensign* 3 (Mar. 30, 1893): 4.

51. Blackwell, "California Veto," 124. See also Severance, "Tricked! Tricked!" 4.

52. Anthony and Harper, *History of Woman Suffrage,* vol. 4, 485; Donald Waller Rodes, "The California Women Suffrage Campaign of 1911" (master's thesis, California State University, Hayward), 7; Williams, *Democratic Party,* 201–202, 199; Alexander Saxton, "San Francisco Labor and the Populist and Progressive Insurgencies," *Pacific Historical Review* 34 (Nov. 1965): 426; *Colusa Sun,* Jan. 11, 1895, and *Los Angeles Express,* Jan. 17, 1895, both in Anthony Scrapbook 24.

53. *Red Bluff News,* Jan. 12, 1895, *Woodland Democrat,* Jan. 29, 1895, and the *Wheatland Democrat,* undated, clippings from small California papers in Anthony Scrapbook 24; F.M.A., "The Outlook in California," *Woman's Journal* 26 (Feb. 16, 1895): 52; *Livermore Herald,* Feb. 2, 1895, Anthony Scrapbook 24.

54. Material quoted is from *San Jose News,* 1895, Anthony Scrapbook 24. See also Anthony and Harper, *History of Woman Suffrage,* vol. 4, 485–86; Ida Husted Harper, *The Life and Work of Susan B. Anthony,* vol. 2 (Indianapolis, Ind.: Bowen-Merrill, 1898), 863; *San Francisco Chronicle,* Jan. 25, 1895; *Los Angeles Times,* Feb. 7, 1895; F.M.A., "Woman Suffrage in the California Legislature," *Woman's Journal* 26 (Feb. 23, 1895): 60; "Suffrage at the Capitol," *Pacific Ensign* 5 (Feb. 14, 1895): 2.

55. Sherry J. Katz, "Dual Commitments: Feminism, Socialism, and Women's Political Activism in California, 1890–1920" (Ph.D. diss., University of California at Los Angles, 1991), 80.

56. Material quoted appears in *Sacramento Bee,* Feb. 2, 1895 (see also Jan. 25, 1895); for arguments by other women suffragists, see the *Bee* for Feb. 6, 7, and 9, 1895.

57. *Sacramento Bee,* Jan. 25, 1895.

58. Anthony and Harper, *History of Woman Suffrage,* vol. 4, 485–86; *Los Angeles*

Times, Feb. 17 and Jan. 25, 1895; "Notes from Sacramento," *Pacific Ensign* 5 (Feb. 21, 1895): 2.

59. For material quoted see Anthony and Harper, *History of Woman Suffrage,* vol. 4, 485–86; Sarah M. Severance, "Our California Letter," *Woman's Journal* 26 (May 4, 1895): 138; and Harper, *Life and Work,* vol. 2, 819–20. See also "The Washington Convention," *Woman's Journal* 27 (Feb. 15, 1896): 50; "National Plan of Work," *Woman's Journal* 27 (Feb. 29, 1896): 70.

60. *San Francisco Star,* June 8, 1895, Anthony Scrapbook 24.

61. Charlotte Perkins Gilman, "The Ethics of Woman's Work," in *Charlotte Perkins Gilman: A Nonfiction Reader,* ed. Larry Ceplair (New York: Columbia University Press, 1991), 77–79.

62. Shaw is quoted in *San Francisco Chronicle,* May 27 and 21, 1895. For information on the Woman's Congress, see *San Francisco Chronicle* and *Call,* May 21–27, 1895, and Anthony Scrapbook 24.

63. *San Francisco Call,* May 24, 1895; *San Francisco Chronicle,* May 21, 25, and 27, 1895.

64. *San Francisco Chronicle,* May 24, 1895.

65. *San Francisco Chronicle,* May 24–26, 1895; *San Francisco Call,* May 24–25, 1895; *St. Helena Star,* May 24, 1895, Anthony Scrapbook 24.

66. Material quoted appears in *San Francisco Chronicle,* May 25, 1895. See also *San Francisco Call,* May 25, 1895.

67. Helen Campbell, "Pacific Coast Woman's Congress," *Woman's Journal* 26 (June 22, 1895): 194; *San Francisco Chronicle,* May 23, 1895; Ethington quotes the *San Francisco Examiner* headline in *Public City,* 360.

68. *Arthur McEwen's Letter* 3 (May 25, 1895): 1; Harper, *Life and Work,* vol. 2, 827–28; Sarah M. Severance, "North California Letter," *Woman's Journal* 26 (June 15, 1895): 186; Sarah M. Severance, "California Notes," *Woman's Journal* 26 (June 29, 1895): 203; Campbell, "Pacific Coast Woman's Congress," 194.

69. *San Francisco Examiner,* May, 1895, Anthony Scrapbook 24; Severance, "North California Letter," 186; *San Francisco Chronicle* and *Call,* May 24–25, 1895.

70. *San Francisco Chronicle,* September 30, 1894; *Sacramento Bee,* Feb. 7, 1895.

71. Material quoted is from *San Francisco Call,* Sept. 13 and 14, 1894. See also Nellie Blessing Eyster, "California Women and Power," *Woman's Journal* 25 (June 16, 1894): 192; *San Francisco Call,* June 2–3 and Sept. 12, 1894; Anthony and Harper, *History of Woman Suffrage,* vol. 4, 478, 480. Regarding antebellum suffrage organizing, see Ellen Carol DuBois, *Feminism and Suffrage: The Emergence of an Independent Women's Movement in America, 1848–1869* (Ithaca, N.Y.: Cornell University Press, 1978), 50, 182. According to Anthony and Harper, Blinn became president of the state suffrage association in 1894, but they failed to mention that she was "president" of only a faction of the association (480).

72. Material quoted is from a news clipping, source not identifiable, dated July 1895 and found in Anthony Scrapbook 24, and from Severance, "North California Letter,"

186. See also *San Francisco Chronicle*, May 21–27, and July 3, 1895; Harper, *Life and Work*, vol. 2, 863–64; *San Francisco Bulletin*, May 27, 1895; *San Francisco Report*, July 2, 1895; *Berkeley Herald*, June 5, 1895; *San Francisco Wasp*, June 29, 1895; *San Francisco Examiner*, July 3, 1895; and *San Francisco Call*, July 3 and 6, 1895, all in Anthony Scrapbook 24; "Suffrage Work in California," *Woman's Journal* 26 (Sept. 7, 1895): 284.

73. Williams, *Democratic Party*, 177–80, 194–98, 200–202, 246–47, 252; Nell Irwin Painter, *Standing at Armageddon: The United States, 1877–1919* (New York: Norton, 1987), 116.

74. McMath, *American Populism*, 186–87; William Deverell, *Railroad Crossing: Californians and the Railroad, 1850–1910* (Berkeley: University of California Press, 1994), 66; Katz, "Dual Commitments," 70–72; Painter, *Standing at Armageddon*, 117–21.

75. Deverell, *Railroad Crossing*, 63–64.

76. Ibid., 63–92; Michael Magliari, "Populism, Steamboats, and the Octopus: Transportation Rates and Monopoly in California's Wheat Regions, 1890–1896," *Pacific Historical Review* 58 (1989): 449–69.

77. Deverell, *Railroad Crossing*, 63–92; McClatchy is quoted in Magliari, "Populism, Steamboats, and the Octopus," 467–68.

78. Alan Trachtenberg, *The Incorporation of America: Culture and Society in the Gilded Age* (New York: Hill and Wang, 1982), 90, 38–100.

79. John Higham, *Strangers in the Land: Patterns of American Nativism, 1860–1925* (New York: Atheneum, 1963), 80–84.

80. For this account of Populism and the 1896 election I turned to Robert C. McMath, Jr., *American Populism: A Social History, 1877–1898* (New York: Hill and Wang, 1993), 180–211.

81. McGreevy, "Farmers, Nationalists," 491–93; Lawrence Goodwyn, *The Populist Moment: A Short History of the Agrarian Revolt in America* (Oxford: Oxford University Press, 1978), 230–63; Robert H. Wiebe, *The Search for Order, 1877–1920* (New York: Hill and Wang, 1967), 76–110.

82. Williams, *Democratic Party*, 246–47, 252; Rogin and Shover, *Political Change*, 22–24.

83. Susan B. Anthony to Clara Bewick Colby, July 29, 1896, Clara Bewick Colby Papers, Huntington Library, San Marino, Calif.; Sarah M. Severance, "North California Letters," *Woman's Journal* 27 (Oct. 3, 1896): 320.

84. Harriet May Mills, "A Triumphal March," *Woman's Journal* 27 (July 11, 1896): 217. See also Harper, *Life and Work*, vol. 2, 860–64; "In Working Trim," *Pacific Ensign* 6 (Mar. 5, 1896): 2; Ellen C. Sargent, "The California Campaign," *Woman's Journal* 27 (Mar. 21, 1896): 95; Adelaide Comstock, "California," *Woman's Journal* 27 (May 9, 1896): 151; Harriet May Mills, "California," *Woman's Journal* 27 (May 23, 1896): 164; for press reports regarding the county conventions, see Anthony Scrapbook 25; Susan Scheiber Edelman, " 'A Red Hot Suffrage Campaign': The Woman Suffrage Cause in California, 1896," *California Supreme Court Historical Society Yearbook* 2 (1995): 49–131, esp. 60–62.

85. Harper, *Life and Work*, vol. 2, 869–74, 883–85; "First Victory in California," *Woman's Journal* 27 (May 16, 1896): 153; Susan B. Anthony, "Cheery News from California," *Woman's Journal* 27 (May 30, 1896): 172; "California," *Woman's Journal* 27 (Aug. 8, 1896): 255, 256; Edelman, " 'Red Hot Suffrage Campaign,' " 62–68, 108–109.

86. Gilman Ostrander, "The Prohibition Movement in California, 1848–1933" (Ph.D. diss., University of California at Berkeley, 1954), 78, 83–84; Anthony and Harper, *History of Woman Suffrage*, vol. 4, 491–93; *San Francisco Call*, Dec. 4, 1896; *San Luis Obispo Reasoner* and the *Salt Lake Herald*, Nov. 10, 1896, in Anthony Scrapbook 25; Edelman, " 'Red Hot Suffrage Campaign,' " 88–92, 108–109.

87. William Issel and Robert W. Cherny, *San Francisco, 1865–1932: Politics, Power, and Urban Development* (Berkeley: University of California Press, 1986), 23–24, 54–56.

88. Material quoted is from *San Francisco Examiner*, July 26, 1896; *San Francisco Call*, Nov. 2, 1896; Sarah M. Severance, "North California Letter," *Woman's Journal* 27 (Nov. 7, 1896): 360. See also "Another Worker," *Pacific Ensign* 6 (July 30, 1896): 4; Anthony and Harper, *History of Woman Suffrage*, vol. 4, 490, 499. For a speech by Naomi Anderson in Los Angeles, see Emma Harriman, "The Afro-American Convention," *Woman's Journal* 27 (Sept. 5, 1896): 287, and *Los Angeles Times*, Aug. 14–15, 1896.

89. Katz, "Dual Commitments," 61–62, 74–77; Mary A. Hill, *Charlotte Perkins Gilman: The Making of a Radical Feminist, 1860–1896* (Philadelphia: Temple University Press, 1980), 167–258; Ann J. Lane, *To Herland and Beyond: The Life and Work of Charlotte Perkins Gilman* (New York: Meridian, 1991), 158–81; Harper, *Life and Work*, vol. 2, 863–64; Saxton, "San Francisco Labor," 425.

90. Harper, *Life and Work*, vol. 2, 881–82; Spencer, *History*, 66–67; "The Campaign Workers," *Pacific Ensign* 7 (Nov. 5, 1896): 4; California WCTU, *Yearbook 1896* (San Francisco: Thomas J. Davis, 1896), 89, 31–38, 55–57; Ruth Bordin, *Woman and Temperance: The Quest for Power and Liberty, 1873–1900* (Philadelphia: Temple University Press, 1981), 121–22; Anthony and Harper, *History of Woman Suffrage*, vol. 4, 481; California WCTU, *Yearbook 1896*, 55–57, 31–38; Ella E. Goodrich, "Santa Cruz Notes," *Pacific Ensign* 5 (Nov. 28, 1895): 3; "Notelets," *Pacific Ensign* 6 (Aug. 27, 1896): 4; Elizabeth M. Voris, "Suffrage Meeting," *Pacific Ensign* 6 (Oct. 1, 1896): 2.

91. *San Francisco Chronicle*, May 21, 1895. See also Sara Hunter Graham, *Woman Suffrage and the New Democracy* (New Haven, Conn.: Yale University Press, 1996), 36–37.

92. Material quoted is from *San Francisco Call*, Sept. 30, 1896, and news clipping, Oct. 1896, Anthony Scrapbook 25. See also Susan B. Anthony to Jane Stanford, Aug. 23, 1896, Ida Husted Harper Collection, Huntington Library; Susan B. Anthony to Clara Bewick Colby, Feb. 28, 1897, Clara Bewick Colby Collection, Huntington Library; Reda Davis, *California Women: A Guide to Their Politics, 1885–1911* (San Francisco: California Scene, 1968), 175, 156–57, 177, 173–74; Harper, *Life and Work*, vol. 2, 875–76; news clipping, Helen J. Waterman Scrapbook 5, California Historical Society; Mrs. Walter S. Morley, ed., *History of California State Society Daughters of the American Revolution* (Berkeley: Lederer, Strect, and Zeus, 1939?), 25–28, 16; *San Francisco Call*, Sept. 19 and Oct. 1 and 27, 1896; *Visalia Times*, Sept. 26, 1896.

93. Harper, *Life and Work,* vol. 2, 887–91; Anthony and Harper, *History of Woman Suffrage,* vol. 4, 493–94; Ethington, *Public City,* 398–401; Edelman, " 'Red Hot Suffrage Campaign,' " 85; for election data from the entire state, see Rodes, "California Woman Suffrage Campaign," 181–82.

94. Anthony and Harper, *History of Woman Suffrage,* vol. 4, 272–73 (see also 493–94). See also Ethington, *Public City,* 400; Harper, *Life and Work,* vol. 2, 887–91.

95. Edelman, " 'Red Hot Suffrage Campaign,' " 85–86; Royce Delmatier, Clarence F. McIntosh, and Earl G. Waters, *The Rumble of California Politics, 1848–1970* (New York: Wiley, 1970), 121–22.

96. Rodes, "California Woman Suffrage Campaign," 181; Edelman, " 'Red Hot Suffrage Campaign,' " 85.

97. Williams, *Democratic Party,* 252–53; Ostrander, "Prohibition Movement," 63–67; Anthony and Harper, *History of Woman Suffrage,* vol. 4, 495–96; *San Francisco Call,* Oct. 17, 1896; for the list of executive board officers, see the letterhead for Lulu Pile Little to Caroline Severance, Sept. 9, 1896, Caroline Severance Collection, Huntington Library.

98. Katz, "Dual Commitments," 63–69. The Friday Morning Club vigorously supported women's suffrage; see Crowther, *High Lights,* 19, and Anthony Scrapbook 25.

99. Material quoted appears in Anthony and Harper, *History of Woman Suffrage,* vol. 4, 497. See also *Los Angeles Herald,* Oct. 31, 1896; Alice Moore McComas, "Southern California Franchise Department," *Woman's Journal* 25 (Sept. 1, 1894): 277. In 1880 Mexicans were 19 percent of Los Angeles's population and in 1900 approximately 4.9 percent. Mexicans dominated the unskilled workforce, but the suffragists may not have approached them at all and concentrated their efforts on the skilled, mostly white working class. See Albert Camarillo, *Chicanos in a Changing Society: From Mexican Pueblos to American Barrios in Santa Barbara and Southern California, 1848–1930* (Cambridge, Mass.: Harvard University Press, 1979), 118–41, 200.

100. *San Francisco Call,* Dec. 25, 1895; *Sacramento Bee,* Feb. 7, 1895.

101. "Why Do Women Want to Vote?" leaflet, San Francisco, 1896.

102. F.M.A., "Woman's Congress of Pacific Coast," *Woman's Journal* 27 (May 30, 1896): 175; M. H. B. Goodcell, "California," *Woman's Journal* 27 (May 30, 1896): 175; "California," *Woman's Journal* 27 (June 20, 1896): 200; "California," *Woman's Journal* 27 (Aug. 1, 1896): 248; for information on the 1896 Woman's Congress, see *San Francisco Call,* May 5–9, 1896; Anthony Scrapbook 25; Ethington, *Public City,* 399–400.

103. News clipping from the *Fresno Morning Republic,* Hester Harland Collection, Bancroft Library.

104. Nancy F. Cott, *The Grounding of Modern Feminism* (New Haven, Conn.: Yale University Press, 1987), 16–20; Melanie Nolan and Caroline Daley, "International Feminist Perspectives on Suffrage: An Introduction," in *Suffrage and Beyond: International Feminist Perspectives,* ed. Caroline Daley and Melanie Nolan (New York: New York University Press, 1994), 17; Joan Wallach Scott, *Gender and the Politics of History* (New York: Columbia University Press, 1988), 167–77.

105. Keith is quoted in *San Francisco Call*, May 6, 1896. See also Virginia Engquist Grabiner, "Woman's Suffrage and Social Control" (Ph.D. diss., University of California at Berkeley, 1976), 86, 89; Sarah M. Severance, "California (North)," *Woman's Journal* 27 (Aug. 8, 1896): 255–56; Sarah M. Severance, "After the Battle," *Woman's Journal* 27 (Nov. 28, 1896): 383; Anthony and Harper, *History of Woman Suffrage*, vol. 4, 492–94; *San Francisco Examiner*, May 8, 1896; Williams, *Democratic Party*, 200–201.

106. *San Francisco Examiner*, Aug. 2, 1896.

107. *San Francisco Bulletin*, May 27, 1895. See also *San Francisco Chronicle*, May 29, 1895; Ida Husted Harper, "Woman Suffrage for the Home," leaflet, San Francisco, 1896; *San Francisco Examiner*, July 26 and Aug. 2 and 23, 1896; news clippings, Harland Collection; *San Francisco Call*, Feb. 11–12 and 19, 1896.

108. *Los Angeles Times*, June 16, 1895, and May 17, 1896. See also the editions of June 11 and 23, 1895.

109. *San Francisco Call*, May 24, 1896. See also the edition of May 20.

110. Material quoted is from *San Francisco Examiner*, Oct. 3, 1896, and *Los Angeles Times*, May 9, 1895. See also Sarah M. Severance, "North California Letter," *Woman's Journal* 26 (June 15, 1895): 186; *San Francisco Chronicle*, May 27, 1895.

111. See Lisa Tickner, *The Spectacle of Women: Imagery of the Suffrage Campaign, 1907–1914* (London: Chatto and Windus, 1987), esp. 163–64, 172–73, 205.

112. The legislator is quoted in "Suffrage at the Capitol," *Pacific Ensign* 5 (Feb. 14, 1895): 2. The cartoon ran in *Los Angeles Times*, May 5, 1895. See also the edition of Feb. 11, 1895.

113. The *Chronicle* is quoted in "California Echoes," *Woman's Journal* 27 (Nov. 14, 1896): 365. See also *Los Angeles Times*, June 18 and Feb. 17, 1895; Edelman, "'Red Hot Campaign,'" 100.

114. *San Francisco Call*, Oct. 11, 1896; *Los Angeles Times*, Mar. 17, 1895.

115. *San Francisco Call*, Sept. 4, 1895.

CHAPTER 3: THE POLITICS OF ALTRUISM

1. See S. Sara Monoson, "The Lady and the Tiger: Women's Electoral Activism in New York City Before Suffrage," *Journal of Women's History* 2 (Fall 1990): 100–135.

2. Material quoted appears in Mary McHenry Keith, manuscript, no pages, Keith-McHenry-Pond Family Papers, Bancroft Library, University of California at Berkeley, and Alida C. Avery, "California," *Woman's Journal* 31 (May 5, 1900): 143. See also Donald Waller Rodes, "The California Woman Suffrage Campaign of 1911" (master's thesis, California State University, Haywood, 1974), 10–11, 24–26; Sherry J. Katz, "Dual Commitments: Feminism, Socialism, and Women's Political Activism in California, 1890–1920" (Ph.D. diss., University of California at Los Angeles, 1991), 259–60; G. W. Littlejohn, "California," *Woman's Journal* 31 (Dec. 1, 1900): 384.

3. See "The Woman's Club," *Land of Sunshine* 8 (May 1898): 283, for the last program of the congress.

4. Garbutt is quoted in Southern California WCTU, *Yearbook 1904* (Los Angeles: Press of Hand and Hand, 1904), 61. See also Mari Jo Buhle, *Women and American Socialism, 1870–1920* (Urbana: University of Illinois Press, 1981), 49–103; California WCTU, *Yearbook 1899* (San Francisco: Thomas J. Davis, 1899), 25–26; California WCTU, *Yearbook 1902* (San Francisco: Salvation Army, 1902), 26–27; Southern California WCTU, *Yearbook 1903* (Los Angeles: Press of Hand and Hand, 1903), 57–58; Katz, "Dual Commitments," 64–66, 79–80, 100–112.

5. Spencer is quoted in "Notes from Congress of Reform," *Pacific Ensign* 10 (Aug. 16, 1900): 1. See also Buhle, *Women and American Socialism,* 118–21; for a more complete definition of the cooperative commonwealth, see Katz, "Dual Commitments," 27. As Katz notes, for socialist women the cooperative commonwealth meant "some form of workers' control ranging from mutual cooperatives to public ownership of the means of production." For further elaboration by the temperance women on socialism, see "A Platform Exercise," *Pacific Ensign* 9 (May 24, 1899): 2–3, and *Pacific Ensign* 7 (Nov. 25, 1897): 2.

6. California WCTU, *Yearbook 1900* (San Francisco: Thomas J. Davis, 1900), 15; Southern California WCTU, *Yearbook 1899* (Santa Ana, Calif.: U. Sid Lemon, 1899), 4; California WCTU, *Yearbook 1905* (San Francisco: Thomas J. Davis, 1905), 18, 51–52; California WCTU, *Yearbook 1899,* 58; Mae M. Whitman, *Pacific Ensign* 15 (Jan. 19, 1905): 2–3; Mary E. Garbutt, "Temperance and Labor," *White Ribbon* 14 (Nov. 1902): 2; Southern California WCTU, *Yearbook 1904,* 61; Southern California WCTU, *Yearbook 1905* (Los Angeles: Press of Hand and Hand, 1905), 57–58.

7. Whitman, *Pacific Ensign,* 2–3; Southern California WCTU, *Yearbook 1904,* 61; Southern California WCTU, *Yearbook 1905,* 57–58; Garbutt, "Temperance and Labor," 2.

8. May Guthrie Tonzier, "To the State Executive W.C.T.U. Committee, California," *Southern California White Ribbon* 14 (Dec. 1902): 1; Dorcas James Spencer, *A History of the Women's Christian Temperance Union of Northern and Central California* (Oakland, Calif.: West Coast Printing, 1913?), 73–75; [unsigned], "At Pacific Grove," *Pacific Ensign* 11 (Aug. 22, 1901): 2; F. J. Wheat, "A Great Conference," *Pacific Ensign* 11 (Aug. 15, 1901): 1; Dorcas J. Spencer, "Impressions of the Conference at Pacific Grove," *Pacific Ensign* 11 (Aug. 22, 1901): 4; Mae M. Whitman, "At Pacific Grove," *Pacific Ensign* 11 (Aug. 22, 1901): 2 (page 2 of that edition in fact carries two articles under the same headline, used twice; one is signed, the other is not).

9. Temperance women and organized women in general shared a culture that frowned upon any public exposure of internal criticism, partly because women's public dissension was often used as "evidence" of their inability to function in public life. Therefore temperance women did not publish any criticism of the 1901 congress. However, it is quite clear, from reading Sturtevant-Peet's remarks, that she had heard several critiques regarding the congress. "Opening Remarks of the State President, Mrs. Sturtevant-Peet, at the Congress of Reform," *Pacific Ensign* 12 (Aug. 28, 1902): 4; Dorcas J. Spencer, "The Congress of Reforms," *Pacific Ensign* 12 (July 24, 1902): 4.

10. Katz, "Dual Commitments," chaps. 1–3; Sherry J. Katz, "A Politics of Coalition: Socialist Women and the California Suffrage Movement, 1900–1911," in *One Woman, One Vote: Rediscovering the Woman Suffrage Movement*, ed. Marjorie Spruill Wheeler (Troutdale, Ore.: New Sage Press, 1995), 245–62.

11. Spencer, *History*, 75.

12. Material quoted appears in *Los Angeles Times*, Apr. 6, 1899. See also the editions of Sept. 25, 1897, and Jan. 1, Mar. 30, and Apr. 6 and 15, 1900; Clara Bradley Burdette, *The Answer to "Clara, What Are You Going To Do with Your Life?": Memoirs of Clara Bradley Burdette* (Pasadena, Calif.: Clara Vista Press, 1951), 176–77; news clipping, Jan. 19, 1900, Friday Morning Club Scrapbook 51, Ephemeral Collection (hereafter FMC Ephemeral Collection), Huntington Library, San Marino, Calif.; for a description of the Los Angeles Ebell Club, see "The Woman's Club," *Land of Sunshine* 8 (Mar. 1898): 194; for examples of other clubs' movement from the arts to politics in California, see Forum Club of California, *Second Annual Report* (Nov. 24, 1897), 6–17, and *Fifth Annual Report* (Nov. 28, 1900), 7–9, 14–16, 23–32, Bancroft Library, University of California at Berkeley; Mrs. J. W. Orr, "The Influence of Woman's Clubs on Social Life," *Pacific Ensign* 8 (May 20, 1898): 1. For a discussion of this movement into reform on the national level, see Karen J. Blair, *The Clubwoman as Feminist: True Womanhood Redefined, 1868–1914* (New York: Holmes and Meier, 1980), 93–113, and Anne Firor Scott, *Natural Allies: Women's Associations in American History* (Urbana: University of Illinois Press, 1991).

13. For material quoted see *Los Angeles Times*, Apr. 6, 1899. See also Katz, "Dual Commitments," 47–49, 70–80.

14. *Los Angeles Times*, July 11, 1904; Florence Collins Porter, "Mrs. Helen Elliott Bandini," *Federation Courier* 12 (July 1911): 12; Kevin Starr, *Inventing the Dream: California Through the Progressive Era* (Oxford: Oxford University Press, 1985), 17–19; Tomas Almaguer, *Racial Fault Lines: The Historical Origins of White Supremacy in California* (Berkeley: University of California Press, 1994), 45–74; Bandini is quoted in F. Arturo Rosales, " 'Fantasy Heritage' Reexamined: Race and Class in the Writings of the Bandini Family Authors and Other Californios, 1828–1965," in *Recovering the U.S. Hispanic Literary Heritage*, ed. Erlinda Gonzales-Berry and Chuck Tatum (Houston: Arte Público Press, 1996), vol. 2, 87.

15. The resolution can be found in Mary I. Wood, *The History of the General Federation of Women's Clubs* (New York: General Federation of Women's Clubs, 1912), 110–11 (see also 71–72, 125–27, 144–48). See also Mildred White Wells, *Unity in Diversity: The Story of the General Federation of Women's Clubs* (Washington, D.C.: General Federation of Women's Clubs, 1953), 54–58, 198–99; Alan Dawley, *Struggles for Justice: Social Responsibility and the Liberal State* (Cambridge, Mass.: Harvard University Press, 1991), 98–105; Robyn Muncy, *Creating a Female Dominion in American Reform, 1890–1935* (Oxford: Oxford University Press, 1991), 3–37.

16. Wood, *History of the General Federation*, 125–26 (see also 144–48).

17. Men also belonged to the Civic League in its early years. Material quoted ap-

pears in *Los Angeles Times,* Oct. 10, 1900. See also "Minutes of the Friday Morning Club," Nov. 10, 1899, Friday Morning Club Archives, Friday Morning Club, Los Angeles; *Los Angeles Times,* Oct. 2, 1900.

18. Clara B. Burdette, *The Rainbow and the Pot of Gold* (Pasadena, Calif.: Clara Vista Press, 1908), 140–42, 121–33, 138–39; Burdette, *Answer,* 3–7, 106–107, 158–59; news clipping, May 4, 1902, FMC Scrapbook, Friday Morning Club Archives; Wells, *Unity in Diversity,* 156–57; Dorothy Grace Miller, "Within the Bounds of Propriety: Clara Burdette and the Women's Movement" (Ph.D. diss., University of California at Riverside, 1984), 23–81.

19. Material quoted appears in news clipping, *California Clubwoman* 1 (May 1900), Box: California Federation of Women's Clubs (hereafter California Federation), Clara Burdette Collection, Huntington Library (hereafter cited as Burdette Collection), and Burdette, *Answer,* 176–77. See also Miller, "Within the Bounds," 53–63; Wells, *Unity in Diversity,* 156–57; Burdette, *Rainbow and the Pot of Gold,* 138–39.

20. Clara Bradley Burdette, typed speech, "Address of Welcome to the Women's Clubs Assembled for State Federation Los Angeles, Jan. 16, 1900 by Mrs. Robert J. Burdette," 4–10, Box: California Federation, Burdette Collection. See also Wells, *Unity in Diversity,* 156–57; Mary S. Gibson, ed., *A Record of Twenty-five Years of the California Federation of Women's Clubs* (n.p.: California Federation of Women's Clubs, 1927), 2–11.

21. Burdette, "Address of Welcome," 6–7. Lowenburg is quoted in *Los Angeles Times,* Jan. 18, 1900.

22. Burdette is quoted in *Los Angeles Times,* Jan. 3, 1900, and Mrs. Robert J. Burdette, "Mrs. Robert J. Burdette's 'Club Creed,'" *Chautauquan* 36 (Feb. 1902): 535. See also Burdette, "Address of Welcome," 4–7; *Los Angeles Times,* Dec. 23, 1899; *San Francisco Examiner,* Mar. 1, 1900; Burdette, *Rainbow and the Pot of Gold,* 142–45, 32–42, 63–66, 72, 86.

23. Burdette, "Address of Welcome," 4–14; Clara Bradley Burdette, typed speech, "President's Address to the California Federation of Women's Clubs, San Francisco, Feb. 4–7, 1902," 1–5, Box: California Federation, Burdette Collection.

24. Gibson, *Record,* 7–8; California Federation of Women's Clubs (hereafter California Federation), *Yearbook 1900–1901* (Los Angeles: Baumgardt, 1901), 6–8; California Federation, *Yearbook 1902–1903* (San Francisco: Murdock, 1903), 10–11; California Federation, *Yearbook 1904–1905* (San Francisco: Town Talk Press, 1905), 13–14; California Federation, *Sixty Year History of the California Federation* (no date or publisher), 6–17; California WCTU, *Yearbook 1900,* 39; California WCTU, *Yearbook 1902,* 35; California WCTU, *Yearbook 1905,* 35; Southern California WCTU, *Yearbook 1900* (Santa Ana, Calif.: U. Sid Lemon, 1900), 39; Southern California WCTU, *Yearbook 1902,* 37; Southern California WCTU, *Yearbook 1905,* 40–42.

25. *Los Angeles Capital,* Aug. 2, 1901; *San Francisco Examiner,* Sunday Magazine, Mar. 3, 1901; Mrs. Henry Christian Crowther, *High Lights: The Friday Morning Club Los Angeles, California, April, 1891–1938* (Los Angeles: Bundy Quill, 1939), 15; news clipping, FMC Ephemeral Collection.

26. "Minutes of the Friday Morning Club," June 29, 1900, Friday Morning Club Archives; *Los Angeles Times*, Apr. 1 and 3, 1899, and Jan. 20, 1900; Bertha Damaris Knobe, "Club Houses Owned by American Women," *Harpers Bazaar* 42 (Aug. 1908): 790–96, esp. 792–93; news clipping, May 1, 1902, FMC Scrapbook, Friday Morning Club Archives; news clippings, Jan. 12, 1900, June 27, 1903, and June 1905? and "The Friday Morning Club," *Pacific Outlook* 20 (1906), all in FMC Scrapbook 33, FMC Ephemeral Collection.

27. Knobe, "Club Houses," 790–96. Knobe lists, in a haphazard fashion, ten club-houses. For other documentation see Mrs. J. C. Croly, *The History of the Woman's Club Movement in America* (New York: Henry G. Allen, 1898), 240–42, 248, 250. For Burdette's role see Wells, *Unity in Diversity*, 156–57; Miller, "Within the Bounds," 63, 87; "Burdette as a Club Woman," *Woman's Journal* 31 (June 23, 1900): 194; "Women's Clubs and Club Women," *Woman's Journal* 32 (Nov. 30, 1901): 380. For more information regarding the Ebell building, see *Los Angeles Times*, Sept. 25, 1897, and *Club Life* 1 (June 1902): 3.

28. Crowther, *High Lights*, 15; Knobe, "Club Houses," 790–96.

29. *Los Angeles Times*, Jan. 1, 1900; Knobe, "Club Houses," 790.

30. Almaguer, *Racial Fault Lines*, 1–19.

31. *Los Angeles Capital*, Aug. 2, 1902. For a similar discussion see "The Clubwoman's 'Burden' and 'Hoe,'" *California Clubwoman* 1 (May 1900): 2–6.

32. Wood, *History of the General Federation*, 129–31; Blair, *Clubwoman as Feminist*, 108–109.

33. Ibid.; news clipping, FMC Scrapbook, Friday Morning Club Archives.

34. *Los Angeles Times*, Feb. 8, 1902, and Apr. 17, 1902.

35. Material quoted appears in *Los Angeles Times*, Apr. 17, 1902. See also Gibson, *Record*, 21; *Los Angeles Times*, Feb. 8 and 11, 1902; *San Francisco Examiner*, Nov. 26, 1901; Sarah Severance, *Pacific Ensign* 12 (June 5, 1902): 5.

36. Material quoted appears in Burdette, *Answer*, 224. See also Wood, *History of the General Federation*, 154–57; Blair, *Clubwoman as Feminist*, 108–10; Gibson, *Record*, 30–32, 34; "Minutes of the Friday Morning Club," Feb. 21, 1902, Friday Morning Club Archives. For a different account of Burdette's activities regarding race, see Miller, "Within the Bounds," 107–11.

37. Bunnell is quoted in *San Francisco Examiner*, Nov. 10, 1901. See also *Los Angeles Times*, Apr. 24 and May 1, 1902.

38. News clippings, Dec. 1902, Friday Morning Club Archives; *San Francisco Chronicle*, Oct. 19, 1902; E. A. Orr to Clara Burdette, Oct. 9, 1902, and M. E. Irine to Clara Burdette, Oct. 6, 1902, both in Burdette Collection, Box: California Federation; Miller, "Within the Bounds," 113–29.

39. *Los Angeles Times*, May 6, 1902.

40. Ibid. See also the *Los Angeles Times* of May 7, 1902.

41. Rudolph M. Lapp, "Mabel Craft Deering: A Young Woman of Advanced Ideas," *California History* 66 (Sept. 1987): 162–69, 233; Nancy Ann Yamane, "Women, Power,

and the Press: The Case of San Francisco, 1868 to 1896" (Ph.D. diss., University of California at Los Angeles, 1995), 231; "But Yet a Woman," *Land of Sunshine* 12 (Dec. 1899): 59.

42. *San Francisco Examiner*, Nov. 9 and 26, 1901. See also the edition of Nov. 8, 1901.

43. Almaguer, *Racial Fault Lines*, 29; Rudolph Lapp, *Afro-Americans in California* (San Francisco: Boyd and Fraser, 1979), 1–31; Lawrence P. Crouchett, Lonnie G. Bunch III, and Martha Kendall Winnacker, *Visions Toward Tomorrow: The History of the East Bay Afro-American Community, 1852–1977* (Oakland: Northern California Center for Afro-American History and Life, 1989), 14, 23.

44. For material quoted see Delilah L. Beasley, *The Negro Trail Blazers of California: A Compilation of Records from the California Archives in the Bancroft Library at the University of California, in Berkeley; and from the Diaries, Old Papers and Conversations of Old Pioneers in the State of California. It is a True Record of Facts, as They Pertain to the History of the Pioneer and Present Day Negroes of California* (1919; reprint ed., Los Angeles: R and E Research Associates, 1969), 226, 228. See also Elizabeth Lindsay Davis, ed., *Lifting as They Climb: A Historical Record of the National Association of Colored Women* (Washington, D.C.: National Association of Colored Women, 1933), 106–18, 188–248, 270–71, 276–77, 284–85; Mrs. James B. Hume, "Federation News," *Federation Courier* 1 (Sept. 1909): 6–7; *Los Angeles Times*, Aug. 30, 1904, and esp. Feb. 12, 1909. See also Paula Giddings, *When and Where I Enter: The Impact of Black Women on Race and Sex in America* (New York: Bantam, 1984), 95–117; Scott, *Natural Allies*, 147–50.

45. For material quoted see Gibson, *Record*, 26–29. See also Almaguer, *Racial Fault Lines*, 32–34; *Los Angeles Times*, May 2, 1902.

46. Gibson, *Record*, 26–29, 32; Starr, *Inventing the Dream*, 93–95; Douglas Monroy, *Thrown Among Strangers: The Making of Mexican Culture in Frontier California* (Los Angeles: University of California Press, 1990); Leonard Pitt, *The Decline of the Californios: A Social History of the Spanish-Speaking Californians, 1846–1890* (Los Angeles: University of California Press, 1966).

47. Severance is quoted in Ella Giles Ruddy, *The Mother of Clubs: Caroline M. Seymour Severance* (Los Angeles: Baumgardt, 1906), 74–75. See also *Los Angeles Times*, Mar. 29, 1902; Charles Lummis, "The Woman Thou Gavest Me," *Out West Magazine* 16 (Apr. 1902): 415–17; Charles Lummis, "The Skin Question," *Out West Magazine* 16 (May 1902), 524–25; "Minutes of the Friday Morning Club," May 10, 1901, Friday Morning Club Archives.

48. Almaguer, *Racial Fault Lines*, 45–74.

49. *Los Angeles Times*, Apr. 22 and 25, 1902. See also Evelyn Brooks Higginbotham, "African-American Women's History and the Metalanguage of Race" in *"We Specialize in the Wholly Impossible": A Reader in Black Women's History*, ed. Darlene Clark Hine, Wilma King, and Linda Reed (Brooklyn, N.Y.: Carlson, 1995), 3–24, esp. 5.

50. *Los Angeles Times*, Jan. 1, 1920. See also news clipping, *News Pilot*, June 3, 1967; Margaret Ann Kerr to Mrs. Boris Gray, June 21, 1967; news clipping, *California Herald*,

July 1967, all in the Friday Morning Club Archives; Eliza D. Keith, *California Ladies' Magazine* 4 (June 1903): 21–23; Mariana Bertola, "Aims and Objects of the Organization," *California Ladies' Magazine* 4 (June 1903): 24; *San Francisco Examiner*, Sept. 9, 1900; Almaguer, *Racial Fault Lines*, 59–60, 64.

51. Material quoted appears in Gibson, *Record*, 32. See also Lummis, "Skin Question," 525; Florence Collins Porter, "Sixth Biennial of the GFWC," *Los Angeles Herald Illustrated Magazine*, May 1902; news clipping, Friday Morning Club Archives; Starr, *Inventing the Dream*, 85–86.

52. The merchants' association is quoted in *Los Angeles Times*, Feb. 1, 1902. See also Starr, *Inventing the Dream*, 85–86; *Los Angeles Times*, May 3, 1902.

53. Starr, *Inventing the Dream*, 75–98; David G. Gutierrez, "Significant to Whom?: Mexican Americans and the History of the American West," *Western Historical Quarterly* 24 (Nov. 1993): 519–39, esp. 520–23; "The Landmarks Club," *Land of Sunshine* 6 (Jan. 1897): 83.

54. Lummis is quoted in Starr, *Inventing the Dream*, 75–95, at 89.

55. Anne Farrar Hyde, *An American Vision: Far Western Landscape and National Culture, 1820–1920* (New York: New York University Press, 1990), 7–10, 161–65, 170, 174; Starr, *Inventing the Dream*, 77–78, 92–95; "The Landmarks Club," *Land of Sunshine*, 6 (Jan. 1897): 83.

56. Starr, *Inventing the Dream*, 75–98; Hyde, *American Vision*, 191, 207, 212–13, 235–38; "The Landmarks Club," *Land of Sunshine* 6 (Feb. 1897): 121; "The Landmarks Club," *Land of Sunshine* 7 (July 1897): 67; "The Landmarks Club," *Land of Sunshine* 15 (Oct. 1901): 260; "The Landmarks Club," *Out West* 16 (Mar. 1902): 303. See also Alan Trachtenberg, *The Incorporation of America: Culture and Society in the Gilded Age* (New York: Hill and Wang, 1982), 11–37.

57. *Los Angeles Times*, Apr. 13 and May 8, 1902; Auguste Wey, "The Camino Real and Its Old Art," *Out West* 16 (May 1902): 480–88.

58. *Los Angeles Times*, May 8, 1902.

59. Material quoted appears in Mrs. A. S. C. Forbes to Caroline Severance, Nov. 22, 1904, Box 16, Caroline Severance Collection (hereafter Severance Collection), Huntington Library. See also typed speech of Caroline Severance, Box 29, Severance Collection; "The Landmarks Club," *Land of Sunshine* 6 (Dec. 1896): 25; Gibson, *Record*, 221–24; *Los Angeles Times*, June 3, 1900, and Apr. 28, 1902; *Los Angeles Examiner*, Feb. 1 and 13, 1904.

60. *Los Angeles Times*, Apr. 28, 1902.

61. Ibid.

62. Richard White, *"It's Your Misfortune and None of My Own": A New History of the American West* (Norman: University of Oklahoma Press, 1991), 363.

63. *Los Angeles Times*, Apr. 28, 1902.

64. Gibson, *Record*, 329–30, 221–24; *Los Angeles Examiner*, Jan. 30 and 31, 1904; Caroline R. Olney to Caroline Severance, June 4, 1904, Box 22, and Mrs. A. S. C. Forbes to Caroline Severance, Oct. 1, 1906, Box 16, both in Severance Collection.

65. For material quoted see California Federation, *Yearbook 1903–1904* (Riverside, Calif.: Press Printing, 1904), 10–11, 15. See also Olney to Severance; speech of Caroline Severance, Nov. 3, 1904, Box 29, 7–8; Mrs. A. S. C. Forbes to Caroline Severance, Nov. 22, 1904, Box 16, all in Severance Collection; *Los Angeles Examiner,* Jan. 30, 1904; Edwin R. Bingham, *Charles F. Lummis: Editor of the Southwest* (San Marino, Calif.: Huntington Library, 1955), 103–11; California Federation, *Yearbook 1902–1903,* 24–25; California Federation, *Yearbook 1903–1904,* 18–20; California Federation, *Yearbook 1904–1905,* 23–24; California Federation, *Yearbook 1905–1906* (Los Angeles: Baumgardt, 1906), 26–30; California Federation, *Yearbook 1906–1907* (San Jose, Calif.: Murgottens, 1907), 26–29, 44–47; California Federation, *Yearbook 1908–1909* (East Oakland, Calif.: C. W. Gordon, 1909), 30–31, 31–32, 53–54, 78–80; California Federation, *Yearbook 1909–1910* (Berkeley, Calif.: Wetzel Brothers, 1910), 60–65; *Los Angeles Examiner,* Jan. 3, 1904; *San Francisco Chronicle,* Nov. 29, 1903.

66. California Federation, *Yearbook 1906–1907,* 37; Dorothea Moore, "The Work of the Women's Clubs in California," *Annals of the American Academy of Political and Social Science* 28 (Summer 1906): 257–60; California Federation, *Yearbook 1903–1904,* 14–15, 10–11; California Federation, *Yearbook 1902–1903,* 18.

67. Kate Cassatt MacKnight, "Report of the Civic Committee," *Annals of the American Academy of Political and Social Science* 28 (Summer 1906), 294–95; Mary Ritter Beard, *Woman's Work in Municipalities* (1915; reprint ed., New York: Arno Press, 1972), 293–94.

68. William H. Wilson, *The City Beautiful Movement* (Baltimore: Johns Hopkins University Press, 1989), 1, 75, 80–81, 84; Judd Kahn, *Imperial San Francisco: Politics and Planning in an American City, 1897–1906* (Lincoln: University of Nebraska Press, 1979), 2–3, 57–59, 63, 74–79.

69. Wilson, *City Beautiful,* 36–49, 128–36.

70. Ibid., 44–45, 49–51, 75, 129–35, 172–73.

71. Beard, *Woman's Work,* 294, 305–308; Gorham is quoted in California Federation, *Yearbook 1905–1906,* 22–24; Darling is quoted in California Federation, *Yearbook 1903–1904,* 10–11; MacKnight, "Report of the Civic Committee," 293.

72. Beard, *Woman's Work,* 294; Gorham is quoted in California Federation, *Yearbook 1905–1906,* 22–24. See also *Los Angeles Times,* May 14, 1902.

73. Mrs. J. W. Orr, "The Influence of Woman's Clubs on Social Life," *Pacific Ensign* 8 (May 20, 1898): 1. See also Selina Solomons, *How We Won the Vote in California: A True Story of the Campaign of 1911* (San Francisco: New Woman Publishing, 1912), 4; Gibson, *Record,* 6–7; Ellen Sargent to Caroline Severance, Mar. 15, 1899, Box 23, Severance Collection; *San Francisco Call,* July 19, 1898.

74. Orr, "Influence on Woman's Clubs," 1. See also Solomons, *How We Won,* 4; Gibson, *Record,* 6–7. Gibson claimed the California Club had five hundred members, but contemporary accounts said four hundred. The first purely civic women's club in the nation was the Civic Club of Philadelphia, organized in 1893. See Wells, *Unity in Diversity,* 30–31.

75. *San Francisco Examiner,* Jan. 4 and Apr. 15, 1900; see also Charles Keeler, "Municipal Art in American Cities: San Francisco," *Craftsman* 8 (Aug. 1905): 584–602, esp. 599–600.

76. *San Francisco Examiner,* Apr. 15, 1900.

77. California Outdoor Art League, form letter, Oct. 20, 1902, and California Outdoor Art League, leaflet, Aug. 12, 1902, both at the Bancroft Library.

78. For material quoted see D. Moore, "Work of Women's Clubs," 258, and *San Francisco Examiner,* Feb. 21, 1900. See also Mrs. Charles F. Millspaugh, "Women as a Factor in Civic Improvement," *Chautauquan* 43 (June 1906): 312–19, esp. 316–17; *San Francisco Examiner,* Jan. 2, 1921; no author or title, *Woman's Journal* 38 (Nov. 16, 1907): 258.

79. For material quoted see *San Francisco Examiner,* Feb. 7, 1900. See also Carolyn Merchant, "Women of the Progressive Conservation Movement: 1900–1916," *Environmental Review* 8 (Spring 1984): 59–60; Gibson, *Record,* 174–77; *San Francisco Examiner,* Feb. 21, 19, and 28, 1900.

80. *San Francisco Examiner,* Mar. 9, 1900; Gibson, *Record,* 175. Scholars feel that the trees were not legally secure until 1954; see Merchant, "Women of the Progressive Conservation Movement," 60.

81. *San Francisco Examiner,* Feb. 21–22, 24, and 28, 1900.

82. Hyde, *American Vision,* 241–43; Susan R. Schrepfer, *The Fight to Save the Redwoods: A History of Environmental Reform, 1917–1978* (Madison: University of Wisconsin Press, 1983), 7–12. The arguments presented in this paragraph and the next two paragraphs were gathered from the *San Francisco Examiner,* Feb. 7, 21–22, 24, and 28, and Mar. 2, 1900.

83. Kahn, *Imperial San Francisco,* 57–79; Philip J. Ethington, *The Public City: The Political Construction of Urban Life in San Francisco, 1850–1900* (Cambridge, U.K.: Cambridge University Press, 1994), 370–87; Kevin Starr, *Americans and the California Dream, 1850–1915* (Santa Barbara, Calif.: Peregrine Smith, 1981), 249–53, 290–93; Michael Kazin, *Barons of Labor: The San Francisco Building Trades and Union Power in the Progressive Era* (Urbana: University of Illinois Press, 1987), 40–41; see also D. Moore, "Work of Women's Clubs," 257–60.

84. Material quoted appears in "Miss Hittell for Telegraph Hill," *Merchants' Association Review* 8 (Sept. 1903): 9. In 1900 Mayor Phelan appointed the first woman to the city's school board, Mary W. Kincaid, former principal of San Francisco's Girls' High School. See Elizabeth Sargent, "California," *Woman's Journal* 31 (Jan. 13, 1900): 15.

85. Keeler, "Municipal Art in American Cities," 584–602, esp. 598.

86. *Los Angeles Times,* May 14, 1902, and Oct. 2, 1904; news clipping, leaflet of the Civic Federation of Los Angeles, Oct. 1903?, FMC Scrapbook, Friday Morning Club Archives; *Los Angeles Examiner,* Jan. 29 and Feb. 19, 1904; California Federation, *Yearbook 1903–1904,* 18–20; California Federation, *Yearbook 1904–1905,* 21–23.

87. *Los Angeles Times,* Oct. 2, 1904.

88. Ibid., Dec. 17, 27, and 28, 1907, and May 27, 1908; Mrs. Herman J. Hall, "Is the Bill-Board Characteristic American Art?" news clipping, FMC Scrapbook, Friday Morning Club Archives.

89. Kanst is quoted in *Los Angeles Express,* May 19, 1908. See also the editions of Dec. 17, 27, and 28, 1907, Apr. 10 and 14, and May 12 and 27, 1908.

90. Dominick Cavallo, *Muscles and Morals: Organized Playgrounds and Urban Reform, 1880–1920* (Philadelphia: University of Pennsylvania Press, 1981), 6, 27 n. 42.

91. For material quoted regarding playgrounds, see "The Child Father to the Man," *Pacific Outlook* 1 (Oct. 27, 1906): 25, 26, and Bessie D. Stoddart, "Recreative Centers of Los Angeles, California," *Annals of the American Academy of Political and Social Science* 35 (Mar. 1910): 435. See also California Federation, *Yearbook 1909–1910,* 77; *Los Angeles Express,* May 30, and June 11, 1908; Everett C. Beach, "The Playground Movement in California," *Sunset Magazine* 26 (May 1911): 521–26; Beard, *Woman's Work,* 131–32; for additional claims regarding playgrounds, see *Los Angeles Express,* July 15 and 22, 1908, and California Federation, *Yearbook 1906–1907,* 26–29.

92. Robert A. Woods and Albert J. Kennedy, eds., *Handbook of Settlements* (1911; reprint ed., New York: Arno Press, 1970), 9–13; Judith Rosenberg Raftery, *Land of Fair Promise: Politics and Reform in Los Angeles Schools, 1885–1941* (Palo Alto, Calif.: Stanford University Press, 1992), 19–20, 27–32; Stoddart, "Recreative Centers," 426; Albert Howard Clodius, "The Quest for Good Government in Los Angeles, 1890–1910" (Ph.D. diss., Claremont Graduate School, Claremont, Calif., 1953), 499–501; California Federation, *Yearbook 1908–1909,* 30–31; Gibson, *Record,* 214–15.

93. Stoddart, "Recreative Centers," 426–30; Beach, "Playground Movement," 524–25.

94. Material quoted appears in American Association of University Women, "History of the San Francisco Bay Branch, 1886–1930" (no place or date, leaflet at California Historical Society, San Francisco). See also *San Francisco Call,* July 19, 1898; *San Francisco Examiner,* Jan. 2, 1921; Beard, *Woman's Work,* 136–37; Ethel Moore, "Playground Development in California," *American City* 6 (June 1912): 851; Caroline Cooke Jackson, Katherine Chandler, and Elisie Wenzelburger Graupner, *A Sketch of the History of the Association of Collegiate Alumnae California Branch, 1886–1911* (San Francisco: Paul Elder, 1911), 28–30; Marion Talbot and Lois Kimball Mathews Rosenberry, *The History of the American Association of University Women, 1881–1931* (Boston: Houghton Mifflin, 1931), 101–102. The San Francisco Council of Women was organized in 1902; see Susa Young Gates, "National Council Notes," *Woman's Journal* 33 (May 24, 1902): 165.

95. Jackson, Chandler, and Graupner, *Sketch,* 28–30; E. French Strother, "Where Shall the Children Play?" *California Weekly* 1 (Mar. 12, 1909): 251; *Woman's Journal* 38 (Nov. 16, 1907): 181; Ida Husted Harper, "Woman's Broom in Municipal Housekeeping," *Delineator* 73 (Feb. 1909): 213–16, 292–94, esp. 215–16; D. Moore, "Work of Women's Clubs," 258; "A Great Woman's Club," *California Weekly* 1 (Oct. 15, 1909): 744; *San Francisco Call,* Dec. 17, 1907, Jan. 11, 1911, and Jan. 8, 1912.

96. "Playgrounds in Oakland," *California Weekly* 1 (Apr. 16, 1909): 326; California Federation, *Yearbook 1909–1910*, 29–30; E. Moore, "Playground Development in California," 851–52; Mrs. Agnes Hill, "Clubs of Alameda District," *Federation Courier* 1 (Mar. 1910): 26; *San Francisco Call*, June 21 and 28, 1909; William Theodore Doyle, "Charlotte Perkins Gilman and the Cycle of Feminist Reform" (Ph.D. diss., University of California at Berkeley, 1960), 59–63, 71–75.

97. Material quoted appears in FMC Scrapbook 33, FMC Ephemeral Collection, and Burdette, *Answer*, 112. See also Mary Austin, *Earth Horizon: Autobiography* (Cambridge, Mass.: Riverside, 1932), 292–93.

98. Bingham, *Charles F. Lummis*, 6–8; Austin, *Earth Horizon*, 292–93; Starr, *Inventing the Dream*, 116–18; Frances E. Willard and Mary A. Livermore, eds., *Portraits and Biographies of Prominent American Women*, vol. 2 (New York: Crowell and Kirkpatrick, 1901), 478; Harris Newmark, *Sixty Years in Southern California, 1853–1913* (New York: Knickerbocker, 1916), 548–49; Boyle Workman, *The City That Grew* (Los Angeles: Southland, 1936), 242.

99. Bingham, *Charles F. Lummis*, 12–14; Austin, *Earth Horizon*, 292–93; Starr, *Inventing the Dream*, 116–18; Workman, *The City That Grew*, 242; *Los Angeles Examiner*, Apr. 9, 1911; Gibson, *Record*, 34–37; "The Landmarks Club," *Land of Sunshine* 6 (Mar. 1897): 157.

100. Gibson, *Record*, 34–39; news clipping, FMC Scrapbook, Friday Morning Club Archives; "Working for Juvenile Court," *Pacific Ensign* 13 (Feb. 26, 1903); *Los Angeles Examiner*, Jan. 5 and 23, 1904; Wells, *Unity in Diversity*, 208; "Women's Clubs and Club Women," *Woman's Journal* 33 (July 5, 1902): 216; Mary E. Odem, *Delinquent Daughters: Protecting and Policing Adolescent Female Sexuality in the United States, 1885–1920* (Chapel Hill: University of North Carolina Press, 1995), 74, 109, 111–12; Janis Appier, *Policing Women: The Sexual Politics of Law Enforcement and the LAPD* (Philadelphia: Temple University Press, 1998), 9–33. For a detailed description of how the juvenile court began in Los Angeles, see Thomas Stuart McKibbon, "The Origin and Development of the Los Angeles County Juvenile Court" (master's thesis, University of Southern California, 1932), 17–19.

101. Gibson, *Record*, 34–39, 213–14; California WCTU, *Yearbook 1902*, 14–15; "Minutes of the Friday Morning Club," Oct. 4, 1901, and Nov. 21, 1902, Friday Morning Club Archives; Mary McHenry Keith manuscript, no pages, Keith-McHenry-Pond Family Papers; "California," *Woman's Journal* 33 (Dec. 13, 1902): 400; "Women's Clubs and Club Women," *Woman's Journal* 34 (Feb. 14, 1903): 56.

102. Gibson, *Record*, 34–39, 213–14; "Working for Juvenile Court," 4; "Women's Clubs and Club Women," *Woman's Journal* 35 (Jan. 2, 1904): 1; Odem, *Delinquent Daughters*, 112; Doyle, "Charlotte Perkins Gilman," 76–79.

103. D. Moore, "Work of Women's Clubs," 260; California Federation, *Yearbook 1904–1905*, 18–19; California Federation, *Yearbook 1905–1906*, 30–32.

104. California WCTU, *Yearbook 1898* (San Francisco: Thomas J. Davis, 1898), 28; "School Suffrage," *Pacific Ensign* 9 (Mar. 9, 1899): 4.

105. Sarah M. Severance, *Pacific Ensign* 10 (May 24, 1900): 5, 6. See also "California," *Woman's Journal* 30 (Mar. 11, 1899): 80; Alida C. Avery, "California," *Woman's Journal* 30 (Mar. 18, 1899): 88; "Officers and Resolutions; National American Woman Suffrage Association," *Woman's Journal* 30 (May 13, 1899): 145; Sarah M. Severance, "California; Governor Gage and California School Bill," *Woman's Journal* 30 (Sept. 23, 1899): 304; California WCTU, *Yearbook 1900*, 56. For more information regarding women on school boards, see Sarah B. Stearns, "Biennial Conference in San Francisco," *Woman's Journal* (June 14, 1902): 186.

106. *Los Angeles Times*, May 2, 1902.

107. For Snyder material see *Los Angeles Times*, May 2, 1902. The *San Francisco Chronicle* is quoted in "Women's Clubs Should Not Ask Charity," *Pacific Ensign* 12 (Oct. 9, 1902): 1. See *San Francisco Examiner*, Nov. 14 and Dec. 30, 1901, and Apr. 7, 1903.

108. Susan B. Anthony and Ida Husted Harper, *History of Woman Suffrage*, vol. 4 (Indianapolis, Ind.: Hollenbeck, 1902), 501–502; Ida Husted Harper, *History of Woman Suffrage*, vol. 6 (New York: Little and Ives, 1922), 39–40.

109. G. W. Littlejohn, "California," *Woman's Journal* 31 (Dec. 1, 1900): 384; Alida C. Avery, "California," *Woman's Journal* 32 (Apr. 27, 1901): 135; "California," *Woman's Journal* 33 (Oct. 11, 1902): 327; *San Francisco Examiner*, Oct. 19, 1901; *San Francisco Chronicle*, Oct. 25, 1902; "California," *Woman's Journal* 33 (Dec. 13, 1902): 400.

110. K. M. Nesfield, "An Ideal Suffragist," *Woman's Journal* 32 (Mar. 2, 1901): 70; "California," *Woman's Journal* 32 (Apr. 13, 1901): 120.

111. For material quoted see *San Francisco Examiner*, Oct. 19, 1901. See also "California," *Woman's Journal* 31 (Dec. 22, 1900): 406–7; "California," *Woman's Journal* 32 (Aug. 3, 1901): 247; Anthony and Harper, *History of Woman Suffrage*, vol. 4, 504–505.

112. Katz, "Dual Commitments," 100, 270–72, 275.

113. Mills is quoted in *San Francisco Examiner*, Oct. 19, 1901. See also Katz, "Dual Commitments," 319–20 n. 48; Caroline M. Severance, "California," *Woman's Journal* 35 (Apr. 30, 1904): 143.

114. Burdette, "President's Address." See also *San Francisco Chronicle*, Oct. 24–26, 1902.

115. The *San Francisco Examiner* is quoted in "California," *Woman's Journal* 33 (Dec. 13, 1902): 400; H.B.B. [Henry B. Blackwell], "Suffrage Prospects on the Pacific Coast," *Woman's Journal* 34 (Nov. 14, 1903): 364; Sara Hunter Graham, *Woman Suffrage and the New Democracy* (New Haven, Conn.: Yale University Press, 1996), 33–36; "Miss Gail Laughlin," *Pacific Ensign* 13 (Nov. 12, 1903): 1.

116. *Los Angeles Times*, Oct. 7, 1904. See also the editions of Aug. 7 and Oct 8, 1904; Harper, *History of Woman Suffrage*, vol. 6, 30–31.

117. *Los Angeles Times*, Oct. 8, 1904. See also Harper, *History of Woman Suffrage*, vol. 6, 31.

118. Material quoted appears in *Los Angeles Times*, Oct. 8, 1904. See also Harper, *History of Woman Suffrage*, vol. 6, 31.

119. For material quoted see *Los Angeles Times*, Oct. 7, 1904; Barbara Sicherman and Carol Hurd Green, eds., *Notable American Women: The Modern Period* (Cambridge, Mass.: Harvard University Press, 1980), 410–11; and "Laughlin," *Pacific Ensign*, 1.

120. "Laughlin," *Pacific Ensign*, 1; Sicherman and Green, *Notable American Women*, 410–11.

121. *San Francisco Chronicle*, Nov. 15, 1903; *Los Angeles Times*, Aug. 7, 1904; Graham, *Woman Suffrage*, 36–37.

122. *San Francisco Examiner*, Oct. 19, 1901.

123. For material quoted see *San Francisco Chronicle*, Oct. 25, 1902, Nov. 20, 1903 (see also the edition of Nov 19, 1903). For an extended discussion of socialist participation in the state suffrage movement during these years, see Katz, "Dual Commitments," 245–73.

124. Mary Simpson Sperry and Hattie J. D. Chapman, "State Reports to the NAWSA: California," *Woman's Journal* 36 (Sept. 16, 1905): 146–47.

125. Southern California WCTU, *Yearbook 1905*, 52–53; Sarah Severance, "An Explanation," *Pacific Ensign* 15 (Apr. 27, 1905): 5.

126. For material quoted see Anna Shaw to Mary McHenry Keith, Dec. 28, 1905, Keith-McHenry-Pond Family Papers; and A.R., "California," *Woman's Journal* 36 (Apr. 22, 1905): 64. See also A.C.A., "California," *Woman's Journal* 36 (Oct. 11, 1905): 180.

127. For material quoted see Harper, "Woman's Broom," 215–16. See also "Official Suffrage Page," *Western Woman* 1 (Dec. 1907): 12.

CHAPTER 4: THE POLITICS OF GOOD GOVERNMENT

1. Josefa H. Tolhurst, "Why?" *Federation Courier* 2 (Apr. 1911): 10. See also "A California Woman's Comment," *Woman's Journal* 42 (Feb. 25, 1911): 59.

2. For the account of the good government movement in California that follows, I used Michael Kazin, *Barons of Labor: The San Francisco Building Trades and Union Power in the Progressive Era* (Urbana: University of Illinois Press, 1987), 113–44; George E. Mowry, *The California Progressives* (Berkeley: University of California Press, 1951), 23–56; Walton Bean, *Boss Ruef's San Francisco: The Story of the Union Labor Party, Big Business, and the Graft Prosecution* (Berkeley: University of California Press, 1952); and Robert M. Fogelson, *The Fragmented Metropolis: Los Angeles, 1850–1930* (Cambridge, Mass.: Harvard University Press, 1967), 205–28. For contemporary discussions of the political machine, see Guido H. Marx, "Some Political Reminiscences," typed manuscript, Mar. 5, 1938, Box 1, Alice Rose Collection (hereafter Rose Collection), Stanford University Library, Palo Alto, Calif.; Ray Stannard Baker, "A Corner in Labor, What Is Happening in San Francisco, Where Unionism Holds Undisputed Sway," *McClure's Magazine* 22 (Feb. 1904): 366–78; Joseph Lincoln Steffens, *The Shame of the Cities* (New York: McClure, Phillips, 1904) and *The Struggle for Self-Government* (New York: McClure, Phillips, 1906).

3. Richard L. McCormick, "The Discovery That Business Corrupts Politics: A Reappraisal of the Origins of Progressivism," *American Historical Review* 86 (Apr. 1981): 260–61.

4. *Woman's Journal* 38 (Nov. 16, 1907): 181.

5. Material quoted appears in *Los Angeles Express*, Feb. 14, 1908. See also *New York Evening World*, Oct. 1908, news clipping, Part II, Box 2, Hiram Johnson Collection (hereafter Johnson Collection), Bancroft Library, University of California at Berkeley; "Official Suffrage Page," *Western Woman* 1 (Dec. 1907): 11.

6. E. French Strother, "Where Shall the Children Play?" *California Weekly* 1 (Mar. 12, 1909): 251; *Woman's Journal* 38 (Nov. 16, 1907): 181; *Yellow Ribbon* 3 (Mar. 1907): 3; "A Great Woman's Club," *California Weekly* 1 (Oct. 15, 1909): 744; Ida Husted Harper, "Woman's Broom in Municipal Housekeeping," *Delineator* 73 (Feb. 1909): 213–16, 292–94, esp. 215–16; Randolph Stephen Delehanty, "San Francisco Parks and Playgrounds, 1839–1990: The History of a Public Good in One North American City," vol. 2 (Ph.D. diss., Harvard University, 1992), 277–93.

7. Delehanty, "San Francisco Parks," 279; *Woman's Journal* 38 (Nov. 16, 1907): 181; *Yellow Ribbon* 3 (Mar. 1907): 3.

8. Guenter B. Risse, "'A Long Pull, a Strong Pull, and All Together': San Francisco and Bubonic Plague, 1907–1908," *Bulletin of the History of Medicine* 66 (1992): 260–86, esp. 268–71.

9. Risse, "'Long Pull,'" 271–79; Bean, *Boss Ruef*, 230.

10. For material quoted see *San Francisco Call*, Feb. 7, 1908; *Los Angeles Express*, Feb. 14, 1908. See also Risse, "'Long Pull,'" 279–83; "Women's Public Health Association," *Woman's Journal* 39 (Dec. 19, 1908): 204; "With Women's Clubs," *Woman's Journal* 39 (May 9, 1908): 76.

11. Kazin, *Barons of Labor*, 130; Mowry, *California Progressives*, 33–36; Bean, *Boss Ruef*, 287–99.

12. TR is quoted in *San Francisco Bulletin*, June 20, 1908; "Proposed Citizens' League of Justice," handwritten note, no author, no date, Box 103, Franklin Hichborn Collection (hereafter Hichborn Collection), Special Collections, University of California at Los Angeles; for the open letter see Citizens' League of Justice, "An Open Letter to San Franciscans: Let Us Think Things Over," typed manuscript, no name, no date, Box 103, Hichborn Collection. See also "Constitution of the League of Justice," *Liberator*, news clipping, Jan. 2, 1909, Box 104, Hichborn Collection; Bean, *Boss Ruef*, 291–93; George Henry Boke, "The Awakening of San Francisco," *Western World Magazine*, news clipping, Box 104, Hichborn Collection. Regarding Roosevelt, see Gail Bederman, *Manliness and Civilization: A Cultural History of Gender and Race in the United States, 1880–1917* (Chicago: University of Chicago Press, 1995), 170–215.

13. Material quoted appears in Elizabeth Gerberding, "Woman's Fight Against Graft in San Francisco," *Delineator* 76 (Oct. 1910): 245 (see also 246, 322–23). See also Citizens' League of Justice to "Dear Madam," Sept. 19, 1908, and Citizens' League of Justice to Mrs. John F. Merrill, Oct. 3, 1908, both in Box 103, Hichborn Collection; *San*

Francisco Bulletin, Mar. 16, 1909; Susan Englander, *Class Conflict and Coalition in the California Woman Suffrage Movement, 1907–1912: The San Francisco Wage Earners' Suffrage League* (Lewiston, N.Y.: Edwin Mellen Press, 1992), 87–90.

14. Gerberding, "Woman's Fight," 245. See also Boke, "The Awakening;" Rev. Samuel C. Patterson to Citizens' League of Justice, Sept. 5, 1908, and Rev. Edward Raley to Citizens' League of Justice, Sept. 7, 1908, and Citizens' League of Justice to William Rader, Nov. 28, 1908, all in Box 103, Hichborn Collection; Citizens' League to "Dear Madam"; Citizens' League to Merrill, all in Box 103, Hichborn Collection; Englander, *Class Conflict,* 87–90; *San Francisco Bulletin,* Mar. 16, 1909.

15. Gerberding, "Woman's Fight," 245–46, 322–23. The description of Gerberding here is based on an interpretation of this source. Suffragist Mary McHenry Keith wrote similar sentiments in a speech entitled "What Women Can Do in the Fight Against Municipal Corruption." Keith was responding to an earlier talk by Francis Heney on machine corruption in which he assigned women to a strictly private role. See "California," *Woman's Journal* 38 (June 8, 1907): 92.

16. Gerberding, "Woman's Fight," 245–46; *San Francisco Bulletin,* Nov. 23, 1908. See also the edition of Nov. 20, 1908.

17. McArthur is quoted in *San Francisco Bulletin,* Nov. 23, 1908; the *San Francisco Call* is quoted in "Women to Fight Graft," *Woman's Journal* 39 (Dec. 19, 1908): 203. See also Gerberding, "Woman's Fight," 322; George Henry Boke, "What the League of Justice Stands for," *California Weekly* 1 (Jan. 1, 1909): 90–91.

18. Gerberding, "Woman's Fight," 246; Citizens' League of Justice to Dr. William Rader, Mar. 3 and 11, 1909, Box 103, Hichborn Collection; *San Francisco Bulletin,* Apr. 19 and June 12, 1909; "California," *Woman's Journal* 40 (July 3, 1909): 107; *San Francisco Call,* June 12, 1909.

19. *San Francisco Bulletin,* Apr. 24, 1909.

20. For a discussion of education as a style of elite politics, see Michael McGerr, "Political Style and Women's Power, 1830–1930," *Journal of American History* 77 (Dec. 1990): 864–85, esp. 871–72.

21. Mowry, *California Progressives,* 29–30, 38–43, 58–61; Albert Howard Clodius, "The Quest for Good Government in Los Angeles, 1890–1910" (Ph.D. diss., Claremont Graduate School, Claremont, Calif., 1953), 125–44; Fogelson, *Fragmented Metropolis,* 212–13; Kazin, *Barons of Labor,* 204.

22. Mowry, *California Progressives,* 44–47; Clodius, "Quest for Good Government," 154–70, 195, 198, 206, 208–10, 214, 393.

23. The material quoted appears in Mowry, *California Progressives,* 41, 46 (see also 40–46). See also Kazin, *Barons of Labor,* 202–204.

24. Lissner is quoted in *Los Angeles Herald,* June 5, 1909. See also Clodius, "Quest for Good Government," 408–12; Tom Sitton, *John Randolph Haynes: California Progressive* (Palo Alto, Calif.: Stanford University Press, 1992), 106–107. The statewide progressive organization, the Lincoln-Roosevelt League, placed women's suffrage in its platform at its organizational meeting in May 1907 but took no further steps for

suffrage. See Meyer Lissner to Viola Kaufman, Aug. 20, 1908, Box 1, Meyer Lissner Collection (hereafter Lissner Collection), Stanford University Library, Palo Alto, Calif.; Mowry, *California Progressives*, 70–72; Donald Waller Rodes, "The California Woman Suffrage Campaign of 1911" (master's thesis, California State University, Haywood, 1974), 33–34.

25. Material quoted appears in "Doctrine of the Minimum," *Pacific Outlook* 7 (Sept. 18, 1909): 3 (see also 2). See also Clodius, "Quest for Good Government," 512–16; "The Purity Remedy," *Pacific Outlook* 7 (June 26, 1909): 1–2; "The Man in the Gutter," *Pacific Outlook* 7 (July 17, 1909): 5.

26. Material quoted appears in "Doctrine of the Minimum," 3. See also Clodius, "Quest for Good Government," 507–10, 30, 54; Sitton, *John Randolph Haynes*, 23, 66; Albert Camarillo, *Chicanos in a Changing Society: From Mexican Pueblos to American Barrios in Santa Barbara and Southern California, 1848–1930* (Cambridge, Mass.: Harvard University Press, 1979), 202–203.

27. *Los Angeles Herald*, Sept. 6, 1908; *Los Angeles Express*, Apr. 3, 1908; Mary A. Veeder, "The Work of a Housing Commission," *California Outlook* 13 (Sept. 14, 1912): 12–13; for subsequent actions of the Los Angeles Housing Commission, see Mary Ritter Beard, *Woman's Work in Municipalities* (1915; reprint ed., New York: Arno Press, 1972), 202, 204, 206, and Johanna Von Wagner, "The Housing Awakening," *Survey* 25 (Mar. 4, 1911): 927–34; regarding the dance hall campaign see *Los Angeles Express*, June 16, 18, and 27 and July 7 and 21, 1908, and *Los Angeles Herald*, Sept. 13, 1908.

28. *Los Angeles Herald*, Dec. 3, 1909.

29. *Los Angeles Herald*, Nov. 13, 1909. See also the edition of Nov. 6, 1909.

30. *Los Angeles Herald*, Dec. 3–4, 1909. See also Meyer Lissner to Caroline Severance, Dec. 23, 1909, Box 20, Caroline Severance Collection (hereafter Severance Collection), Huntington Library, San Marino, Calif. Lissner assured Severance that he had publicly endorsed suffrage before the Political Equality League, although when he did this is not clear.

31. Ella Giles Ruddy to Madam Severance, Dec. 8, 1909, Box 22, Severance Collection; Caroline M. Severance, "California," *Woman's Journal* 39 (Feb. 22, 1908): 31. See also "California," *Woman's Journal* 40 (June 19, 1909): 99; Judith Raftery, "Los Angeles Clubwomen and Progressive Reform," in *California Progressivism Revisited*, ed. William Deverell and Tom Sitton (Berkeley: University of California Press, 1994), 144–74, esp. 152.

32. Gerberding, "Woman's Fight," 322; Citizens' League of Justice to Harris Weinstock, Oct. 11, 1909, Box 103, Hichborn Collection; *San Francisco Bulletin*, Mar. 16 and June 12, 1909; Mowry, *California Progressives*, 36–37; Kazin, *Barons of Labor*, 130, 181–85.

33. Gerberding is quoted in Englander, *Class Conflict*, 91–92; Citizens' League of Justice to Harris Weinstock, Oct. 11, 1909, Box 103, Hichborn Collection; *San Francisco Bulletin*, June 12, 1909.

34. *San Francisco Bulletin*, June 12, 1909; *San Francisco Call*, June 12, 1909; Citizens'

League of Justice to E. W. Scripps, Sept. 8, 1909, Box 124, Hichborn Collection. See also Leo S. Robinson to George H. Boke, Oct. 8, 1909, Box 124, Hichborn Collection.

35. Rodes, "California Woman Suffrage," 41–42, 84–85; Englander, *Class Conflict,* 91–92; Dorcas J. Spencer, *A History of the Woman's Christian Temperance Union of Northern and Central California* (Oakland, Calif.: West Coast Printing, 1913?), 85, 111–12; California WCTU, *Yearbook 1909* (Oakdale, Calif.: Oakdale Graphic, 1909), 17, 18.

36. California WCTU, *Yearbook 1906* (Woodland, Calif.: Home Alliance Print, 1906), 11–12 (see also 19, 28); California WCTU, *Yearbook 1907* (Stockton, Calif.: Enoch Turner, 1907), 35.

37. Sturtevant-Peet is quoted in California WCTU, *Yearbook 1907,* 22–23; Dorr is quoted in California WCTU, *Yearbook 1909,* 28 (see also 17–18, 38). See also Spencer, *History,* 85; *San Francisco Bulletin,* July 13 and 30, 1908; California WCTU, *Yearbook 1908* (San Jose, Calif.: San Jose Printing, 1908), 32. For Gerberding's speech at the 1909 Congress of Reforms, see *California Woman's Home and Club Journal,* Aug. 1909, news clipping, Keith-McHenry-Pond Family Papers, Bancroft Library; Englander, *Class Conflict,* 91.

38. *Los Angeles Herald,* May 26 and 28–30, June 5 and 9, Dec. 30, 1909; Haines Reed to George H. Boke, July 4, 1909, Box 103, Hichborn Collection; Lillian Stark to Professor Boke, Jan. 1, 1910, Box 125, Hichborn Collection; Englander, *Class Conflict,* 91–92; California Equal Suffrage Association, Program of the Annual Convention, Sept. 30 and Oct. 1–2, 1909, Box 124, Hichborn Collection. For information on Carlisle's 1909 campaign, see *San Francisco Bulletin,* Mar. 17, May 3 and 19–20, 1909 and F.M.A., "Mary, Mary, Quite Contrary," *Woman's Journal* 41 (Mar. 12, 1910): 42.

39. Mowry, *California Progressives,* 69–80; *San Francisco Call,* Aug. 28, 1908.

40. For material quoted see "California," *Woman's Journal* 38 (Jan. 19, 1907): 12; Sherry J. Katz, "Dual Commitments: Feminism, Socialism, and Women's Political Activism in California, 1890–1920" (Ph.D. diss., University of California at Los Angeles, 1991), 321–22 n. 52. See also Alice Park, 1914 diary, Box 24, Alice Park Collection (hereafter Park Collection), Hoover Institution on War, Revolution, and Peace, Stanford University; Selina Solomons, *How We Won the Vote in California: A True Story of the Campaign of 1911* (San Francisco: New Woman Publishing, 1912), 5; Lillian Harris Coffin, interview by Alice Rose, May 25, 1939, Rose Collection; Rodes, "California Woman Suffrage," 28–29; Ida Husted Harper, *History of Woman Suffrage,* vol. 6 (New York: Little and Ives, 1922), 31.

41. *Los Angeles Herald,* Apr. 3, 1909. See also the *Herald* for April 7, 1909; William Theodore Doyle, "Charlotte Perkins Gilman and the Cycle of Feminist Reform" (Ph.D. diss., University of California at Berkeley, 1960), 135–39 (Doyle interviewed Coffin); Coffin interview by Rose; Rodes, "California Woman Suffrage," 28.

42. M.C.D. [Mabel Craft Deering], "Annual Convention of the California Equal Suffrage Association," *Yellow Ribbon* 1 (Nov. 1906): 1–2; Alice L. Park, "Work After Election," *Yellow Ribbon* 1 (Nov. 1906): 3; A.S.B. [Alice Stone Blackwell], "From San Francisco," *Woman's Journal* 37 (Apr. 28, 1906): 66; "California Undaunted," *Woman's*

Journal 37 (June 2, 1906): 86; "State Correspondence: California," *Woman's Journal* 37 (July 14, 1906): 112; "California," *Woman's Journal* 37 (Sept. 22, 1906): 152; "State Correspondence: California," *Woman's Journal* 37 (Oct. 20, 1906): 168; Rodes, "California Woman Suffrage," 28–29.

43. Susan B. Anthony and Ida Husted Harper, eds., *History of Woman Suffrage*, vol. 4 (Rochester, N.Y.: 1901), 487–88; Mari Jo Buhle, *Women and American Socialism, 1870–1920* (Urbana: University of Illinois Press, 1981), 105; Katz, "Dual Commitments," 54, 263 n. 47, 241–42.

44. Mowry, *California Progressives,* 60–62, 130; Bean, *Boss Ruef,* 160–61; Dr. John R. Haynes, "The Birth of Democracy in California," typescript, pp. 8–9, Box 1, Rose Collection.

45. Katherine Reed Balentine, *Yellow Ribbon* 1 (Nov. 1906): 2. See also Rachel Foster Avery to Mary Keith, Jan. 31, 1907, Keith-McHenry-Pond Family Papers; "What Kolb-Dill Solons Did to the Suffrage Bill," *Yellow Ribbon* 1 (May 1907): 1–2; Alice L. Park, "California," *Woman's Journal* 38 (Mar. 23, 1907): 48; Solomons, *How We Won,* 5.

46. "California," *Woman's Journal* 38 (Jan. 19, 1907): 12; *Yellow Ribbon* 1 (Mar. 1907): 3. See also "California," *Woman's Journal* 38 (May 4, 1907): 72; Mrs. Florence Collins Porter, "Convention of the Los Angeles County Equal Suffrage League," *Yellow Ribbon* 1 (Nov. 1906): 3.

47. Mrs. William Keith, "The New Politics," *People's Forum* 1 (Sept. 1907): 12–13. See also Madame C. M. S. Severance, "Convention Address Before the Los Angeles Suffrage League," *Yellow Ribbon* 1 (Nov. 1906): 1–3; "That Tveitmoe Man," *Western Woman* 1 (Aug. 10, 1907): 6; "Thoughts for Feminine Reflection" and "Civic League," *Western Woman* 1 (July 11, 1907): 9; Rodes, "California Woman Suffrage," 36.

48. "Mrs. Keith's Bomb," *Woman's Journal* 39 (Jan. 18, 1908): 10; *Woman's Journal* 39 (Nov. 21, 1908): 185. See also "With Women's Clubs," *Woman's Journal* 39 (May 9, 1908): 76.

49. For suffragists' involvement in city affairs in Palo Alto, see "Editorial Notes," *Woman's Journal* 39 (Feb. 29, 1908): 33; "With Women's Clubs," *Woman's Journal* 39 (Mar. 28, 1908): 50; "California," *Woman's Journal* 39 (Apr. 18, 1908): 63; "Notes and News," *Woman's Journal* 39 (May 16, 1908): 80; "California," *Woman's Journal* 39 (Dec. 12, 1908): 200; *Los Angeles Express,* Feb. 14, 1908; Rodes, "California Woman Suffrage," 36.

50. "With Women's Clubs," *Woman's Journal* 39 (May 9, 1908): 76. See also *San Francisco Bulletin,* July 9 and Oct. 2, 1908; Rodes, "California Woman Suffrage," 37–39; *San Francisco Call,* Sept. 4–5, 1908; "Editorial Notes," *Woman's Journal* 39 (Sept. 19, 1908): 149; "California," *Woman's Journal* 39 (Sept. 26, 1908): 155; William Deverell, "The Neglected Twin: California Democrats and the Progressive Bandwagon," in *California Progressivism Revisited,* ed. Deverell and Sitton, 72–98, esp. 76.

51. The women are described in *San Francisco Call,* Aug. 28, 1908 (see also the editions of Aug. 20, 25, 29, and 31, 1908). The version of the Pease statement used here appears in "Not Thanks, But Justice," *Woman's Journal* 39 (Sept. 12, 1908): 147, but somewhat different wording appears in "California," *Woman's Journal* 39 (Sept. 5,

1908): 143, and "California," *Woman's Journal* 39 (Sept. 19, 1908): 151. See also Solomons, *How We Won*, 9–10; *San Francisco Bulletin*, July 9, 11, and 23 and Aug. 18, 1908; Rodes, "California Woman Suffrage," 38–39.

52. *San Francisco Call*, Aug. 29, 1908.

53. *San Francisco Call*, Aug. 28, 1908. See also Mowry, *California Progressives*, 64–65, 69–70, 80–81; Spencer C. Olin Jr., *California's Prodigal Sons: Hiram Johnson and the Progressives, 1911–1917* (Berkeley: University of California Press, 1968), 53; Lou Young, "Legislation," *Southern California White Ribbon* 20 (July 1908): 5; Hester T. Griffith, "President's Letter," *Southern California White Ribbon* 21 (Mar. 1909): 3; California Federation of Women's Clubs (hereafter California Federation), *Yearbook 1905–1906* (Los Angeles: Baumgardt, 1906), 65–66; California Federation, *Yearbook 1908–1909* (East Oakland, Calif.: C. W. Gordon, 1909), 30–31, 82; *San Francisco Bulletin*, Jan. 23, 1909.

54. Rodes, "California Woman Suffrage," 41–42; *Los Angeles Herald*, Oct. 3, 1909.

55. California Equal Suffrage Association, Program of the Annual Convention, Sept. 30 and Oct. 1–2, 1909, Box 124, Hichborn Collection.

56. Material quoted appears in "California State Report," *Woman's Journal* 40 (Aug. 14, 1909): 131. See also Katz, "Dual Commitments," 326–27 n. 61; for other examples of links see Mrs. William Keith, "The New Politics," *People's Forum*, 1 (Sept. 1907): 12–13; *San Francisco Bulletin*, July 11, 1908; Mrs. Seward Adams Simons, "Why Women Should Have the Privilege and Responsibility of the Ballot," leaflet, Political Equality League, Los Angeles, 1911, 10.

57. Mowry, *California Progressives*, 105–32; California Republican State Convention, "Platform Adopted by the Republican State Convention at San Francisco, Sept. 6, 1910," Box 3, Rose Collection; Mary McHenry Keith, "The Political Situation," undated handwritten manuscript, Keith-McHenry-Pond Family Papers; Harper, *History of Woman Suffrage*, vol. 6, 36–38; Rodes, "California Woman Suffrage," 43–44; Marshall Stimson, "Autobiography," typed manuscript, p. 186, Marshall Stimson Collection (hereafter Stimson Collection), Huntington Library.

58. "Woman's Suffrage," *California Weekly* 2 (Sept. 9, 1910): 657; editorial response to a letter to the editor, *California Weekly* 1 (Oct. 22, 1909): 760. See also A. J. Waterhouse, "She Was Very Commonplace," *California Weekly* 1 (Feb. 5, 1909): 167; *California Weekly* 1 (Sept. 17, 1909): 676; Ellen C. Sargent to editor and response, *California Weekly* 2 (Feb. 25, 1910): 216; A. J. Waterhouse, "Ma, She's Busy," *California Weekly* 2 (Mar. 18, 1910): 263; "A Straight Tip," *California Weekly* 2 (Apr. 15, 1910): 321; "And Why Not?" *California Weekly* 2 (Apr. 22, 1910): 339; A. J. Waterhouse, "The Question of Woman's Vote," *California Weekly* 2 (May 6, 1910): 375; editorial response to a letter, *California Weekly* 2 (May 13, 1910): 394; A. J. Waterhouse, "Woman's Intellectual Place," *California Weekly* 2 (May 20, 1910): 407; "The Line of Advance," *California Weekly* 2 (Sept. 23, 1910): 691.

59. For material quoted see A. L. Shinn to "Dear Friend," Aug. 10, 1910, Box 10; S. V. Wright to Hiram Johnson, Aug. 17, 1910, Box 11; Hiram Johnson, typed speech, Oct. 14, 1910, pp. 13 and 15, Box 12; news clipping, *Riverside Daily Press*, Apr. 12, 1910, Box 12;

Hiram W. Johnson, "The Big Issue," printed speech, delivered in Los Angeles, June 3, 1910, Box 12, all in Johnson Collection. See also Alfred Bourne Nye to Hiram Johnson, Feb. 18, 1910, Part 1, Box 9, also in Johnson Collection.

60. Hiram Johnson to Meyer Lissner, Nov. 6, 1911, Part 2, Box 1, and Hiram Johnson to Ben Lindsay, Oct. 27, 1911, Part 2, Box 1, both in Johnson Collection.

61. Hiram Johnson to Ben B. Lindsay, Oct. 27, 1911, Part 2, Box 1, and news clipping, *Evening World,* Dec. 1910, both in Johnson Collection; "The Ladies' Privilege," *Pacific Outlook* 10 (Jan. 28, 1911): 2–3; "Line-up on Women's Vote," *Pacific Outlook* 10 (Feb. 11, 1911): 3; Solomons, *How We Won,* 13; Rodes, "California Woman Suffrage," 50–56; *Los Angeles Times,* Jan. 8 and 27, 1911; Mowry, *California Progressives,* 147.

62. For material quoted see Meyer Lissner to Hiram Johnson, June 21, 1910, and Elizabeth Lowe Watson to Hiram Johnson, Sept. 5, 1910, both in Johnson Collection. See also Mowry, *California Progressives,* 70, 139–43; Olin, *Prodigal Sons,* 43–44; "California," *Woman's Journal* 38 (Oct. 19, 1907): 166–67; "California," *Woman's Journal* 40 (May 8, 1909): 75; "California Men for Suffrage," *Woman's Journal* 41 (Sept. 10, 1910): 147; Tolhurst, "Why?" 10; *Los Angeles Express,* Sept. 13, 1910.

63. Mowry, *California Progressives,* 119–20, 133.

64. Kazin, *Barons of Labor,* 53–59; Jules Tygiel, *Workingmen in San Francisco, 1880–1901* (New York: Garland, 1992), xi–xxviii; Jules Tygiel, " 'Where Unionism Holds Undisputed Sway': A Reappraisal of San Francisco's Union Labor Party," *California History* 62 (Fall 1983): 196–215; William Issel and Robert W. Cherny, *San Francisco, 1865–1932: Politics, Power, and Urban Development* (Berkeley: University of California Press, 1986), 85–88, 154–55.

65. Kazin, *Barons of Labor,* 113–20, 128–39, 181–85; Tygiel, *Workingmen,* xi–xxviii; Tygiel, " 'Where Unionism Holds Undisputed Sway,' " 196–215; Issel and Cherny, *San Francisco,* 88–91, 155–61.

66. M.C.D. [Mabel Craft Deering], "Annual Convention of California Equal Suffrage Association," *Yellow Ribbon* 1 (Nov. 1906): 1–2; "California," *Woman's Journal* 37 (Oct. 20, 1906): 168; Katz, "Dual Commitments," 265–69.

67. Katz, "Dual Commitments," 241–362; Kazin, *Barons of Labor,* 204.

68. Englander, *Class Conflict,* 42–58; Rebecca J. Mead, "Trade Unionism and Political Activity Among San Francisco Wage-Earning Women, 1900–1922" (master's thesis, California State University, San Francisco, 1991), 32, 38, 54–57.

69. Katz, "Dual Commitments," 321–22 n. 52; Doyle, "Charlotte Perkins Gilman," 135–39; Solomons, *How We Won,* 4–5; Mary McHenry Keith, "California in 1901–1920," typed manuscript, Box 3, Keith-McHenry-Pond Family Papers; news clipping, *Everywoman* 1 (Mar. 3, 1906): 1, Keith-McHenry-Pond Family Papers; Deering, "Annual Convention," 1–2; Englander, *Class Conflict,* 77–110; Mead, "Trade Unionism," 110–22.

70. *San Francisco Call,* Sept. 23, 1908.

71. *San Francisco Call,* Oct. 4, 1908.

72. Ibid. See also *San Francisco Call,* Aug. 28, 1908.

73. Englander, *Class Conflict,* 58–98; Mead, "Trade Unionism," 120–22. For an excellent discussion of working-class feminism, see Annelise Orleck, *Common Sense and a Little Fire: Women and Working-Class Politics in the United States, 1900–1965* (Chapel Hill: University of North Carolina Press, 1995).

74. Mead, "Trade Unionism," 63–65, 75–76, 86, 89.

75. Frances Noel, interview with Irving Bernstein, Nov. 24, 1952, Frances Noel Collection (hereafter Noel Collection), Special Collections, Library of the University of California at Los Angeles; Katz, "Dual Commitments," 271, 329–40 n. 70, 603–604 n. 8, 612–14 n. 26, 632–34 n. 55.

76. Katz, "Dual Commitments," 324–25 n. 60, 600–601 n. 4, 569–72, 579–80, 603–604 n. 8.

77. Mead, "Trade Unionism," 138–48; Katz, "Dual Commitments," 579–80; Mowry, *California Progressives,* 70, 92–94, 143–45; Olin, *Prodigal Sons,* 46–49; E. T. Earl to Edward Dickson, Feb. 13 and Mar. 11, 1911, Box 2, Edward Dickson Collection (hereafter Dickson Collection), Special Collections, Library of the University of California at Los Angeles; Meyer Lissner to Hiram Johnson, Mar. 23, 1911, Box 2, Lissner Collection.

78. California WCTU, *Yearbook 1910* (San Francisco: K. L. Mackey, 1910), 18–19 (see also 31–33, 47). See also Katz, "Dual Commitments," 575–76, 164, 579; Mead, "Trade Unionism," 142; California WCTU, *Yearbook 1911* (San Francisco: K. L. Mackey, 1911), 34; Southern California WCTU, *Yearbook 1906* (Los Angeles: Press of Hand and Hand, 1906), 54; Southern California WCTU, *Yearbook 1907* (Los Angeles: Press of Hand and Hand, 1907), 32, 78–79; Southern California WCTU, *Yearbook 1908* (Los Angeles: Press of Hand and Hand, 1908), 27–28, 62–63; Southern California WCTU, *Yearbook 1909* (Los Angeles: Press of Hand and Hand, 1909), 37–38, 79–80; Southern California WCTU, *Yearbook 1910* (Los Angeles: Press of Hand and Hand, 1910), 84–85; Southern California WCTU, *Yearbook 1911* (Los Angeles: Press of Hand and Hand, 1911), 33–34, 69, 81; "State Social Science Institute," *White Ribbon* 20 (Jan. 1909): 5; Mary Garbutt to Caroline Severance, Jan. 17, 1909, Box 17, Severance Collection; Agnes H. Downing, "Temperance and Labor," *White Ribbon* 22 (July 1910): 6; Mary E. Garbutt, "What Is the WCTU Doing for Wage Earning Women?" *White Ribbon* 22 (Sept. 1910): 5.

79. Garbutt, "What Is the WCTU Doing," 5; Mary S. Gibson, ed., *A Record of Twenty-five Years of the California Federation of Women's Clubs* (n.p.: California Federation of Women's Clubs, 1927), 33–39, 178; California Federation, *Yearbook 1902–1903* (San Francisco: Murdock, 1903), 8–10, 20–21; California Federation, *Yearbook 1903–1904* (Riverside, Calif.: Press Printing, 1904), 18–20, 25–26; California Federation, *Yearbook 1904–1905* (San Francisco: Town Talk, 1905), 21–23; California Federation, *Yearbook 1906–1907* (San Jose, Calif.: Murgottens, 1907), 26–29; California Federation, *Yearbook 1909–1910* (Berkeley, Calif.: Wetzel, 1910), 34–36; Mrs. Henry Christian Crowther, *High Lights: The Friday Morning Club Los Angeles, California, April 1891–1938* (Los Angeles: Carl A. Bundy Quill, 1939), 31; Katz, "Dual Commitments," 615 n. 29. San Francisco women also organized a Consumers' League, but it had an erratic existence. See Mead, "Trade Unionism," 237 n. 129. See also Kathryn Kish Sklar, "Two

Political Cultures in the Progressive Era: The National Consumers' League and the American Association for Labor Legislation," in *U.S. History as Women's History: New Feminist Essays* ed. Linda K. Kerber, Alice Kessler-Harris, and Kathryn Kish Sklar (Chapel Hill: University of North Carolina Press, 1995), 36–62.

80. Mead, "Trade Unionism," 142, 134–36, 1–2.

81. *Los Angeles Express,* Jan. 19–20, 1911; *San Francisco Examiner,* Jan. 12 and 20, 1911; Mary Ware Dennett, "National Headquarters Letter," *Woman's Journal* 42 (Jan. 28, 1911): 28; A.S.B. [Alice Stone Blackwell], "The Victory in California," *Woman's Journal* 42 (Feb. 11, 1911): 44; "California Next?" *Federation Courier* 2 (Feb. 1911): 4–5; College Equal Suffrage League of Northern California, *Winning Equal Suffrage in California* (n.p.: National College Equal Suffrage League, 1913), 25–27. The *Los Angeles Times,* an adamantly antisuffrage newspaper, chose to portray the suffragists' diversity as a weakness. See the *Times* for Jan. 16 and 19, 1911.

82. Material quoted appears in Lucretia Watson Taylor, "California," *Woman's Journal* 42 (Mar. 25, 1911): 93–94. See also Katz, "Dual Commitments," 277–78, 333–34 n. 78; Rodes, "California Woman Suffrage," 137–41; Equal Suffrage Campaign Committee, typewritten list (1911?), Elizabeth Boynton Harbert Collection (hereafter Harbert Collection), Huntington Library; Hester Griffith, "State President's Letter," *White Ribbon* 23 (Aug. 1911): 2.

83. For material quoted see Gibson, *Record,* 61 (see also 60–63, 70–73, 342–43, 235). See also *San Francisco Examiner,* May 14 and 16–17, 1911; *Los Angeles Times,* May 17, 1911; Katherine Edson to Meyer Lissner, May 9, 1911, Box 15, Lissner Collection; Rodes, "California Woman Suffrage," 140; California Federation, *Yearbook 1911–1912* (Ontario, Calif.: Ontario Publishing, 1912), 85–86.

84. Nancy F. Cott, *The Grounding of Modern Feminism* (New Haven, Conn.: Yale University Press, 1987), 1–50.

85. John Hyde Braly, *Memory Pictures: An Autobiography* (Los Angeles: Neuner, 1912), 226 (see also 227–43). See also Mowry, *California Progressives,* 131–32; Harper, *History of Woman Suffrage,* vol. 6, 40–42; Francesca Pierce, "California," *Woman's Journal* 41 (Apr. 16, 1910): 63; "California Men for Suffrage," *Woman's Journal* 41 (Sept. 10, 1910): 147; "California," *Woman's Journal* 41 (Nov. 5, 1910): 190–91; "A Man's Club," *Woman's Journal* 42 (Aug. 26, 1911): 265; *Los Angeles Times,* Apr. 6, 1910.

86. "Man's Club," 265.

87. *Los Angeles Express,* Dec. 17, 1910; Braly is quoted in "The Los Angeles Banquet," *Woman's Journal* 41 (Dec. 31, 1910): 256. See also "Solons Feasted," *Woman's Journal* 41 (Dec. 17, 1910): 244.

88. *Los Angeles Express,* Dec. 17, 1910. See also Katz, "Dual Commitments," 276.

89. For material quoted see "California," *Woman's Journal* 42 (Apr. 15, 1911): 115, and *Los Angeles Times,* Aug. 2, 1911. See also "Man's Club," 265; on the tendency of political campaigns run in an elite style to suffer defeat, see McGerr, "Political Style," 864–85; "Suffrage Mass Meeting Called," *California Outlook* 11 (July 29, 1911): 15; *Los Angeles*

Times, Aug. 24, 1911; *Los Angeles Tribune,* Aug. 22, 1911; Rodes, "California Woman Suffrage," 114–15; "Concentrate on California," *Woman's Journal* 42 (Sept. 9, 1911): 281. See *Los Angeles Express,* Sept. 25, 1911, for a description of a similar incident; suffragists held an "open-air" meeting on the tennis courts of a private home.

90. Katz, "Dual Commitments," 291–95; Ellen Carol DuBois, "Working Women, Class Relations, and Suffrage Militance: Harriot Stanton Blatch and the New York Woman Suffrage Movement, 1894–1909," *Journal of American History* 74 (June 1987): 34–58, and "Harriot Stanton Blatch and the Transformation of Class Relations Among Woman Suffragists," in *Gender, Class, Race, and Reform in the Progressive Era,* ed. Noralee Frankel and Nancy S. Dye (Lexington: University Press of Kentucky, 1991), 162–79.

91. Ella G. Ruddy to Caroline Severance, June 17 and July 1, 1911, Box 22, Severance Collection. During the 1911 campaign, two Political Equality Leagues existed; Ruddy claimed in her June 17 letter that her league performed "only out-of-door work during the campaign." See also "J. H. Braly's Speech," *Woman's Journal* 42 (Nov. 4, 1911): 346–47.

92. Katz, "Dual Commitments," 291–95; Solomons, *How We Won,* 53; "California News," *Woman's Journal* 42 (July 22, 1911): 230–31; *Los Angeles Times,* July 2 and 13, and Aug. 22, 1911.

93. *Woman's Journal* 39 (Feb. 8, 1908): 21; "College and Alumnae," *Woman's Journal* 39 (Feb. 15, 1908): 25; "California," *Woman's Journal* 39 (Mar. 7, 1908): 40; "Learned It From the Journal," *Woman's Journal* 39 (Mar. 28, 1908): 49; Sara Hunter Graham, *Woman Suffrage and the New Democracy* (New Haven, Conn.: Yale University Press, 1996), 45–46, 60. Several sources that discuss the College Equal Suffrage League of Northern California give different dates for its founding. See College Equal Suffrage League, *Winning,* 10; Solomons, *How We Won,* 6; Rodes, "California Woman Suffrage," 30.

94. *San Francisco Examiner,* Oct. 12, 1911; College Equal Suffrage League, *Winning,* 65 (see also 37).

95. Material quoted appears in College Equal Suffrage League, *Winning,* 40–41 (see also 36–42). See also "California News," *Woman's Journal* 42 (July 22, 1911): 230–31; Elizabeth Lowe Watson, "California News," *Woman's Journal* 42 (Aug. 12, 1911): 256.

96. College Equal Suffrage League, *Winning,* 83–84.

97. Fannie Lyne Black, "Personal Views by District Presidents," *Federation Courier* 3 (Sept. 1911): 21; Wiley J. Phillips, "Franchise for Women," *White Ribbon* 23 (Sept. 1911): 3. See also College Equal Suffrage League, *Winning,* 65.

98. Material quoted appears in College Equal Suffrage League of Northern California, "Arguments for Equal Suffrage," leaflet (1911?), California Historical Society, San Francisco. See also College Equal Suffrage League, *Winning,* 24; Maud Younger, "Why Wage-Earning Women Should Vote," leaflet, California Equal Suffrage Association, San Francisco, 1911, and "Justice, Simple Justice!" leaflet, both in Keith-McHenry-

Pond Family Papers. See also *San Francisco Examiner,* Sept. 2, 1911. For information regarding union women and Asians, see Englander, *Class Conflict,* 48–51, and Mead, "Trade Unionism," 127–31.

99. Rodes, "California Woman Suffrage," 163–66, 173; for discussion of suffragist characteristics, see pp. 85–87 in Rodes; *Los Angeles Times,* Oct. 3–4 and 9, and Nov. 20, 1911; *Los Angeles Express,* Sept. 6, 1911; "Field Notes," *Federation Courier* 2 (May 1911): 15; College Equal Suffrage League, *Winning,* 105. For another description of suffragists' demographics, see Ronald Schaffer, "The Problem of Consciousness in the Woman Suffrage Movement: A California Perspective," *Pacific Historical Review* 45 (Nov. 1976), 469–94.

100. Mary McHenry Keith, "The American Revolution," leaflet, and Keith, "The Political Situation," handwritten manuscript, both in Keith-McHenry-Pond Family Papers. For other anti-Asian sentiments by Keith, see *San Francisco Call,* Sept. 1, 1911.

101. Black, "Personal Views by District Presidents," 21–22. See also "The San Francisco Man: A Fable," leaflet, California Equal Suffrage Association, San Francisco, 1911.

102. Material quoted appears in "List of Suffrage Stereopticon Slides," typewritten list, Keith-McHenry-Pond Family Papers. See also Jane Addams, "Jane Addams Wants to Vote," leaflet (1911?), California Equal Suffrage Association, California Historical Society; E. L. Watson to Mr. and Mrs. McBean, July 20, 1911, and E. L. Watson to Jennie McBean, Aug. 24, 1911, Keith-McHenry-Pond Family Papers; College Equal Suffrage League, *Winning,* 94–96. The slide paraphrased something Charlotte Perkins Gilman once said that California suffragists frequently quoted: "Politics governs even the purity of the milk supply. It is not outside the home but inside the baby." For an example of this quote on a suffrage poster, see Keith-McHenry-Pond Family Papers. For examples of other California suffrage leaflets on the theme of municipal housekeeping, see "Mothers, Fathers, and All Good Citizens," leaflet (1911?), Political Equality League, Los Angeles, Huntington Library; "Women in the Home," leaflet (1911?), California Equal Suffrage Association, San Francisco, Keith-McHenry-Pond Family Papers.

103. "List of Suffrage Stereopticon Slides," Keith-McHenry-Pond Family Papers. See also Mrs. Seward Adams Simons, "Why Women Should Have the Privilege and Responsibility of the Ballot," leaflet, Mar. 1911, Political Equality League, Los Angeles, Huntington Library.

104. See Ellen Carol DuBois, "Woman Suffrage Around the World: Three Phases of Suffragist Internationalism" in *Suffrage and Beyond: International Feminist Perspectives,* ed. Caroline Daley and Melanie Nolan (Washington Square, N.Y.: New York University Press, 1994), 252–74, esp. 262.

105. College Equal Suffrage League, *Winning,* 96–98; Rodes, "California Woman Suffrage," 162; *San Francisco Examiner,* Sept. 1 and Oct. 13, 1911; Englander, *Class Conflict,* 128–43; Bertha Damaris Knobe, "The Co-Citizens of California: The Spectacular Campaign by Which Four Hundred Thousand Women Won the Vote," *Collier's* 48 (Oct. 28, 1911): 20, 31–32.

106. Katherine Philips Edson, "Votes for Women," typed manuscript, 6–7, Kather-

ine Philips Edson Collection (hereafter Edson Collection), Special Collections, Library of the University of California at Los Angeles. See also Peter Clark Macfarlane, "A California 'Stateslady': An Everyday American of To-morrow," *Collier's* 52 (Nov. 1, 1913): 5–6, 29; *Pacific Empire Press Reporter* 1 (May 28, 1913): 8–9; Jacqueline R. Braitman, "A California Stateswoman: The Public Career of Katherine Philips Edson," *California History* 65 (1986): 82–95, 151–52.

107. Edson, "Votes for Women," 6–7.

108. Ibid., 6–7 (see also 19–20); Mrs. Seward Adams Simons, "Some Reflections Upon Mrs. Scott's Address," *California Outlook* 11 (Oct. 7, 1911): 11–12.

109. Whitehead is quoted in Katz, "Dual Commitments," 249 (see also 241–59). See also J. Stitt Wilson, "Votes for Women," leaflet (1910?), no publication information, Huntington Library.

110. Mrs. Seward A. Simons, "Equality of Opportunity Needed," leaflet (1911?), Political Equality League, Los Angeles, p. 3, Clara Burdette Collection (hereafter Burdette Collection), Huntington Library; Edson, "Votes for Women," 8.

111. Simons, "Equality of Opportunity," 7. See also Helen MacGregor Todd, "The Political Rights and Duties of Women," *California Outlook* 11 (Sept. 30, 1911): 19–20, and Clifford Howard, "Why Man Needs Woman's Ballot," (leaflet), 1911, Political Equality League, Huntington Library, Los Angeles.

112. Simons, "Why Women Should Have the Privilege," 15 (see also 6–7). See also Edson, "Votes for Women," 10–17; Simons, "Equality of Opportunity"; Lillian Harris Coffin, "The Woman Suffrage Amendment," *California Weekly* 3 (Dec. 30, 1910): 75, 76, 79; *San Francisco Examiner*, Sept. 12, 1911.

113. James J. Rawls and Walton Bean, *California: An Interpretive History*, 6th ed. (New York: McGraw-Hill, 1993), 252–57; Mabel Craft Deering, "The Women's Demonstration: How They Won and Used the Vote in California," *Collier's* 48 (Jan. 6, 1912): 17–18; Mowry, *California Progressives*, 135–49; Rodes, "California Woman Suffrage," 180–87.

114. Katz, "Dual Commitments," 297–98, 356–57 n. 140; *Los Angeles Times*, Nov. 5 and 21, 1911. During the heated mayoral campaign that followed, some contested these findings. Mrs. George E. Cole, president of the Woman's Progressive League, announced she was "sick and tired" of the statement that socialists "gave the women the ballot." Cole thought she had figures to prove them wrong, but whether she was correct is not clear. See *Los Angeles Times*, Nov. 29, 1911, and *Los Angeles Express*, Nov. 30, 1911.

115. Deering, "Women's Demonstration," 17–18; See also Katz, "Dual Commitments," 297–98, 356–57 n. 140; Englander, *Class Conflict*, 136–37, 157; Mead, "Trade Unionism," 121–23.

116. Material quoted appears in College Equal Suffrage League, *Winning*, 101–102 (see also 98–102, 104–106). See also Louise Michele Newman, *White Women's Rights: The Racial Origins of Feminism in the United States* (New York: Oxford University Press, 1999), 152.

117. Material quoted appears in *Los Angeles Times,* Oct. 14, 1911. See also Gibson, *Record,* 69–70; *San Francisco Examiner,* Oct. 19 and Nov. 13, 1911.

118. Mowry, *California Progressives,* 47–52.

119. Ibid., 46–49. See also Kazin, *Barons of Labor,* 203.

120. Mowry, *California Progressives,* 49–50; Kazin, *Barons of Labor,* 204–206; Stimson, "Autobiography," 334–406.

121. Mowry, *California Progressives,* 50–55; Kazin, *Barons of Labor,* 206–207.

122. "The Nightmare that Passed," *California Outlook* 11 (Dec. 9, 1911): 2.

123. Deering, "Women's Demonstration," 17. See also Mowry, *California Progressives,* 47–56; Kazin, *Barons of Labor,* 202–208; Katz, "Dual Commitments," 299–302; *Los Angeles Times,* Oct. 25–27 and 29, and Nov. 1–2 and 8, 1911.

124. *Los Angeles Express,* Dec. 2, 1911. See also *Los Angeles Times,* Oct. 28–29 and 31, Nov. 4, 6–7, 10, 12, 20, and 23, and Dec. 2 and 5–6, 1911; *Los Angeles Express,* Oct. 28 and 30–31, Nov. 2–3, 9–10, 22–24, and 29–30, 1911; "Tremendous Vote by Los Angeles Women," *Woman's Journal* 43 (Dec. 23, 1911): 401, 403; "The Nightmare That Passed," *California Outlook* 11 (Dec. 9, 1911): 2; "What the Women of Los Angeles Did with Their Ballots," *California Outlook* 11 (Dec. 16, 1911): 13.

125. *California Outlook* 10 (June 17, 1911): 8; Olive Percival, Friday Morning Club Scrapbook 1905, Ephemeral Collection, Huntington Library. See also *California Outlook* 11 (Dec. 9, 1911): 11; *Los Angeles Herald,* Apr. 4, 1909.

126. "A California Woman's Comment," *Woman's Journal* 42 (Feb. 25, 1911): 59.

127. *Los Angeles Times,* Oct. 31, 1911. See also "Test of Women's Vote," *California Outlook* 11 (Nov. 11, 1911): 3–4; Kazin, *Barons of Labor,* 206; Stimson, "Autobiography," 362–63.

128. *Los Angeles Times,* Nov. 21 and Oct. 31, 1911. See also *Los Angeles Express,* Oct. 30–31, 1911.

129. *Los Angeles Times,* Oct. 31, 1911. See also the editions of Nov. 21 and 26, 1911, and *Los Angeles Express,* Oct. 30–31, 1911.

130. *Los Angeles Times,* Nov. 20, Oct. 31, and Nov. 11, 1911. See also *Los Angeles Express,* Oct. 30 and Nov. 10, 1911 (see the latter for the front-page story).

131. *Los Angeles Times,* Nov. 23, 1911; *Los Angeles Express,* Nov. 23, 1911. See also *Los Angeles Express,* Nov. 28–30, 1911.

132. *Los Angeles Express,* Nov. 23, 1911.

133. *Los Angeles Times,* Nov. 8 and 12, 1911. See also *Los Angeles Express,* Nov. 3, 1911, and "What the Women of Los Angeles Did," 13–14.

134. *Los Angeles Times,* Nov. 8, 1911; *Los Angeles Express,* Dec. 2, 1911.

135. *Los Angeles Express,* Nov. 9, 1911, and *Los Angeles Times,* Dec. 11, 1911. See also the *Express* for Nov. 10 and Dec. 11, 1911, and the *Times* for Nov. 7 and 12, 1911. For information on McCan, see *California Outlook* 11 (Nov. 18, 1911): 5, 11.

136. Quoted from *Los Angeles Times,* Dec. 11, 1911. See also "Woman's Progressive League of California," *California Outlook* 11 (Nov. 18, 1911): 5; *Pasadena Daily News,* Oct. 13, 1911.

137. *Federation Courier* 3 (Dec. 1911): 17.

138. *Los Angeles Times*, Nov. 26, 1911; Meyer Lissner to Hiram Johnson, Nov. 21, 1911, Box 3, Lissner Collection.

139. *Los Angeles Times*, Oct. 1, 1911.

140. Sarah Severance to Caroline Severance, Dec. 28, 1911, Box 23, Severance Collection.

EPILOGUE

1. Susan E. Marshall, *Splintered Sisterhood: Gender and Class in the Campaign Against Woman Suffrage* (Madison: University of Wisconsin Press, 1997), 189–90.

2. Christine A. Lunardini, *From Equal Suffrage to Equal Rights: Alice Paul and the National Woman's Party, 1910–1928* (New York: New York University Press, 1986), 2–5, 20–21; Nancy F. Cott, *The Grounding of Modern Feminism* (New Haven, Conn.: Yale University Press, 1987), 53–81.

3. A.S.B. [Alice Stone Blackwell], "Drawing the Lines," *Woman's Journal* 42 (Oct. 21, 1911): 332.

4. Ibid. See also Sherry J. Katz, "Dual Commitments: Feminism, Socialism, and Women's Political Activism in California, 1890–1920" (Ph.D. diss., University of California at Los Angeles, 1991), 542 n. 32.

5. Mary S. Gibson, ed., *A Record of Twenty-five Years of the California Federation of Women's Clubs, 1900–1925* (n.p.: The California Federation of Women's Clubs, 1927), 181–202.

6. Ibid., 187–95.

7. Ibid., 190–202; Mrs. Charles Farwell Edson, "Woman's Influence on State Legislation," *California Outlook* 14 (June 14, 1913): 7–8, 19; Sherry Katz, "Socialist Women and Progressive Reform," in *California Progressivism Revisited,* ed. William Deverell and Tom Sitton (Berkeley: University of California Press, 1994), 117–43; George E. Mowry, *The California Progressives* (Chicago: Quadrangle, 1963), 150–57; Spencer C. Olin Jr., *California's Prodigal Sons: Hiram Johnson and the Progressives, 1911–1917* (Berkeley: University of California Press, 1968), 104. See also Gayle Gullett, "City Mothers, City Daughters, and the Dance Hall Girls: The Limits of Female Political Power in San Francisco, 1913," in *Women and the Structure of Society: Selected Readings from the Fifth Berkshire Conference on the History of Women,* ed. Barbara J. Harris and Jo Ann McNamara (Durham, N.C.: Duke University Press, 1984), 149–59, 281–84.

8. Mowry, *California Progressives,* 150–57; Olin, *California's Prodigal Sons,* 104.

9. Gibson, *Record,* 202–209; "California," *Woman's Journal* 46 (Jan. 23, 1915): 29; "California," *Woman's Journal* 46 (Feb. 20, 1915): 59; Mary Roberts Coolidge, "What California Women Have Done with the Vote," *Woman's Journal* 47 (Dec. 16, 1916): 402; Katz, "Dual Commitments," 474–75 n. 96, 535–37 n. 23; Mrs. Seward A. Simons, "A Survey of the Results of Woman Suffrage in California," (leaflet), May 1917, California Federation of Women's Clubs, Katherine Philips Edson Collection, Special Collec-

tions, Library of the University of California at Los Angeles. See also Gayle Gullett, "Women Progressives and the Politics of Americanization in California, 1915–1920," *Pacific Historical Review* 64 (Feb. 1995): 71–94; Mowry, *California Progressives,* 195–220; Olin, *California's Prodigal Sons,* 103–11; Katherine Philips Edson to Carrie Chapman Catt, May 13, 1915, Edson Collection.

10. Ellen Carol DuBois, *Feminism and Suffrage: The Emergence of an Independent Women's Movement in America, 1848–1869* (Ithaca, N.Y.: Cornell University Press, 1978), 17–18.

INDEX